The Nation's Crucible

PETER J. KASTOR

The Nation's Crucible

THE LOUISIANA PURCHASE AND
THE CREATION OF AMERICA

Yale University Press
New Haven &
London

Published with assistance from the foundation established in memory of Philip
Hamilton McMillan of the class of 1894, Yale College.

Set in type Sabon by Keystone Typesetting, Inc.
Printed in the United States of America.

Library of Congress Cataloging-in-Publication Data
Kastor, Peter J.
The nation's crucible : the Louisiana Purchase and the creation of America /
Peter J. Kastor.
p. cm.
Includes bibliographical references and index.
ISBN 0-300-10119-8 (alk. paper)
1. Louisiana Purchase. 2. United States — Territorial expansion. 3. Nationalism —
United States — History — 19th century. 4. Political culture — United States —
History — 19th century. 5. National characteristics, American. 6. United States —
Politics and government — 1801–1815. 7. United States — Politics and
government — 1815–1861. 8. Louisiana — History — 1803–1865. 9. Frontier and
pioneer life — Louisiana. 10. Louisiana — Race relations. I. Title.
E333.K37 2004
973.4′6 — dc22
2003066259

A catalogue record for this book is available from the British Library.

The paper in this book meets the guidelines for permanence and durability of the
Committee on Production Guidelines for Book Longevity of the Council on
Library Resources.

10 9 8 7 6 5 4 3 2 1

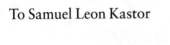

To Samuel Leon Kastor

Contents

Acknowledgments

This project began with a question, and not just the standard one for many graduate students: "What are you going to write your dissertation about?" Although that question was floating around my head in the summer of 1993, it was not the question that required the most immediate answer.

"Can I have a job this summer?" was the question I asked at the Papers of James Madison. Tucked away on the fifth floor of Alderman Library at the University of Virginia, the Papers of James Madison is one of those anonymous editorial projects that are in fact vital for so many historians. Fortunately for my checkbook, the Madison Papers had work for me. I had spent the previous summer at the Madison Papers, with most of my time spent printing, filing, and labeling the microfilmed correspondence of American consuls. In the summer of 1993, I would be transcribing correspondence from the winter of 1803–04. And that correspondence provided an answer to the question I had not dared to ask: exactly what *would* I explore in my dissertation?

What amazed me was both the flurry of activity in Washington in 1803–04 as the United States prepared to take charge of the land it had acquired through the Louisiana Purchase and the sheer unpreparedness of the Jefferson administration. What followed was a predictable story. The subject seemed interesting, but had anybody written about it? When the answer turned out to be "no," the possibility of a dissertation topic suddenly came into view. Those events in the summer of 1993 eventually led to a dissertation that was the first version of this book.

A decade later, the process of discovering that topic is still clear in my mind, as is the environment that made that possible. At the University of Virginia I found not a single institution, but rather a home to distinct communities, each of which provided the means and the inspiration for this study. That good fortune continued at Washington University in St. Louis, where I converted the dissertation into a book.

First and foremost, the faculty at the Corcoran Department of History showed an unending commitment to the intellectual development of its graduate students. I am particularly grateful to J. C. A. Stagg and Peter S. Onuf, the first my advisor of record and the second a mentor whose assistance was (and continues to be) all the more impressive because I was *not* officially his student. I feel a similar debt of gratitude to Edward L. Ayers, who despite tremendous commitments found time to be an outside reader, to employ me on his pathbreaking digital project, the Valley of Shadow, and to provide crucial lessons in teaching when I was one of the large cadre of teaching assistants for his survey course in U.S. history. Other members of the department proved vital in other ways. Cindy Aron, Stephen Innes, Melvyn Leffler, and Joe Kett all taught courses that, though not actually focusing on the early American republic, shaped the way I thought about teaching and studying history.

When I arrived at UVa in the fall of 1991, I came with a larger class of graduate students than the department expected. Ed Ayers, then the director of graduate studies, described the process of teaching and funding all those students as "trying to shove a watermelon down the throat of a giraffe." Perhaps so, but I found myself with a wonderful group of fellow graduate students who, for all the seriousness that's supposed to be attached to graduate work, never took themselves seriously. These people made graduate school enlightening and even fun.

Meanwhile, the staff at the Corcoran Department of History possessed the good spirits and keen attention that kept all those graduate students from losing their minds. Lottie McCaulley, Kathleen Miller, Elizabeth Stovall, and Ella Wood made certain we didn't slip through the cracks and listened to a lot of griping as well as a lot of gossip.

I got to know the staff best during my final years in Charlottesville, when I provided computing support for the history department. That job was only one of a number of opportunities in digital technology at UVa. The Electronic Text Center, the Institute for Advanced Technology in the Humanities, and the Multimedia Resource Center (now part of the Robinson Media Center) all fostered innovative ways of thinking about technology, scholarship, and teaching. Meanwhile, funding from the School of Arts and Sciences funded my technology work in the History Department. The paychecks I received from these institutions kept me fed, and the skills I learned proved vital to my professional development. They created tremendous opportunities, not the least of which was to make me a candidate for the technology-based postdoctoral fellowship that first brought me to St. Louis.

While the faculty, the graduate students, the staff, and the technology institutions at UVa each created distinct and important places in the realization of this project, none proved more important for the day-to-day research than the Madison Papers itself. Not only did the Madison Papers house a remarkable collection of published and microfilm sources, but if I wasn't sure what source to use, somebody at the Madison Papers would know exactly where to go. Jeanne Cross, Mary Hackett, David Mattern, Susan Perdue, Jewel Spangler, and above all J. C. A. Stagg were my guides through the complex sources on early American policymaking. I emphasize the importance of the Madison Papers because editorial projects remain the unsung heroes of the historical profession. These endeavors continue at their quiet pace, and anybody who has gone from individual archival collections to annotated published collections understands the value of these projects.

In addition to the help I received in Charlottesville, I was fortunate to work in archival collections with magnificent facilities and, more importantly, superb staff. The Library of Congress and National Archives continue to amaze me with their commitment to delivering materials of all sorts to the American public. Meanwhile, after listening with dread to stories of the difficulties my friends encountered at local archives, I was delighted with my experiences at Louisiana State University, Tulane University, and the Historic New Orleans Collection, the three institutions where I conducted most of my research while in Louisiana. The staff at all three were always helpful and knowledgeable. I am also grateful to James and Charlene Lewis as well as Juliette Landphair for providing housing during my extended stays in Louisiana.

I converted my dissertation into a book manuscript at Washington University in St. Louis, where I arrived in the summer of 1998 on a two-year appointment in American Culture Studies. I immediately found myself in the company of mentors who went out of their way to support me, in no small part *because* I was supposed to be there such a short time and they wanted that time to be productive. Wayne Fields and David Konig (both of whom eschew the title of "mentor") have provided me with everything I could want in the form of colleagues who encouraged my work while teaching me innumerable lessons. Both Wayne and David are from that rare breed of talented scholars and committed teachers who also recognize their responsibility as university citizens. Meanwhile, Carolyn Gerber, Brian Hamman, and Deborah Jaegers have contributed to the collegiality and commitment to intellectual development that are the foundations of American Culture Studies.

Although American Culture Studies was my official place at Washington University, the History Department immediately made me feel at home. This was partly the work of the chair, Derek Hirst, who let me teach what I wanted and who encouraged my professional development. But it also came through the kindness of the other faculty, who rather than protecting their turf welcomed me as a like-minded soul. That my appointment at Washington University became permanent is largely the work of these people in the History Department and American Culture Studies.

Once ensconced at Washington University, I found an ideal home for this project at Yale University Press. Forthright from the start about how my manuscript needed to change in order to become a book, the team at Yale also moved through the publishing process with remarkable efficiency. I am particularly grateful to Lara Heimert and Keith Condon. More recently, Ann Hawthorne proved to be a wonderful editor. Meanwhile, proofreading and indexing this book became far easier thanks to Kevin Butterfield, a graduate student at Washington University. His superb work as an editorial assistant reflect his expertise in the world of academic publishing and his promise as a historian. Finally, I need to thank the outside readers, both of whom provided magnificent commentary on earlier versions of this book. I was delighted when I learned that Dan Usner was one of those readers, because his own work helped spark my initial interest in Louisiana's history. I am equally grateful to Jay Gitlin, who was busy finishing his own book for Yale University Press. As I worked on my study of Louisiana's role in American nationhood, I lamented the absence of a more thorough study of local political culture in Francophone North America. Jay's book will finally fill this gap, in the process raising important questions about the way we understand the end of European rule in North America.

Some of the material in this book first appeared as " 'Motives of Peculiar Urgency': Local Diplomacy in Louisiana, 1803–1821," *William and Mary Quarterly,* 3d. ser., 58 (2001): 819–48. I thank the editors of the *Quarterly* for permission to reprint the substance of that article, and I remain grateful to their superb editors for suggesting changes to the article that proved equally useful for this book. I also received important suggestions when I presented ideas from this book to the Society for Historians of the Early American Republic, the Southern Historical Society, the Society for Historians of American Foreign Relations, and the Consortium on Revolutionary Europe, as well as the Southern History Seminar and the Early American Seminar at the University of Virginia.

On a final academic note, I need to go back to the beginning. I wouldn't say I really knew what an academic historian did when I was in college, but I did know I loved studying history. And that pleasure came from the courses I took at Franklin & Marshall College. Franklin & Marshall continues the often-overlooked tradition of liberal arts colleges, institutions that have remained true to their commitment that undergraduate education happens through close contact between faculty and students. My only regret is that my undergraduate advisor in the history major, John Andrew, did not live to see this book. He endured my senior thesis, which was far too long, and his good humor would have found something amusing in the fact that other people now have to endure what I write.

And on a personal note, there are of course thanks for my family, the sort of thanks that never do full justice. But I will restate what those people should already know. That I am doing anything productive at all happened through the unending patience and support of my parents, Mae and John Kastor. They put up with a lot, and always encouraged me to follow an interest in history that they shared themselves. Within months of stumbling upon Louisiana as a dissertation topic, I made an even more important discovery: in the summer of 1993 I met my wife, Jami Ake, whose support saw me through the difficulties of graduate school, my first academic job, and completing this book.

So why isn't this book dedicated to them? Because for all they did, their contributions to this book are more difficult to pinpoint than that of my son, Sam Kastor. Sam had the kindness to be born about a week late: he waited exactly twenty-four hours after I mailed the first draft of my manuscript to Yale University Press before sending Jami into labor. By the time the readers' reports came back, Sam had already displayed a disposition so cheery that it could always overcome the exhaustion of editing a book manuscript. And for that I'll always be grateful.

Introduction

There once was a place called the Neutral Ground. It was a somewhat misshapen rectangle, the two longest lines following the twists of the Sabine River to the east and an obscure tributary called the Arroyo Hondo to the west. These waterways vanished into the numerous streams flowing into the Gulf of Mexico, with the Gulf Coast itself forming a southern border. To the north, the Red River closed off the Neutral Ground. The name was attractive, for the Neutral Ground imposed a vision of conciliation and peace on the Texas-Louisiana border. The name was also misleading, for people were anything but neutral when it came to the Neutral Ground.[1]

Much of the Neutral Ground occupied a region now known as Texarkana, encompassing portions of Texas, Arkansas, and Louisiana. In the early nineteenth century, the final status of this land was anybody's guess. The United States, Spain, and the Caddo Indians all claimed the territory as their own. The Neutral Ground came into being in 1806 to avert a war among these parties, and for the next fifteen years it was sustained by the conflict and uncertainty that reigned in the region. In creating the Neutral Ground, delegates from Spain, the United States, and the Caddo agreed to prohibit European soldiers from entering the region and to permit only a few traders to pass through. This was hardly the work of world statesmen. Only the Caddo chief, Dehahuit, was an experienced negotiator. The two non-Indian officials—Colonel Simón de Herrera y Leyva of Spain and Brigadier General James Wilkinson of the United States—had no such credentials. They approached the situation as novices, fumbling for a means to contain the tensions that seemed likely to explode in a Spanish-American war.

The frontiers of North America abounded with areas similar to the Neutral Ground, places where no particular system of power reigned supreme.[2] And while the Neutral Ground was emblematic of that sort of cultural adaptation and innovation, it was hardly indicative of the accommodation that so often appears to have emerged on the frontiers of North America. All three of the negotiators had clear agendas that they attempted to impose on the border-lands. All three sought control rather than amity. Nor was the context any more peaceful. The contest for the Neutral Ground came in the midst of international tension, suspected slave revolt, and unprecedented contact be-tween people of different backgrounds. Upheavals within the British, French, and Spanish empires seemed close at hand even as people came to terms with the relatively new polity of the United States.

The sense of volatility in Louisiana radiated outward, and nowhere was it more apparent than in Washington, D.C. Secretary of State James Madison expressed his own feelings in December 1806 while drafting a proclamation intended for his close friend, President Thomas Jefferson. At the same time that Wilkinson, Herrera, and Dehahuit worried about stability on Louisiana's frontier, Madison fretted about the residents of the Mississippi Valley. "Sun-dry persons, citizens of the U.S. or residents within the same, are conspiring and confederating together," Madison observed. He advised Jefferson to re-quire "all good and faithful citizens" to assist in putting down this "insurrec-tionary combination."[3] The specific machination to which Madison referred was the Burr Conspiracy, a separatist movement attributed to the former vice president of the United States and the source of no end of concern to Ameri-cans during 1806 and 1807. But Madison also drew on five years of experi-ence governing Louisiana as secretary of state, experience which indicated to him that the United States had only the most tenuous hold on the people and the land it had acquired from France in 1803. The Neutral Ground crisis, coming in such close proximity to the Burr crisis, intensified Madison's convic-tion that domestic and international threats might yet rob the United States of Louisiana or pull the Southwest into a vortex of violence, chaos, and disunion.

What accounts for Madison's concern? Circumspect though he was in even his most optimistic moments, personality alone is insufficient, because Madi-son's fears were hardly unique. Rather, a host of problems combined to con-vince observers throughout the United States that powerful forces were con-spiring to keep Louisiana disconnected and unstable. As a result, domestic troublemakers like Aaron Burr and diplomatic tensions on the borderlands were interconnected challenges to a federal system still struggling to establish how it would do business.

Those concerns first exploded onto the national landscape in 1803, when France ceded its North American holdings to the United States. The Louisiana Purchase reconfigured the domestic and international order in the same way it transformed the boundaries of North America. Imposed on the United States with terms very different from those the Jefferson administration sought, the Louisiana Purchase suddenly added a vast landscape to the national domain. And as people scrambled to figure out what Louisiana would be, they changed what it would mean to be American.[4]

Louisiana commanded national attention because the transfer of land brought with it a quandary: What would become of the people and the land in Louisiana? The search for an answer bedeviled policymakers and average citizens alike long after diplomats signed off on the Louisiana Purchase.

This study chronicles the struggle to incorporate Louisiana and its residents. The nominal chronological boundaries are two treaties, the Louisiana Purchase of 1803 and the Transcontinental Treaty, negotiated in 1819 and ratified by the United States in 1821. The years between those two treaties had been marked by a flurry of activity as people attempted to foster or to undermine incorporation, the process by which Louisiana became a permanent component of the American union and was understood as such by people throughout the Americas and Europe. Because incorporation was very much in the eye of the beholder, I treat this term less as an absolute threshold than as a structural and perceived development.

The incorporation of Louisiana was also a matter of central concern in the first two decades of the nineteenth century. Regardless of their location or background, people saw Louisiana as one of the greatest tests of American nationality on matters ranging from political economy to individual loyalty to race. Nor were they far from the mark. The task of incorporating Louisiana proved critical to the process of nationbuilding, precipitating a fundamental reconsideration of nation and citizen. When scholars discuss the concept of nationhood, they tend to emphasize the constructed nature of national communities.[5] The history of Louisiana in the early American republic provides the blueprint for that construction project, revealing the meanings of nationhood at a time when people debated the form, the purpose, or even the viability of union.

The incorporation of Louisiana — and the struggle for nationhood — often turned on the relationship between the foreign and the domestic, the foreigner and the citizen. In the process, incorporation gave concrete meanings to those words in a way that had been absent in the United States. The Louisiana Purchase posed a fundamentally nationalist challenge: Could the American national community (rather than the borders of the United States) expand sufficiently to contain the sudden influx of new citizens concentrated on a distant frontier who had not undergone any form of naturalization? It was *demographic* expansion, rather than *geographic* expansion, that was the subject of so much concern. After all, the Louisiana Purchase marked not only the largest addition of new territory since independence, but also the first addition of large populations, whether Indians who were in obvious control of certain areas, or white and black residents who had not been transplanted from other parts of the United States.

The federal government's efforts to achieve incorporation proved so difficult and so important because constructing a definition of nationhood had been among the central concerns in the brief history of the United States. Those arguments took form on the frontiers of the union. So too did the solutions. Nowhere else did settlers so conspicuously claim that local and regional peculiarities could coexist with national attachments. The tension between periphery and center, such a common subject in the historiography of the United States, often proved to be more apparent than real as people developed elaborate mechanisms to connect Louisiana with the rest of the nation.

The process of incorporation occurred in the formal arena of government and concerned public administration, diplomacy, and politics. But it also occurred in less obvious settings like the contest between masters and slaves or the correspondence between Washington and New Orleans. Those locales — the physical world of face-to-face confrontation and the written world of print culture — suggest the intricacy as well as the breadth of nationbuilding.

And in the end, the laboratory of Louisiana validated nationhood itself. The chaos that seemed everywhere in 1803 gave way to signs of regional stability, racial supremacy, and political integration by 1820. Louisiana was hardly calm, of course, for political and racial unrest remained a feature of daily life in the decades that followed. Yet in comparison to the white resentment, nonwhite violence, foreign intervention, and domestic disunion that so many predicted in 1803, Louisiana seemed particularly well connected to other states and territories.

In telling this tale of incorporation and nationbuilding, I have generally eschewed "identity," a word that seems almost inseparable from considerations of nationalism. Although I do use the word occasionally, I prefer the term "attachment." Identity rests on fundamentally recent conceptions of self and society. This was the case in large part because they operated before the word "identity" had even entered the public vocabulary with meanings similar to that of the current use of that term. Add to this the fact that people cast a much wider net when they considered the incorporation of Louisiana. They were equally concerned with political, administrative, commercial, diplomatic, and legal structures. Attachment therefore keeps the discussion of Louisiana more grounded, for attachment was the word people used at the time.[6]

This inherently pragmatic outlook on nationhood helps explain a perplexing problem. Scholars have devoted considerable energy to asserting that people could think in nationalist terms during the early American republic despite the reality of distinct and often separate political, economic, and cultural communities.[7] While scholars have acknowledged that nationalism faced opponents, they have rarely investigated why its advocates would select a national framework. What were the benefits? Likewise, what were the specific intellectual tools that could enable people to believe that nationhood was a reality? Nationhood was never an obvious choice, nor was it some natural impulse as it so often appears in the scholarly literature on nationalism. Nationhood in the early American republic was instead a pragmatic option that people selected from among a variety of forms of social organization — whether local, regional, racial, or ethnic. Nationhood had to be argued rather than simply embraced, and in some cases it had to be imposed by force. In the turmoil that followed the Louisiana Purchase, white residents of Louisiana shifted from a fundamentally localist perspective to one that fused local concerns with a national outlook for highly pragmatic reasons.

Federal policymakers were no less pragmatic. Nationhood always had several intertwined objectives to officials in Washington and their delegates on the frontier. The first four — securing federal sovereignty over clearly defined borders, promoting a republican political culture, cultivating the sentimental attachment of white residents, and excluding nonwhites from the national community through a system of racial supremacy — were ends unto themselves. The fifth — the creation of effective systems of public administration at the state and federal levels — may have been the means to those ends, but it was no less important. For federal leaders, Louisiana would be where they developed their own visions of public administration.

Of course, people throughout North America responded to these federal goals in different ways. White Louisianians and free people of color saw considerable opportunities in nationhood. Indians often supported incorporation, but only so long as it redefined American federalism in significant ways that collided with the goals of federal policymakers. Finally, slaves mobilized against nationhood, either individually or in groups. The vision of incorporation that eventually came to dominate in Louisiana left no room for the liminal status that nonwhites had enjoyed under European colonial rule. In the nineteenth century racial dynamics in Louisiana underwent profound changes that historians have attributed to sources ranging from divergent legal traditions to land hunger to the fear of slave revolt to the simple cultural arrogance of many Anglo-Americans.[8] But nationhood itself deserves a fair share of the blame.[9]

Fueling the pragmatic decisions of frontier residents was the fact that precedents from the French and Spanish colonial heritages were always nearby in Louisiana. So too was the influence of the revolutions in France, Haiti, and Spanish America. All these models provided alternatives to the vision of incorporation fostered by the federal government.

The tradeoffs and balancing acts of revolutionary principles fueled the complexity that reigned in Louisiana. Even the demographic divisions within Louisiana can prove confusing. I use "Louisianians" to refer to those people who lived in Louisiana before 1803 and who found their nationality transformed by the Louisiana Purchase. Though never a wholly unified group, these people did enjoy a unique status within the United States as a result of the Purchase. I have specifically avoided the word "Creole" (a term that scholars often apply indiscriminately to the local population) to describe the predominantly Francophone population, because so many leading Louisianians came from the Caribbean or from France. I reserve "Creole" for people born in Louisiana, a people of predominantly French or African ancestry but with a substantial mixed-race population as well as a significant Hispanic influence that resulted from a generation of Spanish rule in Louisiana.[10]

The Americans to whom I refer were the predominantly Anglophone citizens of the United States from outside Louisiana, even though these labels would be something of an insult to many Louisianians in the early nineteenth century who so forcefully argued that they, too, were Americans. By the 1820s few people would question whether Louisianians were also Americans. In the first two decades after the Louisiana Purchase, however, nobody was so certain. With their own feelings of exclusion from the national community, even white Louisianians acknowledged that being an "American" involved more than individual citizenship or statehood.

The "Louisiana" I discuss is both the current state of Louisiana and its jurisdictional predecessor, the Territory of Orleans. There was also, of course, a greater Louisiana, encompassing the entire landmass the United States purchased from France in 1803. Residents of Upper Louisiana (a term applied during the colonial period to the land that now constitutes the states north of Louisiana and along the eastern plains), the majority of them Indians, underwent their own ordeal in the years following the Louisiana Purchase. Conditions were dramatically different, however, and Upper Louisiana's rough admission into the United States remains a subject awaiting investigation.

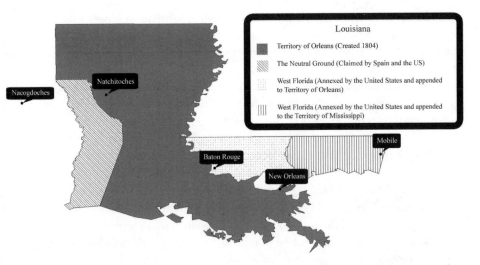

Louisiana (including contested claims). The dark portion was under unchallenged American sovereignty. The internal divisions reflect individual parishes, the seat of local administration.

This book is divided into four parts. Part I provides a brief background. Chapter 1 considers general conditions on both sides of the Atlantic before 1803, while chapter 2 chronicles the particular circumstances in which the United States acquired Louisiana in 1803. Part II investigates the period from 1803 through 1808, when the Louisiana Purchase unleashed numerous, often conflicting, visions of incorporation. Although a series of changes to the domestic apparatus seemed to establish the federal hold and white supremacy by 1808, part III shows how a series of crises at home and abroad from 1809 through 1815 upset the institutional development that was supposed to secure incorporation. Finally, part IV investigates the period from 1815 through 1820, when whites in Louisiana completed the process of constructing the legal, political, administrative, racial, and military structures of racial supremacy.

Parts II–IV correspond roughly to three different Republican administrations, a correlation that is more coincidental than causal. Thomas Jefferson occupied the presidency during the period of greatest domestic uncertainty in Louisiana, James Madison during the period of greatest international activity, and James Monroe during the period of resolution on foreign and domestic fronts. These developments say less about the three presidents than they do about shifting circumstances in Louisiana, the Americas, and Europe. Indeed, the incorporation of Louisiana occurred during a period of tremendous consistency in Washington, as Jefferson, Madison, and Monroe pursued almost identical priorities. Among these three Virginians, it was Madison who made the greatest impact, first by asserting his own supremacy in crafting a foreign and domestic policy as secretary of state, later as a president who proved hesitant to surrender that authority.

As the dynamic between Louisiana and Washington suggests, this is very much a story of federal relationships. The logic of such an approach is obvious during the territorial period, when federal officials exercised direct control over Louisiana. The importance of the national perspective after 1812 is more subtle. Experience at the state level influenced both the way Americans conceived of politics and actual governance at the national level. Yet the reverse can just as easily be said for frontier states like Louisiana, where the lengthy experience of territorial government, and the ongoing contact with the federal regime, established the rules by which state polities would operate.

This is not a social history of Louisiana, and its analysis of culture is rather narrowly focused, largely because Louisiana's social and cultural history has already been richly treated.[11] Instead, this book exploits Louisiana as a focal point for connecting the seemingly disconnected matters of frontier settlement, nationalism, and federalism.

Previous scholarship on these component topics has produced a fundamentally misleading vision of the early American republic. First, studies of frontiers and borderlands have systematically overstated the ease of American expansionism, both as policymaking program and as sentimental appeal. Second, the nationalist tactics that preserved the nation as it expanded were grounded in pragmatism, not in sentiment. Finally, the ideologies of American nationhood emerged from the process of governance, not the other way around, and the most dynamic developments occurred at the federal rather than the state level.

Nationhood was most powerfully argued on frontiers in general and Louisiana in particular, but in ways that indicate the problematic ways that scholars have conceived of North America in the late eighteenth and early nineteenth centuries. In making this statement, I realize that I am harkening back to Frederick Jackson Turner, who first argued that America was defined in a singular place called the "frontier." And yet I am hardly the first to do so. Much as historians might criticize Turner's racial and ethnic tunnel vision, they nonetheless tend to share his conception of expansion as an inevitable expression of American culture, an impulse that Anglo-Americans enacted with unquestioning and often brutal zeal. They tend to describe a simple trajectory of geopolitical and cultural imperialism on the part of the United States, allowing little room for the very negotiation, contingency, and accommodation that they consider so common to frontiers. Scholars of early American politics and diplomacy acknowledge the limited territorial aspirations of federal leaders, and yet they invariably revert to the notion of a confident, ambitious, expansionist American state.[12] Meanwhile, most of the recent studies of the politics of frontiers in the early American republic have focused on the fringes of Anglo-American settlement in the first new states to be carved from the land between the Appalachian Mountains and the Mississippi River. Studies of intercultural contact have generally been limited to the collision of westward-moving settlers of unchallenged American nationality colliding with eastward-looking Indians, rather than the collision of peoples from numerous backgrounds that occurred in places farther west.[13]

Most historians studying the creation of the federal system in the United States have focused on a history of ideas, and usually political ideas.[14] More recent work in political culture has extended this process by asking how people outside the policymaking elite interpreted those terms through daily public activity.[15] The actual process of creating a functioning government from those principles—whether on frontiers or at the centers of power—is an afterthought, with case studies serving more as illustrative examples of political ideas than as formative realities in their own right.[16] This fundamentally political and ideological focus goes a long way toward explaining why so much of the work on the Jeffersonian Republicans is limited to the 1790s, when the Republicans formulated their principles, but before electoral victories in 1800 forced Republicans to implement those ideas. The result is that we know a great deal about what the Federalists and Republicans believed, but not much about what they actually did. We know how they secured office, but not how they executed power.

The story of early national Louisiana provides a different lesson from the traditional vision of American continental empire. The federal system and the American nation, as well as the Jeffersonians who governed it throughout the first quarter of the nineteenth century, emerged from the particular challenges of expansion. Equally important, federalism and nationalism emerged no more in the political than in the administrative arena, where the functional realities of governance and protean concepts of nationalism interacted. Those nationalist principles were essential for expansion in general and for the incorporation of Louisiana in particular, for Louisiana's unity with the rest of the United States entailed more than the constitutional relationships that so often take center stage in studies of the Louisiana Purchase.[17] The very weakness of nation and state that came with expansion forced the United States into situations in which frontier residents played a vital role in shaping those systems.

Those practical matters, so often presented as mere illustrations by historians, were hardly an afterthought at the time. To the contrary, this book describes a policymaking dynamic operating in the opposite direction. It was institutional practice that determined the way people conceived of politics. It certainly structured the outcome of the federal regime. Rather than operating as examples of political ideas, the specific activities of the policymaking process shaped the way people conceived of the republic. This dynamic held true for residents of Louisiana and for federal leaders in Washington. Not only did people, regardless of race or background, encounter what it meant to be American through contacts with the formal institutions of government, but federal governance also transformed the way federal leaders approached their job. This was especially true after 1800, when partisan disputes had little direct impact. On a daily basis, most federal policymaking concerned foreign affairs and frontier governance, arenas in which Federalists had no substantive influence. Nationhood after 1800 emerged through an internal debate between settlers and a series of Republican administrations that sustained a consistent vision over a quarter-century. Not only did the Federalists fail to generate any sticking power on the frontiers of the union, but their dwindling fortunes in Congress meant that federal policymaking was a wholly Republican pursuit until the Republicans themselves disintegrated in the 1820s.

This book also focuses on these policymaking concerns because administrative matters remain one of the great unknowns of the early republic. What claim to be studies of "government" in the early republic are usually discussions of political debate, constitutional relationships, or legal practice. Each critical in its own way, these subjects nonetheless ignore the functional realities of governance, the process by which government agencies, constitutions, and laws actually manifested themselves.[18] Meanwhile, historians of American statebuilding tend to ignore the century after independence altogether.[19]

This study also does not limit the purview of policymaking to public officials. Although most of the players were white men, Indians, slaves, free men of color, and women of all backgrounds made active attempts either to shape incorporation on their own terms or to reject it altogether. Racial policymaking was critical to federal leaders, but people in Louisiana situated race alongside other factors as they decided how they would respond to the Purchase. The following chapters therefore chronicle the policymaking process from both ends, connecting federal leaders in Washington to residents of Louisiana. The Neutral Ground should not be confused with the Middle Ground, that masterful conceptualization of human relations which Richard White applied to points north of Louisiana. After all, Americans never did grasp the principles of the Middle Ground, but the harsh geopolitics of the Neutral Ground made perfect sense. The Neutral Ground of this study also resided in a climate of greater social, political, and diplomatic contestation, where people of all sorts were trying harder to build walls of separation than to build forms of community. And it was that process of distinguishing peoples that lay at the foundation of nation.

The notion of Louisiana as a national test case is hardly new; observers in the early nineteenth century certainly conceived of the Lower Mississippi Valley in such terms. Yet this national perspective was lost on subsequent generations of scholars, most of whom have treated Louisiana as fascinating but anomalous. Discussions of Louisiana tend to be comparative, referring to the rest of the nation only to call attention to Louisiana's peculiarities. The result: a world that seems so corrupt, so unusual, so definitively aberrant that Louisiana suffers in scholarly isolation. So while this study calls for rethinking nationhood in the early republic, it also argues for a new understanding of Louisiana during these vital decades.

Scholars have yet to investigate these issues or to explain Louisiana's ungainly fit into the United States. Most historians of the early American republic prefer instead to see Louisiana in wholly diplomatic terms and end their discussion of it in 1803 with the Louisiana Purchase, returning to the Southwest briefly in 1819 to discuss the Transcontinental Treaty.[20] Historians of American politics and ideology have likewise afforded Louisiana a brief and distant consideration. They consider the Louisiana Purchase within the national debate over expansion or the struggle to preserve a vigorous republic. They, too, lose interest after 1803 and, like diplomatic historians, return to the Mississippi Valley in 1819, in this case to consider the fate of Missouri.[21]

In the same way that historians of the early republic often ignore Louisiana, so too have Louisiana scholars shied away from the early republic.[22] They have focused on the colonial and antebellum eras to the exclusion of the early republic in particular or politics in general. They tend to collapse the dramatic changes separating the early republic from the antebellum era, distinctions that other historians have chronicled in rich detail for the rest of the nation. The world of corruption and quadroon balls, of cotton fields and Creole cuisine that historians and novelists alike use to describe antebellum Louisiana was either in its infancy or absent altogether from the Louisiana of the early republic.

The familiar story of Louisiana in the decades following the Purchase is one of struggle between arrogant Creoles and insensitive Americans. It is a tale crafted by Louisiana's first historians, men only a few years removed from the Purchase itself.[23] George Washington Cable provided a literary counterpart in his novel *The Grandissimes*. Over a century after Cable set to work, few question that the Creoles of Louisiana resented American rule just as they resented the influx of American newcomers. And over a half-century after historian Joseph Tregle coined the term "ego politics" to describe the divisive politics of antebellum Louisiana, historians continue to extend the term backward to the early republic.[24]

I take issue with this synthesis on a series of points. Louisianians and Americans often came to blows, but this contest was never a simple battle for ethnic supremacy. I draw this conclusion from casting Louisiana in a national context, for just as Louisiana provides insights to the early republic, so too does a national perspective demand a more complex interpretation of Louisiana's internal history. What looks like ethnic hatred at close range becomes a struggle over citizenship, nationhood, and the status of territories when seen alongside similar contests in the rest of the United States.

These similarities do not mean that Louisiana was identical to other states and territories or that the population of Louisiana joined the United States quietly. Far from it; people often assumed that these divisions were rooted in cultural differences separating the people of Louisiana from other American citizens. As Judith Schafer put it so succinctly in her study of Louisiana slave law, "most often . . . [Louisiana] was simply *different*."[25] But it was the way people saw those differences at the time that proves so revealing, for it rested on their own understanding of culture, history, nationhood, and even difference itself.

Instead of engaging these questions and topics, scholars of Louisiana have instead detailed a process of "Americanization" in which Louisiana came to fit an American norm. This word adorns the title of books and articles. These Americanization studies describe a local population steadfastly defending its commercial, political, and social traditions against encroaching Americans. In this model, American expansion brought with it the imposition of an amorphous Anglo-American "culture," usually to the detriment of borderland residents.[26] I have avoided "Americanization" because the term supposes a clear threshold before which Louisiana was foreign and after which it was "American." The Americanization model also tends to treat Louisiana as a static "French" society rather than a dynamic colonial society that shaped the particular conditions of multiracial and multiethnic contact on the frontiers of North America. Nor was the "American" influence so monolithic as it might appear from the periphery. The definition of American was hardly fixed in stone.

The dynamic quality of nationhood goes a long way toward explaining why Louisiana became such a steadfast part of the union despite customs from the French and Spanish colonial past that clashed with American norms. White Louisianians found the means to accommodate their own status as American citizens with their sense of themselves as minorities of various forms. They also welcomed changes that brought the promise of commercial opportunity, regional development, and racial supremacy.

For all these reasons, I find "incorporation" more useful than "Americanization." I am less concerned with ways in which Louisiana was distinct from or similar to the rest of the United States than I am with how people at the time conceived of Louisiana's place within the nation as a whole. Did people in Louisiana believe they shared anything with other residents of the United States, and did others in the United States share that opinion? What qualities differentiated peoples, and were they fixed? The answers provide clues to the way men and women in the early nineteenth century interpreted various forms of differentiation. Incorporation was on the lips and in the writing of people throughout Louisiana and the United States. Cabinet members and common citizens, presidents and local public officials, senators and slaves all asked what incorporation would mean. Each group offered a different answer.

Incorporation was less a struggle for homogeneity than a struggle for attachment and connection: the emotional attachment of new citizens, the geopolitical attachment of new territory, the legal attachment of property (whether land or slaves) to its owners, the commercial attachment of merchants in regional or national trading networks. Different groups responded in kind, proposing their own visions of nationality and attachment. White Louisianians, like policymakers in Washington, hoped to create bonds that would overcome not only geographic distance but also the distance created by separate histories. Free people of color attempted to ingratiate themselves both locally and nationally, claiming that race need not be a barrier to nationality. Indians and slaves proposed other models, rejecting systems of attachment that brought only greater travail. Indians sought autonomy, establishing limited contacts with the U.S. government while attempting to keep white authority at arm's length. Slaves were even more explicit. Whether through escape on the Neutral Ground or through violent revolt, they rejected both attachment and nationality on federal terms.

Although Indians and slaves revealed the fissures in American nationhood, they failed to achieve their own visions of freedom. Whites created effective mechanisms to preserve the attachment of Indians and slaves even as they excluded those people from the national community. Despite all the noise of discontent and signs of instability, Louisiana is most striking for the *absence* of resistance to American authority, separatist appeal, and ethnic political polarization among white residents. Louisiana is equally striking for the *presence* of accommodation and the desperate struggle of white Louisianians to insert themselves into social, commercial, and political networks. In less than a generation, Louisiana went from a place that seemed on the brink of separa-tism or racial revolt to one of the most loyal states in the union with one of America's most repressive slave regimes. Making Louisiana such a stable fix-ture in the American union involved the cold rule of law and the sentimental attachment of individuals, the diplomacy of nations, and the self-promotion of local entrepreneurs. It also involved a series of events occurring simulta-neously in the borderlands surrounding the Mississippi Valley, in the Carib-bean, in Washington, D.C., and in Europe.

In the strictest narrative terms, this is the story of how a foreign and poten-tially fractious population on the southwestern periphery became one of the most steadfast and prosperous members of the American union. Madison's own comments captured this trajectory, which proved fitting considering his role as the most important figure in Washington when it came to Louisiana. As secretary of state he orchestrated the purchase of Louisiana and then oversaw its administration. As president he sustained his influence on affairs of the Lower Mississippi Valley. In 1819 former President Madison wrote to his successor, James Monroe, confessing his considerable relief that American negotiators had finally reached an agreement with Spain acknowledging once and for all the boundaries of the Louisiana Purchase. "It will be a most happy termination of our business," he wrote. Diplomacy alone did not account for this change of heart, for he and other policymakers saw a region where whites displayed unquestioned loyalty, contributed to mechanisms of slave control, and helped the federal government strip Indians of their power.[27]

How observers interpreted that change would inform their understanding of the profound issues that emerged from the reconfiguration of empires that occurred in North America during the late eighteenth and early nineteenth centuries. The same year that Madison wrote to Monroe, the governor of Louisiana, Jacques Philippe Villeré, expressed similar optimism in his annual message to the state legislature. A Creole, Villeré proclaimed Louisiana a firm member of the "great American family," its population delivered from the "idle prejudices between citizens of different origins."[28] Villeré's assertion was well founded. Madison's change of view from 1806 — when he wrote so anx-iously about the prospect of unrest in Louisiana — to 1819 was indicative of the transformation that so many of his countrymen underwent in their atti-tudes toward Louisiana. The fourth president's letters to Jefferson and Mon-roe — his predecessor and his successor — captured the shift from uncertainty to calm, from the fear of potential disunion to the belief in growing attach-ment. In moving from one pole to the other, Americans were forced to con-sider what lay at the core of who they were as individuals, as members of states, and as citizens of the United States.

On the fringe of a nation where nationality itself was under debate, in a world gripped by revolutions, Louisiana seemed replete with possibilities. Just how the nation would expand was anybody's guess in 1803, and everybody offered a plan. Those same possibilities could portend opportunity or destruction depending on individual perspectives. These matters were so important because they forced people to reconsider what defined the United States. In 1776 residents of the former British colonies wrestled with the problem of creating a nation; in 1803 they faced the equally vexing question of expanding a nation. After precipitating this crisis of nationality, however, the Louisiana Purchase eventually reinforced union. In the process, it was Louisiana that helped Americanize the United States.

PART I

Empires, Republics, and Nations
(1763–1804)

I

America

Pierre Clément Laussat was a newcomer, and his sojourn was not long. He reached North America in March 1803, dispatched by Napoleon Bonaparte to assume the office of prefect for Louisiana. The product of a wealthy family, Laussat had nonetheless weathered the French Revolution almost unscathed and had enjoyed midlevel appointments under both royalists and revolutionaries.[1]

Once in Louisiana, Laussat ensconced himself in New Orleans, for almost a century the center of European government in Louisiana. While colonial governors enjoyed their own residence, they shared their workplace with administrative, judicial, and military personnel. Throughout the eighteenth century a variety of ramshackle structures had been the center of colonial governance in Louisiana. In 1795 the Spanish began work on a new administrative headquarters called the Hotel de Ville. The building housed the Cabildo, the city's municipal government, from which the building eventually acquired its informal title. Although the Cabildo served primarily as a home to city administration, it also provided a focal point for power throughout the colony.

In the summer of 1803 came news that France had sold Louisiana to the United States, and would resume direct authority only to hand over the territory to its new owner. Enter Pierre Clément Laussat, who faced the difficult task of explaining this turn of events to the residents of Louisiana. He chose to treat the Louisiana Purchase as if it had been written exclusively with their interests in mind. Laussat explained that "the epoch will soon arrive, in which you will choose for yourselves a form of government; which while it will be conformable to the sacred principles of the social compact of the federal union, will be adapted to your manners, to your necessities, to your climate, to your customs, soil and local circumstances."[2]

Laussat saw an active role for the Louisianians, and he wanted to minimize any local resistance to the transfer. He need not have worried. Louisianians grasped at incorporation with a zeal that was as likely to alarm Americans as it was to please them. Laussat nonetheless appreciated the question posed by the Louisiana Purchase: How could the Louisianians become Americans? For his part, Laussat proposed a smooth process in which Louisianians accepted their new nationality while the United States respected local culture. He had indeed captured the goal of many Louisianians.

Finding a place for the residents of Louisiana, first in European empires and then in the United States, came in the wake of a lengthy debate as Americans, Louisianians (whether of European, African, or combined descent), and Indians attempted to establish what constituted membership in a nation. This debate happened on both sides of the Mississippi River, two facets of a continental movement to reform colonial relationships that involved peoples of all backgrounds. All these people had fundamentally pragmatic means for defining what might separate or divide the peoples of North America. Indeed, this question of how people in the Americas would be bound to one another and to the governments that ruled them connected the United States to Louisiana long before the Louisiana Purchase.

Though operating at a time when localism framed the way most people understood the world — before the ideologies, technologies, and politics that created modern nationalism — residents of North American frontiers and people concerned with the fate of those frontiers consistently considered the world in terms that wedded the local to the national and the transatlantic. Without acting in concert, people in the United States and Louisiana attacked what they saw as the worst vestiges of their imperial pasts. Motivated by highly pragmatic goals, these people sought larger communities of interest. Whether they wanted reform within imperial systems or rejected colonial rule altogether, they sought forms of association that would serve highly practical tasks ranging from individual opportunity to national liberty.

Nations and Citizens

Throughout the ferment of the British imperial crisis, the American Revolution, and the first years of the independence, people in what became the

United States struggled to establish a common basis for their existence as a nation. By 1800 advocates of union had established a nationalist philosophy that sought to reconcile the goal of unity with the reality of distinctiveness. Meanwhile new arrivals and frontier settlers concluded that nationhood was the only viable definition of individual and national identity, for nationhood was the one system that delivered the specific benefits that immigrants and frontiers settlers considered most important.

These issues had their roots in the 1760s, when irate British colonists in North America discovered that their claims about power and authority, participation and exclusion, representation and government found support in the protean concepts of nationalism. Contemporary European arguments that nations embodied distinct peoples conformed with the political arguments of Americans, who charged that British policy imposed unnatural distinctions within the extended British nation. When the colonists eventually rejected their status within the British empire, they placed the same nationalist theories at the center of their own self-creation.[3]

In this context, the Declaration of Independence was more than a statement of jurisdictional and political autonomy. It had to be in order to account for the jarring shift from shrill claims of British citizenship to the proclamation of independent nationhood. Opening with a discussion of the need "for one people to dissolve the political bonds which have connected them to another," the Declaration asserted that the residents of the thirteen colonies were indeed distinct from the people of the British Isles. Political jurisdiction needed to reflect that social reality. Jefferson's assertion was somewhat hyperbolic. It was hardly the first time he wrote in such terms, and it was certainly not the last. Yet Jefferson was not alone. Other advocates of independence throughout the British colonies made the same argument that national boundaries had to be coterminous with distinctive peoples.[4]

Two assumptions in the Declaration underscored these principles. First, the Declaration charged that British rule became null once the foundation of British nationhood collapsed ("one people" separated from "another"). Second, the Declaration projected a unity onto the American colonies ("one people"). But nationhood was an intellectual aspiration rather than a reality in a collection of independent-minded state legislatures, separatist schemes, cultural diversity, vast geographic distances, and people who were more likely to identify themselves by localities or by states. The self-styled Americans had to lay claim to their own national identity if they were to achieve not only independence from Britain but unity among themselves.[5]

Much of the argument for nationhood was in direct response to the very pragmatic problems that some saw in a loose association of polities and individuals. The concept of nation — a collection of peoples bound by some level of sameness — would provide vital ammunition for union — a political structure — during the Federalists' successful bid for the Constitution. A nationalist constitutional order could not exist without a nationalist intellectual framework.

In the end, the nationalist principles that rationalized independence from Great Britain proved equally effective in refuting antifederalism. In the absence of the ethnic, historic, religious, or linguistic foundations that European nationalists used to fashion national communities, Americans emphasized the political principles of the Revolution and the attachment of individual citizens. That attachment might take the form of personal allegiance to states or to the national polity, or (most often) attachment to republican government.[6] This consensus remained in place despite the fact that Americans disagreed radically about what "republican" actually meant.[7] Nationhood proved all the more attractive in the United States because, in the absence of a king, national principles provided the unifying identity without which people could not believe a nation actually existed.[8]

This vision of an American national community does not mean that the American Revolution and the federal structure drew their inspiration exclusively from principles of nationalism. It does mean, however, that principles of nationality dovetailed nicely with other concerns, and many advocates of a permanent union among the newly independent states drew from those principles with growing frequency.[9]

Such a vision was intellectually consistent for Americans at the same time that it was practically feasible given the diversity of their world. It also constituted a crossroads between two different foundations of nationhood. The concept of American nationality combined principles of the Enlightenment inherited from the eighteenth century with notions of affection and sentimental attachment that eventually became more pronounced in the nationalist movements of the nineteenth and twentieth centuries.[10]

People who did not share the political values at the foundation of American nationality were, by definition, foreigners. This principle was readily apparent in the status of Loyalists, nonwhites, and women. After initially assaulting Loyalists as traitors by virtue of their opposition to the new regime, American legislatures and courts eventually classified them as aliens because of their attachment to a foreign nation, namely Great Britain.[11] By claiming that Indians or people of African descent were incapable of appreciating the most basic concepts that all citizens had to understand, whites could uphold their own notions of nationhood. Every person was either an equal citizen or an alien. There could be no middle ground.[12] But the neat rules of citizenship begin to break down when it came to matters of gender. Although women derived their citizenship from male heads of households, the problems of female attachment became the subject of public scrutiny during that first test of nationhood, the American Revolution, when husbands and wives chose different sides.[13]

Americans turned considerations of independence, states' rights, Loyalism, and slavery into considerations of their definition as a nation. Despite the political sources of American nationhood, at no time were suffrage and citizenship one and the same. This does not mean that Americans failed to appreciate the power of voting or that they failed to demand suffrage. Indeed, stripping free people of color from access to suffrage was a crucial step in the process by which state legislatures made clear that freedom would not mean membership in the national community for African Americans. Given such limitations on the voting population, people sought other means to prove their membership in the national community.[14]

This system was at once conveniently satisfying and fraught with tensions. Slaves and free people of color became exactly the sort of permanent aliens that white revolutionaries hoped to avoid through the expulsion of Loyalists and Indians.[15] The persistence of slavery, African-American exclusion, and female coverture did not undermine the notion of equal citizenship for white men. To the contrary, citizenship itself rationalized inequality. The white men who crafted the state and federal constitutions had exactly the intellectual tools they needed to conceive of a world in which inequality within the national community did not in fact exist. Differentiation might be present in the form of divergent state constitutions and a diverse white population, but inequality was not.[16]

For all the ability of white men in the United States to believe in a single national community, legal and constitutional structures nonetheless sustained a bifurcated system of citizenship that was at once uniform and diffuse. Not only did whites belong to two political communities at once — one federal and one state — but the federal Constitution referred to citizens without defining them. Only in the Bill of Rights did American legislators begin to define what political rights unified all Americans and, in turn, helped to determine who was foreign.[17]

State governments addressed these issues with varying clarity and concern. The federal government would tackle the challenges of nationhood most consistently in response to the reality of expansion geographically on the periphery through westward migration and demographically at the center through immigration that occurred primarily in large cities. By the 1790s both forms of expansion proved critical to the discussion of nationhood. Territorial policy and naturalization law therefore served the same function by nationalizing places as well as people. The Naturalization Acts of 1790, 1795, 1798, and 1802 all upheld the principle that a foreigner could not become a citizen until he understood the principles, liberties, and responsibilities that formed the political basis of American nationality.[18] Territorial policy served a similar role, providing for a probationary period during which institutions of republicanism took root in new polities. Once the probationary period ended, both new citizens and new polities entered the national community as equals. Jurisdictional equality was no less dangerous to the viability of the union than individual equality.[19]

When Federalist lawmakers attempted during the 1790s to extend the naturalization of immigrants or to extend territorial rule, they drew from their own assumption that loyalty was mercurial, that allegiance was suspect, and that political resistance was tantamount to treason. The Jeffersonian opposition responded that this policy would only undermine nationhood by fostering resentment and, inevitably, separatism. They proposed instead a policy that would stimulate attachment by promoting equality. They argued that by making the state apparatus stronger, the Federalists only made the nation weaker.[20] Meanwhile, territorial residents and naturalizing aliens believed that *both* parties waited too long. Their complaints only reaffirmed the commonality that joined Federalists and Republicans. Despite their radically different visions of individual adaptability and group development, policymakers shared a belief in the necessity of a homogeneous society with a uniform republican outlook, even as they disagreed on the very definition of republicanism.[21]

Debates over naturalization and territorial expansion during the 1790s helped distill vital principles that had been brewing among the Jeffersonian Republicans. As they struggled to wrest control of the federal government from their Federalist opponents, the Republicans developed a platform that they hoped would foster national cohesion through the loyalty of equal white citizens. They saw this conflict as one between liberty and tyranny. Yet this was also a conflict over the shape of nations, and it needs to be understood as such. Would the United States be unified by force or by loyalty? At a more fundamental level, would the nation-state be defined first as a nation or as a state? In the end, Republicans chose the former, in large part because they doubted that the U.S. government had the resources to extract unity through coercion. Federalists chose the latter. They decided that a powerful federal government would define, protect, and preserve the United States. This outlook proved to be their undoing. Nationhood on Republican terms proved infinitely more attractive, especially to immigrants and western settlers.

It was therefore entirely appropriate that in his first inaugural address in 1801, Thomas Jefferson said, "Let us, then, fellow-citizens, unite with one heart and one mind. . . . We are all republicans, we are all federalists." This statement, so often interpreted as an appeal for political reconciliation, was also a nationalist manifesto. It reaffirmed the notion of a politically if not culturally homogeneous population of white men joined by a national commitment to republican government. It was an aspiration as much as a statement, for the viability of nationhood remained in question.

Jefferson's statements also constituted a reply to a question Supreme Court Justice James Wilson posed in 1793 when he asked, "Do the people of the United States form a Nation?" It was an appropriate question in an appropriate venue. The American constitutional structure reinforced the tension between state and national identities. Wilson's answer was, implicitly, "yes." But what else could he conclude? Indeed, the force with which men like Wilson argued for the existence of nationhood suggests the anxiety that nationalism could create. It was not sufficient for a government to wield power; the absence of any commonality among the citizens of a nation was intellectually untenable and at the same time would inevitably (they believed) lead to separation and suffering.[22]

Empires and Colonists

At the same time that Americans struggled to create a system of nationality, citizenship, and attachment, white Louisianians launched their own campaign to redefine these terms within the Spanish empire. In the process, they found themselves grappling with many of the same issues that proved so vital to Americans, in large part because they drew on the same intellectual principles and responded to similar circumstances. While developments throughout Europe and the Americas shaped white Louisianians' understanding of nationhood, the problematic effort to superimpose Spanish authority on Louisiana was the most important factor. For close to four decades Louisianians attempted to carve a place for themselves within the Spanish empire. They crafted definitions of an imperial polity that shared the American notions of equality but rejected the principle of homogeneity that was so essential to the way Anglo-Americans were defining their national community. They eventually created an outlook that merged the familiar perspective of localism with a remarkably internationalist, cosmopolitan means to resolve their problems.[23]

France, Spain, and Great Britain had all treated (and traded) the Mississippi Valley in the same strategic terms. Each power saw the region as a riverine thoroughfare that would also safeguard other, more important possessions. France began this trend at the end of the seventeenth century, creating the first permanent European colonization scheme in the Lower Mississippi Valley primarily to guarantee trade from Canada. The French soon found that Louisiana generated administrative headaches instead of profits, and when France lost its Canadian possessions during the Seven Years' War, Louisiana instantly lost whatever value it had. As a result, in 1763 France ceded Louisiana (the French holdings west of the Mississippi) to Spain, while Spain ceded West Florida (the name of the Gulf Coast territory from Baton Rouge to Pensacola) to Great Britain. It was a brief tenure for the British. The Spanish restored their sovereignty by force during the American Revolutionary War, and when the British acknowledged American independence in 1783, West Florida lost its value as a bulwark against Spain in the South. For Spain, Louisiana would continue to serve as a buffer to protect more vital possessions in Texas, New Mexico, and Mexico against Britain and, later, the United States.[24]

Louisiana may have been valuable, but it was never profitable. The paucity of white migration, imperial neglect, and repeated interracial warfare between European settlers and Indians combined to create social instability and economic torpor throughout the first half of the eighteenth century. By the time France ceded Louisiana to Spain in 1763, the European and African populations were finally reproducing, albeit at a slow rate. Population growth and the foundations of a profitable agricultural economy at last enabled whites to sever the ties with local Indians that had sustained Europeans during the first years of settlement.[25] Spanish officials arrived in 1768 to find a colony that had coalesced around Francophone and Afro-Louisianian cultures consisting primarily of French immigrants, African-born slaves, and a growing number of native-born Creoles. Convinced that the European presence was in a precarious state, white residents concluded that commercial development would provide the basis for individual as well as collective survival.[26]

Spanish officials hoped to orchestrate a peaceful exchange that would consolidate imperial power in North America. That process got off to a shaky start. In 1768 a small confederacy within the Creole elite deposed the first Spanish governor. Spanish officials had to use force to restore control. They rushed troops to Louisiana, conducted a quick inquiry, and executed five leading planters. A sixth was found dead in his prison cell, and family members privately suspected that Spanish officials had ordered his murder.[27]

The 1768 Revolt, much like the reaction to the Stamp Act over a thousand miles away, was not a fundamental assault on imperial rule. It was instead a call for reform led by local elites who considered themselves entitled to economic opportunity and political power. While some Creoles hoped that France would restore its possession of Louisiana, others wrote to Spanish officials explaining their actions. It was also a fundamentally localist movement, in much the way that a good deal of the resistance in the British colonies emerged from local interpretations of imperial policy. White Louisianians charged the Spanish regime with enacting policies that would be the colony's undoing. By eliminating the Superior Council (a committee of local planters who advised French colonial governors) the Spanish seemed intent on crushing the political aspirations of the local elite. By imposing new commercial restrictions they threatened the prosperity that Louisianians had only just established after decades of struggle. By revising racial laws that created new opportunities for slaves to acquire their freedom the Spanish undermined both racial supremacy and plantation agriculture.[28]

The 1768 Revolt proved to be an anomaly. Never again did white Louisianians rise up against Spanish officials, nor did they make covert attempts to transfer their nationality. Louisianians resigned themselves to membership in the Spanish empire. Independence was neither an intellectual nor a practical possibility for a provincial colony that remained dependent on its imperial masters for vital resources. Nonetheless, white Louisianians resisted the status imposed upon them by the Spanish. Like British colonists in North America, they interpreted imperial regulation over seemingly mundane matters as sources of future disaster. White Louisianians feared that Spanish policy would jeopardize their fragile economy and social structure.[29]

But the Creoles of Louisiana did ask a question of their Spanish rulers that was similar to that facing the British Parliament and Crown and, eventually, the United States: Could an empire function with an entrenched system of jurisdictional inequality? White Louisianians never carried this question to the extreme that the Americans did. They were less concerned with individuals than with polities, assuming that Louisiana's subservient status relative to other Spanish holdings would forever retard regional development.[30] Loyalty was useful but hardly essential to the empire's self-definition. Perhaps most important, the Spanish continued to employ the traditional European notion that the Louisianians' status as colonial subjects emanated downward from the crown, not upward from the Louisianians themselves. Like colonies the world over, Louisiana existed to serve the greater interest of the empire.

Demographic changes in Louisiana during the 1780s and 1790s only reinforced Louisiana's distinctiveness and insecurity. While Creoles still constituted a majority, thousands of Acadians (later known as Cajuns), French Caribbeans, and migrants from France itself arrived in Louisiana. Most of these people were themselves refugees from revolutionary change, whether the Acadians who felt the political and economic squeeze of the British regime in Canada, the Caribbeans who feared the racial revolt in Saint Domingue, the French who fled the assault on the privileges they had known in monarchical

France, or a growing number of British Loyalists who opted for Spanish West Florida, already the site of both French and Spanish communities. All these groups had their own agendas and experienced more than their share of disagreements. At the same time, all demanded equality before the law, commercial access, and opportunities for political advancement.[31]

The increasingly diverse group of white Louisianians continued to search for a viable identity within the Spanish empire. As such, they were only the latest colonials to consider where they fitted within broader cultural or political landscapes.[32] Meanwhile, the French and American revolutions offered attractive visions of imperial reform that collided with Spanish policy. Both the United States and France attempted to establish uniform codes of national citizenship and rejected notions of peripheral inequality.[33]

Louisianians accommodated themselves because Spanish imperial officials never sought the cultural and political homogeneity for the residents of Louisiana that Americans attempted to impose on immigrants. Although they never let Creoles assume high offices, the Spanish kept the number of their own functionaries to a minimum and let Creoles dominate many local offices, especially in New Orleans, where the growing population demanded increased administrative capacities. Equally important, the Louisianians sustained their own linguistic and legal customs. Spanish policy in turn fueled the assumption among Louisianians that neither administrative cohesion nor individual attachment required cultural homogeneity.[34]

White Louisianians and Spaniards also found common ground over external threats that often seemed more dangerous than internal divisions. The Spanish delivered renewed guarantees of defense against both Indians and slaves, promises that became increasingly important as Louisiana's enslaved population grew during the 1790s.[35] During the American Revolution, the Franco-Spanish alliance in support of American independence led Spanish officials and white Louisianians to join in opposition to British operations in the Mississippi Valley and along the Gulf Coast.[36] During the 1790s, apprehension among merchants, planters, and clerics in Louisiana about the leveling impulses of the French Revolution eroded loyalties that some white Louisianians felt toward the Paris regime.

The very weakness of nationalist sentiment in the eighteenth century goes a long way toward explaining the plasticity of local affiliations in Louisiana. White Louisianians might share personal and familial connections in France, but the same localism that guided the way Louisianians acted toward Spain also helps account for why they did not take stronger action to become French. In the same way that policymakers in the United States had to argue the case for their countrymen to create an American union, residents of Louisiana showed none of the sentimental attachments to their land of ancestry that are the hallmark of more recent nationalist movements. Instead, Louisianians could pick and choose their attachments.

So if white Louisianians were neither Spaniards nor Frenchmen, what were they? First, neither term is entirely appropriate, for the very notion of being a "Frenchman" or a "Spaniard" was as novel as it was to consider oneself an "American."[37] Like many people throughout the United States, white Louisianians had a localist outlook that emerged from shared experiences as well as linguistic and ethnic commonalities within the Francophone population. Yet the Louisianians also certainly thought in terms of larger communities. They were colonial provincials attempting to maximize their possibilities within larger polities. As a result, Americans and Louisianians conceived of citizenship and nationhood in very similar ways. By 1800 both groups saw advantages in equality among white male citizens and benefits from broad networks of interest. For Americans, equality would preserve the union and a republican political culture; for Louisianians, equality would establish prosperity and local power.

Slavery and Freedom

For settlers of European birth and ancestry in the United States and in Louisiana, the creation of national communities was in large part contingent on white supremacy. In the United States, nationhood demanded the definition of non-Europeans as quasi-alien and, in turn, the complete exclusion of those people from the national community. Things were more complicated in Louisiana, where a variety of factors created a different racial order within which slaves and free people of color proposed their own models for social organization. Two profoundly different Afro-Louisianian communities emerged, one seeking membership in an imperial polity, the other committed to its destruction.

Slavery was no less cruel in Spanish Louisiana than in French Louisiana, or for that matter in the United States. Nonetheless, the legal status of slaves and other nonwhites was indicative of the different visions of citizenship in the United States and Spanish colonial Louisiana. Unlike the United States, where the predominant effort focused on creating a clear line of demarcation between citizens and aliens (whether unnaturalized whites or excluded people of color), Louisiana was home to a more complex caste system in which people of European, African, and Native American ancestry all knew different forms of inequality beneath an imperial leadership that ruled supreme.[38]

Slavery in Louisiana was almost as old as the colony itself. The shortage of white settlers led French colonial officials to enslave Indians soon after creating the first farms near the Gulf Coast. Africans and Caribbean Creoles of

African descent soon replaced Indians as the primary source of slaves, and the colony's prosperity grew in almost direct proportion to the availability of unfree labor.[39] The Louisiana that France sold to the United States in 1803 was home to almost 11,000 slaves and 1,500 free people of color, nearly equaling the white population of approximately 15,000.[40]

Nonwhites and people of mixed-race ancestry secured opportunities in Louisiana unparalleled in the United States. Slaves had considerable freedom of movement. Slaves were assumed to be people, each with a soul, and as such they could sue to purchase their own freedom, even without their masters' consent. These liberal manumission laws created the largest and most prosperous free black population in slaveholding North America. Free people of color owned property (including slaves), established contacts with white businessmen, and participated in social activities open to all free people.[41]

Most free people of color lived in New Orleans, a city that both reflected and fueled Louisiana's growth in the last decades of the eighteenth century. What had been a struggling village on the point of collapse only a few decades before was by 1800 a thriving entrepōt. In a variety of trades, the majority of New Orleans' artisans were free people of color. Free men of color served in local militias during the American Revolution. The militia eventually emerged as a crucial institution, one that free men of color used to establish membership in the polity and a hierarchy among themselves. Free people of color could worship freely at the cathedral that stood in New Orleans' central square.[42]

Unlike in the United States, where American nationhood demanded the exclusion of nonwhites, free people of color in Louisiana became increasingly enmeshed in the free population of Louisiana. The same individual and jurisdictional inequality that proved so infuriating to white Louisianians also validated the status of free people of color as unequal members of the broader imperial polity.[43]

Like enslaved Louisianians, free people of color engaged at the local level the questions of unity that were of such concern to American policymakers at the federal level. The question that free people of color faced was whether to join with slaves in opposition to racial hierarchy, or to find common cause with whites in the interest of creating a single community of free individuals. Although most whites suspected them of favoring the former course, the vast majority of free people of color chose the latter. They found the means to bind themselves to white Louisianians through commercial activity, kinship (both literal and fictive), and even through efforts to preserve the slave regime. Solidarity among free people of color and connections with white Louisianians became mutually reinforcing. Both provided prosperity as well as subtle forms of political muscle.[44]

Conditions in Louisiana had emerged as a product of particular frontier conditions and the complex interaction of French and Spanish imperial policies. The very instability of the French grip on Louisiana fueled a fluid social context in which people of European, African, and Native American ancestry interacted in ways that would have been impossible elsewhere. Differences separating French and Spanish racial policies from British codes only exacerbated Louisiana's differences from the British colonies east of the Mississippi. But race also responded to differing visions of nationhood, and the very demand for equality that proved so advantageous to American citizens also created new systems of oppression that had no parallel in Louisiana.

These matters became all the more complicated as the demographic and social dynamics of Louisiana changed. Access to new slaves had dwindled during the last years of French rule in Louisiana. Indeed, the 1768 Revolt emerged in no small part from the anger of white settlers at Spanish officials who seemed hesitant to support a rejuvenated slave trade. In the 1780s and 1790s, however, Spanish Louisiana became the home to a booming slave trade. As the number of white settlers and African slaves increased, and as Spain built a more effective infrastructure, slaves lost whatever leverage they had possessed. Although slaves continued to possess legal rights in Spanish Louisiana that had no counterpart in the United States, the system of intercultural exchange that had sustained the colony of Louisiana for decades increasingly gave way to the beginnings of a plantation economy.[45]

This population of Afro-Louisianians was hardly a community, for linguistic and ethnic differences combined to separate slaves from one another.[46] Nonetheless, news of the French Revolution and of the racial revolt in the French colony of Saint Domingue inspired enslaved Afro-Louisianians to new forms of organization and mobilization. The most striking example of the newfound alliances came in 1795, when slaves in Pointe Coupée (a plantation district on the western banks of the Mississippi not far from Baton Rouge) began planning a revolt, the details of which remain elusive. The conspirators included Afro-Louisianian Creoles and African newcomers, who like Anglo-Americans sought independence through unity.[47]

Although white settlers and Spanish officials effectively crushed the conspiracy, the mobilization in 1795 served notice that slaves could overcome internal differences in the interest of realizing political goals. In the most local terms, slaves were articulating the benefits of union that white Americans hoped to impose on a continental scale. They, too, sought networks of interest that would overcome the profound cultural differences between Africans and Creoles of African descent. And like their white counterparts—who seemed to occupy such a different world—enslaved Afro-Louisianians developed their plans in the specific context of the friction that shaped the imperial structure of Europe and the Americas in the late eighteenth century.

Slaves in Pointe Coupée made their appeal on the basis of class rather than race. As a result, the largest following they drew from the free population consisted of disaffected white settlers, most of them poor men who concluded quite accurately that elite Louisianians were reaping the real benefits of tighter integration in the Spanish imperial economy. By contrast, few free people of color joined with the slaves, choosing instead to mobilize alongside whites to preserve the racial regime. Their reasons varied. Most free people of color were of mixed-race ancestry, and many felt more closely connected to their free white neighbors than to the Afro-Louisianian slaves. Still others were committed to establishing themselves as members of an imperial community that, if not equal, nonetheless provided opportunities for all its free subjects.[48]

And like slaves, white Louisianians, or American policymakers, free people of color found their own actions guided by revolutionary models. The revolution in France, with its guarantees of equality, and the revolt of slaves and free people of color that it inspired in the Caribbean colony of Saint Domingue, provided the rhetoric to assault racial supremacy. But like white Louisianians, free people of color were careful in what they borrowed from outside revolutions. They tended to identify with the first stage of the revolt in Saint Domingue, when free people of color had demanded equality within the French empire without necessarily advocating the end of slavery. As the Caribbean movement became increasingly radical, many free people of color in Louisiana remained steadfast in their support of slavery, whether because they did not want to lose their own human property, because they feared a violent revolt, or because they recognized that condemning insurrectionary slaves provided an ideal means to reinforce linkages with white Louisianians.[49]

Just as the concept of nationhood in the United States proved crucial to the construction of racial hierarchy, the different principles of European empires would lead to profoundly different structures in Louisiana. Residents of these European imperial polities were first and foremost subjects rather than citizens. That status not only accorded considerable powers to the monarchs of France and Spain; it also presumed inferiority to the imperial centers. Yet even though the codes of race were different in Louisiana, the way that race informed matters of unity and difference was not.

Villages and Confederacies

The largest concentrations of Louisianians — whether free or enslaved — were in New Orleans and on the plantations that followed the twists and turns of the Mississippi River. At the very center of Louisiana, these people attempted to recast the systems of power within the Spanish empire. A similar movement was afoot on Louisiana's periphery, where Spain's power in North America was sorely tested by the Indians of Louisiana. But the Indians' responses were entirely in keeping with those of other residents in North America. Like the leaders of the United States, Indians concluded that autonomy required new forms of unity among themselves. Like the Louisianians of European and African ancestry, Indians began to create new communities of interest that would serve their agendas.

In addition to a variety of independent villages, Louisiana was home to two major Indian confederacies: the Choctaw in the East and the Caddo in the West. Choctaw and Caddo can be misleading titles, for they impose forms of unity that were, respectively, collapsing and beginning. Connected by linguistic similarity and commercial affiliation, the Choctaw and Caddo villages were as internally distinct as most other Indian societies of North America. The same population growth and economic consolidation that proved so beneficial for whites and free people of color created a crisis for Indians. If they were not always able to press their own terms on the French and the Spanish, Indians in Louisiana did at least enjoy forms of leverage that those in other parts of the Americas had lost as Europeans consolidated their power.

Although the Choctaw had occasionally unified during the eighteenth century in opposition to whites, those bonds were disintegrating, and whole villages were moving to the more sparsely populated reaches of western Louisiana. As with whites, slaves, and free people of color, experiences with French and Spanish colonial rule established Native Americans' priorities as well as their views on race. The Choctaw were familiar with whites, and they had suffered accordingly. They had dominated the banks of the Lower Mississippi when French settlers arrived in the late 1600s and early 1700s. Within a century disease and intermittent warfare left their numbers decimated and their regional power destroyed.[50]

Scattered in the area that now constitutes Texarkana, the Caddo were more fortunate. During the era of French rule their land became a buffer between the French and Spanish empires. The Caddo navigated between the two empires, both in their settlement and in their diplomacy. The situation changed after 1763, and the Caddo received a taste of the Choctaws' experience when they were squeezed between Texas and Louisiana during the four decades of Spanish rule. Just as white Louisianians struggled to come to terms with their change from French to Spanish subjects in 1763, so too did the Caddo seek ways to respond to the changing face of European power in the Americas. And at the same time that American nationalists concluded in the 1780s that unity would preserve both domestic tranquility and international security in the United States, some of the Caddo were advocating unity for much the same purpose. The most militant responses came from the Kadohadacho villages of the Red River Valley. Like the emerging political elite of the United States, Kadohadacho leaders found that unity among Indians delivered power to themselves.[51]

This was less an ethnic or racial appeal to unity than a pragmatic and political one. The foreign threat for the Kadohadacho took various forms. Although the Spanish constituted the most prevalent danger, violent disputes with the Osage Indians living to the north of the Caddo indicated not only the limits of pan-Indian unity, but also the ways that tension among some Indians could create unity among others.

The Caddo were hardly unique in their efforts to achieve unity during the last decades of the eighteenth century. Not only were Americans like Jefferson and Madison unrelenting in their call for union, but Indians throughout North America were also claiming that unity might serve domestic and foreign goals. Militants from the Eastern Woodlands to the Gulf Coast were claiming that unity would promote spiritual revitalization while providing the means to resist white dominance. Like the residents of the United States, these militants established an increasingly distinct definition of the foreign, abandoning some of the older give-and-take that had characterized intercultural contact.[52]

The Caddo also provide a cautionary tale. They were never so radical as other Indian militants, nor did they reject out of hand the notion that connections to whites could bring benefits. Like free people of color, they constructed different alliances in different contexts. Nor were the identities for any of the people in Louisiana ever so fixed as to be unshakable. Not only was Louisiana home to a large population of mixed ancestry, but people saw no reason why they could not change their attachments if need be. The real change in the eighteenth century was not so much the creation of nations as it was the recognition that broader networks of interest could serve specific goals. People in Louisiana and the United States had reconceived their own notions of community in response to those conditions. In 1803 the geopolitical situation changed. The question facing people on both sides of the Mississippi was how much things would change within an American Louisiana.

2

Acquisition

A thousand miles from the Cabildo where Laussat delivered his predictions for an American Louisiana, another official was preparing his commentary on Louisiana at a very different center of government. That official was Thomas Jefferson, and the commentary took the form of a letter to his son-in-law, Thomas Mann Randolph. It was 5 July 1803, and the federal capital was returning to business after celebrating the twenty-seventh anniversary of independence. Jefferson informed Randolph that American negotiators had "signed a treaty with France, ceding to us the island of N. Orleans and all of Louisiana. . . . This removes from us the greatest source of danger to our peace."[1] Perhaps so, but Jefferson was not altogether satisfied with the treaty. It did not achieve vital diplomatic objectives and came with troubling domestic ramifications.

More than anything, the Louisiana Purchase came as a surprise, and not necessarily a welcome one. Not only did the treaty fail to indicate how the people of Louisiana would fit into an American national community, but it did not even define what "Louisiana" actually was. That the Louisiana Purchase would fuel dispute was only partly a result of its text. In 1802 and 1803, the Jefferson administration attempted to settle affairs on the Mississippi River in a way that would meet its definition of American security. In the end, however, it was the European powers that determined the fate of Louisiana, and France eventually imposed on the United States a Louisiana Purchase quite different from what the Jefferson administration had wanted. That the Louisiana Purchase the United States ratified in 1803 was so different from the one the federal government had sought was the crucial factor in shaping the relationship between Louisiana and the United States.

In the immediate aftermath of the Purchase, members of the Congress and the administration attempted to create a government for this new acquisition. The administration's foreign policymaking as well as Congress' domestic policymaking emerged from the same concerns about expansion, naturalization, and nationhood that had shaped American political debate during the quarter-century since independence. And the ramifications of those events in 1803–04 had tremendous sticking power. Not only did the text of the Louisiana Purchase itself prove critical, but the initial plan for an American government in Louisiana established the contours of politics and administration in the years that followed.

As Americans grappled with the Louisiana Purchase, they immediately learned that the extended debates over geographic expansion in the eighteenth century had left policymakers ill prepared for the more difficult task of adjusting to a sudden increase in population. On subjects both foreign and domestic, people in the United States saw the Louisiana Purchase in a context of expansion that posed numerous dangers. And yet these fears seem disconnected from Jefferson's own comments to Randolph, in part because Jefferson's exuberance was vague and in part because people would eventually have difficulty remembering the uncertainty of 1803. The ambivalence that Americans expressed toward the Purchase in 1803 emerged from sentiments that had been brewing since the 1770s. Those concerns made command of the Mississippi a necessity, but would also make incorporating Louisiana seem an insurmountable challenge.

"One of the Principal Channels of Future Commerce"

The ink was hardly dry on the Declaration of Independence before Americans began to consider their future in the Mississippi Valley. As settlements in Tennessee, Kentucky, and the Old Northwest (now the Midwest) grew with bewildering speed, a coalition ranging from key figures in the nation's emerging political elite to anonymous western settlers concluded that unrestricted passage down the length of the Mississippi River would be critical to preserving domestic harmony. If western settlers could not transport their goods down the Mississippi for transshipment into the Gulf of Mexico and the Atlantic, economic pressures would endanger a republican social order and a stable union. Western settlers actively cultivated these fears to ensure that federal policymakers protected their interests.[2]

Policymakers in the United States focused particular attention on the mouth of the Mississippi and the port cities of New Orleans and Baton Rouge that controlled its approaches. They were hardly the first to do so. European powers had eyed the region for over a century, and the Spanish who governed Louisiana were well aware of the Mississippi's strategic value. Beginning in 1784, the Spanish excluded Americans from trade down the lower Mississippi River, a policy that for western settlers constituted a corollary to the restrictive policies that the British imposed on merchants along the eastern seaboard attempting to trade in the British West Indies. As a result, one of the first tasks of American diplomats was to negotiate treaties with Spain and Great Britain that would secure American trading privileges down the Mississippi and across the Atlantic. These negotiations bore fruit first in the Jay Treaty of 1794, an agreement with Great Britain that proved so controversial it fueled the creation of organized parties; and the Treaty of San Lorenzo in 1795, a less controversial agreement between the United States and Spain that guaranteed American merchants unobstructed passage down the length of the Mississippi and the free deposit of American goods in New Orleans for transshipment to the Atlantic. The Treaty of San Lorenzo also ceded most of what now constitutes Alabama and Mississippi to the United States, with the crucial exception of the Gulf Coast.[3]

Pleasure with the Treaty of San Lorenzo was short-lived, however, for in 1801 Americans learned that Spain had retroceded Louisiana to France in a secret agreement the previous year. Napoleon had little interest in promoting French settlement in Louisiana — he knew that Louisiana had been an unprofitable colony — but he believed it would provide vital raw materials and foodstuffs to France's immensely lucrative holdings in the Caribbean. As a result, the Treaty of San Ildefonso (the instrument of the retrocession) preserved Spanish administration of Louisiana. Americans worried that France or Spain might argue that the retrocession invalidated the Treaty of San Lorenzo. Louisiana now belonged to one unreliable nation and was governed by another. The news came within months of Jefferson's inauguration as president, and the precarious status of American trade down the Mississippi soon commanded his administration's agenda.[4]

American policymakers found their fears confirmed in October 1802, when the Spanish intendant at New Orleans abruptly suspended the American right of deposit. In addition to augmenting their fears of Spanish caprice on the right of deposit, the retrocession reinforced growing Republican disillusionment with the government of Revolutionary France. Reports from Paris indicated that "France . . . could not suffer the Americans to navigate the Mississippi, nor enjoy a right of Deposit." Worse still, France seemed intent on reestablishing itself as a major force on the American mainland. Reports soon reached the United States that as many as 1,500 French soldiers were earmarked for assignment in Louisiana. Americans assumed, incorrectly, that the French emperor intended to place a massive army on the North American mainland.[5]

No matter who controlled the Mississippi, it seemed unlikely they would satisfy American goals or acknowledge American commercial aspirations.[6] Developments overseas overlapped with equally troubling domestic news. The Kentucky legislature passed a resolution condemning the Spanish action, claiming that without the right of deposit western settlers would suffer disastrous losses on their cotton crop. Federalists as well as Republicans projected this concern onto the entire West, and in the Mississippi Crisis (as the situation soon became known) they saw nothing less than a fundamental threat to the preservation of the union.

The response to this situation reflected diplomatic priorities and also helped to establish the dynamics within the newly installed Jefferson administration. As they conferred over how best to respond, Jefferson and Secretary of State Madison assumed control of the Republican foreign policy to the exclusion of their colleagues. Jefferson was convinced that his own vice president, Aaron Burr, had conspired against him in the 1800 election, and Burr immediately found himself excluded from Jefferson's confidence. Secretary of the Treasury Albert Gallatin, whom Jefferson trusted as much as Madison, played a secondary role, usually concurring with his colleagues rather than driving debate. Secretary of War Henry Dearborn and Secretary of the Navy Robert Smith had less influence. Although international tensions had obvious repercussions for their departments, they concerned themselves with administrative and operational matters rather than with formulating policy. They saw in this crisis only the latest example of a mercurial European power ignoring treaty obligations in pursuit of its own economic interests.[7]

Meanwhile the most ardent Federalists advocated a quick military response to the Mississippi Crisis, an invasion that would settle the matter once and for all. Although members of the administration considered war a possibility if they were unable to resolve the situation through negotiation, they also knew that the United States lacked the military power to make invasion a viable option. Jefferson and Madison rejected the possibility of war or of a European alliance so long as a diplomatic strategy would serve both their short-term goals in the Southwest and their long-term vision of an international system governed by treaty.

The Republicans hoped to resolve the crisis by ending European control of the Mississippi. The administration had broached the possibility of buying a vaguely defined "Louisiana" from France as early as 1801. That purchase would consist of the small region commanding the mouth of the Mississippi.[8] In reaction to the events of 1802, Jefferson and Madison renewed their efforts to acquire that territory through purchase. They defined their objectives in limited terms. They sought New Orleans and the Gulf Coast, especially West Florida. This territory would consolidate the federal government's hold east of the Mississippi, and included territory that the Spanish had refused to cede in the Treaty of San Lorenzo. It would require only the most minimal changes to the federal structure, for the territory could easily be added to the Mississippi Territory.[9]

The administration also hoped to exploit the uneasy peace in Europe, which in 1801 had ended eight years of warfare between the allies and opponents of revolutionary France. But the American minister to France, Robert R. Livingston, found himself ignored by French leaders, who were far more concerned with other Europeans, whether friends or foes. Repeated delays in Paris led Jefferson and Madison to dispatch James Monroe as minister plenipotentiary to bolster American diplomatic efforts. Monroe's departure in March 1803 presented Jefferson and Madison with their last opportunity to influence the negotiations. In lengthy, detailed instructions signed by Madison but written with Jefferson's extensive involvement, the two men reviewed their central objectives. As much as any document, the instructions revealed what the administration sought in the Southwest. This document underscored Jefferson and Madison's focus on regional security concerns, established the limits of their territorial ambitions, and confirmed their vision of diplomatic relations. The instructions also provide the key to understanding the administration's pleasure and frustration with the subsequent fruits of the Paris negotiations.[10]

At the core, the instructions reiterated the necessity of acquiring New Orleans and West Florida. This objective appeared twice, first as an injunction to the diplomats and later as an unequivocal statement in the draft treaty. "The object in view," Madison wrote in his opening paragraph, "is to procure by just and satisfactory arrangements, a Cession to the United States of New Orleans, and of West and East Florida." The draft treaty opened by stating that "France cedes to the United States, for ever, the territory East of the River Mississippi, comprehending the two Floridas, [and] the Island of New Orleans . . . France reserving to herself all her territory on the West side of the Mississippi." To achieve this end, Madison outlined a variety of possible diplomatic configurations. Livingston and Monroe could offer commercial and diplomatic incentives. They could purchase other portions of French Louisiana that they might later exchange. Livingston and Monroe could offer $10 million, but should haggle for a lower price. Madison intended these options to create the circumstances in which Livingston and Monroe would finally be able to secure the purchase of the vital territory at the mouth of the Mississippi.[11]

Livingston and Monroe's instructions expressed only modest territorial objectives. They were not a blueprint for Manifest Destiny. This is a matter of no small importance, because historians have often situated the Louisiana Purchase within a broader synthesis of expansion.[12] Conceiving of the Louisiana Purchase as a link in an unbroken chain of expansionism contributes to an attractive portrait, one that creates a simple and direct history of territorial acquisition connecting the Revolution to the Louisiana Purchase to the Mexican War. Yet by collapsing expansion into a single rubric, scholars have ignored both the complexities of expansion in 1803 and the changes that came in the half-century that followed.

Developments in both Europe and the Caribbean that had made the French so intent on keeping Louisiana in 1802 made them equally eager to sell the colony a year later. The massive army that Napoleon had dispatched to restore white authority in Saint Domingue disintegrated through a combination of disease and an effective revolutionary army. Meanwhile the precarious peace in Europe — which had enabled Napoleon to focus his attention and resources on the Caribbean — collapsed as well. During the winter of 1802–03 Napoleon decided he could not meet the expenses of both an overseas empire and a European war. First among the losses was Saint Domingue, where Napoleon decided to abandon his attempt to preserve French control. And without Saint Domingue, there was no reason to keep Louisiana.[13]

Napoleon had only to read the pleadings from Livingston to realize that he had an eager buyer in the United States. Nor did Napoleon fail to grasp that American control of the Mississippi would isolate British holdings in Canada.[14] No sooner did Monroe reach Paris in April 1803 than French negotiators announced their intention to the stunned American diplomats. Although Americans knew of the circumstances in Saint Domingue, they thought the situation would provide new leverage in securing New Orleans, not a reason for Napoleon to dispense with his entire North American possessions.[15]

In less than a month, French and American diplomats hammered out a treaty in which France ceded all its territory on the North American continent to the United States in exchange for $11.5 million plus an American promise to annul $3.5 million in French debts. The French would expel the Spanish (the immediate source of the Mississippi Crisis) and resume direct control over Louisiana in preparation for final transfer to the United States. Much of the treaty's structure mirrored the plan Madison had established in his instructions to Livingston and Monroe. The French officials who made the final decision to sell Louisiana agreed to these terms because few of the provisions clashed with their own goals. But the timing and the thrust of the Louisiana Purchase remained the product of French decisionmaking. Nothing revealed this disparity as clearly as the scope and the price tag, both of which exceeded any of the administration's plans. The United States did not buy Louisiana so much as France sold it.[16]

French and American diplomats finished negotiating the Louisiana Purchase on 30 April 1803, backdating their signatures two days later on the final instruments of the cession. On 13 May Livingston and Monroe wrote a triumphant letter to Madison informing him that "we have the pleasure to transmit to you . . . a Treaty which we have concluded with the french Republic for the Purchase & Cession of Louisiana." This was also a defensive letter, since both men knew the Louisiana they had bought bore little resemblance to the one the administration wanted. "An acquisition of so great an extent was, we well know, not contemplated by our appointment; but we are persuaded that the Circumstances and Considerations which induced us to make it, will justify us, in the measure, to our Government and Country."[17]

Two months later, following the treaty's lengthy passage across the Atlantic, Jefferson wrote his letter to Thomas Mann Randolph announcing receipt of the Louisiana Purchase. For all Jefferson's exuberance in that letter, Livingston and Monroe's caveats were a better indicator of what would follow. They predicted both the domestic reaction and the problems of governing "so great an extent." In the following months, critics of the Purchase charged that territorial acquisition would destroy the union. Meanwhile, pamphleteers who endorsed the administration's plans were hard pressed to develop theories that would make a virtue of the land acquired through the Louisiana Purchase.[18] Even the most fervent defenders of the Louisiana Purchase were guarded in their language, for they shared the sentiment of many other Americans who associated considerable problems with the acquisition of new land and new peoples.

"The Inhabitants of the Ceded Territory Shall be Incorporated"

News of the breakthrough in Paris came as a shock to Americans. The Louisiana Purchase as dictated by France was neither what they had sought nor what they had expected. Despite their initial happiness, members of Congress and the administration feared that specific provisions and the occasionally vague language in the treaty would shackle American diplomats, inhibit an orderly transfer, or fail to secure American territorial claims. Far from resolving the question of Louisiana's national status, the terms of the treaty only created new doubts about the boundaries of national sovereignty and, as a result, the definition of nations. In response to that treaty, Americans focused not just on the acquisition of places but also on the acquisition of people.

At the most fundamental level, the treaty offered the vaguest definition of Louisiana, ceding to the United States the land that France had acquired through the retrocession—a political jurisdiction rather than a fixed geographic space. Although Americans had no doubt of their acquisition of New Orleans, gone were the guarantees of an American title to West Florida. Worse still, the United States was in no position to impose its own vision of Louisiana on the world. Although the Spanish grudgingly acknowledged the French cession of New Orleans and the land west of the Mississippi to the United States, they refused to relinquish sovereignty over the Gulf Coast. The United States and Spain found themselves engaged in a dispute over exactly what constituted "Louisiana," an argument that continued for years.

Spanish policymakers were already infuriated with France for selling Louisiana. They also saw in the Louisiana Purchase only the latest example of American territorial ambitions. Reports from North America only reinforced their belief in unchecked American aspirations.[19] If American policymakers were unwilling to see themselves as threatening, the Spanish failed to appreciate the security concerns that motivated American policymakers. Overreaction became a force unto itself. With both sides projecting avarice on their opponents and seeing none in themselves, they exacerbated the tensions in the Mississippi Valley. But the rising diplomatic tensions only reinforced the fact that the struggle to accomplish the objectives that Jefferson and Madison outlined in the instructions to Livingston and Monroe was infinitely more important in shaping their policy in the Southwest than plans for an American empire west of the Mississippi. The West that mattered most to policymakers was in the Ohio and Mississippi Valleys. They hoped to keep white settlers in that region content and secure through the diplomatic incorporation of Louisiana.[20]

Along with the absence of a settlement on West Florida was the presence of a vast new domain. The United States had acquired millions of acres stretching from the Gulf of Mexico to Canada, from the Mississippi River to the Rockies. Such an acquisition may have satisfied Jefferson's most ambitious fantasies, and historians have often interpreted it as such, but even the president expressed reservations. There was more to worry about in the Louisiana Purchase than just boundaries, although the boundary problem was trouble enough. The treaty required the United States to grant preferential trade agreements at a time when Americans were particularly resistant to any treaty that seemed to reduce the federal government's policymaking independence. The Louisiana Purchase further required the United States to respect European agreements with Louisiana's Indians, which came just as the federal government was becoming more confident in its ability to press its own terms on the Indians of North America.

Of all the passages in the Louisiana Purchase, however, none proved so explosive as Article III, the passage that most directly addressed the residents of Louisiana. More than any other legislation, treaty, or public pronouncement, the single lengthy sentence that constituted Article III governed the way people conceived of Louisiana in the years that followed and determined the debate over incorporation.

With stark language, Article III dictated what would become of Louisiana's residents:

> The inhabitants of the ceded territory shall be incorporated in the union of the United States, admitted as soon as possible, according to the principles of the federal constitution, to the enjoyment of all the rights, advantages and immunities of citizens of the United States; and in the mean time they shall be maintained and protected in the free enjoyment of their liberty, property, and the religion which they profess.[21]

Exactly what would happen to the Louisianians had been a matter of minor concern in the administration only a year before, in large part because American policymakers expected to acquire only a small number of people through the cession of New Orleans and West Florida, people who in turn would most likely be enveloped by the existing polity of the Mississippi Territory. Diplomatic imperatives in the Southwest were also so pressing in 1802 and 1803 that the Jefferson administration actually gave little thought to the questions of citizenship that played such a vital role in early American nationbuilding. Madison's only attempt to address the question of Louisiana's residents came in Article VII of his draft treaty:

> To incorporate the inhabitants of the hereby ceded territory with the citizens of the United States on an equal footing, being a provision, which cannot now be made, it is to be expected, from the character and policy of the United States, that such footing will take place without unnecessary delay. In the mean time, they shall be secure in their persons and property, and in the free enjoyment of their religion.[22]

In the instructions to Monroe and Livingston that accompanied the draft treaty, Madison explained that Article VII had been "suggested by the respect due to the rights of the people inhabiting the ceded territory, and by the delay which may be found in constituting them a regular and integral portion of the union." He wanted to apply principles enumerated in the Bill of Rights even if he was unprepared to advocate statehood. Full federal citizenship similar to that of other territorial residents was also inappropriate, since the residents of Louisiana were foreigners. In the absence of a state constitution or even an organic act like the Northwest Ordinance, Article VII would preserve the most important rights that came with federal citizenship. Citizenship itself, however, would happen sometime in the future and would be the subject of domestic policymaking. In the meantime, the federal government would enjoy an interval to develop a cohesive policy for naturalizing the residents of Louisiana.[23]

The differences between Article III and the draft Article VII may seem of a minor semantic nature, but they reflected fundamentally different expectations. Critical to the draft Article VII was the use of the future tense, implying that the residents of New Orleans would undergo the same probationary period embodied by federal naturalization policy.[24] While the Louisianians were not ready to be Americans, Jefferson and Madison expressed optimism that such a transformation would inevitably occur. The absence of *permanent* alienation or legal inferiority enabled Jefferson and Madison to see the provision in marked contrast to the colonial systems that other nations established over newly acquired territory. Colonial relationships were anathema to the Republicans' territorial policy, and they hoped Article VII would extend that principle to Louisiana. Nonetheless, Madison specifically rejected *immediate* citizenship.[25]

Article III determined what the Louisiana Purchase would mean in the years following 1803. It was the reference point by which people determined whether the Louisiana Purchase was beneficial or dangerous. It was the text that people imported to serve their own visions of what place Louisiana — and above all its occupants — would occupy in an American national community. It also provided the word — incorporation — that people would use repeatedly in the years that followed both to establish their priorities and to evaluate conditions in Louisiana.

Despite these challenges posed by the wording of the Louisiana Purchase in general and Article III in particular, Jefferson and Madison were eager to see the Louisiana Purchase take effect. Whatever problems they saw would have to be the subject of future discussion. In the meantime, it was vital for the United States to secure what it could and tackle the realities of governing Louisiana. In August 1803 Jefferson called a special meeting of Congress to consider the Louisiana Purchase. In the months that followed, he actively attempted to secure a quick settlement of the Louisiana Purchase, with Kentucky's Senator John Breckinridge introducing legislation almost unchanged from the drafts he received from the president.[26] Jefferson acknowledged that the Purchase required the work of both houses, for while the Senate alone could approve the treaty, the Purchase had such profound domestic ramifications that the House would also need to consider how to extend federal sovereignty.

"Are They Citizens of the United States, or Can Congress Make Them Such?"

It was in this atmosphere of urgency and ambivalence that federal leaders attempted to determine exactly how things would work in Louisiana. The debate would reach its greatest intensity during the fall and winter of 1803–04 as members of Congress debated first the implementation of the Louisiana Purchase and then the plan for Louisiana's government. They immediately concluded that the domestic policymaking structure would be hard pressed to resolve the problems they saw in the treaty. Some policymakers remained convinced that the United States could not incorporate the foreigners of Louisiana in ways that were in keeping with American principles of nationhood and naturalization. Although members of Congress were eventually able to construct arguments for the viability of incorporation, it was not an easy task. They claimed that American nationhood could accommodate the Louisianians, but that only through aggressive policymaking would the United States preserve the attachment of its new acquisition.

This proved to be the case; the first reports from Louisiana were not good. Private correspondence and published travel narratives of outsiders visiting Louisiana described a society so fundamentally corrupt that white residents of Louisiana would be incapable of joining an American national community premised on republican principles.[27] As Congress turned to the problem of governing Louisiana, critics raised issues that had plagued Americans for decades. In the process, they showed a prescience that was missing within the cabinet. Jefferson and Madison's focus on resolving disputes with France and Spain prevented them from perceiving the considerable challenges facing the federal government as it attempted to incorporate the people of Louisiana. Decades of ambivalence about expansion fueled the debate. Obviously, the United States had been the site of new settlements, but always within fixed boundaries and with a predominantly Anglo-American population. Policymakers had never considered expansion on the scale of the Louisiana Purchase, whether that meant acquiring so much land or incorporating so many foreigners.

As Senator William Plumer of New Hampshire wrote, "our Republican government derives its authority & momentum from the frequent meetings of the mass of people in towns & county assemblies. An extension of the body politic will enfeeble the circulation of its powers & energies in the extreme." From this foundation he felt "confident that the ratification of the treaty & the possession of that immense territory will hasten the dissolution of our present government."[28] Plumer, like so many other Americans, was convinced that the grip on Louisiana was extremely fragile. White resentment or nonwhite revolt seemed the most likely source of domestic separatism, either of which could in turn lead a foreign power to recognize the ease with which it could seize Louisiana.

The debate on governance for Louisiana would also show just how irrelevant the constitutionality of the Louisiana Purchase as a foreign treaty (the constitutional issue of greatest concern to most scholars) would be in practice when compared with the difficulties of incorporating the residents of Louisiana. For a brief period, Jefferson hoped to circumvent constitutional problems altogether and drafted two versions of a constitutional amendment, but he eventually abandoned the effort, concluding that constitutional revision was neither feasible nor necessary. Allies and opponents followed suit. The real question facing policymakers was not whether the Constitution provided the power to acquire new land, but whether it provided the means to govern that land effectively. Members of Congress certainly seemed less concerned with the constitutionality of executive action than with governance. In October 1803 the Senate ratified the treaty, and both houses approved the actual transfer of power after a relatively brief debate. It was when Congress turned to the more practical affair of what the United States would actually do in Louisiana that the problems began.

With the Louisiana Purchase a reality, a five-member Senate committee began drafting a governance plan for Louisiana. Once again the administration hoped to drive the agenda. At its first meeting, committee member John Quincy Adams reported that John Breckinridge, the administration's unofficial representative, "had a form of government ready prepared" based on Jefferson's own provisions. Adams would find serving on the committee a frustrating experience. "My ideas are so different from those entertained by the committee," he explained, "that I have nothing to do but to make fruitless opposition."[29]

In January 1804 the committee submitted a plan that divided Louisiana into northern and southern districts, upheld immediate citizenship for its residents, and created a few appointed offices. It was hardly an unprecedented act; policymakers had models in the Northwest Ordinance of 1787 and the legislation that created Louisiana's neighbor, the Mississippi Territory, in 1798. But the fundamental problem posed by the Louisiana Purchase soon became apparent. Although members of Congress had shown few reservations about the constitutionality of *geographic* expansion, imposing a government that would be able to handle subsequent migration and to govern small populations, they immediately expressed ambivalence about *demographic* expansion through the sudden, unnaturalized acquisition of foreign peoples. In this context, no previous plan for governing western peoples provided an appropriate model for Louisiana. The problem in Louisiana was the existing population, a force of demographic expansion. The closest thing to a precedent was the Quebec Act of 1774, by which the British established a colonial regime in Canada that sustained certain French institutions. But the Quebec Act preserved the colonial systems of power along a European imperial model, exactly the sort of relationship the United States hoped to eliminate.

The contentious nature of this debate emerged from a quarter-century in which Americans had argued about how best to manage geographic as well as demographic expansion. While some Americans were finding ways to rationalize expansion as a means to preserve republicanism and unleash individual energy, they had to develop arguments responding to a corpus of political philosophy claiming that large republics would inevitably descend first into corruption and then into disintegration. The struggle in Washington was to construct a public policy that would reap the advantages of expansion while providing safeguards against its dangers.[30]

The plan for Louisiana needed to do more than provide a skeletal government of the sort created by the Northwest Ordinance. It would have to double as a form of naturalization, and it was here that members of Congress ran into trouble. As Vice President Aaron Burr wrote on 18 January 1804, two days after the Senate began debate on the bill, "it is doubted whether the Louisianians can be received into the Union without an amendment to the Constitution. Consider of this. Again; are they citizens of the United States, or can Congress make them such?"[31] The constitutional matters that Burr mentioned coexisted with other concerns about attachment and citizenship; and rightly so. It was essential to establish a place for the Louisianians. Burr asked whether the treaty was sufficient, whether a diplomatic act that proclaimed people to be citizens could replace the naturalization process that was supposed to convert foreigners into Americans.

With the committee's plan for Louisiana government before the House and Senate, policymakers were bitterly divided at every step in ways that defied the emerging contours of party politics. The administration and some congressional Republicans were steadfast in their support of the bill. Federalists by and large opposed it. But the bulk of the opposition came from the mid-Atlantic states rather than from the Federalist stronghold in New England. In addition, a vocal contingent of Republicans openly expressed doubts. Whether they considered the bill too restrictive or too generous, they worried that it flew in the face of the most basic principles of citizenship and nationhood.[32]

Critics went on the offensive as soon as the bill appeared. The Federalist *Alexandria Advertiser* was not far from the mark when it reported that "the Democratic members appeared to be sorely pressed to answering the Federalists."[33] Detractors from both parties often claimed that French and Spanish colonial rule as well as intellectual infection from the worst elements of French Revolution had left the Louisianians unprepared to be Americans. They were "incapable of performing the duties or enjoying the blessings of a free government," said Timothy Pickering of Massachusetts. "They are too ignorant to elect suitable men."[34]

In making this argument, Pickering was only the latest Federalist to claim that frontier residents were unprepared for elective office. But while he echoed the arguments Federalists had invoked in the 1790s, he operated from a different foundation. Previously, it was the recent quality of settlement as well as the apparent rough nature of the settlers that justified an appointed system of government. But men like Pickering were well aware that the French and Spanish had been settling the Lower Mississippi Valley for over a century, and that New Orleans was no less sophisticated than cities throughout the United States. However numerous and established they might be, it was the fact that Louisiana's white residents were unfamiliar with American government that made them "too ignorant to elect suitable men."[35]

The critics did more than invoke the nativist themes that had infused Federalist rhetoric since the Alien and Sedition crisis. They also introduced what became a common refrain in American discussions about Louisiana. Incorporation might be a treaty requirement, but it was a policymaking impossibility. Members of Congress could not conceive of equality for an unnaturalized population. Samuel White, a Federalist senator from Delaware who had actually served on the committee that drafted the governance bill, explained that "as to Louisiana, this new, immense, unbounded world, if it should ever be incorporated into this Union, which I have no idea can be done but by altering the Constitution, I believe it will the greatest curse that could at present befall us; it may be productive of innumerable evils."[36] Like so many others, constitutionality was less important to White than the realities of governance. As Congressman John Smilie, a Republican from Pennsylvania, claimed, "neither the conquest nor the purchase can incorporate them [the residents of a new territory] into the Union. They must remain in the condition of colonies, and be governed according."[37] Smilie captured the fundamental problem posed by Louisiana. Expanding American *territory* would be difficult; expanding the American *nation* might be impossible.

Critics decried this notion. "The people of that country are free," John Cocke of Tennessee told his Senate colleagues. "Let them have liberty & a free government. This bill I hope will not pass — it is tyrannical."[38] John Quincy Adams launched a more withering attack on the bill. Prevented from shaping the bill in committee by Breckinridge's efforts to push through the administration's plan, Adams chose instead to try altering the bill in the Senate chamber with statements that reversed Smilie's logic but were no less condemning. "This is a Colonial system of government," he told his Senate colleagues. "It is the first the United States have established — It is a bad precedent."[39] The absence of elected offices did more than create inequality; it imposed unacceptable distinctions within the national community.

Smilie's colleague from Pennsylvania, John Lucas, stated that "it could not be said that a people thus inured to despotism, were prepared on a sudden to receive the principles of our Government." Lucas was no reactionary Federalist, nor was he a nativist. Born Jean Lucas, he was a loyal Republican, a Frenchman by birth, and a beneficiary of rapid naturalization in the United States. Yet Lucas worried that Article III was inconsistent with American principles and law. Foreigners could not truly be Americans unless they underwent naturalization. Like himself, the Louisianians would have to be transformed and remade.[40]

As reservations abounded in both houses of Congress, Representative Samuel Mitchill of New York asked Federalist and Republican critics an important question: What other options were available? To ignore Article III might lead France to renounce the treaty. If the Louisianians remained unintegrated or became disaffected as a result of the absence of elected office, they could potentially undermine the entire project of a peaceful and unified nation. The government's first objective should be to get a government in place that was consistent with the treaty before the Southwest descended into chaos. "What . . . shall we do with them?" Mitchill asked, referring to the Louisianians.[41]

The bill's supporters struck a compromise that they hoped would counter the Federalist claims and, more importantly, satisfy Republican critics. They presented a vision of citizenship that was adapted to Louisiana and was rooted in the protection of basic civil liberties without abandoning a probationary period. Rather than take Article III at its word, they attempted to interpret it in ways consistent with Madison's draft Article VII. They also dismissed the Federalist claims that neither the nation nor the state could successfully expand. Although they never expressed doubts that the Louisianians could acculturate themselves and become loyal Americans, the bill's advocates believed this process would take time and would pose unprecedented challenges for the federal government.[42]

Mitchill once again crystallized the opinions of those around him. He proposed that the Louisianians "serve an apprenticeship to liberty; that they are to be taught the lessons of freedom; and by degrees they are to be raised to the enjoyment and practice of independence."[43] Article III would be a means as well as an end. In the short term, it would ameliorate any residual anger among the Louisianians by guaranteeing a set of specific civil liberties. In the future, the Louisianians would become Americans as they incorporated American political principles into their daily lives.

In proposing this system, advocates of the governance plan restated many of the principles that had first appeared in debates over naturalization and territorial government during the quarter-century preceding the Purchase. Federalists remained convinced that the Louisianians were in fact foreigners and would always consider themselves as such. The bill's allies in both the administration and Congress were steadfast in the belief that, given time, the Louisianians would lose their most dangerous political and social beliefs. These men defined incorporation as a process rather than a single act. Equality would make the Louisianians into Americans in the eyes of the law at the same time that equality would make them appreciate the advantages of membership in the American national community. Beyond preserving the amity of Louisianians, equality would make them Americans like any others. Equality would enable the nation to expand both as a geographic entity and as a community of citizens.

The governance bill made the territorial system itself substitute for federal naturalization. Institutions implanted and directed by the federal government would teach residents what they had not learned as unnaturalized aliens. This system appeared in embryonic form in Article VII of Madison's draft treaty, which assumed some form of mass naturalization that would accompany political integration. Now policymakers attempted to construct a revised approach in reaction to the demands imposed upon them by Article III.

For Madison, the congressional debate was an irritating process, all the more so because he believed that the absence of a governance bill was a major impediment to his own efforts to begin the process of incorporation by creating a territorial structure. Writing to Livingston in February 1804, he commented that the members of Congress "dwell with Particular tediousness on the Bill providing a Govt for Louisiana."[44] Although Madison was forced to acknowledge that the lengthy debate was a natural result of "the novelty & nature of the subject," he and other members of the administration believed the threat came less from Article III than from the lack of a decision on the matter. Louisiana seemed to be in a precarious situation, its residents undefined within the federal system, and the land itself under the acquisitive gaze of European powers. The jury-rigged naturalization process in the governance bill satisfied most of his objectives for governing Louisiana and offered a viable solution to the problems of immediate citizenship.[45]

Madison was relieved when Congress finally passed "An Act erecting Louisiana into two Territories, and providing for the Temporary Government thereof" on 26 March 1804. Upper Louisiana became the District of Louisiana. Lower Louisiana became the Territory of Orleans. In keeping with the original text of the bill and following the precedent established in other territories, neither section possessed elected offices. The District of Louisiana reverted to the authority of the governor of the Indiana Territory. In Orleans the governor, secretary, thirteen-member Legislative Council, and an unspecified number of judges would, like all federal appointees, require approval by the Senate but would then serve at the president's discretion. This system would keep the local population in check until its attachment to the United States could be fixed.[46]

The Governance Act also prohibited foreign slave trade in Louisiana. American policymakers believed the ban would bolster the American hold on Louisiana and benefit the nation at large. While nobody in the cabinet and few in Congress considered eliminating slavery in Louisiana (as they had in the Northwest Territory), they were confident they could control its growth.[47] Equally important, the exclusion would prevent the arrival of slaves from Saint Domingue. Policymakers decided that if new slaves reached Louisiana they would do so through the internal slave trade. This process could be beneficial in its own right. It would at once establish commercial bonds connecting white Louisianians to the rest of the nation and dilute the population of slaves raised under the dangerous French and Spanish racial systems. Louisiana also created a pressure valve for the East by diffusing the massive slave populations in states like Virginia and the Carolinas. And in a classic example of the way people could merge self-interest with public interest, the eastern plantation elite faced a lucrative opportunity. If Louisiana did indeed prosper, planters in the West would need to purchase slaves from the East, not only creating a market but also raising prices for slaves.[48]

Yet for all their defensive claims to the contrary, the Louisiana Purchase was an uncomfortable fit to many policymakers, and the ban on the foreign slave trade stands as a case in point. While American settlers immediately saw opportunities awaiting them in Louisiana, policymakers approached expansion with considerable trepidation. Pamphleteers proclaimed the virtues that would come from such a vast national reserve. Yet their often shrill enthusiasm was as much an attempt to overcome uncertainty as it was a statement of confidence.[49] In the end, the pamphleteers correctly predicted how Americans would eventually remember the Louisiana Purchase, but for the wrong reasons.

That Americans could accommodate the Louisiana Purchase does not mean they sought it. The tremendous benefits that Americans eventually reaped from the Great Plains, the Rockies, and the Pacific Northwest were unimaginable in 1803. The hyperbole of the pamphleteers was telling, as was their timing. These arguments came *after* the Purchase, rather than before. The same commentators, and others like them, never raised their voices before 1803 in a demand for wholesale expansion west of the Mississippi.[50]

The incongruities between the contents of public pamphlets and the private correspondence of American policymakers suggest two portraits of the Louisiana Purchase and American expansion. The one that remains most vivid today is an unquestionably confident outlook on the new western domain driven by the boisterous enthusiasm of pamphleteers and western settlers. Another, more circumspect reaction becomes apparent from a different document—the Purchase itself—and a different set of actors—members of the administration and Congress.

The Governance Act, together with the Louisiana Purchase, defined federal policymaking and local activity in the years that followed. The Louisiana Purchase unleashed profound concerns about the dangers of unchecked expansion, while the Governance Act showed how policymaking itself might present means for the United States to respond to these challenges. Meanwhile, the very ambiguity of these documents that proved so troubling to federal leaders provided exactly the circumstances that people in Louisiana hoped to exploit.

The Governance Act could not have come a moment too soon, for the United States was in fact governing Louisiana. An ersatz administrative system was already in place, operating without form or much direction. Residents of Louisiana had also begun to articulate their own definitions of nationhood even as members of Congress were attempting to provide resolution on the issue through the Governance Act. As they came to terms with the provisions of the Governance Act, people in both Washington and Louisiana would continue their efforts to revise the Louisiana Purchase.

PART II

Louisiana Purchase
(1803–1808)

3

"Numerous and Troublesome Neighbors"

William C. C. Claiborne rode into New Orleans in December 1803. He came at the head of an army, a general by his side. It was not a long trip, only about 200 miles from Washington, Mississippi, the territorial capital, where Claiborne had served as governor since Jefferson selected him for the post almost two years before. But it had been a lengthy venture over difficult roads before the final descent down the Mississippi River. Though not officially relieved of his post in the Mississippi Territory, Claiborne nonetheless left matters to his subordinates, focusing all his energies on Louisiana.

The general was James Wilkinson, the senior officer in the U.S. Army and the immediate commander of the republic's western forces, who brought with him a detachment of troops. Claiborne and Wilkinson served as co-commissioners to receive Louisiana, and while Wilkinson's own ambitions knew few bounds, the general never challenged Claiborne's authority. Wilkinson left over a year later for an appointment in Upper Louisiana, but the troops he brought with him soon settled in to stay, the vanguard of what eventually became the nation's largest peacetime military concentration. The troops had numerous responsibilities: defending New Orleans against foreign adventurism, preserving the subjugation of slaves, asserting federal authority over Indians, and defending the American possession in the event of resistance from local whites. In these capacities, the army would continue the tradition of government on the frontiers of North America, where troops served numerous civil as well as military roles in European colonies and American territories.[1]

Claiborne never admitted as much, of course, preferring instead to emphasize that civil government, rather than military force, would bring Louisiana into the American national community. Indeed, the soldiers served mostly ceremonial purposes, in large part because the transfer of power proved to be a peaceful affair. Together with local militiamen, U.S. soldiers participated in the elaborate rituals that marked the transfer of power in Louisiana on 30 December 1803.[2] Pierre Clément Laussat was there, delivering Louisiana to the United States before making his own hasty departure from Louisiana in April 1804 to assume another colonial prefecture, this time in Martinique.

Claiborne immediately turned to the most mundane affairs of government. On 29 December, for example, he issued a set of regulations for the Port of New Orleans. Like most public documents in American Louisiana, the regulations were bilingual, with a vertical line separating English from French. Claiborne spoke neither French nor Spanish (a matter of no small irritation to Louisianians), so at the bottom of the French version of the regulations was a brief line reading "P. Derbigny, Interprète du Gouvernement."[3] The line referred to Pierre Derbigny. Like Claiborne (and, for that matter, Laussat), Derbigny was a newcomer to Louisiana. A Frenchman by birth and an attorney by trade, Derbigny supplemented his income with work as a translator during Laussat's brief restoration of French sovereignty.

Claiborne and Derbigny were soon at odds, and although the port regulations were not the direct cause of the problem, they were symptomatic. People throughout Louisiana exploited the particulars of American nationhood, the weakness of the American empire, and the novelty of the Louisiana Purchase to resist incorporation by attacking the administrative structures that the United States attempted to install. Whites Louisianians, slaves, Indians, free people of color, and even malcontent Americans all attempted to realize their vision of a reconstituted Louisiana, in the process creating an atmosphere of uncertainty and potential violence. From 1803 through 1808 these resisters assaulted incorporation in all its forms.

"We Have Thanks to Return; We Have Complaints to Make"

The problems of Article III immediately became clear. Free residents of Louisiana — whether whites or free people of color — articulated their own visions of nationhood, which, though embracing attachment, imposed political demands that collided with the federal government's administrative agenda. They demanded incorporation in ways that seemed more likely to frighten federal leaders than to please them.

Although the free residents of Louisiana began to articulate their concerns as soon as the United States took charge, the real spark of political mobilization was the Governance Act of 1804. With its paucity of political opportunities and the complete lack of elected offices, Louisianians had ample evidence that American merit was nothing more than ethnic cronyism. This turn of events came as a rude awakening to elite or aspiring Louisianians, men like Pierre Derbigny who predicted that the Louisiana Purchase would create new opportunities for patronage and public office. If anyone correctly foresaw attitudes in the newly created Territory of Orleans, it was John Quincy Adams, who in the debates over the Governance Act had predicted resentment toward what he characterized a "colonial" system of government. His own reservations about a political system that smacked of colonial rule mirrored those of people in the Southwest. The administration and its allies in Congress may have seen incorporation as a process, but the Louisianians were convinced it was an act.

Contemporary observers as well as subsequent historians often mistook this anger for proof that the Louisianians sought a return to European colonial status. This conclusion makes sense when the mere presence of local unrest is interpreted as an ethnic struggle between Louisianians and Americans, but it cannot be sustained given the absence of any significant campaign to secure a retrocession to France or Spain. There are other, more illuminating ways to interpret the Louisianians' actions. The first is to consider their experiences in the eighteenth century. Many Louisianians brought from Spanish colonialism the need to secure concessions from distant political capitals. They had resisted the Spanish less because they were foreign than because Spain had failed to deliver political and commercial opportunities to Louisiana. The second is to see the Louisianians as dissatisfied westerners, for they used arguments identical with those of other westerners who claimed that territorial rule imposed both inequality and unnatural divisions within the nation.

In the "Remonstrance of the People of Louisiana against the Political System Adopted by Congress for Them," native-born Louisianians, French émigrés, and transplanted Americans articulated their own vision of citizenship in an expanding nation. Completed in May 1804, it became the Louisianians' first assertion of their political presence within the American system. The Remonstrance stated that the Louisianians were "persuaded that a free people would acquire territory only to extend the blessings of freedom, that an enlightened nation would never destroy those principles on which its Government was founded, and that their Representatives would disdain to become the instruments of oppression." In the absence of a state constitution or an acceptable form of territorial government, Article III would be "our constitution." They explained that "we knew that it was impossible to be citizens of the United States without enjoying a personal freedom, protection for property, and, above all, the privileges of a free, representative Government." Louisianians claimed that the Governance Act denied them the privileges of federal citizenship, in direct contravention of Article III as well as the precepts of nationhood.[4]

Again and again, the authors of the Remonstrance returned to Article III, much like the men who had debated the Governance Act in Congress only a few months before. "To be incorporated into the Union must mean to form a part of it," the Louisianians said. This statement did not mean that the Louisianians demanded immediate statehood. Instead, they sought a modified territorial system with elected offices and representation in Congress.[5]

The Remonstrance claimed that the 1804 Governance Act "does not 'incorporate us in the union,' that it vests us with none of the 'rights,' gives us no advantages, and deprives us of all the 'immunities' of American citizens." The Louisianians did more than invoke the terms of Article III; they detailed their understanding of what it meant to be Americans. The Remonstrance charged that the 1804 Governance Act constituted a betrayal of American treaty obligations and of American principles. Referring to the Declaration of Independence, the federal and state constitutions, and the published statements of national leaders, the Remonstrance argued that citizens of the United States possessed the inviolable right to shape the political decisions that affected them.[6] That the Governance Act created no elected offices was bad enough. Worse still, the Governance Act singled out Louisiana for cruel economic injustice. Disgruntled Louisianians claimed that the ban on the foreign slave trade only further marginalized them within the national community and threatened to preserve the economic underdevelopment that white Louisianians associated with European rule. The end result was a territorial system that perpetuated both individual and jurisdictional inequality.[7]

The Louisianians closed with a provocative question, one that struck at the core of American nationhood. "Are truths, then, so well founded, so universally acknowledged, inapplicable only to us?" they asked. "Do political axioms on the Atlantic become problems when transferred to the shores of the Mississippi?" Their answer was a resounding "no." Louisianians claimed that their own resistance to oppression defined them as Americans. In this statement they deployed the same argument that people throughout the United States had used when they vied for membership in a national community.[8]

Pierre Derbigny, Jean Noël Destrehan, and Pierre Sauve came to Washington in the winter of 1804–05 to deliver the Remonstrance. For the Creoles Destrehan and Sauve, the trip was a journey of exploration as they ventured for the first time into the republic they had joined. For Derbigny, it was only the latest in a series of attempts to establish himself in the United States. On the eve of the transfer of power, Derbigny had anglicized his name to "Peter" in a letter to Gallatin seeking employment as a county clerk. Derbigny reminded the secretary of the treasury that the two men had met a decade before in Pennsylvania during Derbigny's lengthy migration from France to New Orleans. Gallatin had been a rising congressman at the time and Derbigny a fledgling attorney. "I was then a complete youth, morally and physically speaking," Derbigny explained. Derbigny assured Gallatin that he had matured since then, and remained faithful to the American laws and political principles he had learned during his visit to the United States. Derbigny hoped to make himself a candidate for public office through direct correspondence or, better still, through references from men like Gallatin and Claiborne. This campaign failed to generate results, and when the government excluded Louisianians from high-level appointments, Derbigny assumed the pseudonym "Louisianais" to write a scathing attack on federal appointment policy. That same year he signed the Remonstrance and joined the trio of men who delivered it to Washington. Peter Derbigny died, and Pierre Derbigny was reborn.[9]

Derbigny, Destrehan, and Sauve sought meetings with every influential person they could find in the capital. They even managed to secure an audience with Jefferson, only to conclude that the president was unresponsive to their concerns. Jefferson preferred to leave the matter to Congress, stating in his 1804 annual message that "the form of government thus provided having been considered but as temporary, and open to such improvements as further information of the circumstances of our brethren there might suggest, it will of course be subject to your consideration."[10]

Although the delegates from Louisiana were unsuccessful with the president, among their first converts was William Plumer, a Federalist senator from New Hampshire whose only great distinctions were a detailed journal of Senate proceedings and the dubious honor of being the only senator never to serve on a committee. Proving that attitudes toward Louisiana were not prescribed in either geographic or partisan terms, Plumer concluded "they are all gentlemen of the first respectability in that country. Men of talents, literature & general information—Men of business, & acquainted with the world. I was much gratified with their company."[11]

But Plumer made other comments that explain the trajectory of public debate in 1803–04. "They are all frenchmen," he explained, despite acknowledging that Destrehan and Sauve were Creoles. Like so many other observers, he lumped the entire Francophone population into one group. Equally important, he found the men so agreeable because "they have little of French flippery with them—They resemble New England men more than the Virginians."[12] In the same way that some Republicans in Congress had spoken in favor of the Louisianians only a few months before because they seemed so much like themselves, Plumer generalized his own region into the ideal norm for the whole nation. Federalists and Republicans, northerners and southerners, all American commentators found in the Louisianians an ideal opportunity to accentuate their own political and regional virtues in opposition to the flaws they saw among others.

Despite Plumer's comments, Derbigny, Destrehan, and Sauve were no more satisfied by Congress than they were by Jefferson. Representative Joseph Nicholson of Maryland, who presented the Remonstrance to the House, gave them a halfhearted introduction. He explained to his colleagues that the Remonstrance "may contain expressions that the House will have to pardon, ascribing them to the feelings of the inhabitants so peculiarly situated, and not to any want of respect for the Government of the Union." He concluded that the Louisianians "labored under an idea that their morals, manners, and customs, had been misunderstood, and consequently complained of, and that the law of last session was passed by Congress under those mistaken impressions."[13]

A House committee charged with investigating the Louisianians' claims was equally critical. The committee attacked the "manifest absurdity" of the accusations. The report stated that the "memorialists may have appreciated too highly the rights which have been secured to them by the treaty of cession."[14] In his proclamation to the Louisianans less than two years earlier, Laussat had promised that the Louisianians would have a government adapted to their "manners . . . necessities . . . climate . . . customs . . . and local circumstances." Now those very distinguishing characteristics — what scholars would now refer to collectively as "culture" — were working against the Louisianians.

Derbigny, Destrehan, and Sauve returned to New Orleans in the spring of 1805, convinced that the federal government had no intention of responding to their grievances. The intersection of resistance and incorporation became clear when the three men wrote a lengthy report from Washington in 1805. They explained that "we found already established a prepossession of the most unfavorable kind. . . . Days and weeks passed on without an appearance of their bestowing a thought on us. In vain by our constant attendance at every sitting of Congress, and by the frequent visits we paid to the members charged with our affair, did we seek to rouse their attention." Their reception, like the Governance Act itself, showed that policymakers may have accepted that the Louisianians were citizens, but still did not consider them fellow-countrymen.[15]

Although they condemned the administration for ignoring their concerns, the Louisianians offered "a tribute which we ought to pay to all those inhabitants of the United States, who have condescended to take an interest in the fate of Louisiana; and to feel a solicitude for the welfare of her inhabitants. We have thanks to return; we have complaints to make." By laying claim to the American right of dissent, the Louisianians made an end run around their critics. Their resistance made them American. It was the government's desire to stifle them that smacked of alien principles. In 1804, even as he mobilized in opposition to the Governance Act, Derbigny referred to the Louisiana Purchase as "our political emancipation." By joining the budding political opposition, he intended to make that emancipation a reality.[16]

Nor was the Remonstrance the only sign of white discontent. Although it posed the clearest assault on the federal government's vision of incorporation, it seemed so threatening because of other disputes within Louisiana. At the same time that white Louisianians demanded reform in the civil polity, they were mobilizing for change in the religious polity. With the departure of Spanish officials came the departure of most of Louisiana's priests as well as the destruction of the Diocese of Louisiana and Florida. White Louisianians demanded that American officials settle disputes within parishes. Most notably, American officials and New Orleans Catholics alike worried about an ongoing argument between Father Antonio de Sedella and Father Patrick Walsh for control of New Orleans' largest and most prominent congregation, headquartered at the massive St. Louis Church, which, under the old diocese, had been a cathedral.[17] Similar disputes emerged in other parts of Louisiana as disagreements between priests engulfed whole parishes.[18] Claiborne doubted his powers to interfere in church activities, while the only bishop in the United States, John Carroll, waited for years to learn from the Vatican whether his jurisdiction overlapped with that of the expanded United States.[19]

These religious conflicts only exacerbated the anticatholicism so prevalent among the overwhelmingly Protestant federal leadership. Federal officials were convinced that Catholicism retarded republicanism, while the Catholic church continued to provide the means for foreign intervention. Nor was the departure of Spanish ecclesiastical authority much better, for the confusion that came in its wake was generating angry disputes throughout Louisiana.

Even as they professed their attachment to the United States, white Louisianians were upsetting the administration's plans. Worse still, the mobilization of whites provoked even more frightening activities by nonwhites. As white men began to gather in opposition to the Governance Act, free men of color planned to do the same. Claiborne and New Orleans mayor Etienne Boré quickly called a meeting with a delegation of nine free men of color, warning them that the government would use force to suppress any mass meeting of free people of color. Claiborne and Boré were successful in preventing the mass meeting, but their means suggested the cracks in the system of racial supremacy that both men hoped to impose in American Louisiana. By inviting the free people of color to an official meeting, they were forced to create a space in the polity for nonwhites.[20]

Notwithstanding whites' fear of free people of color, their comments were conformist. Indeed, free people of color proved eager to establish their own respectability through measured public activity and deferential political pronouncements. In January 1804 some of those same free men of color had signed a petition in which they "begged leave to approach . . . with Sentiments of respect & Esteem and sincere attachment to the Government of the United States." They explained:

> We are Natives of this Province and our dearest Interests are connected with its welfare. We therefore feel a lively Joy that the Sovereignty of our Country is at length united with that of the American Republic. We are duly sensible that our personal and political freedom is thereby assured to us for ever, and we are also impressed with the fullest confidence in the Justice and Liberality of the Government towards every Class of Citizens which they have here taken under their Protection.[21]

Free men of color also petitioned Claiborne to preserve a special unit of the territorial militia. For almost three quarters of a century free men of color had served in a special militia unit. Originally created by the French to reinforce the small number of white soldiers in Louisiana, by 1803 the unit served mostly ceremonial purposes. Excluded from many of the acts associated with both citizenship and masculine society (i.e., political participation, service on juries, public celebrations), free men of color used this institution to uphold their status as civic-minded men. These same principles had inspired free men of color to send the statement of attachment to Congress in January 1804 and to begin plans to mobilize in the spring before Claiborne and Pitot made clear that they would permit no such activity.

The free residents of Louisiana frightened American policymakers. Their attachment to the United States seemed suspect. Their political demands upset administrative agendas. Yet they also showed how attractive the vision of nationhood and incorporation could be to free people on the frontiers of the union. The political terms that had emerged in the United States since independence gave these residents of Louisiana the tools they needed to demand membership in a national polity. Other residents sent a very different message.

"A Spirit of Revolt and Mutyny"

While Derbigny, Destrehan, and Sauve were traveling east in 1804 and 1805, other migrants were heading west in pursuit of freedom and independence. These were not Anglo-Americans, but rather the enslaved Afro-Louisianians who hoped to capitalize on the Louisiana Purchase by fleeing to the contested Texas-Louisiana borderland. With Louisiana wedged between the two Spanish possessions of Texas and West Florida, slaves found they could successfully elude capture by escaping American jurisdiction. Their action was only a facet of a broader movement. Whether individually or in groups, whether in New Orleans or on the territorial periphery, slaves immediately set about assaulting the federal regime that American policymakers hoped to create.

Free people and slaves understood that incorporation assumed a stable slave system. For slaves, the simplest way to challenge that system was to run away. For the federal government, more was at stake in preventing slave runaways than in preserving the labor of individual slavemasters. Article VII of Madison's draft treaty guaranteed the preservation of individual property in Louisiana, a provision that emerged unchanged in Article III of the Louisiana Purchase. American rule was a sham if public officials could not guarantee the property rights of its citizens. For slaves to resist that authority in any form was no less threatening to incorporation than the prospect of white disaffection. Members of the New Orleans City Council were so worried that slaves hired by the day would attempt to flee that they required slaves to wear "a collar or shoulder belt and a plate made of tin or other metal, on which will be engraved the name of his master and in default of this distinctive sign, the owner of the negro will be fined the amount of one dollar."[22]

Slaves also subverted American efforts to resolve the disputed western border, an equally important requirement for the successful conclusion to the Louisiana Purchase. As runaways disappeared into the Texas-Louisiana borderland, they generated uncertainty and fear on both sides. Americans became convinced that the Spanish were providing a haven for subversive slaves and Spanish officials worried that the Americans might use the hunt for runaways as the pretext for military intervention. In 1804 Claiborne complained to the marquis de Casa Calvo, a former governor of Spanish Louisiana who remained in the area after the transfer of power, that "the inhabitants of the District of Natchitoches manifest . . . much inquietude" as a result of the haven afforded runaways in Spanish Texas. Claiborne charged that "no existing degree of his Catholic Majesty promised freedom & protection to Negro's escaping from the service of their masters." Claiborne concluded with the cryptic but chilling comment that "if the protection be offered by the Commandant of Nacogdoches to a Single Slave deserting the service of his master, the consequences . . . will be injurious to the citizens of the United States, and may tend to disturb the good understanding between our two nations."[23] In 1807 Claiborne informed Madison that runaway slaves still "receive the protection of the Spanish Agents," warning the secretary of state of "the very serious injury which is likely to result therefrom to the inhabitants of the Territory of Orleans."[24]

Captain Edward Turner, who commanded troops and served as civil commandant in Natchitoches, a settlement in northwestern Louisiana, was less diplomatic in his language. He reported that "the Spaniards are undoubtedly meditating mischief in this quarter; their Emissaries have been at work among the Indians and Negroes."[25] Turner saw a direct correlation between runaways, slave revolts, and national security. Meanwhile, members of Congress received reports of depredations against American citizens in the Southwest committed by an interracial gang of brigands from Spanish America. Thus runaways could create an atmosphere of chaos and disorder that would destroy the American hold on Louisiana.[26]

It was through the lens of international affairs and incorporation, not just of racial supremacy, that whites considered the dangers of slave revolt. So too for slaves, who understood that the contested borderlands could facilitate their own plans for escape or revolt. The linkage between slavery and foreign policy is not the standard stuff of American history. Historians of American foreign relations usually restrict their study to the actions of white policymakers, leaving little room for slaves as actors on the diplomatic stage. The focus on transatlantic affairs, with particular attention to American relations with France and Britain, further reduces the need to discuss slavery. Historians of slavery in the United States have their own reasons for steering clear of diplomacy. They have examined states like Virginia, the Carolinas, and Tennessee, often to the exclusion of the Southwest. More important, they have rarely shown interest in diplomacy or international relations. That perspective precludes consideration of individual experiences throughout the borderlands. Slaves, slaveowners, and public officials on the nation's periphery all made their decisions in a context of international relations. These concerns followed the geography and timetable of American expansion. Although these concerns faded once Americans established control over the Gulf Coast and the Florida Peninsula, the diplomatic context of slavery continued westward, first to Texas and later to the new borderland created by American acquisitions during the Mexican-American War.[27]

Likewise, it was an international event — the Saint Domingue revolt — that continued to shape racial conflict in Louisiana. A growing number of refugees came to Louisiana, their slaves in tow. After initial attempts to exclude these slaves in 1803, Claiborne eventually relented.[28] The arrival of the newcomers immediately aroused concern. In 1804 rumors abounded of a mysterious "stranger" known only as a "dangerous character from St. Domingo." Operating outside the control of white officials, he seemed intent on fomenting a revolution on American shores.[29] Other white observers saw evidence of more widespread black organization. Residents of Pointe Coupée rushed a petition to Claiborne with 105 signatures reporting that "the revolution of St. Domingo and other Places has become common amongs [*sic*] our Blacks — A Spirit of Revolt and Mutyny has Crept in amongst Them."[30] Claiborne did not need much convincing. He saw a "Spirit of Insurrection among the Negroes at Point Coupee." The value of the troops who had accompanied Claiborne and Wilkinson to New Orleans became readily apparent, and Claiborne immediately sent a detachment to guard against revolt.[31]

The fear and the reality of servile insurrection were hardly a product of the Louisiana Purchase. It had been a driving force in both the United States and colonial Louisiana. Racial unrest also struck close to home for members of the administration only a few years after a short-lived insurrection in Richmond in the summer of 1800 under the apparent leadership of a slave named Gabriel Prosser.[32] Slave revolt challenged the meaning and even the possibility of incorporation through the extension of federal sovereignty and administration. Policymakers believed that a successful incorporation of Louisiana rested on unquestioned American sovereignty and a cohesive national community of white citizens. Slaves undermined both these objectives.

Public officials were equally convinced that whites might assist in racial revolt. In July 1804, for example, police in New Orleans arrested a white man named Regnier for offering fencing lessons to free people of color. Of particular importance was the fact that Regnier had "lived several years in St. Domingo," which whites interpreted as proof that he might be training an army for a slave revolution on the American mainland.[33] The following year, New Orleans mayor John Watkins reported to the City Council that

> [the] wretch named Grandjean [a white migrant from Saint Domingue], one day took Célestin [a slave he had hired from a Mr. Duverne] into his confidence and revealed the plot relating to a general freedom of slaves, the success of which was to be accomplished at the cost of lives and fortunes of the whites. Célestin, actuated by a natural feeling of honest and as a faithful slave, immediately related to Mr. Duverne the details of this story.[34]

Council members later elaborated that Grandjean was conspiring with local slaves "to incite the slaves [of New Orleans], set fire to the city and murder its white inhabitants."[35] Grandjean was arrested, and although the immediate threat seemed to be over, his activities and — perhaps more important — Célestin's account of that activity convinced local officials that racial revolt might come from a variety of sources.

Célestin faced the choices that slaves made as they decided how best to respond to the American regime. In the same way that whites spared no invective in their efforts to demand protection from potentially insurrectionary slaves, Célestin may have exaggerated his own reports, in this case to accentuate his own attachment to the white regime. Célestin apparently decided that he was more likely to benefit from uncovering the conspiracy than from joining it. He proved right. Public officials decided to make an example of Célestin, offering to purchase his freedom and "give him back the liberty he has refused at the price of the white persons' blood."[36] Célestin was one of a large number of slaves who secured their freedom through legal means. In the confusion that came with the transfer of Louisiana from Spain to France to the United States, local officials continued to respect Spanish procedures permitting slaves to petition for their own emancipation. From 1804 through 1806, almost 200 slaves purchased their own freedom.[37] That these actions were legal did little to assuage white observers — many of them Louisianians — intent on preserving a line between American and foreign that overlapped with free and slave, white and black.

Somewhere between the legal process of self-purchase and extralegal acts of running away or fomenting revolt were other forms of resistance that, if not a direct assault on white supremacy, nonetheless constituted attempts by slaves to determine the nature of power in Louisiana. In August 1806 members of the City Council observed that "negroes working by the day have the impertinence to refuse frequently and by sheer caprice the kind of work which is proposed to them by the citizens." Outraged council members decided that the government needed to guarantee actively that slaves would obey whites, whether those whites were their masters or potential employers.[38] They did so from heightened fears generated by events in Saint Domingue, but they also did so because of the very real resistance in Louisiana.

"My Words Resemble The Words My Forefathers Have Told Me"

The challenge for slaves was to establish their individual freedom in a world of white domination. The task that Indians set for themselves was to preserve their collective autonomy. They took steps to establish a vision of federalism that, if it acknowledged American sovereignty against European territorial claims, nonetheless demanded that the United States treat Indians as partners in regional governance, while Indians would also continue to enjoy exclusive powers in their own villages. At the same time that American officials hoped to make Indian governance a discrete facet of domestic policy, conditions on the borderlands enabled Indians to position themselves as independent actors in complex foreign relations. The Indians' success or failure depended on complex configurations of local demographics and international affairs. Regardless of circumstances, however, the Indians of Louisiana threatened the domestic security and the racial supremacy that were essential to incorporation.

On the eastern borderlands, the beleaguered Choctaw attempted to cultivate influence at the same time that interracial contact created outbursts of violence. When the Choctaw tried to ingratiate themselves with the United States by providing intelligence on Spanish moves in West Florida, for example, they did little more than alarm American officials that Indians might undermine attachment. In 1805 a Choctaw chief approached Indian Agent John Sibley, eager to prove his loyalty with news that only increased concerns in Washington that Indians would deliver destruction on Louisiana. Sibley reported that the Spanish had informed the Choctaw that "the Americans holding this country were all wind; that if they were wise, they would abandon us and attach themselves to them, (the Spaniards,) for their old friends would not forsake them." Worse still, the Choctaw reported that the Spanish claimed they would "soon build a fort in Opelousas, and another at Attakapas, and one at or near Natchitoches, and proceed on towards New Orleans." In the ultimate act of subversion, the Spanish wanted the Indians to purchase equipment from Americans that would eventually be used to build these forts.[39]

As the Choctaw situated themselves in the uncertain diplomatic conditions in Louisiana, so too were they forced to confront the territorial regime that Americans were struggling to build. In the summer of 1807, residents of Opelousas killed a Choctaw Indian and seemed likely to stage additional attacks on neighboring villages. Claiborne found himself dispatching troops to prevent any violence, and issued an apologetic statement to the Indians stating that "I have heard news which much grieves me. Some Blood has been shed and a warrior of your tribe dangerously wounded . . . if he should die, all I can promise is, that the white man who did the Mischief, shall be tried and punished agreeable to the Laws of this Territory." But Claiborne also admitted to Secretary of War Henry Dearborn that "my own opinion, is that differences between the frontier settlers, and the small tribes West of the Mississippi, will frequently arise, until Treaties are entered into with them."[40]

Although Claiborne managed to contain white violence, he and other officials continued to blame the situation on the Choctaw. In September 1807, Indian Agent Henry Bry wrote to Dearborn that the Choctaws "are very numerous & troublesome neighbours. They commit depredations on the property of the industrious planters; Complaints of that kind are daily brought before me."[41] Of course, white officials were slow to acknowledge any complicity among their own settlers. As on so many other frontiers, white settlers managed to function as perpetrators while describing themselves as victims.

The Choctaw had little recourse in eastern Louisiana. The Spanish would not invade, nor would the United States meet its own promises to contain white settlers. Without much leverage of any sort, they could not press their demands on either party. Things were different in the West, where the Caddo exploited similar tensions to much greater advantage.

The immediate source of dispute remained one of borders. The United States and Spain continued to argue about the precise extent of the Louisiana Purchase. Meanwhile, Spanish officials had reason to believe that the United States had launched a concerted effort to undermine imperial authority in the West. The United States had dispatched two surveying expeditions into Louisiana, one under the command of Meriwether Lewis and William Clark in 1804–1806 and another under Zebulon Pike in 1806. The Spanish correctly predicted that these expeditions would cross onto Spanish soil. The Spanish were particularly concerned that the United States intended to build a broader military alliance with the Indians who controlled the North American interior.[42]

Nor were the Spanish fears entirely without foundation. Despite his claims — both public and private — of the scientific and commercial goals of these expeditions, Jefferson had indeed dispatched his western expeditions to establish friendly relations with the Indians of Louisiana, which the Spanish interpreted as efforts to destabilize their own regime. Dire reports reached Washington from the Territory of Orleans, and by May the administration feared that a Spanish invasion was imminent.[43]

Federal attempts to control Indians and Indian land often proved more difficult than anybody serving the federal regime had predicted. The situation reached a boiling point in the summer of 1806, when Jefferson dispatched yet another expedition to the borderlands, this one ascending the Red River under the command of surveyor Thomas Freeman and physician Peter Custis. The expedition passed through the very region under dispute, and the Caddo found themselves hosting the expedition. Spanish troops descended on the Red River Valley, intent on deterring what looked like American adventurism. The explorers returned to New Orleans, where they alarmed public officials with stories of Spanish hostility.[44]

The Jefferson administration, locked in unsuccessful negotiations with Spain over the boundaries of Louisiana, could not resolve the situation. Meanwhile, Claiborne struggled without success to reach a settlement with Spanish officials in Texas. It was in this diplomatic vacuum that General James Wilkinson, Colonel Simón de Herrera y Leyva, and Dehahuit launched their own diplomatic initiatives. Wilkinson had returned to Orleans in the summer of 1806 under the nominal excuse that the dangers facing the territory required him to take direct control of federal troops. He acknowledged that he was "ignorant . . . of the negotiation with Spain, & the consequent determination of Government."[45] White and Indian negotiators hammered out a resolution that prohibited new white settlement and kept white armies clear of the Caddo villages.[46] The agreement called for both nations to stand down their forces and await a final diplomatic settlement between Washington and Madrid. The agreement also created the Neutral Ground, the buffer zone between Texas and Louisiana that served the objectives of Americans, Spaniards, and Indians alike.[47]

The situation was tailor-made for James Wilkinson. For years he had sought commercial opportunities in Spanish America with a determination that would eventually lead to charges of treason. Throughout the fall of 1806 he was in contact with Spanish officials, selling them information on developments in the United States. That these personal ambitions corresponded with the American national interest in ending the rising conflict with Spain only made the situation more logical to Wilkinson.[48]

The Neutral Ground appeared equally advantageous for the Caddo. Dehahuit had seen white regimes come and go in Louisiana, but he was determined to preserve the unity and the independence of the Caddo. Like other Indian leaders, or for that matter Anglo-American federalists, Dehahuit concluded that union and independence were mutually reinforcing. He explained his vision of the borderlands during a meeting with Claiborne at one of the Caddo villages on 5 September 1806. Dehahuit chose to explain things this way. "My words resemble the words my forefathers have told me they used to receive from the French in ancient times," he informed the governor. "If your nation has purchased what the French formerly possessed, you have purchased the country that we occupy, and we regard you in the same light as we did them."[49] Though offered as a promise of loyalty, Dehahuit's speech was also a succinct statement of fact. Dehahuit gave notice to the United States that he understood international boundary disputes and intended to use the situation to his advantage. That he referred to the French rather than to the Spanish was no less important, for during the period of French rule, a period marked by similar boundary disputes between France and Spain, the Caddo had enjoyed the sort of autonomy they hoped to restore. He was willing to acknowledge American territorial pretensions in exchange for an American agreement to meet the Caddo on their own terms. While he accepted American trade, he demanded that the federal government resist any direct involvement in Caddo political affairs. To this end the Caddo even flew the U.S. flag in Dehahuit's village.[50]

The Neutral Ground preserved the peace, but it did not make anybody happy. The Caddo continued to worry about both collision and collusion among whites. The United States and Spain continued to view each other with suspicion, convinced that the other party intended to steal what it did not own. And even in resolving these issues, the federal government was forced into the very position it opposed: dependence on Indians that enabled Indians to function as independent actors rather than domestic dependents.

"That Portion of Our Territory Which Is Kept in Possession of Spain"

Indians were not alone in challenging federal sovereignty on the borderlands. On both the eastern and western fringes of Louisiana, whites attempted to replace national unity with local separation or unrest. Aaron Burr descended on Louisiana, embodying the fears of disunion that had gripped so many Americans since 1776. Unruly American settlers in West Florida challenged the authority of both the United States and Spain. Meanwhile, elite whites threatened to upset the political order in the heart of Louisiana. These actions only spiked the rising tensions between the United States and Spain. Together with the Caddo and the Choctaw, white troublemakers challenged the ability of world powers to control their domestic affairs and to settle their foreign disputes. Worst of all, they also showed that the United States could not even restrain its own citizens.

The first of these controversies emerged in West Florida. The fact that West Florida did not fall under American sovereignty was an obvious sore spot for the Jefferson administration, which saw the Gulf Coast in geopolitical terms. But West Florida was a local problem as well, undermining governance on both sides of the Mississippi. These problems began with something as seemingly simple as a road. In 1805 Jefferson designed a road, or rather a lengthy thoroughfare, that would connect Federal City to Crescent City, running from Washington to the Creek Indian agency in Tennessee to Fort Stoddart in Mississippi to the Mouth of Pearl River and finally to New Orleans. Jefferson faced a problem: Spanish possession of the Gulf Coast prevented any direct or secure route through the Southwest. In 1807 Postmaster General Gideon Granger expressed similar frustration that he could not establish postal routes through "that portion of our Territory which is kept in possession of Spain." Granger expressed little concern for the diplomatic dimensions of policymaking on the southwestern frontier. He focused instead on the practical impediments to an efficient federal apparatus. Until the United States had secured its claim, the postmaster and his delegates would have to negotiate with the Spanish directly for permission to travel through West Florida. So Granger instructed Blaise Cenas, the postmaster for Balize, an outpost near New Orleans, "to procure some intelligent and faithful surveyor to lay out a Road" that would reach north to the Mississippi Territory rather than through West Florida. This lengthy and indirect route would have to serve until the United States could secure its claim to the Gulf Coast.[51] Roadbuilding was no small affair, nor was postal delivery. Many Americans considered them nationalizing technologies that would connect people to one another through trade, contact, and communication.[52]

Diplomatic conditions also threatened economic conditions for American settlements in Mississippi and Alabama in much the same way that Spanish control of New Orleans before 1803 had endangered settlers in Kentucky and the Ohio Valley. Spanish officials impeded American trade through Mobile, either denying entry or imposing import taxes that American merchants considered excessive. Secretary of War Henry Dearborn considered this a "humiliating" situation, echoing the sentiments of other policymakers who interpreted these actions as nothing less than an assault on national independence. Locally, however, there were more immediate and tangible dangers. Settlers on the southern frontier were isolated and dependent on Spanish authority for their own prosperity. Spain still stunted the economy of the southwestern borderlands.[53]

For all the complaints of American officials that Spanish possession of West Florida endangered incorporation, West Florida constituted a problem in governance for the Spanish that was quite similar to the problems of incorporating Louisiana. Like the United States, Spain governed an unfamiliar population. Although most of the European settlers in the Gulf Coast during the seventeenth and eighteenth centuries came from Spain and France, they and their descendents were soon joined by Anglophone newcomers in the late eighteenth and early nineteenth centuries who eventually constituted the majority in pockets of West Florida, especially around Baton Rouge. The first of these migrants consisted of Loyalists.[54] American settlers eventually followed, including a number who both resisted Spanish laws and upset the tenuous peace on the borderlands. The most famous of these troublemakers were the Kemper brothers—Nathan, Rueben, and Samuel—who beginning in 1805 created a series of violent disturbances. As rumors abounded that Americans from the Mississippi Territory would enter West Florida in support of the Kempers, the Spanish dispatched troops. Although the American invasion never came, an armed gang from Mississippi entered West Florida with the

Kempers in the lead, stealing both horses and slaves and killing a Spanish soldier.[55]

The ability of lawbreakers to move back and forth from Spanish West Florida to American Louisiana made incorporation an extremely unattractive option. So long as the United States could not realize its vision of sovereignty, these men could maintain their own freedom. In 1808, for example, Lieutenant John Owings of the U.S. Navy landed in West Florida to seize a deserter. Vicente Folch, the governor of Spanish West Florida, who had feared American activity in the Southwest for years, considered this act a breach of sovereignty. Claiborne pressured Master-Commandant David Porter, who commanded the New Orleans naval station, to return the deserter and suspend Owings. For his part, Porter doubted the law-enforcement capabilities of the Spanish government in West Florida. He suspected that settlers had moved onto foreign soil only in order to elude American law enforcement or to begin new illegal activities under the weak and corrupt Spanish regime.[56] These troublemakers — whether whites or Indians — unleashed sporadic episodes of violence and resistance.

At least the white threat in the East came from rabblerousers of undistinguished background. More troubling were activities of men from the pinnacle of the American aristocracy. Edward Livingston was certainly the last man whom Jefferson expected to cause problems. The youngest brother of Robert R. Livingston, he had been a rising star in the Republican leadership a few years before. No sooner had Livingston become both mayor of New York (an office appointed by the governor) and U.S. attorney (a reward from Jefferson) than he suddenly found himself liable for public funds that a clerk had legally borrowed but failed to reimburse. Pursued by creditors throughout New York, Livingston abandoned the east coast for Louisiana, hoping to rebuild his shattered political and economic fortunes.[57]

Jefferson and especially Gallatin were already losing faith in Edward Livingston. Livingston only hurt himself by joining a team of American attorneys in writing an opinion on behalf of the Spanish minister, Carlos Martinez de Yrujo, on the matter of Franco-Spanish spoliations.[58] What might have been a minor irritant anywhere else in the United States was evidence of potential disloyalty in Louisiana, where Americans were deeply afraid of Spanish intervention. When Congress passed the Governance Act and Livingston found himself still excluded from public office, he sided with the indignant Louisianians. Livingston found support from Daniel Clark, the last American consul in New Orleans. In 1803 Clark's contacts with the Louisianians had provided crucial information to the administration. But with American sovereignty came the elimination of the consul's office and an end to the pay and the perquisites that Clark had known.

When Clark, like Livingston, was excluded from subsequent appointments, he, too, cast his lot with irate Louisianians. They advised white Louisianians to resist the Governance Act and eventually helped write the Remonstrance. In 1808 Clark rose to the defense of four Indians imprisoned in New Orleans for breaking a city ordinance against vagabonds. "Under the pretext I do not know of which interest of humanity," Mayor James Mather reported, Clark "presented himself at my office to notify me that he would have them released by a *Writ of Habeas Corpus* and complained about the despotism exercised upon these individuals, whose detention, he said, was illegal and arbitrary." The parish judge upheld the writ, released the Indians, and left Mather even more infuriated with Clark. Mather further added that on "the same day, Mr. Livingston came to my office and asked me several questions concerning his removal of earth, and concerning the permissions which he maintained that I had given to this effect. He finished by threatening me to have the Superior Court pronounce a new injunction against the inhabitants of the City." Through no apparent connivance, Clark and Livingston showed the City Council that local malcontents were prepared to resist government supervision of public lands. The coincidence of their activities only heightened the council's intransigence and the Jefferson administration's concern.[59]

Livingston's greatest act of defiance came in 1807, when he defended claims to the private ownership of the New Orleans Batture, a stretch of alluvial soil fronting the Mississippi River that had traditionally been subject to public use. When Livingston published a pamphlet on the matter, council member Jean Thierry complained about how Livingston "deluges the public" with false accusations. Council members described Livingston's actions as an "attack, directed in contempt of the most formal Laws by a man, whose purpose is to disorganize the administration of the City by absorbing the greater part of its revenues into lawsuit expenses intended by him for the ruins of the Corporation."[60] Claiborne lamented that "I once thought that Mr. Livingston would be an acquisition to Louisiana, where men of Science & political Information are so much wanting; But I fear he will become a troublesome member of our political society, and I do sincerely regret, that he ever left New-York."[61]

The relationship between Claiborne and Clark was even more volatile. In 1807 Claiborne was wounded in a duel between the two men, the result of increasingly vehement public attacks over the preceding three years.[62] Suddenly the diplomatic disputes between the United States and Spain provided some advantage, for the two men were able to pass over to Florida, avoiding laws against dueling in the United States. Claiborne later stated that he was ashamed of the incident. "My feelings have led me to an act which I fear may subject me to your censure," he informed Jefferson. Claiborne offered Jefferson an "apology for my imprudence." Although he did not receive any direct punishment, his superiors in Washington provided little absolution. In fact they provided no comment at all, a powerful silence to Claiborne, who eagerly sought the administration's approval. Dueling undermined the peaceful resolution the administration hoped to institutionalize in Louisiana.[63]

At the very moment that Clark and Livingston reached the zenith of their opposition politics, another American created even greater fears. Beginning in the fall of 1806, disturbing reports filtered back to Washington about Aaron Burr. Unceremoniously evicted from the Republican ticket in the 1804 election, indicted for the murder of Alexander Hamilton, Burr traveled west. Observers throughout the United States were convinced that Burr was at the center of a broad conspiracy to launch a separatist movement in Louisiana, creating a separate republic that would probably include New Orleans and might extend as far west as Spanish Texas.

On 25 November James Wilkinson reported that Burr "had proceeded too far to retreat," and it was only a matter of time before he led a force of 2,000 men to secure Louisiana's separation. A month later Jefferson wrote to Claiborne that "you already have a general knolege of the insurrection prepared by Colo. Burr. his object is to take possession of N. Orleans, as a station from whence to make an expedition against Vera Cruz & Mexico."[64] Wilkinson had good reason to send these reports. An initial ally of Burr's (this alliance may also explain why Wilkinson returned to the Territory of Orleans in 1806), by the winter of 1806–07 he was busy distancing himself from the conspiracy. When he was not zealously pursuing suspected Burrites, Wilkinson was at work on the Neutral Ground agreement, calling conspicuous attention to his own attachment to his patrons in Washington. Still convinced that the Louisianians had only the faintest attachment to the United States, many Americans concluded that Burr would find ready supporters among them.[65]

Louisiana seemed able to corrupt upstanding men like Edward Livingston or to seduce disreputable men like Aaron Burr. But this capacity for corruption only made sense to American observers. Since 1803 they had concluded that French and Spanish procedures, the power of the Catholic church, and local racial practices had ruined white Louisianians. Those forces seemed so powerful that they would consume Americans as well.

The Burr Conspiracy remains the most famous example of resistance in Louisiana and is usually the starting point for scholars who investigate challenges to the Republicans' efforts in the trans-Mississippi West. But the activities of Aaron Burr seemed so dangerous only because they came in a context of resistance that was already under way when Burr traveled west. From New York aristocrats to slaves, people in Louisiana were challenging the federal government's vision of incorporation. They confirmed the worst fears of American policymakers, who worried that expansion on the scale of the Louisiana Purchase was impossible given the goals and structures of the federal system. But they had also shown something else. For all their attention to Louisiana and their debate over the Governance Act, federal policymakers had not actually built a government in Louisiana. The Governance Act provided the means, but the resistance within Louisiana would prove no less important as men in Washington and Louisiana attempted to make federal governance a reality.

4

Codes

James Monroe was worried. At the very moment of Dehahuit's emergence on the world stage — the negotiations in 1806 that culminated in the Neutral Ground agreement — Monroe believed his own diplomatic career was falling apart. Of course, Monroe would not compare himself to an Indian, nor had he ever set foot in the West that was Dehahuit's home. In fact, by 1806 Monroe had not set foot in North America for almost three years. He had become a journeyman diplomat, traversing the capitals of Europe in a frustrating effort to impose American terms on European leaders, most of whom considered the United States a distant, irrelevant country that was almost comic in its efforts to establish a voice in world affairs.

Monroe left Paris soon after the Louisiana Purchase to assume the post of American minister to Great Britain. But in 1805 he went to Spain in an effort to end the deadlock over the boundaries of Louisiana. He failed to make headway toward a resolution of either Anglo-American commercial disputes or Spanish-American border disputes. It was in Madrid that Monroe received a copy of Jefferson's 1805 annual message, a document focusing on the diplomatic problems with Spain and Great Britain. Dejected though Monroe might be, he expressed considerable bravado when commenting on Jefferson's message. In a letter to Madison, Monroe explained that Jefferson's message "opens the question between the U States and this country [Great Britain], and also with Spain, in a manner to shew that our government understands its rights and interests and will vindicate them, while it makes it equally evident that if a misunderstanding takes place between us and either of them, it will be owing to such power and not to us."[1]

Monroe's unflinching tone was characteristic of his correspondence as well as his behavior. Besides, Monroe was convinced that there was no other viable stance for the United States to take. Every piece of evidence he received from either side of the Atlantic indicated that the United States faced tremendous dangers. He knew the diplomatic problems firsthand. Meanwhile, Jefferson and Madison had kept him apprised of an administration thrown on the defensive by the domestic difficulties in Louisiana. Unruly Creoles and Francophone migrants, slaves and free people of color, Caddo and Choctaw, Burr conspirators and West Florida rebels had successfully exploited the contingency on the frontier to advance their own agendas. Not only did American policymakers conclude that foreign and domestic threats were mutually reinforcing, but people within Louisiana recognized that international affairs could serve their own purpose, whether to build attachments or to attack them.

With the federal administration in Louisiana under assault, federal policymakers renewed their efforts to co-opt white Louisianians, contain American troublemakers, reinforce racial supremacy, and promote national security. Through international treaties, an expanded bureaucracy, and new rules of conduct, the federal government set out to get incorporation back on track. The codes and institutions they created were amendments of a sort to the Louisiana Purchase, attempts to clarify provisions that had seemed either vague or dangerous in 1803. In the process of revising the Purchase, white Louisianians and American officials would also continue the process of learning that they shared a great deal when it came to their visions of Louisiana's future.

The government of territorial Louisiana may not have been fully "adapted to your manners," as Laussat had promised the Louisianians in 1803, but it was adapted to the particular challenges of incorporating Louisiana. Yet this was hardly an aberrant government within the United States. It was instead the quintessential example of Republican policymaking, not only because it epitomized the Jeffersonians' vision of governance, but also because Louisiana so dominated the administration's agenda that it shaped every facet of foreign and domestic policy.

Treaties and Jurisdictions

The effort to reinvigorate incorporation began in Washington and involved both the administration and Congress. Jefferson and Madison moved to isolate the newly independent republic of Haiti and to secure a treaty that would establish boundaries of a Louisiana that included West Florida. While the administration attempted to foster Louisiana's diplomatic incorporation in ways that would reduce foreign threats, members of Congress attempted to promote diplomatic and administrative incorporation in ways that would promote domestic harmony. They hoped to create a system that would cultivate the attachment of whites while providing for Louisiana's permanent attachment to the United States.

The administration's diplomatic efforts were actually as old as the Louisiana Purchase itself. Since the summer of 1803, Jefferson and Madison had engaged in a fruitless search for proof that West Florida had indeed been covered by the Louisiana Purchase.[2] It was a dubious claim at best. Besides, Spanish officials made clear that they had no intention of surrendering the Floridas, regardless of American claims.[3] Monroe himself endured what he considered personal humiliation at the hands of a Spanish government that, like the British, was unwilling to bend to American pressure. In his 1806 annual message, the best Jefferson could say of the situation was that "what will be that of the negotiations for settling our differences with Spain, nothing which had taken place at the date of the last despatches enables us to pronounce." Unable to appreciate (or unwilling to acknowledge) Spanish concerns about what looked like American adventurism, Jefferson instead emphasized the danger facing the United States. He portrayed the Spanish as a dangerous, aggressive neighbor that had "advanced in considerable force, and took post at the settlement of Bayou Pierre, on the Red River." It was this vision of continental and transatlantic affairs that informed Monroe's own analysis in his letter to Madison.[4]

James Monroe's travels in Europe were only part of the effort to change this state of affairs. Still unconvinced that any real benefits would come from wholesale expansion, federal policymakers considered returning the vast majority of the Louisiana Purchase—especially the land north of the Territory of Orleans—in exchange for the Floridas. In February 1807 Congress even authorized an additional $2 million that would serve primarily as a bribe to solicit French pressure on Spain to sell or cede the Floridas to the United States.[5] When Bonaparte proved uninterested in Spanish-American affairs, the United States found itself incapable of pressing its agenda in Madrid.

The lack of a diplomatic settlement of Louisiana's borders perpetuated a status quo that worked against the federal government's domestic agenda. Spanish possession of West Florida and the ill-defined border of western Louisiana provided safe havens for runaway slaves and white lawbreakers. These circumstances contributed to the low point in the administration's foreign policy. Monroe eventually returned to London, where he helped negotiate an 1806 treaty with Great Britain that proved so objectionable to American observers that the Senate roundly rejected it. The failure of those initiatives

reflected the simple fact that European powers could ignore American initiatives whenever they wanted. And when the United States attempted to assert
diplomatic muscle in 1807, the results were disastrous. The Embargo of
1807–1809, which shut down American foreign trade in an effort to coerce
changes in Britain, proved so unsuccessful in both policymaking and popular
terms that it threatened all the Jeffersonians' political and diplomatic gains
since 1800.

The administration was more successful in the Caribbean, in no small part
because it was operating from a position of strength. The Republic of Haiti
declared its independence from France on 1 January 1804. Two months later
Jefferson expressed his desire for an international agreement "not to suffer the
former slaves to have any Kind of Navigation whatsoever or to furnish them
with any Species of Arms or Ammunition."[6] Although Madison did not leave
a similar paper trail expressing opposition to the new regime in Haiti, he
tacitly affirmed the president's attitude by implementing a diplomatic policy
that excluded Haiti from the community of nations. Congress followed suit in
February 1806 with a law prohibiting any trade with Haiti (still referred to as
"St. Domingo" in the federal record, in large part because the bill rationalized
the ban by claiming that the island remained a French colony).[7]

The administration's effort in Haiti proved effective because the infant republic in the Caribbean was even more vulnerable than the United States.
Unlike Spain, which could ignore American demands, Haiti had no real power
and few friends in Europe. Besides, the administration had eager allies within
Congress. The effort to isolate Haiti remained among the most consistent and
successful elements of Republican foreign policy. This proved to be the case in
no small part because the isolation of Haiti seemed critical to the incorporation of Louisiana, for Haiti constituted an obvious model for slaves who
hoped to overturn the racial supremacy of American Louisiana.[8]

In the Caribbean and in Europe, the administration intended to secure the
incorporation of Louisiana by eliminating foreign threats. Madison in particular hoped that diplomatic progress on the administration's terms would eliminate at least some of the challenges to the territorial government he was struggling to build. Meanwhile he was equally dependent on Congress, which was
already at work reforming its initial plans for the government of Louisiana.

When Derbigny, Destrehan, and Sauve left Washington in 1805 after delivering the Remonstrance, they were disappointed by federal legislators. Yet
the delegates from Louisiana had underestimated the power of their argument. The Remonstrance had indeed highlighted shortcomings in the 1804
Governance Act. Although the authors of the congressional report rebuked
the Louisianians for their demanding tone, they agreed with them in spirit.
They suggested that "the United States cannot have incurred a heavy debt in

order to obtain the Territory of Louisiana merely with a view to the exclusive or especial benefit of its inhabitants." At the same time the committee "earnestly recommend[ed] that every indulgence, not incompatible with the interests of the Union, may be extended to them." The report concluded that "only two modes present themselves whereby a dependent province may be held in obedience to its sovereign State—force and affection." This statement recapitulated the Republicans' vision of nationhood, in which affection would create a more powerful union than force could ever sustain. The report took for granted the principle that the United States existed through the attachment of its citizens.[9]

On 2 March 1805 Congress passed a second Governance Act creating an elected House of Representatives that would work in conjunction with the appointed Legislative Council, as well as a nonvoting delegate to Congress. Residents of Louisiana now had elected offices to govern them locally and a voice in Congress to represent them nationally. The act also replaced the District of Louisiana with a freestanding Territory of Louisiana, which, although it lacked elected offices, had its own government distinct from the Indiana Territory. James Wilkinson was the territory's first governor. He moved to St. Louis, only to return south the following year, ostensibly to take command of troops in the area as tensions with Spain increased.[10]

The 1805 Governance Act also stated that the Territory of Orleans could petition for statehood once the free population exceeded 60,000. Though crushing the hopes of Louisianians eager for immediate statehood, it provided conditions for statehood in place of the administration's vague promises best captured in Madison's draft treaty in March 1803. Perhaps most important, Congress had finally integrated Orleans into the mainstream of territorial policy. If Louisiana had diminished political rights, at least its unequal status now conformed with that of other territories.

The 1805 Governance Act and the administration's diplomatic initiatives were supposed to create a foundation that would contain the resistance that abounded in Louisiana after 1803. The next step was to create rules that would govern the new American territory. Although the administration and Congress would influence this process, it was primarily a local endeavor within Louisiana, one that showed just how much the administration had overestimated the resentment of white Louisianians.

Property

No sooner did Congress create the bicameral legislature for Orleans than that body set to work drafting codes to define human property as well as the rules of commercial transaction. The United States might be incapable of establishing its claims to property on the North American continent, but it did establish individual property in ways that expressed a response to threats of white resistance and nonwhite revolt. Together with supplemental legislation, the Land Title Act of 1805, the Black Code of 1806, and the Louisiana Civil Digest of 1808 sought to define property in ways that would promote regional stability, white attachment, and racial supremacy against the considerable threats that came in the wake of the Louisiana Purchase.

Congress began the process by reasserting the linkage between individual and national property through the Land Title Act of 1805. Passed on 2 March, the same day as the 1805 Governance Act, the Land Title Act conveniently nullified all Spanish claims after the retrocession to France (an adroit political maneuver which reinforced the American argument that in the retrocession Spain surrendered any legitimate claim to Louisiana). Spanish grants issued after 1 October 1800 required reauthorization by federal land commissioners.[11] Individual ownership of the land was less important than the fact that ownership emanated from federal authority. Even as Spanish and American diplomats argued over the boundaries of Louisiana, land surveyors struggled to make American sovereignty an operational reality. Nor were these two processes merely coincidental. An effective survey within Louisiana would reinforce diplomatic efforts to determine exactly what Louisiana was. Secretary of the Treasury Albert Gallatin was also keen to replace the long, narrow strips of most French and Spanish land claims, a highly efficient way to provide the greatest access to riverine transport, with the square blocks that formed the basis of land distribution on the western frontier. How better to incorporate Louisiana than to change the landscape itself? Gallatin wondered. What would make it more American than a series of blocks with clear title granted to American citizens?[12]

While Congress defined landed property, territorial legislators attempted to define human property. Whereas in other states the laws of race emerged piecemeal over decades, the Black Code of 1806 attempted to provide a comprehensive redefinition of social behavior. At its core the Black Code was designed to reinforce the control of masters over their slaves and to create a clear stratification within the free community by establishing the superiority of whites over free people of color. "As the person of a slave belongs to his master," read Article 16, "no slave can posses any thing in his own right, or dispose in a way of the product of his industry, without the consent of his master." Article 18 carried this notion further. "The condition of a slave being merely a passive one, his subordination to his master and to all who represent him, is not susceptible of any modification or restriction."[13] Along related lines, Article 40 stated: "Free people of color ought never to insult or strike white people, nor presume to conceive themselves equal to the white; but on the contrary that they ought to yield to them in every occasion, and never speak or answer to them but with respect, under the penalty of imprisonment according to the nature of the offense."[14]

The Black Code was an injunction as much for white Louisianians as for Afro-Louisianians. Fearful that existing customs might create the conditions for slave revolt, the legislature made clear to slaveowners exactly what behavior was acceptable. "Every inhabitant is prohibited from suffering in his camp, other assemblies than that of his own slaves, under the penalty of paying all the damage which might result to the owner of any strange slave in consequence of such an admittance."[15] The conspiracies of 1804 and 1805 (whether real or imagined) had left their mark on Louisiana's legislators.

In the process of drafting the Black Code, Louisiana legislators hoped to redefine the relationships between race and slavery. Instead of a world consisting of black, white, and mixed-race people, they attempted to make Louisiana a place of whites and nonwhites. While legal distinctions between slaves and free people of color remained in place, both groups were distinctly outside the community of citizens. The Black Code also assumed that race rather than slavery, freedom, or birthplace dictated social status. This provision constituted a radical shift from the French and Spanish system, where the mulattos who made up the bulk of the free people of color were a distinct caste, entitled to a distinct range of privileges. White Americans and Louisianians together struggled to eliminate the legal basis of those racial gradations. Although Louisiana would long maintain a social-caste system in which people of mixed race occupied different levels of status, legislators nonetheless hoped to clarify the legal status of whites and nonwhites, ending both the ambiguity and the resistance of the preceding years. This change did as much to bolster white claims to equal citizenship as it did to exclude nonwhites.

"White" and "nonwhite" were, of course, no less constructed in Louisiana than anywhere else. In fact the Black Code was an explicit effort to design that construction. And although historians have shown that the one-drop rule was a product of twentieth-century racial politics, the Black Code showed that at the turn of the nineteenth century whites in Louisiana believed that African ancestry meant exclusion from the national community.[16]

Subsequent legislation reinforced the Black Code as well as the linkages to the administration's Caribbean policy. As an 1806 law explained, "whereas serious inconveniences might arise, if measures were not taken to prevent the introduction of people of color from Hispaniola, and from the French American Islands," the territorial government explicitly prohibited entry to free people of color from the French Caribbean. A law the following year went even further, prohibiting all free people of color from migrating to Louisiana under penalty of fine, imprisonment, and re-enslavement. In 1807 the legislature also passed new rules granting masters greater control over the emancipation of their slaves, dictating that "no person shall be compelled either directly or indirectly, to emancipate his slave or slaves." This legislation closed the loopholes that so many slaves had exploited after 1803. It also set out to prevent any increase in the number of free people of color. So, too, did the restrictions on migration, but those restrictions had other purposes. Free people of color had been the first revolutionaries on Saint Domingue, demanding that France sustain equality among all free people regardless of race. Despite the fact many free people of color who left Saint Domingue had done so to flee the revolution, many white Louisianians were convinced that these newcomers would lead a slave revolt in Louisiana.[17]

Although the coalition that supported the Black Code was a textbook case of white solidarity, white solidarity alone does not account for the Black Code. The law was a response to the mobilization of slaves and free people of color, but it was also an attempt to determine who would be a member of the national community. In the Black Code, legislators sought to define and secure nationhood, using ancestry to establish Afro-Louisianians in a permanent, quasi-foreign status while also establishing the administrative structures to preserve that system. Crucial to this process was its effect in reinforcing the claims of white Louisianians, for if the Black Code constructed an impenetrable wall that excluded nonwhites, it provided an equally strong inclusion of whites. In constructing the code, white Louisianians became among the first people of non-British European ancestry to assert that whiteness trumped any other form of difference.[18]

The Land Title Act and the Black Code preserved property. This was no small affair in the early American republic, where property was essential to the way people conceived of liberty.[19] Enforcing these codes involved only one problem: there *was* no law in Louisiana. The same legal ambiguity that served the interests of slaves and free people of color soon began causing considerable dispute among whites. Although there was no resolution so neat as the Black Code, passage of the Black Code did coincide with a certain clarification—if not a resolution—on other matters of property.

Two years after passing the Black Code, the territorial legislature approved *A Digest of the Civil Laws Now in Force in the Territory of Orleans . . . Adapted to Its Present System of Government.* The work of James Brown (an American from Kentucky) and Louis Moreau-Lislet (a recent arrival from Saint Domingue), the *Civil Digest* was supposed to synthesize the laws in force. The title was perfect, since Louisiana was very much a place where law had "adapted" to changing circumstances. The subtle intricacy and multinational ancestry of the *Civil Digest* did justice to a region where settlers and rulers from France, Spain, and finally the United States all left their imprint on legal culture.[20] Claiborne had his reservations not only about its origins, which he considered foreign, but also about its apparent threat to incorporation by keeping Louisiana's law out of the American mainstream. Nonetheless, the need for a legal code of any form was essential, and Claiborne recognized the *Civil Digest* as a logical compromise.

The Black Code and the *Civil Digest* have been the subject of considerable scholarly inquiry. Legal historians have explored the *Civil Digest* to determine the roots of Louisiana law, which remains an anomaly in American jurisprudence. Meanwhile, scholars have situated the Black Code within a broader consideration of the extent to which different European colonial systems fostered different conceptions of race.[21] Both pursuits have often proved frustrating, in large part because it requires a balancing act between continuity and change, benefits and drawbacks. While the Black Code preserved opportunities for slaves and free people of color unprecedented in the United States, it signaled a retreat from some of the possibilities under French and Spanish rule.[22]

The broader contours of legal systems are no less ambiguous. At first glance the question of law in territorial Louisiana *appears* to be the quintessential manifestation of cultural conflict or cultural difference, and rightly so. Nowhere else were the lines between Americans and Louisianians so clearly defined, and in few other circumstances did both sides see such direct relationships between public institutions and ethnic differences. Colonial Louisiana and the United States *did* have different legal and racial traditions that came into conflict after the Louisiana Purchase. Federal officials in Washington and Louisiana *did* believe that French and Spanish policies had fostered the atmosphere of racial unrest in Louisiana.[23] Likewise, irate Louisianians *did* protest federal efforts to replace their legal traditions with the common law. And yet federal policymakers agreed to the *Civil Digest* despite its preservation of legal procedures that kept Louisiana out of the American mainstream, while white Louisianians did accept — and even welcome — numerous changes to their local traditions that came about through the Black Code, the Land Title Act of 1805, and the *Civil Digest* of 1808.

Above all, however, it was the ambiguity of social conduct that worried the order-conscious, often litigious white men who debated public affairs in Louisiana. While many of Louisiana's Francophone attorneys and merchants worried that they would suffer from their unfamiliarity with Anglo-American legal norms, many were also eager for legal reform.[24] Frustrated by the imprecision of the colonial legal system, they believed that the transfer of power provided an unprecedented opportunity to create a more effective legal system, to professionalize their occupation, and to advance their own status.[25] Despite their commitment to the common law, American policymakers were equally eager for a settlement that would finally establish the rules governing the very principles established by the Land Title Act and the Black Code. In addition, Louisianians expressed no opposition to a compendium on criminal law, written by Americans Lewis Kerr and James Workman and New Orleans mayor John Watkins, which imposed American principles of criminal procedure at the expense of colonial legal customs at the very moment the *Civil Digest* protected older practices in civil jurisdiction. Although differences in legal culture fueled the angry debate in Louisiana, the struggle for an effective political economy was no less important in the consideration of legal reform. What legal tradition would serve as the basis of that system might be subject to debate, but the need for reform was not.[26]

Once again the national perspective proves instructive. The Black Code coincided with similar legislation in other southern states designed to reaffirm the exclusion of slaves and to prevent an increase in the number of free people of color. At a time when people throughout the United States were hard at work defining both citizenship and nationhood, a time when whites were increasingly fearful of racial revolts, these sorts of laws became all the more important.[27] The territorial legislature passed the Black Code so quickly because white Louisianians were eager for a more restrictive slave system.[28] Federal policymakers were none too pleased, because the Black Code removed the ambiguity from the Louisiana Purchase itself. Whereas Article III referred only to "the inhabitants of the ceded territory," a passage that free people of color had been quick to exploit, the Black Code and the *Civil Digest* explicitly quashed their aspirations to membership in the national community.

The Land Title Act responded to similar pragmatic concerns. White Louisianians were eager for the settlement of disputed claims. Meanwhile, the Jefferson administration retreated from its initial efforts to orchestrate wholesale changes in land ownership and, in turn, a change in local culture. The same absence of formal, written grants that brought Louisianians into dispute made it impossible for the administration to demand the sort of documentation required in the 1805 Land Title Act.[29] In April 1806 Gallatin admitted that "in many instances no legal evidence of a permission to settle can be produced, and . . . great hardship would follow."[30] Faced with the true scope of ascertaining land ownership in Louisiana, Gallatin recommended, and Congress enacted, a more lenient policy. On 17 April 1806 Congress passed legislation permitting people without documentation to use three years of "quiet possession" as the basis for a legal claim. While Gallatin and his surveyors were still committed to a full accounting of the land in Louisiana, they abandoned their more ambitious desire to impose the norms of American claims. Instead, the old long lots would have to coexist with newer squares the government superimposed on public lands.[31]

White Louisianians and American policymakers continued to eye each other suspiciously, and they usually did so through their response to legal codes that seemed to invoke culture. Yet they were just as likely to relax their concerns for cultural homogeneity in response to greater threats. From 1805 through 1808 legislators in Washington and in New Orleans crafted codes to secure the diverse elements of incorporation. In the process, however, they had also begun to rehabilitate their own relationships after the disputes in 1803–04 embodied in the Remonstrance. This was only the first in a series of collaborative efforts that would show just how much white Louisianians and American policymakers shared similar visions of legal reform, political development, political economy, and racial supremacy. That sort of attachment between white Louisianians and white Americans was in itself a necessary part of incorporation.

"The Blessings of Law and Social Order"

The codes could not function by themselves. They might express the goals of white policymakers, they might establish a prescriptive groundwork for behavior, but their power was limited by the willingness of people to observe those rules and the government's capacity to enforce them. So at the same time that public officials in Washington and Louisiana attempted to craft texts that would promote their vision of incorporation, they also attempted to build institutions in Louisiana that would militate against both internal unrest and external attack. Indeed, the creation of new law tells only a fundamentally political story, rather than an administrative story that situates institution-building in the broader process of providing specific services and constructing functional linkages between Louisiana and the rest of the United States. Not only would the government's ability to impose its will test the real significance of the documents of reform crafted from 1805 through 1808, but the means the territorial regime pursued were no less important than the ends.

The challenge facing federal leaders was to create appointed offices which would not undermine a government that remained responsive to its citizens.[32] The problems of governance in Spanish Louisiana provided a cautionary tale for leaders of the young republic, since they seemed to show how the absence of a republican political culture could not just undermine politics but also retard prosperity.[33] When the Louisiana Purchase forced the United States to build a government west of the Mississippi, policymakers attempted to graft this system onto the new, extended national frontier. Similar attempts to build territorial governments during the 1790s fueled the growing rift that eventually turned into organized partisanship. Despite the fact that Federalists and Republicans offered radically different plans for western governance, this debate rested on a consensus about the *purpose* of government. They remained committed to the notion that a vigorous public policy was essential to the stability and prosperity of white settlers on the western frontier.[34]

In the end, creating a government in territorial Louisiana was a fundamentally Jeffersonian pursuit. Not that the Federalists did not care about territorial affairs, far from it; but the Federalists' political influence was already waning when the United States acquired Louisiana. Losses in the 1802 and 1804 elections reinforced Republican strength in Congress. Despite opposition to the Governance Act of 1804 from within Republican ranks, the Jefferson and Madison administrations were free to direct territorial governance as they saw fit. The governments in the Territory of Orleans and eventually the state of Louisiana were the apotheosis of the Jeffersonians' vision of western public policy. The considerable challenges that came with extending American government to encompass a distant land and a foreign people reveal how American government operated and how it interacted with politics.

Understanding the government the Republicans built in the Territory of Orleans begins with one federal entity and one man: the State Department and William C. C. Claiborne. That this system of government depended on an individual and a single federal department indicates the confluence of structural and personal factors in the American territorial regime. It also provides a case study in the operational realities of governing the frontiers of the union.

In the five decades between the creation of the federal government in 1789 and creation of the Interior Department in 1849, the State Department handled territorial affairs. That Madison was already Jefferson's most trusted ally only reinforced his constitutional powers, for Madison assumed that the War, State, and Treasury Department officials who also served in the Territory of Orleans would follow the priorities established by the State Department. And although Jefferson replaced Burr with George Clinton, he saw no reason to let the former New York governor join the president's circle of confidants.

At the other end of the policymaking structure was William C. C. Claiborne, who enjoyed similar authority over the officials in Louisiana. Claiborne was only twenty-eight years old when he crossed the Mississippi River to take charge in Louisiana. Never a particularly deep or original thinker, Claiborne had nonetheless known both electoral and appointive success. A Virginian by birth, Claiborne was often on the move. After a brief stint in New York and abbreviated legal studies in Richmond, Claiborne settled in Tennessee, eventually winning the congressional seat vacated by Andrew Jackson in 1797 after Jackson's election to the Senate. In Congress Claiborne joined his uncle, Thomas Claiborne, a representative from Virginia. For some reason, nobody challenged Claiborne's election, despite the fact that he was two years short of the twenty-fifth birthday that would qualify him for election to the House. Four years later, as Jefferson attempted to clear the territories of their Federalist governors, the new president nominated Claiborne to take charge in Mississippi. By 1803 Claiborne was an experienced frontier governor serving just across the river from Louisiana. Claiborne was ideally situated (both geographically and politically) to serve as a commissioner to receive Louisiana on behalf of the United States.[35]

Claiborne's initial months in Louisiana proved devastating. No sooner did he bring his wife and young daughter to join him than both died of yellow fever.[36] The deaths of Elizabeth and Cornelia Claiborne came soon after Jefferson had selected Claiborne as the first and only governor of the Territory of Orleans, a title he received soon after the 1804 Governance Act created the position. Still struggling to recover from his personal loss, Claiborne worried about his abilities to reform a population that he considered corrupted by a colonial regime that was "a Despotism, partly Civil, partly Military, and in some degree ecclesiastical."[37]

While Claiborne's tenure in Louisiana eventually proved to be longer than that of most territorial governors, his responsibilities were normal. Functioning like the narrow passage in the center of an hourglass, Claiborne was the primary conduit between Washington and Louisiana. And in the same way that sand squeezes its way through an hourglass, Claiborne's office became the locus of considerable pressure. Claiborne proved to be an ungainly gatekeeper, retarding contact between Washington and Louisiana as often as he promoted it.

Claiborne had proposed his own host of institutional changes in his very first address to the territorial legislature in 1806. Claiborne emphasized the need to pursue "the preservation of Order in Society, and the advancement of the general weal." He advocated reform in fields ranging from prisons to roads to schools.[38] But most important to territorial leaders — whether appointed or elected — was the construction of a policymaking infrastructure that would enable them to translate priorities into reality.

Claiborne ruled a dynamic territorial government that grew and reshaped itself with each passing year. The rudimentary collection of civil and military

officials on hand for the transfer of power in 1803 gave way to a more sophisticated system the following year, when the Governance Act of 1804 established the three familiar branches of American government: an executive (in
the person of the governor), a legislature (the thirteen-member Legislative
Council), and a judiciary (a three-member Superior Court meeting in New
Orleans). In 1805 Congress created the elected territorial House of Representatives. Equally important, soon before the bicameral legislature came into
being, the Legislative Council augmented the judicial structure by adding
forms of local government that attempted to make systems left from the colonial era conform with Jeffersonian norms. The Cabildo that had governed
New Orleans under the Spanish gave way to the Conseil de Ville, or City
Council, consisting of a mayor appointed by the governor, a recorder, a trea-
surer, and fourteen aldermen.[39] A group of twelve counties, based loosely on
old parishes that had doubled as civil and ecclesiastical districts under the
French and Spanish, became jurisdictions for justices of the peace who served
local judicial functions. As demands on the judicial system increased, the
twelve counties gave way in 1807 to nineteen parish courts and five judicial
court districts. The goal was to reduce the strains on public officials. The result
was to increase the possibilities for patronage.[40]

This separation of powers was limited to the pinnacle of territorial government, however, and try as they might the governor and the territorial legislature were unable to create such clear demarcations at the local level. While the
legislature came closest to independence, the line between judicial and executive responsibility was often hard to detect. Judges served as chiefs of individual police juries, the primary administrative agency at the parish level. Like the
governor, judges could organize the construction of roads and levees. Like the
legislature, they could impose taxes on real and personal property.[41]

An example of the practical realities of judicial governance came in 1808,
when members of the New Orleans City Council accused Orleans Parish judge
James Workman of improperly granting a tavern license to a woman named
Mercier. Later that year the council claimed that Workman had no right to
receive a portion of the sales taxes levied in the city. Council members charged
that this transfer of funds "would entail a conflict of functions, incompatible
with the spirit of American Government, in giving the Judge a prerogative
which, in the hierarchy of powers, is not even accorded to the grand Jury."
Nobody on the council questioned Workman's right to levy taxes outside the
city. Indeed, they saw little difference between his administrative responsibilities and their own. Their criticism stemmed from his effort to impose that
authority on the city, which had its own administrative agencies.[42]

The growing pains of this new system belied the similarities with the colonial structure or, for that matter, with local governance throughout the United States. Colonial Louisiana had been home to a similar mixture of powers at the local level. Meanwhile, the numerous responsibilities of local officials only reflected a nationwide reality that was hardly limited to western territories. The federal Constitution prescribed the responsibilities of only a fraction of the men serving the federal government: the president and vice president, Supreme Court justices, and members of Congress. Beyond that was anybody's guess. The civil and military officials employed by the federal government did not observe those clear distinctions, nor were they expected to so.[43] And while state constitutions were more precise than their federal counterpart when it came to the selection of local officials, they were equally vague on the boundaries of authority. Outside the few large cities that dotted the American landscape, judges and justices of the peace unified the powers that were divided only with the subsequent advent of county councils and boards of commissioners.[44]

The goals, structures, and leadership of western government always encompassed both civil and military activities. As much as any institution, the military and paramilitary bodies in Louisiana became the instruments for three of the most vital facets of incorporation: co-opting white Louisianians, controlling slaves and Indians, and suppressing unruly Americans. It was, after all, the U.S. Army that patrolled for slaves on one hand while arresting Aaron Burr on the other. In its public capacity, the military proved crucial to implementing the legislation of 1805–1808. In more subtle forms, however, the military would be the means for crafting an effective public policy that convinced both white Louisianians and American policymakers that Louisiana was securely incorporated.

By 1806 Louisiana was home to the largest single contingent of the U.S. Army as well as a sizable contingent from the U.S. Navy. The administration kept such a large force in the Southwest primarily to deter French, British, and, above all, Spanish acquisitiveness. Yet military personnel never believed that their responsibilities in Louisiana were limited to defense against foreign nations, since the foreign threats did not always come from overseas. As quasi-alienated people who lived on American soil, Indians and slaves could easily become violent enemies. The newly created territorial militia served a supplementary role, patrolling New Orleans and Louisiana's rural plantation districts, acting as a deterrent against potential revolt or a means to end any actual uprising.[45]

Nor was the Navy's mission without a similar racial dimension. The pirates and smugglers who abounded on the Gulf Coast and in the swamps and bayous of the Mississippi River welcomed runaway slaves and free people of color. Navy officers were equally eager to recapture runaway slaves who attempted to reach freedom in the holds of the numerous merchantmen sailing to northern ports like Philadelphia, New York, and Boston, or escape to Spanish Florida (a regular destination for vessels coming through New Orleans).[46]

Despite this military presence, municipal officials in New Orleans still considered the city vulnerable.[47] Members of the City Council responded by creating a paramilitary organization in 1809 called the "City Guard." The first urban police force in the South, the Guard was more closely akin to the militia in both organization and spirit than the informal constables on the streets of northern cities. Guardsmen patrolled the city on horseback and on foot, complete with swords and firearms. Elaborate uniforms made all residents aware that they were under the watchful eye of an armed constabulary. The City Guard was no less important than the territorial judiciary when it came to enforcing the Black Code.[48]

The Guard was responsible for all forms of law enforcement, but it was "specially required to search and pursue fugitive negroes."[49] Council members intended the Guard to be proactive and ruthless in its suppression of slave resistance in any form. As an incentive, members of the Guard could augment their regular salaries with bonuses for every runaway slave they captured. Like the army and the militia, the Guard would preserve the "respect" that the Black Code required of all slaves and free people of color.[50]

Reforming the territorial militia into an effective institution of racial supremacy meant purging free men of color from its ranks. Whites in Louisiana, whether Americans or Louisianians, showed little sympathy for free men of color who hoped to preserve the special militia unit in which they served. Claiborne, his superiors in Washington, and many white Louisianians shared the same fear of armed and organized black troops, especially in the wake of events in Saint Domingue.[51] Meanwhile, white militiamen also believed that the unit mocked their status as Americans at a time when many white Louisianians already felt slighted by their new fellow-countrymen.[52] Claiborne was reluctant to eliminate the organization outright, however, fearing that "to disband them would be to raise an armed enemy in the very heart of the Country."[53] So white Louisianians dissolved the free black militia through omission. The unit was noticeably absent from territorial militia legislation, a tacit means for the legislature to keep the militia white only. Angry free men of color met to plan how best to revive the unit, a tactic that only heightened white fears. They continued to offer their services as allies to the territorial regime, whether that meant defending the United States against foreign enemies or reinforcing the military response to slave revolts.[54]

No American governor—whether of a state or a territory—was ever entirely pleased with the militia. Nonetheless, at least Claiborne had a militia. The Governance Acts of 1804 and 1805, together with federal policymaking and territorial codes of conduct, had provided the means to create a system for public administration. The Louisiana Purchase had extended the structure of republican government west of the Mississippi. Now that government needed men to fill its public offices.

"A Good Sort of Man"

The West was ruled by appointees. This simple fact held true in European colonies as well as in American territories. The men who populated the government of Louisiana joined a federal bureaucracy that followed principles of hierarchy and authority peculiar to the early American republic. The process of selecting appointees, while only subtly different from systems in the colonial world, nonetheless were sufficiently in keeping with the principles of American republicanism for policymakers to believe they had created a revolutionary form of government that matched their revolutionary system of politics. That conclusion was convenient indeed, but it was essential for public officials intent on convincing themselves that they had engineered the means to avoid corruption.

These administrative principles stood in marked contrast to the increasingly democratic relationship between elected officials and their constituencies elsewhere in the United States. The networks of kinship and connection that sustained this workforce also inverted the principles that became the cornerstone of the bureaucratic state in the late nineteenth century, principles that historians eventually imported to describe corruption and inefficiency in the early American bureaucracy. Nor was this the more explicitly political system of patronage developed by the Jacksonians a generation after the United States took charge in Louisiana, a system that Progressive reformers later used to condemn patronage more generally.[55] Systems of merit and accountability that appeared ludicrous by century's end seemed essential to an effective government to Louisiana — or, for that matter, anywhere on the frontiers of the early American republic.

When the departure of European authority created an administrative vacuum in Louisiana, federal officials turned to principles that had guided the appointment process at state and federal levels since independence. Public officials of all political persuasions had asked what made a good public servant. Always in the back of their minds was the memory of British bureaucrats, who became stereotypes of the dangers that republics faced from corrupt and self-interested men or from published travel narratives that provided exaggerated tales of Spanish inefficiency. Since independence, Americans had developed a set of criteria that they hoped would produce a class of reliable, virtuous appointees who would not question the ultimate authority of the people. Background, education, social sophistication, political alignment, and individual success formed a definition of merit that became the hallmark of federal appointment. In the absence of the quantifiable measures of talent that have come to play such an important role in public appointments, public officials continued to rely on a set of criteria that remained intentionally vague.[56]

Nor was this a small collection of men. Although the federal presence in states remained limited, the Territory of Orleans was home to thousands of federal employees, whether civil officials, soldiers, or sailors. The largest contingent — enlisted men in the military — were not subjects of appointment. Nonetheless, hundreds of men selected by the administration and approved by the Senate served at some point in the Territory of Orleans. And as the number of appointments grew in Orleans and the Territory of Louisiana (the jurisdiction created from the northern majority of the Louisiana Purchase), the Louisiana Purchase began to exert its influence on the entire federal structure. Western government propelled American government, consuming federal resources and attention in a way that no state could rival.[57]

As Benjamin Morgan put it when he arrived in New Orleans in the summer of 1803, "it will require the talents of virtuous good men to make the laws of freemen palatable to them."[58] But who would be these "virtuous good men"? What emerged was a collection of appointees connected by kinship. The kinship might be literal, but it was more likely to be a fictive kinship premised on eighteenth-century notions of merit and connection. This system first took form in state governments. Federal leaders, most of whom learned about government at the state level, applied identical principles to the territorial workforce. The "kin" from which they drew could share blood, friendship, class, political affiliation, or, ideally, a combination of these. Kinship alone did not qualify a man for appointment, but it could raise him above candidates with similar backgrounds. Few contemporaries failed to recognize the way that connections and cronyism delivered patronage to people who might lack reliability, experience, or intelligence. At the same time, a system of kinship seemed logical and beneficial; and the only criticism came from people who were rejected for appointment. In a time of suspect loyalties, how better to guarantee reliable delegates than to choose people bound by lineage and political belief? Those connections served a particularly important function on the frontier.

That appointed officials assumed considerable independence in developing public policy has often been attributed to delays in communication or to nepotism, and rightly so. But this autonomy was not some passive acceptance of the problems posed by distance, nor was it simply a means for men in power to reward friends and relatives. Instead, political kinship provided an active mechanism that would create a responsive, supple government that transcended the delays of correspondence. In governing a vast republic, there seemed to be no better way to guarantee a consistent policy than to appoint familiar individuals. Personal acquaintance and social connection provided the coherence to policymaking that the delays of nineteenth-century communication could not. A broadly defined kinship provided the best conditions for a frontier administration that understood its objectives without explicit instructions.[59]

The Federalists are better known than their opponents for using the federal government as a nationalizing force in the context of the Federalist administrations. But the Republicans pursued a similar policy, and although Alexander Hamilton was the most aggressive in equating the state with the nation, Jeffersonians also believed that statebuilding could catalyze nationbuilding. Patronage provided the means for public officials to bind local elites to the national or state cause. To American policymakers, this system seemed a revolutionary improvement from the inherited titles of Europe. Of course, this system was also convenient. It enabled American policymakers to believe they had made a clean break from European models. Senior officials might be selecting appointees from a limited list of familiar white men of elite means, but they also believed they were preserving both good government and a republican political culture.[60]

Jefferson and Madison deployed these strategies when they began to look for men to fill the public roles in Louisiana, starting with the governor. They initially considered more experienced and more familiar men, ranging from Monroe to the marquis de Lafayette. Though not related to either Jefferson or Madison through blood, Monroe and Lafayette shared a political kinship. Their republican scruples and their personal loyalty were above doubt.[61] Jefferson made his own preferences brutally clear in August 1804, when he sent Claiborne his commission as governor of the Territory of Orleans. He explained that the "office [of governor] was originally destined for a person whose great services and established fame would have rendered him peculiarly acceptable to the nation at large" (whether Jefferson was referring to Monroe, Lafayette, or some other candidate remains open for debate). He continued that "circumstances however exist which do not now permit his nomination . . . that therefore being suspended, and entirely contingent, your services have been so much approved as to leave no desire to look elsewhere to fill the office."[62] Such frank explanations and backhanded compliments were rare for Jefferson or his cabinet, men who usually treated appointment letters as an opportunity to crystallize loyalty through excessive praise.

So if Claiborne's initial selection can be attributed to his convenient proximity, what accounts for his longevity in the Territory of Orleans? The members of Jefferson's administration certainly received plenty of complaints about Claiborne, and they had their own doubts about his ability. In 1807 Jefferson explained to John Dickinson that "there were characters superior to him whom I wished to appoint, but they refused the office: I know no better man who would accept of it, and it would not be right to turn him out for one not better."[63] Yet the fact that other men were unavailable is not sufficient, and Jefferson's lukewarm commentary only raises the question why Claiborne lasted in office for so many years.

The letter to Dickinson that poses so many questions also suggests an answer. In the same paragraph that provided such an uninspiring account of Claiborne's appointment, Jefferson added that the governor "has always been a firm republican." Whether he meant a man of republican convictions or a member of the Jeffersonian Republicans is uncertain and almost irrelevant, for by 1804 Jefferson saw little difference between the two. Equally important, Claiborne was a Virginian (although he had moved to Tennessee as a young man). This fact was a matter of no small importance in an administration that had made a practice of selecting Virginians for many of the most sensitive positions in the government. Nor were the two factors so far apart in the administration's calculation. Often suspicious of the political sentiments in other states, Jefferson and Madison saw many of their fellow Virginians as among the most steadfast republicans (and Republicans) in the nation. Claiborne's performance as the governor of the Territory of Orleans received mixed reviews, but criticism was never so severe that the administration considered removing him. Claiborne never suffered a catastrophic controversy of the kind that undid other territorial governors. And while the administration may have questioned his competence from time to time, it never doubted his loyalty.

Loyalty was of particular importance in Louisiana. While men in Washington were arguing about how best to achieve a geopolitical attachment consistent with American foreign goals or to sustain the individual attachment of white Louisianians, a governor who would remain attached to the priorities as well as the authority of federal leaders was vital. Claiborne seemed to fit the bill, and federal leaders employed similar criteria when selecting his colleagues and his subordinates.

Another member of the federal community in New Orleans captured the general view of Claiborne. In 1810 Master-Commandant David Porter, commander of the New Orleans naval station, confided to a friend that Claiborne "is considered a *good sort of man* and tells a number of good *long* stories." While this comment was as much criticism as compliment (Porter questioned

Claiborne's intelligence and considered him too eager to court the Louisianians' favor), it captured the administration's reasons for renewing Claiborne's commission throughout the territorial period. The key to an effective public administration was to find "a good sort of man" whose qualities made him likely to understand and support the administration's objectives. And for all his criticism, Porter was the product of the same system that produced Claiborne. Porter had risen through appointment and through the active patronage of his commanders.[64]

The same patronage that had served Porter and Claiborne provided the model that Claiborne hoped to institute in Louisiana. His own position secure, Claiborne functioned as the administration's proxy, selecting or nominating hundreds of men to fill numerous offices.[65] Some of these men were blood relations, others simply friends or longtime associates. His brother, Ferdinand, secured appointment as a judge and as a colonel in the territorial militia. Ferdinand also enjoyed electoral success in the Mississippi Territory, eventually serving as speaker of the territorial house of representatives. Another relative, Richard Claiborne, became a judge and later a federal district court clerk in Louisiana. As his kin traveled across the Mississippi, Claiborne remained confident that this process of selection guaranteed a reliable government in the Territory of Orleans. Were these men "cronies"? Not according to Claiborne, who saw no reason why the appointment of close friends collided with the public good. To the contrary, he acted from a tradition of public administration which validated that very system of appointment.[66]

At the same time that Louisiana normalized an enlarged federal presence, so too did it normalize executive supremacy over that workforce. Only a decade before, the Constitution's silence on matters of administration had led Congress to challenge the administration for control of the nation's infant bureaucracy. Whatever their other differences, both the Adams and Jefferson administrations demanded direct authority over territorial governments. The immediate needs of governance left no room for delayed consideration by Congress. The debate over the Governance Acts of 1804 and 1805 provided the only extensive congressional involvement in the administration of Louisiana. Even the power detailed to Congress by the Constitution — Senate approval of federal appointees — gave way to the pressing need to create governments in the West. As Jefferson dispatched lists of men to fill the ever-growing number of civil and military appointments in Louisiana, Senate consideration of those nominees only became more brief.[67]

Jefferson's nominees shared many of Claiborne's qualifications. The administration's choices were always Republicans, often Virginians, and usually connected by friendship or blood kinship to the national elite. Those not from

Virginia were often from Tennessee (Claiborne's case) or, better still, from Kentucky. The Kentuckians made particular sense. The state itself was kin to Virginia, only a generation removed from membership in a greater Virginia that reached clear to the Mississippi River. Likewise, Jefferson, Madison, and Monroe (the Virginians who directed territorial policy as presidents and secretaries of state) saw in the Kentuckians a perfect combination of reliable Virginia sensibilities enhanced by practical experience on the frontier.[68]

The intersection of regional origins and political contacts became readily apparent in the lives of the administration's first appointees. One of the few northerners to secure an appointment in Louisiana was Judge John Prevost, stepson of Vice President Aaron Burr. While any affiliation with Burr would eventually scotch the possibility of public appointment, Prevost's selection in 1804 made sense. Prevost enjoyed numerous connections with the Republican leadership. He was godfather to James Monroe's daughter, a fact that preserved his reputation even after Burr's collapsed.[69] Those connections also defended Prevost from Claiborne, who in 1811 asserted that the judge was "labouring incessant to effect my political Ruin." When Prevost eventually resigned his judgeship, Jefferson selected Kentuckian Lewis Kerr, who shared his own quasi-familial connection to the administration. Claiborne considered Kerr, a close friend from his days as Mississippi governor, a "member of my family." It was not a very amicable "family," for Claiborne and Kerr eventually became political enemies. But Claiborne's statement was particularly appropriate, for it captured the notion that kinship of all sorts was essential to effective government.[70]

These appointments of course were never without specific benefits, either to patron or client. Congressman John Randolph emphasized the crasser motives of office-seeking in April 1806, when he announced on the House floor that "it is well known, that the antechambers of our great men were crowded with applicants for offices in Louisiana. I have understood that for every office there were at least one hundred and fifty applicants. Thus much for the idea which has been thrown out of the existence of a scarcity of characters to supply these offices."[71] The same principles of appointment applied to Hore Browse Trist, whose family had enjoyed a long acquaintance with both Jefferson and Madison. The port collector in Natchez in 1803, he was the logical choice to assume that post in New Orleans. Trist may have been reliable, but he was also nearly bankrupt and desperately in need of the salary he received from the Treasury Department.[72] His was a short tenure. When Trist died in 1804 during the same yellow fever epidemic that killed Elizabeth and Cornelia Claiborne, Gallatin quickly chose William Brown, Trist's brother-in-law, to take his place.[73] Hore Browse Trist's patronage was of the kind more familiar to historians, with personal connections securing public office that would deliver direct rewards to himself and his family. At the same time that officeseekers sought personal advancement and family security by currying patronage, the administration was not averse to using patronage for explicitly political purposes, whether to benefit or to punish. The Jeffersonians had neither patience nor sympathy for Federalist officeholders, and during the Jefferson administration they set out to purge the federal government of Adams' appointees.[74] Nonetheless, it is too simple to see the appointment process exclusively in terms of a crass search for individual advancement or political benefit. Jefferson and his cabinet members certainly did not, nor did their Federalist predecessors. American policymakers, like their European imperial counterparts, instead approached the matter of appointment with a thoroughly pragmatic perspective that combined gifts to friends, rewards to political allies, and the creation of a reliable federal regime.

Whole families reinforced this system. Henry Clay soon emerged as a major conduit of power in Louisiana without himself traveling there. Relatives from Kentucky moved to Louisiana throughout the 1800s, where Clay's name helped them secure offices both high and low. Both his brother, John, and his business associate James Brown made the arduous journey to Louisiana to exploit the opportunities they saw in the Southwest. For Brown, those opportunities abounded. He soon built a lucrative legal practice and eventually cemented his relationship with Clay by marrying his sister, Nancy. As much as anybody, Brown seemed an ideal candidate for patronage. Not only had he shown his ability to thrive in Louisiana, not only was he bound by kinship to reliable figures in Washington, but his personal experience seemed to provide exactly the sort of personal background that was in such short supply west of the Mississippi. No stranger to the process of developing frontiers, Brown was a Virginian by birth who had established his reputation in Kentucky. As a member of the state's legal aristocracy, he had helped cement public authority against the challenges of frontier settlers who hoped for a more democratic and less legalistic public culture. As one of the authors of Kentucky's 1799 constitution, Brown had specific experience building new governments. From 1799 until his departure from Kentucky five years later, Brown developed his legal practice while teaching law and politics at Transylvania University. For all these reasons, Jefferson and Madison did not hesitate to cultivate James Brown as a member of their political kin. No sooner was the territorial system in place than they selected him as the first territorial secretary, soon promoting him to district attorney. Along the way, Gallatin selected Brown for a brief service as a land commissioner. But Brown's most important contribution came in 1808, when he coauthored the *Civil Digest*.[75]

The Clay-Brown connection established sources of contact that paralleled the official avenue of administrative communication. When James Brown was not writing directly to his superiors in the administration, he could sustain contact through Henry Clay. During his first year in Louisiana, Brown could also write to the two senators from Kentucky: his brother, John, and his cousin, John Breckinridge. Both men left the Senate in 1805, but Brown traded Senate influence for direct influence in the administration when John Breckinridge became Jefferson's attorney general. The obvious way to consider these relationships is as part of a system that delivered political influence to men like Brown. From Washington, however, those familial connections also reinforced the administration's influence over its own delegates. Nor was Breckinridge unconcerned with Louisiana's government. In 1803–04 he had represented the administration's interests on the Senate committee that devised the first draft of Governance Act.[76]

Clay also exerted influence beyond his own blood kin. For example, Claiborne and Territorial Secretary Thomas Bolling Robertson invoked Clay's name in recommending a relative named Francis Watkins for appointment as a midshipman aboard the naval vessels in New Orleans. They wrote to David Porter that the seventeen-year-old "possesses a good moral character, and (as we learn) has received the advantage of a liberal Education."[77]

The Brent and Graham families offer a similar case in point. John Graham served as secretary in the Territory of Orleans from 1805 to 1807, a post he left to become chief clerk at the State Department. Graham's predecessor as chief clerk was none other than his cousin, Daniel Brent. At different times and in different ways, both men helped create the administrative networks that would bind New Orleans to Washington. As a State Department employee, much of territorial secretary Graham's correspondence crossed his cousin's desk. When Graham came to Washington, he brought with him the contacts he had established in Louisiana.[78] Although Claiborne admitted that he "cannot take the liberty to recommend a Successor" for Graham, Madison eventually decided to fill the vacancy with Thomas Bolling Robertson, a member of another influential Virginia family.[79]

Equally useful was Daniel Brent's relationship with his uncle, John Carroll, who in 1808 became the first archbishop in the United States. Carroll used Brent as a conduit for assuring the administration that "if any clergyman acting . . . under my authority should ever betray disposition, or countenance measures unfriendly to the Sovereignity of the United States, or if ever he should hold correspondence of a suspicious nature with a foreign nation, he shall be deprived of any commission from me and of the care of the soul."[80] If political kinship served the Catholic church, it also presented the administration with the unofficial means to establish its influence over ecclesiastical affairs.

As the administration began to branch out in selecting men for Louisiana, it sought men who seemed to possess the cultural background to fit in with the Francophone majority. Among the first of these was none other than James Pitot, a French immigrant from Saint Domingue who in 1802 had written a travel narrative critical of the Spanish government in Louisiana. Pitot's scientific experiments with sugar had brought him close to a breakthrough in refining that set the stage not only for the introduction of modern crystallized sugar, but also the explosive growth in sugar plantations throughout southern Louisiana. Claiborne appointed the Frenchman mayor of New Orleans in 1804, and eventually named him judge for Orleans Parish.

François-Xavier Martin presented even more attractive credentials. Martin was, like Pitot, a Frenchman by birth. He had come to the New World via the French colony of Martinique and settled in New Bern, North Carolina, eventually building a printing business sustained primarily by the lucrative contracts he received for publishing laws and other public documents.[81] An attorney himself, Martin served in the state legislature before receiving an appointment as judge in the Mississippi Territory. In 1810, only a year after arriving in Mississippi, Martin moved to New Orleans, where he joined the Superior Court. He was an ideal choice, not only providing the sort of judicial expertise that was sorely lacking but also possessing the same background as so many ambitious Louisianians. Familiar to the administration and unquestioned in his loyalty, Martin was a far more attractive candidate for patronage than Francophone Louisianians like Derbigny. When William Blackledge of the Mississippi Territory formally recommended Martin for appointment, he described him to James Madison as "a Frenchman by birth . . . [who] has been upwards of twenty years in the United States and uniformly Republican, tho never busying himself much with politics; and is remarkable both for his industry & sobriety." In addition to his ideal combination of public-mindedness without political ambition, Martin, Blackledge added, was a "master of both the English & French languages, [and] he has pretty good acquaintance with the Spanish language."[82]

Pitot and Martin were unusual cases, indeed the ideal cases as far as the administration was concerned. Not only were they American citizens, but both men had published documents that explicitly stated their understanding of how things ought to work in a Jeffersonian polity. Pitot was already at home in Louisiana. Martin was familiar with the area and had crucial judicial experience. Perhaps most important, both men seemed ideally situated to cultivate the attachment of the Francophone immigrants who constituted such a large part of Louisiana's emerging political leadership.

These connections between Washington and Louisiana did more than foster political fortunes. They enabled public officials to envision a national government (not just a federal one) in which officials were connected to one another despite the chasm of geographic distance and the delays of nineteenth-century correspondence. While the Republicans rejected Federalist arguments that the government constituted the foundation of nationhood, they nonetheless believed that a viable union depended on an effective administrative apparatus.[83]

"Men of Integrity, of Understanding, of Clear Property and Influence"

As the Jefferson administration set out to build an administrative structure in Louisiana, one thing was clear: the administration's selection criteria left little room for Louisianians. There were no long-standing kinship bonds to connect Louisiana with the United States, nor was there a wealth of personal contact that might enable the administration to believe it could predict the Louisianians' actions. Yet American policymakers and the white Louisianians whom they hoped to make their partners in incorporation believed that appointed office remained a remarkably effective way to promote attachment. Indeed, in some arenas of institutional development, patronage was the only indication of success. Selecting men for appointment to the institutions of government honed the Jeffersonians' notion of political kinship. It also exemplified incorporation's role as both a means and an end. Creating the institutions would serve the broad goals of preserving domestic order, racial supremacy, and national security. But finding a place for Louisianians within those institutions would be a means to the intercultural socialization that was itself a cornerstone of attachment.

Establishing the criteria for appointment began with the legislature. Jefferson decided to appoint six Louisianians to the Legislative Council, enough to represent local views but still not a majority on the thirteen-member body. He decided that candidates from Louisiana should "be . . . I think men of integrity, of understanding, of clear property and influence among the people, well acquainted with the laws, customs & habits of the country, and drawn from the different parts of the Orleans district in proportion to their population."[84] Always eager to please, Claiborne responded quickly with a lengthy memorandum that dissected the qualities of the leading candidates. Chief among these were men of "Republican principles," in much the same way that Jefferson rationalized Claiborne's appointment by explaining that Claiborne "has always been a firm republican." Meanwhile, Claiborne avoided recommendations of men "whose political sentiments" remained a mystery.[85]

James Wilkinson sent his own, unsolicited list. Although he suggested

different candidates and struck a generally more negative tone when it came to
the Louisianians' talents, he based his decisions on the same criteria. He referred to one man as "a young man of good Reputation of whose abilities I am
quite ignorant." Wilkinson saw more direct connections between foreign attachments and poor talents. Indeed, he concluded that for many elite Louisianians, their egos and ignorance went along with their French loyalties. For
example, when discussing Etienne de Boré, who had already served as mayor
of New Orleans, Wilkinson wrote: "he is principally distinguished by his
vanity & a blind attachment to the French Nation." Nor was he much kinder
about Jacques Pitot, whom he considered guilty of "pedantry & arrogance. . . .
He thinks the French the first of nations & himself the first Frenchman."
Wilkinson dismissed many white Louisianians on account of "poor morals."
In contrast to these men, Wilkinson described Evan Jones, a transplant from
the United States who had lived in Louisiana for years, as "an American by
birth and attachment." Claiborne would have disagreed, however, for Jones
soon emerged as one of his most vocal opponents.[86]

Both men had something to prove. Claiborne and Wilkinson made conspicuous reference to their own struggles to import the administration's standards
in recommending Louisianians for public office. In the process, the governor
and the general set out to reinforce their own status as reliable officials.

Appointments to the Legislative Council were the administration's first tentative attempt to adapt their principles of merit to a situation where kinship
would be a product of — rather than a prerequisite for — government service.[87]
Nominations became an annual process in which Claiborne attempted to discern the "political sentiments" and the reliability of local residents. In his 1810
nominations, for example, Claiborne recommended Matharin Guerin as an
"excellent Citizen," Manuel Andry as "a man of integrity," and Jean Blanque
as a merchant of "high credit . . . a man of Genius and Education, & possess[ing] considerable influence in the City & vicinity of New Orleans." Cumu-
latively these references formed a rough set of criteria for public officials.
Claiborne and others like him were engaged in a process of professionalizing
the public workforce.[88]

Louisianians who received federal appointment were quick to insinuate
themselves with American officials, and vice versa. These Louisianians recognized that appointment constituted the most important form of advancement
under the territorial regime, while federal leaders hoped that the Louisianians
would provide contacts with the local population. Patronage would soon
divide onetime allies. After initially concluding that Jean Nöel Destrehan opposed the territorial regime, Claiborne found that the Creole was a willing
client. To this knowledge he added that Destrehan had the qualifications of

"hold[ing] large Estates in this Territory, and enjoy[ing], deservedly, the esteem of their Neighbors."[89] Destrehan joined the Legislative Council, serving occasionally as its president. His path marked a contrast with that of Pierre Derbigny, Destrehan's traveling companion along with Pierre Sauve on the venture to Washington with the Remonstrance in 1804–05. Sauve later joined Destrehan on the Legislative Council. Derbigny left the world of public administration for the world of electoral politics, running successfully for a seat in the territorial house of representatives. Claiborne did show some limited patronage to Derbigny, but only through an appointment to the relatively powerless Board of Regents for the territory's public school system.

Julien Poydras became the administration's point man among the Louisianians. A Frenchman by birth, he settled in Saint Domingue, that other home to Louisiana's newcomers, and in 1768 came to the American mainland, reaching Louisiana just as the Spanish began their troubled reign. By 1803 he exemplified the aspirations of Louisiana's elite, thriving as both a planter and a merchant. A generation of residence in Louisiana had enabled Poydras to ingratiate himself with the Creoles, who constituted a majority of Louisiana's white population.

Poydras had his own qualms about the territorial system, but he was also eager to work with the American regime and to defend the administration publicly.[90] Claiborne responded in kind, immediately appointing Poydras the civil commandant for Pointe Coupée, a task of no small importance to the federal government given the slave conspiracy of 1795 and the signs of racial revolt in 1804. In Pointe Coupée Poydras tried without success to organize public schools. But although public education failed, Poydras' efforts provided yet more evidence of his attachment and commitment to an American Louisiana. Poydras was soon on the Legislative Council, where he was elected its president. Extending his reach to quasi-public institutions, Poydras secured an appointment from Claiborne to the board of the Louisiana Bank, one of the few financial institutions on the southwestern frontier.[91] Influential with his fellow Louisianians yet comfortable with American policymakers, Poydras was the logical choice for appointment as the territorial delegate to Congress in 1809.[92]

Men like Poydras attempted to establish themselves as political kin, loyal clients eager to serve their federal patrons. Poydras put this relationship in his own terms, explaining that Louisiana was "an adopted child of a great family." He could not have been more in tune with the administration, which held that allegiance to the Jeffersonian Republicans would form a "family" of like-minded thinkers. This family in turn would create a pool of acceptable appointees. Louisianians approached this process in the same pragmatic terms that had prevailed when the Francophone population had attempted to use commercial, social, and political connections to secure patronage from their Spanish rulers. In both cases, Louisianians named the price of their own co-optation and made certain that unfamiliar rulers knew they were ready to deal.[93]

While appointment or election to the legislature provided only a limited number of slots, the same military that was supposed to exclude nonwhites became an effective tool for incorporating whites. And the number of those appointed offices grew by leaps and bounds. The positions in the legislature remained finite, and were highly contested properties. It was in the appointed officialdom scattered throughout the Territory of Orleans that Louisianians found additional offices. The territorial militia presented opportunities for patronage that delivered not only contact with the American regime but also status for ambitious white Louisianians. In 1805, for example, Claiborne selected the Creole Jacques Philippe Villeré to be one of the first colonels in the territorial militia. It was not the first time Villeré had served unfamiliar rulers. His own father had been the conspirator who died so mysteriously in a Spanish jail following the 1768 Revolt. His mother fled Spanish Louisiana for French Saint Domingue with her children, but Villeré eventually returned to Louisiana, where he pledged his loyalty to the Spanish and eventually received a commission in the militia. Villeré ingratiated himself with Claiborne, establishing himself as a member of the governor's political kin. Villeré in turn extended that relationship to his blood kin, eventually securing militia appointments for his two sons. By 1809 the majority of the senior officers in the militia were still Americans, but Claiborne had carefully selected a cadre of Louisianians for senior rank, while Louisianians soon accounted for the majority of junior officers.[94]

Americans believed that the U.S. military would serve much the same purpose. They actively recruited Creoles for commissions as officers in the vast army stationed in the Southwest, sent them to West Point, or had them appointed midshipmen in the navy. In 1804, before he became embroiled in either the Neutral Ground negotiations or the Burr Conspiracy, James Wilkinson discussed the prudence of offering a commission to Michael Walsh. Young Michael's uncle was Father Patrick Walsh, the Irish-born vicar-general who was engaged in one of the feuds that seemed to be tearing apart Louisiana Catholicism. This appointment in the civil arena presented an opportunity for the United States to extend its influence into the ecclesiastical elite.[95]

In keeping with the broad contours of incorporation, the workforce of incorporation would be both a means and an end. In the most immediate sense, the federal government needed to populate an American regime in Louisiana that would implement the very codes passed by the territorial regime while defending the territory until the United States could secure treaties that guaranteed the security of a Louisiana that fitted the administration's definition. But it soon became clear that the government of Louisiana would also be a means, for in serving this territorial regime white Louisianians made their bid for incorporation and federal leaders hoped to provide an education in American political principles.

Politics and administration were never far apart in this story of influence, connection, and kinship. Martin Duralde provides a telling case in point. An amateur scientist and advocate of educational reform, Duralde seemed the ideal candidate for public office. With each year Claiborne referred to Duralde with growing affection, a friend whose personal connection to the governor made Duralde a superior candidate for public office. Duralde joined the American family in very real — and very confusing — terms during these years. Not only did Henry Clay's brother, John, marry Duralde's daughter, Julie, but Henry Clay's daughter, Susan, married Duralde's son (to make matters more confusing, the son's name was also Martin). A third Duralde child, Clarissa, soon established an even more important bridge. In 1807 she married the widower William C. C. Claiborne, three years after the governor's wife and daughter had died. In 1808 the couple welcomed a son, named William.[96] Claiborne explained the marriage to Jefferson in terms entirely appropriate to Louisiana. He explained that Clarissa "is a native of Louisiana . . . and united to other qualities, which to me were interesting, *those* of a sincere Attachment to the Government of the United States, and to the American Character."[97]

In August 1811 Clay wrote to Attorney General Caesar Rodney on behalf of his growing brood in the Southwest. He endorsed his brother's recommendation for appointment as register in the Port of New Orleans. He also provided an introduction for the elder Duralde, whom he called "a French gentleman, wealthy and respectable." Both the administration and the Duraldes benefited from this relationship. Clay served as a guarantor to the administration, vetting his blood relatives as well as the Duraldes. And yet it was an incorrect introduction, for Duralde was not French. He was in fact of Spanish ancestry. But many Americans used the word "French" for want of a better description of the residents of Louisiana. The key for them was to acknowledge that he was somehow foreign, and then belie that fact by emphasizing the Duraldes' membership, both literal and figurative, in an American family. These comments bore a striking resemblance to those of William Plumer, who in 1804 had described the men who delivered the Remonstrance as "Frenchmen," only to modify that statement by associating Frenchness with the Jeffersonian Republicans.[98]

Public advancement came quickly for the Duralde men. With a combination of offices similar to Julien Poydras, Claiborne appointed Martin Sr. to one of the coveted positions on the Legislative Council and selected him to help plan the schools for Attakapas Parish. Martin Jr. eventually received appointment as a federal marshal.[99] Claiborne informed his new father-in-law that the younger Martin "is capable and will receive *further patronage* if he embraces the present occasion to place himself in a situation to improve his mind." Education remained a vital prerequisite for professional advancement, but background, reputation, and experience were equally important factors for men seeking patronage.[100]

Claiborne further explained to Duralde Sr. that an appointment as marshal was "a most honorable trust and always conferred on the most deserving Citizens. In the U.S. there is no Office more sought after, nor is there an Officer more respected than a Marshal."[101] While this may have been something of an exaggeration designed to make a father proud of his son, Claiborne also reasserted the importance of merit in the administrative process. These decisions were never easy, because defining the qualities of a "most deserving Citizen" could generate no end of controversy.

Even as Louisianians expanded the boundaries of appointment, one group of men found themselves left permanently in the cold. Although Claiborne offered appointments to some of his most outspoken critics among the Louisianians, he was scrupulous in excluding Americans who had crossed his path. As the bureaucracy around them grew, men like Edward Livingston and Daniel Clark found themselves excluded. Claiborne had no mandate to secure the attachment of these Americans.

At a time when hierarchies faced new challenges in American electoral politics, the world of appointment retained older systems of deference and patronage. The vast collection of appointed officials in the territories, whose number exceeded that of the nation's elected officials, continued to position themselves as obedient clients. Poydras' selection as congressional delegate was the subject of particular relief to federal policymakers. Not only did he seem friendly to the administration's definition of incorporation, but his selection indicated a sea change within the territorial legislature. In 1806 the legislature's first delegate to Congress, Daniel Clark, seemed like a direct rejection of the administration's priorities. Claiborne in particular saw things that way. When the legislature replaced him with Poydras, however, Claiborne and his superiors in Washington saw that Louisianians knew how to pick the right people.

Despite the considerable failings of institutional policymaking—an anemic school system, continuing disagreement about civil-religious relations, threats of racial revolt, and unending disputes about land ownership — Louisiana seemed more firmly attached to the United States by 1810 than it had only five years before. Courts and armed forces had done more than reassert white supremacy: they had imposed restrictions on slaves and free people of color unprecedented during the colonial era. White Louisianians had effectively insinuated themselves into the elected and appointed structures of government, finding opportunities in direct proportion to the limitations on Afro-Louisianians. At the same time that they built institutional connections with the territorial and federal leadership, they continued their public pronouncements of their attachment to the United States. This effort went together with institutional developments, different facets of the same campaign of attachment. Institutional development became yet another means for white Louisianians to prove that they were neither foreigners nor strangers. The successful process of institutionbuilding coincided with renewed efforts by white Louisianians to prove their attachment and to promote incorporation.

Among the Louisianians' most zealous converts was Claiborne himself. By 1806 Claiborne had concluded that "there are indeed some ancient prejudices which are difficult to remove," at the same time that "I persuade myself that the time is not distant when the Louisianians generally will be zealous members of our republic."[102] Claiborne eventually recanted many of his early opinions about the Louisianians. "Soon after receiving possession of Louisiana, & early in January 1804," he confided to territorial judge John Johnson, "I wrote an Official Letter to the Government, in which I took a general view of the state of the District." In his effort to undo any harm to his reputation that had come from those comments, Claiborne argued that "there was not a sentiment, which evidenced the smallest ill-will towards the people of the Country."[103]

Of course, marriage to a Louisianian only accelerated his change of heart, and it was a fusion of institutional developments and social connections that bound Claiborne to Louisianians. But bad fortune — or, rather, bad health — continued to follow the Claiborne family. Clarissa Duralde Claiborne died in November 1809.[104]

Soon after his second wife died, William C. C. Claiborne suggested that his own son would be a logical candidate to join the administration's political kin. He hoped that "at some future day, his virtues, talents & attachments to civil & Religious freedom . . . [would] recommend him to the patronage of his Country." In the meantime, however, Claiborne had an eighteen-month-old infant. To whom did Claiborne turn when discussing the child? To his new-found kin of all sorts in Louisiana. Although he still had doubts about Louisiana's male clergy, Claiborne had come to see the Ursuline Convent as a vital institution in New Orleans, and thanked its lady abbess for "the interest you take in the welfare of my dear little William, [which] furnishes additional proof of your kindness toward me."[105] Claiborne often entrusted his son with his father-in-law, Martin Duralde. "Present me affectionately to my Mother," Claiborne wrote, referring to his mother-in-law almost two years after Clarissa's death. "Kiss for me again and again my dear little William."[106]

Martin Duralde was by then an institutional man, having helped promote both civil government and public education. Sentimental attachment and institutional development went hand in hand, both working together to convince whites that internal factors would accelerate the incorporation of Louisiana. They would soon learn, however, that the foreign developments which had always guided Louisiana's fate would continue to determine its incorporation.

PART **III**

Crisis
(1808–1815)

5

Local Diplomacy

Three years after James Monroe wrote with dismay about his country's affairs, President James Madison wrote about the subject with confidence. When Madison submitted his first annual message to Congress in May 1809, he announced that "it affords me much satisfaction to be able to communicate the commencement of a favorable change, in our foreign relations."[1] He referred not to the Lower Mississippi Valley or to Spanish-American affairs, which had dominated so much of Jefferson's foreign policy, but to relations with Great Britain. Madison was also making a virtue out of adversity. Only a month before, he had extricated the United States from the Embargo, a disastrous policy which he himself had helped engineer and which Jefferson, exhausted by his final year in office, had left as one of a number of difficult legacies for his successor.[2]

That Madison could avoid discussing issues related to tensions with Spain resulting primarily from the borderlands surrounding the Mississippi Valley indicated the considerable successes that American policymakers associated with the administrative changes of the preceding years. The stabilization of Louisiana through foreign policy and domestic policymaking enabled President Madison to believe he could focus his efforts elsewhere, in contrast to the time that Secretary of State Madison had been forced to devote to Louisiana.

In his communication with the Territory of Orleans, Madison also began shifting from the official, workaday tone of his correspondence as secretary of state to the more formal tones of president. In July 1809, for example, he wrote to the New Orleans City Council, thanking the members for a message congratulating him on his election.[3] Madison further explained in rather self-serving terms that "the peace & plenty which have distinguished our Country, amid the convulsions and calamities forming the general character of the times . . . claim for the policy which has preserved those blessings, the approbation you bestow on it." He then thanked the council for its part, explaining that "such marks of attachment to the solid interest of our Country, and of the confidence in the public Councils, are the more to be valued, as the trials imposed on us by foreign Injustice, have not ceased." He concluded by stating that "never was such a connection more distinctly pointed out by nature itself; nor can the reciprocal benefits of it ever cease whilst the laudable and enlightened sentiments which you proclaim, shall continue to pervade the great Body of our fellow Citizens."[4]

Madison would soon find himself dealing with the City Council in more trying circumstances. At the same time that Madison was composing his reply, thousands of refugees were descending on New Orleans, and council members would soon demand the assistance of the new administration. And as relations between the United States and Spain disintegrated, Madison became increasingly dependent upon the council in ways that would test the functional realities of the "attachment" linking the governments in New Orleans and Washington.

Madison and the New Orleans City Council were only two elements of local diplomacy, a system in which international relations on the borderlands ran parallel to, but were never entirely distinct from, the elite negotiations that are the familiar stuff of diplomatic history. Local diplomacy was more than a diplomatic process. It was also a vital and telling extension of the federal policymaking structure. Instead of acting through officials dedicated exclusively to diplomatic negotiations, officials in Washington had to rely upon— and contend with—civil and military officials on the periphery charged with numerous responsibilities. Although federal leaders never surrendered authority altogether, their delegates enjoyed considerable latitude so long as their own interpretation of national policies coincided with sentiments in the cabinet. Local diplomacy was also the system through which private individuals exploited diplomatic affairs to advance their own agendas, whether in opposition to or in agreement with the administration.

Local diplomacy did not suddenly appear in 1809, nor was it limited to Louisiana. But the level of international activity, tension, and conflict increased during Madison's presidency, accentuating the connections between foreign policymaking and domestic governance while also reinforcing local diplomacy as the logical means to implement the administration's priorities. The mature territorial system that federal policymakers and white Louisianians had constructed by the end of the Jefferson administration created additional mechanisms for diplomatic activity. As foreign and domestic crises challenged the incorporation of Louisiana, public officials and private individuals responded with local diplomacy. Equally critical to this change was Napoleon's decision in 1808 to break his alliance with Spain, dispatch troops to the Iberian peninsula, and place his own brother on the Spanish throne. The immediate effect was to freeze American relations with Spain as the Madison administration avoided recognizing either the Napoleonic regime or the Spanish monarchy's government-in-exile. In contrast to this static diplomatic situation, the Napoleonic invasion cast social and political ripples throughout the Americas that had a profound effect on Louisiana.

American foreign relations took form within a broad array of political, racial, and administrative realities. The task facing officials in Washington and residents on the frontier was to make local diplomacy work to their benefit. This project naturally unleashed tension as numerous groups articulated their own foreign policies. Consequently, U.S. foreign policy on the southwestern periphery was anything but tidy. It was also anything but peripheral.

Diplomats

The basis of local diplomacy resided within the overlap of domestic and foreign threats, the structure of the federal government, and the realities of nineteenth-century communication. Rather than see domestic and international tasks as existing in conflict, public officials believed they were complementary and mutually beneficial given Louisiana's multinational circumstances. First among these was William C. C. Claiborne, who had actively negotiated with Spanish, French, and Indian leaders since 1803. He considered these activities an essential aspect of his role as governor. Why would he see things otherwise? After all, like all territorial officials Claiborne's superior was the nation's chief diplomat, the secretary of state. That simple relationship between the territorial government and the State Department created an inseparable linkage between frontier governance and foreign policy.

A perspective that linked foreign policy and domestic governance was by no means limited to territorial governors like Claiborne.[5] When Jefferson and, later, Madison and Monroe argued as presidents that foreign policy needed to serve domestic ends, they did so from their own experiences as secretaries of state, when they had doubled as civil administrators with direct charge over the nation's far-flung territories. The vast majority of civil officials — from governor to coroner — reported to the secretary of state, and all of them became potential instruments of foreign policy. Equally important, the State Department's expansive bureaucracy on the territorial periphery stood in marked contrast to a diminutive staff at the political center of Washington, D.C., consisting of only a few clerks and couriers to assist the secretary of state.[6] The problem of communication had bedeviled every power that had attempted to govern large portions of the Americas, but the anemic diplomatic resources of the United States reinforced the need for civil officials to perform diplomatic roles.

Granted, the mixed responsibilities of the State Department were not the only reason American leaders saw connections between foreign and domestic affairs. Americans consistently argued that foreign policy needed to serve domestic goals.[7] Likewise, the attempt to create an American foreign policy responded to the same political and constitutional concerns that shaped domestic debates. Nonetheless, the absence of any clear administrative distinction between domestic and foreign policy reinforced the intellectual connection that many Americans saw between a vigorous foreign policy and a harmonious union.

And while secretaries of state acted through the civil officials who populated the territorial government, the heads of the Treasury, War, and Navy Departments created their own networks in the Southwest during the Jefferson administration. They, too, recognized that the Louisiana Purchase had unleashed new conditions that blurred the lines between domestic and foreign policy. Men in Louisiana serving all these departments struggled with the consequences of international change. All of them eventually found themselves negotiating with foreign representatives.[8] The considerable delays in communication that necessitated political kinship also fueled local diplomacy. With a transit time between Washington and New Orleans of almost a month, correspondence with the periphery of the United States took almost as long as diplomatic correspondence with Europe.

Madison proved particularly eager to deploy local diplomacy and became confident in his abilities to do so. By the time he became president, Madison had more experience with federal governance than any of his predecessors. Not only had he crafted the structure of that government at Philadelphia in 1787, but he had served in both Congress and the administration. This extensive experience may also help account for why he intended to settle matters himself rather than delegate much power to his subordinates. Aside from Albert Gallatin, who continued to serve as head of the Treasury Department, Madison had little time for his own cabinet. Madison also continued the tradition of ignoring his vice president. George Clinton may have been less controversial then Aaron Burr, but Madison's decision to retain him as vice president did not reflect any reduction in the antipathy that had developed between them during Jefferson's second term. Meanwhile, Madison doubted the loyalty of Secretary of State Robert Smith, the competence of Secretary of War William Eustis, and the sobriety of Secretary of the Navy Paul Hamilton. He had made these appointments out of political necessity, and saw little reason why they should enjoy any real policymaking discretion of the sort he was willing to allow local officials. Only when people began to appropriate diplomatic contingency to realize objectives contrary to those of the administration did Madison and his subordinates attempt to restrict local diplomacy.

The Port

Local diplomacy was most constantly on display in the Port of New Orleans, and rightly so. As the major entrepōt near the Gulf Coast, New Orleans was a center of international contact and controversy that in turn spread throughout the mouth of the Mississippi. After 1809, however, developments in the Caribbean and across the Atlantic forced officials in Louisiana to shape the way the United States would handle foreign affairs as well as immigration policy.

Among the most important newcomers to reach Louisiana through the Port of New Orleans were migrants from Saint Domingue. These people arrived in three concentrated clusters. The first came in 1793, soon after slaves committed themselves to violent revolution. Most of these refugees settled in the port cities of the Atlantic seaboard. The second and largest wave left Saint Domingue in 1803, when slaves and free people of color crushed the French army and Napoleon made clear his intention to abandon his Caribbean colony (one result of which was the Louisiana Purchase itself). While some refugees went to Louisiana, thousands more chose Cuba, where they found not only a friendly reception from whites but also a familiar system of Caribbean plantation agriculture.[9]

The Napoleonic invasion of the Iberian peninsula converted the Saint Domingue migrants from guests to pariahs. Infuriated royalists drove them from the island, unleashing a wave of refugees who descended on Louisiana in 1809 and 1810, the vast majority arriving in the summer of 1809. The impact on Louisiana's demography was stunning. Just over 9,000 people from Saint Domingue (2,731 whites, 3,102 free people of color, and 3,226 slaves) reached Louisiana, constituting over 12 percent of the total population for the Territory of Orleans.[10] As James Sterrett observed in June 1809, "We are in a fair way of being over run with french people & Negroes from St. Yago, Havana and other posts in Cuba."[11] These people soon became known as "the Foreign French," a nickname that was often not meant as a compliment.

New Orleans mayor James Mather proposed a broad-based support effort that entailed "the necessity of opening a subscription, not only here but in the various Parishes of the Territory to bring together a great deal of help."[12] In these observations, Mather assumed that the municipal government would coordinate the diplomatic and naturalization roles that local officials had always considered to be their purview. When refugees demanded to be let ashore with their slaves, however, public officials vacillated, constrained by the prohibition on the importation of slaves in the 1804 Governance act as well as the 1808 federal ban on the foreign slave trade.[13] In 1803 Claiborne had allowed refugees to bring their slaves. But their numbers had been small. The situation in 1809 seemed entirely different and far more dangerous.

Slaveowning refugees found allies among Creoles who were eager for access to new slaves despite their fear that slaves from Saint Domingue would cause a similar revolt in Louisiana.[14] In June 1809 Congress decided to allow the refugees to enter with their slaves. The following month, but *before* receiving news of the federal legislation, Claiborne implemented an identical policy. It was a difficult decision for Claiborne, who felt a certain ambivalence about asserting complete policymaking independence. Nonetheless, he concluded that diplomatic contingency demanded policymaking autonomy. That Claiborne acted before receiving approval from Washington indicated the role he assumed for himself. That he chose the same policy as members of Congress and the administration protected him from any rebuke. The similarity to circumstances in 1806, when Wilkinson and Jefferson had proposed simultaneous resolutions to the western boundary dispute, was more than coincidental. So long as people at both ends of the policymaking continuum reached the same conclusions, officials in Washington did not insist on a hierarchical chain of authority.[15]

In the process of implementing these *local* rules, officials in Louisiana created new *federal* policies. The Naturalization Act of 1802, the latest federal statement on immigration, provided no restrictions on what property immigrants could bring. In 1809 Louisiana created its own naturalization law. This policy was in keeping with the standard established by other slave states, which enacted similar provisions establishing local rules of naturalization and, in turn, international relations.[16]

Consider the timing of Claiborne's decisions. On 15 May 1809 he wrote to Secretary of State Robert Smith asking for the administration's advice on what to do with the refugees. That same day, however, he began writing to civil and military personnel informing them that they should stop incoming vessels carrying Saint Domingue slaves. While allowing for instructions and alterations from Washington, Claiborne nonetheless felt secure initiating his own interpretation of federal objectives.[17] Claiborne also took it upon himself to write thinly veiled orders to the American consuls in Havana as well as Kingston. "I will thank you Sir," Claiborne wrote to William Savage, the consul at Jamaica, to "inform such as should pass by the way of Jamaica, that it is advisable for them, to seek an Asylum elsewhere, than in the Territory of Orleans."[18]

In their dealings with the Saint Domingue migrants, civil officials concluded that foreign policy on the Mississippi River and the Gulf Coast had to contribute to fixing the attachment of white Louisianians. To this end, they attempted to foster an environment in which the United States controlled commerce without angering local merchants. This policy clashed with the objectives of naval officers, who believed that placating white Louisianians and white refugees from Saint Domingue impeded foreign policy. They specifically rejected any concessions that seemed to waver from a strict implementation of federal sway. When it came to pirates and smugglers, civil officials and naval officers alike bemoaned the lawbreakers and their allies within Louisiana's white population. During the Embargo, for example, both naval officers and civil officials had condemned local residents who circumvented federal law.[19]

But the treatment of European vessels was another matter, one that by 1810 generated considerable disagreements within the federal apparatus as naval officers, civil officials, and private citizens argued over the meaning of neutrality. Operating in the Port of New Orleans, the mouth of the Mississippi, and the Gulf Coast, naval officers pursued an aggressive policy that included seizing European vessels that they suspected of smuggling or of breaking the federal laws prohibiting foreign warships from operating out of American ports.[20] When naval officers were not condemning European mariners, they were blaming white Louisianians themselves for undermining American diplomatic goals. Many officers seemed to share the opinion of Master-Commandant David Porter, who commanded the New Orleans naval station from 1808 to 1810. "Information that I have collected enables me to state that those . . . branches of illicit commerce engaged the attention of many merchants at this place," Porter informed Hamilton on New Year's Day in 1810.[21] Porter claimed that Louisianians who held public office were in collusion with the criminals. He aimed particular scorn at the federal marshal, Michael Fortier, complaining that so long as "the Marshall is a frenchman there will be allways a large Majority of frenchmen on the Juries and a frenchman can never be convicted however heinous his crime." Like so many others, Porter invoked the general term "Frenchmen" to describe all white Louisianians as somehow foreign.[22]

Worse still, naval officers believed civil officials failed to appreciate the situation or to respond appropriately. When Porter left New Orleans in 1810, a gathering of his officers claimed that his task was all the more difficult "amidst all the clamour and opposition it excited among a particular class of persons, has met with the approbation of all good citizens and merits the highest applause."[23] The "particular class of persons" to which naval officers referred consisted of white Louisianians, Saint Domingue migrants, merchant masters, and European consuls, all of whom complained about the navy's foreign policy. When the navy seized the French vessel *Franchise*, for example, white Louisianians defended the vessel's captain in the *Louisiana Gazette*, stating that "Capt. Chevalier is . . . an honorable man, perhaps a member of the *Legion of honor*, and of course, could nor would not be connected in any *illicit trade*, nor commit any depredations on the commerce of the United States."[24] And when the *Franchise*'s captain charged Porter with stealing a crucifix from his cabin, the French minister to the United States demanded that Hamilton remove Porter from his post.[25]

Civil officials agreed that white Louisianians undermined American neutrality and commercial law.[26] Nonetheless, they were slow to act in ways that would antagonize the local population or foreign representatives. Claiborne made his opinion known in 1810 when the navy seized another French ship, a suspected privateer called the *Duc de Montebello*. Pierre Derbigny rushed an angry letter to the governor on behalf of the *Duc de Montebello*'s captain, who held Porter responsible for $10,000 in damage.[27] Speaking in the role he assumed for himself as the senior diplomat in the region, Claiborne apologized to the French consul at New Orleans that "Porter being rendered entirely independent of my orders or Controul, it only remains for me to lay your Communications before the President of the United States."[28]

There was no love lost between Claiborne and Derbigny, who had openly criticized the governor since 1804. Nor were white residents of Louisiana united in their opposition to the navy's policy for Creoles, Frenchmen, and the foreign French. But these local dynamics only made Claiborne more steadfast in advocating a conciliatory stance. Within this complex ethnic and political environment, co-opting men like Derbigny was a matter of vital importance. Claiborne was actively seeking Louisianians for civil appointments, the very appointments that proved so irritating to Porter. A year after Porter complained about a "Frenchman" serving as marshal, Claiborne selected his brother-in-law, Martin Duralde Jr., for the task. Though exactly the sort of Creole whom naval officers detested, he was also exactly the sort of political kin who Claiborne believed would create a reliable territorial government.

Secretary of State Robert Smith, who had served as Jefferson's secretary of the navy, apparently did not attempt to resolve the dispute in New Orleans through negotiations with his successor at the Navy Department, Paul Hamilton. Nor did Madison settle affairs by overriding his subordinates. Their silence on the matter may have been frustrating, but it is also telling. Although members of the administration lamented the international controversies, they seemed to accept a bifurcated diplomatic system in which the navy suppressed illegal commerce while civil officials promoted domestic loyalty. With only silence from Washington, local diplomacy filled the vacuum; in the absence of explicit instructions or prohibitions, naval officers and civil officials continued to collide as they pursued two different policies, two different visions of incorporation.

Whether it was the influx of Saint Domingue refugees or the dispute over commercial and strategic policy in the port, settling these *local* matters proved crucial to creating *federal* policies. Both controversies forced federal officials to reconsider the implementation of their diplomatic objectives. Jefferson and later Madison had taken few steps toward a practical isolation of the regime of former slaves in the newly independent Republic of Haiti. Now officials at all levels developed the contours of that policy. In the summer of 1809, for example, both territorial secretary Thomas Bolling Robertson and New Orleans mayor James Mather negotiated with the French consul to settle the disposition of refugees. When British naval officers detained a vessel carrying the last French troops from Saint Domingue, Mather even positioned himself as a broker between the British and the French consul.[29] Territorial officials in Louisiana did not fail to recognize the diplomatic import of their actions. To the contrary, they considered the diplomatic situation too pressing to await a decision in Washington.

Likewise, the disputes between civil officials and naval officers constituted more than petty bureaucratic squabbles. Although there was ample recalcitrance to go around, the struggle in New Orleans existed within a specific structural and diplomatic context. Commercial policy remained at the core of American foreign policy. In addition, scrapes between American and European vessels raised international tensions, undoing the work of American diplomats overseas while convincing members of the Jefferson and Madison administrations of European belligerence. Given the uncertain boundaries of administrative capacities in the early republic and the ambiguous line between domestic and foreign relations, the disputes in the Port of New Orleans constituted an attempt to settle how the federal regime would operate. European consuls and merchants responded in kind. They recognized that trading on the Gulf Coast meant dealing with officials in Louisiana. The question in New Orleans was which foreign policy would prevail and how the policymakers in Washington would balance conditions on the frontier with the nation's broader diplomatic strategy.

The Border

That men outside the administration and Congress could develop and implement their own foreign policies proved equally evident on the Texas-Louisiana borderlands, but with very different results. Unlike the Port of New Orleans, where competing diplomatic agendas both within and among nations created no end of controversy, the western borderlands became the site of a diplomatic consensus that crossed national and racial lines. The accord emerged despite the fact that Spanish, American, and Indian leaders had abundant reasons to distrust one another.

In 1806 American, Spanish, and Caddo negotiators had created the Neutral Ground, the buffer zone between Spanish Texas and American Louisiana, to preserve the peace. Their relief proved short-lived. The Neutral Ground became a haven for American squatters, runaway slaves, and white criminals hoping to elude arrest on either side. Angry white slaveowners and local officials pursued their prey into the area. On the increasingly crowded frontier, the Caddo decided that the Spanish and American governments were unable to keep their own people in check.[30]

Claiborne wrote to Madison in 1808 pleading for the secretary of state to apply diplomatic pressure on Spain. Madison offered neither assistance nor advice (Claiborne's requests were overwhelmed by more pressing matters, including the Embargo and the presidential election). In the meantime, public officials and Louisiana slaveowners continued to complain that the Spanish-American diplomatic stalemate undermined their efforts to establish an effective slave system.[31] And in a classic example of the disjuncture between elite negotiations and local diplomacy, the French invasion of the Iberian peninsula, which suspended negotiations between Washington and Madrid, actually created the conditions for American officials to press their claims. As the Spanish imperial regime collapsed around him, Texas governor Manuel Salcedo was too busy preserving his authority in Mexico to settle disagreements with the United States. He agreed to surrender runaway slaves in exchange for an American promise to do the same. Unlike Jefferson and Madison, who refused to recognize either the Napoleonic regime or the monarchy in exile, Claiborne had no qualms about contacting the monarchist Salcedo so long as doing so preserved the slave regime. He had done so previously, and despite his irritation with the Spanish, he continued to believe that this sort of contact was beneficial.[32]

As news of Indian discontent spread, local civil and military personnel sought a new policy on the borderlands. In the spring of 1810 Colonel Thomas Cushing had reached the conclusion that "the intruders—have taken their present position in full confidence that neither nation can remove them without a breach of the Agreement entered into by General Wilkinson & Colonel Herrera; and that, if they should be permitted to remain, a numerous & lawless banditti will soon be collected."[33] With the Neutral Ground threatened, local diplomacy again provided a solution. Spanish, American, and Caddo representatives agreed that troops from both white nations could remove the intruders. "Should you approve of the plan," Cushing wrote to Secretary of War William Eustis, "and authorize a Co-operation on our part, an early check may be put to an evil which, if permitted to progress, may produce very injurious Consequences at a future day."[34] In June 1810 Eustis gave Cushing vague instructions permitting him to remove the intruders. Cushing elaborated on those instructions by dispatching twenty-five men under a young lieutenant named Augustus Magee, who joined an identical number of Spanish troops to drive the squatters from their settlement and burn their makeshift homes.[35]

This sort of cooperative behavior indicated a diplomatic trajectory in complete opposition to that which prevailed in high-level diplomatic relations between the United States and Spain. Army personnel were not without their suspicions of Spanish intentions, nor were they convinced that the Spanish could preserve order in their own territory. Likewise, they had no love for the Caddo. Instead, driven by what they saw as the vital objective of regional stability, army officers negotiated with officials whom the administration did not recognize and reached diplomatic accords with people they did not trust. They pursued these policies because they saw a different cause-and-effect relationship from the one that was apparent from Washington. In an effort to defuse local conflicts that might otherwise lead to violence, army officers ignored the cessation of official elite Spanish-American relations. Their motivation stemmed from fears that remained in place *because* of their chauvinism (whether national or racial) rather than *despite* it.[36]

By 1810 two of the three people who had originally negotiated the Neutral Ground were gone. Herrera was no longer in the area. Wilkinson had left as well. The general had his own problems, facing two investigations, one for the death by disease of almost half the men stationed at the American outpost at Terre aux Boeufs (an encampment Wilkinson had personally selected), the other for suspected complicity in the Burr Conspiracy.[37] Only Dehahuit remained, still committed to finding a resolution that would preserve Caddo security and autonomy. But the Neutral Ground had always been a product of established diplomatic practice rather than of particular individuals, so it remained an appealing model for all concerned. William Eustis eventually ordered a general policy of ejecting intruders from Indian land.[38] Eustis' decisions only clarified and legitimized a system that was already in place. Throughout the year that followed, American army officers entered the Neutral Ground to root out squatters or retrieve runaway slaves. Spanish army officers in Texas, like the Caddo themselves, permitted these ventures so long as there was no evidence of greater American adventurism in east Texas.

The Caddo were only the latest in a series of Indians to find that disputes between the United States and European powers enabled Indians to realize their own diplomatic goals and sustain their own diplomatic style, replacing the bureaucratic authority of the United States with face-to-face negotiation that demanded the autonomy of their negotiating partners. Yet Madison never acknowledged local diplomacy as an "Indian" system. There was more to this attitude than willful ignorance. Madison and his cabinet had reasons to see the Neutral Ground agreement as a useful model for a distributed system of federal power that preserved the administration's goals.[39] That Madison committed his administration to removing intruders from Indian villages did not indicate any dramatic change in the nation's Indian policy. Instead, particular diplomatic conditions and domestic administrative needs combined to convince the administration that it should pursue this policy. The administration's ongoing endorsement of the frontier autonomy that sustained the Neutral Ground actually attested more to the limitations of local diplomacy than to its possibilities. So long as local officials made decisions that were in keeping with the broad contours of the administration's diplomatic and domestic objectives, men in Washington provided either retroactive approval or silent consent.

This state of affairs could not have produced a better outcome for the Caddo in general or Dehahuit in particular. Well aware of the strategic advantage he enjoyed, Dehahuit made clear to American and Spanish officials that if they wanted to keep the peace, they had to satisfy the Caddos' needs. In the interest of creating a buffer zone, Spain and the United States acknowledged the Caddos' autonomy as well as their diplomatic legitimacy. The diplomatic disputes in turn helped forge the internal structure among the Caddo, reinforcing Dehahuit's power over neighboring villages.

Army officers were not oblivious to the developments in West Florida, nor were they unaware of the international implications of tension in the Southwest. But they consistently agreed that the greatest danger to the region came from the western borderlands. As a result, they constructed their own policy.[40] But Madison welcomed local diplomacy in the West for the specific reason that it freed him to focus on other matters. Louisiana was indeed at the center of the administration's concerns in 1810. It was simply that the locus of the administration's attention was to the east of Orleans, not the west.

"The Kingdom of Spain Is Nomore"

The local diplomacy that sustained the Neutral Ground proved particularly attractive in 1810 because formal relations between the United States and Spain had collapsed. While Madison found his own policy with Spain and the Spanish empire frozen by the absence of an acceptable negotiating partner, officials on the southwestern frontier could maintain active diplomatic relations specifically because they were not accredited diplomats. Madison soon decided that local diplomacy might provide the means to realize his goals in West Florida. As the president and his advisors would learn, however, local diplomacy had its limitations.[41]

The French invasion generated revolutionary governments throughout Spanish America, most of them issuing statements of loyalty to the ousted Bourbon regime (among those royalists were the residents of Cuba who evicted the Saint Domingue refugees). West Florida was different. Like the Francophone residents of Louisiana, the residents of the Gulf Coast chafed at the political and commercial limitations they associated with Spanish rule. It was the troublemakers who became the most famous (or infamous), men like the Kempers, who assaulted the Spanish regime both literally and figuratively.[42] The Kempers' activities make for a gripping narrative, and their resistance to Spanish authority has been the subject of the most whiggish historians of American progress on the frontier and a useful case study for critics of expansionism. Forced to contend with men like the Kempers and aware of the administration's public statements, Vicente Folch, the Spanish governor of West Florida, concluded that Americans were bent on nothing less than the domination of all Spanish possessions in North America.[43]

Most ambitious Anglo-Americans followed a less radical course very similar to that of white Louisianians. Just as Francophone Louisianians west of the Mississippi attempted to ingratiate themselves with Americans in an effort to secure prosperity and patronage, so Anglophone residents of the Gulf Coast strove for influence within the Spanish imperial regime. For example, in the summer of 1809 John McDonogh sent "a present of Wine" to Folch. A merchant and slave trader who had recently moved from Maryland, McDonogh was eager to win Folch's favor.[44] In 1807 another American named Frederick Kimball boasted that "I now float Nearly as high on the wings of Spanish Government as any Man in it." Kimball was no fan of the Spanish regime. Far from it, he criticized Spanish officials at every turn. A year before, he had considered leaving West Florida for Louisiana, writing: "I am so tired with our present Government that I am fixing to go and Explore Lusiana to see if I like that part of the world for a man is not nor cannot be happy here that is known to be a friend to Amarica." Nonetheless, he reconciled himself to the situation in West Florida so long as it benefited his commercial interests.[45]

American settlers in West Florida, like Louisiana Creoles, often attributed these problems to the Spanish administration of property, both landed and human. They were frustrated by the difficulty of establishing uncontested land claims (the source of the Kemper revolt in 1805). They lamented the scarcity of credit, and much as Kimball might boast of his influence, he was frustrated by the fact that "the thing Called money is not to found in the floridas."[46] They cast an envious eye toward Louisiana, where the territorial legislature was hard at work creating new systems to preserve slavery. In the end, Frederick Kimball said goodbye to West Florida and decided to seek his fortune across the river in American Louisiana. The neighbors he left behind continued to complain that only Spanish policy prevented them from realizing the potential bonanza on the Gulf Coast.[47]

It was men like these who joined the West Florida Convention, a collection of dissatisfied settlers who gathered in the summer of 1810. Similar bodies had taken form throughout the Spanish empire, but they consisted primarily of Hispanic Creoles instead of the transplanted Americans who took charge of the Convention. On 23 June 1810 Conventioneers presented a new plan of governance for West Florida that wedded the caution of men like Rhea with the opportunism of men like the Kempers. The Convention proposed to take charge of West Florida, yet still swore loyalty to Spain. Spanish officials could keep their offices so long as they swore allegiance to the new regime.[48]

Not all Americans sided with the Convention. One gathering of West Florida residents explicitly rejected the Convention and questioned its motives. They wrote to Philip Hickey, who had been a loyal servant of the Spanish regime, describing the Convention in terms very similar to the alarmist reaction of white Louisianians and American officials to the white troublemakers in Louisiana. The petitioners explained that "the present critical situation of our country is viewed with painful anxiety by every person concerned in its welfare, with an inconsiderable population of various descriptions, differing in manners in Language and in habits, in a great measure unacquainted with each other, and unaccustomed to any participation in the councils or administration of the government which has hitherto protected us." Adding trouble to this situation were "some characters [who] have stepped forward and indeavored to sew the seeds of anarchy amongst us." The petitioners called on Hickey to preserve Spanish sovereignty. Apparently they did not know that Hickey himself had joined the Convention.[49]

American civil and military officials worried that the Convention would spread chaos and violence throughout the borderlands.[50] Madison was determined to defuse the crisis on the Gulf Coast in a way that would satisfy American concerns, and he hoped that local diplomacy would provide the means. In July 1810 Smith dispatched Mississippi territorial judge William Wykoff and former Georgia governor George Mathews to establish contact with the Conventioneers, "diffusing the impression that the United States cherish the sincerest good will . . . that in the event of a political separation from the parent Country, their incorporation into our Union would coincide with the sentiments and policy of the United States." Smith informed his delegates that they should also "draw their [the members of the West Florida Convention] minds to a contemplation of the obvious and very disagreeable consequences, as well to them as to us, should the dissolution of their ties to the parent Country be followed by a connection with any of the European powers."[51]

For all the intrigue of their instructions, Wykoff and Mathews were not covert agents in the modern sense of the term. Although Madison certainly hoped that Wykoff and Mathews would solicit a request for annexation by the West Florida Convention, he was more concerned that the United States avoid any official recognition of the Convention. Wykoff and Mathews were instead a new by-product of local diplomacy: unofficial delegates who could negotiate without binding the administration or providing the de facto recognition of the West Florida Convention that would come with sending accredited diplomats. Neither Jefferson nor Madison had ever deployed local diplomacy in such a direct or secretive way. In 1810 Madison tested just how much power the administration could wield through unofficial negotiations.[52]

It was the West Florida Convention that upset Madison's plans. On 26 September 1810 the Convention declared itself the government of an independent republic on the Gulf Coast. The Conventioneers set about building a political system and a government of their own. In keeping with the violent masculinity of so many leaders of the Convention, the emphasis of this government was military. The first order of business was to acquire a cache of military supplies and build an army. Conventioneers even attempted to create a rudimentary navy to secure the ports and rivers, waterways where Spanish commercial policy had raised so much anger among the Anglo-American residents of West Florida and Mississippi. Conventioneers then invited Fulwar Skipwith to serve as president of the new republic. Skipwith was no novice to the world of international affairs, nor was he disconnected from the United States. The scion of an elite Virginia family, he had served as the American consul to Martinique and Paris before establishing a plantation in West Florida in 1809. He had tried to position himself for appointment as governor of the Territory of Orleans, only to be dismissed by Jefferson for lacking "the habits and feelings, and the tact" for the job.[53]

On 3 November an exuberant Reuben Kemper wrote that "The kingdom of Spain is nomore."[54] From Washington's perspective, this was a statement of fact testifying to the collapse of Spanish authority. To Kemper, however, it was a celebration of the new polity on the Gulf Coast, one that delivered power and legitimacy to him. As a principal advocate of West Florida's independence and a member of its new government, Kemper had transformed himself from frontier outlaw into revolutionary leader. The question that remained unanswered was whether this new republic could withstand the competing ambitions of France, Spain, and the United States, all of which claimed the region as their own.

When news of the declaration of independence on the Gulf Coast reached Washington, Madison faced both the crisis he had long feared and the opportunity he had long sought. A weak, independent Florida created a vacuum of power that could easily serve as a pretext for French or British intervention. Madison responded by abandoning the uncertainty of local diplomacy, and on October 27 he issued a proclamation announcing the American annexation of West Florida. Madison backed up this decision by dispatching troops to seize West Florida and civil officials to extend federal sovereignty. Writing with excessive, almost forced assurance, Madison claimed that West Florida "has, at all times, as is well known, been considered and claimed by [the United States]" and had remained under Spanish authority only through "the acquiescence of the United States in the temporary continuance of the said Territory under the Spanish authority." He added that the Napoleonic invasion and, more important, the subsequent collapse of Spanish authority in 1810 *required* the United States to seize West Florida in 1810 in the interest of regional stability. "A failure of the United States to take the said Territory into its possession," Madison explained, "may lead to events ultimately contravening the view of both parties."[55]

Much as Madison might assume authority in Washington, he would need to depend on local officials to execute his orders. And because of a fluke in the timing, they would be junior officials indeed. Claiborne was on the East Coast, in the midst of an extended trip to visit his family in Virginia and confer with officials in Washington. Madison cut short the governor's sojourn, but Claiborne would be hard pressed to reach the Southwest in time to oversee the timely implementation of Madison's proclamation. Meanwhile the mass of troops in the Southwest were still without a commander. Wade Hampton, who had recently been appointed to replace James Wilkinson, encountered innumerable delays traveling by sea from South Carolina.[56]

On 1 December Claiborne finally reached Washington, Mississippi, his territorial capital before moving to New Orleans. Claiborne coordinated with David Holmes, then in his second year as Mississippi's territorial governor, and a pair of army colonels—Leonard Covington and Zebulon Pike—to move troops from both sides of the Mississippi. It was a rushed affair, without any of the methodical ease that Madison had wanted.

For all the problems that Madison faced in dispatching forces to the Southwest, his choice of direct action seemed to bring immediate benefits. American soldiers and civil officials from the territories of Orleans and Mississippi descended on the Gulf Coast, quickly establishing their authority over Baton Rouge and the surrounding territory. By January 1811 Captain John Shaw, David Porter's successor in New Orleans, could write confidently to Secretary of the Navy Hamilton: "So ended the Floridian Republic, much indeed to the well wishes of the good citizens in General."[57]

"The Confusion Was Great beyond Description"

A week after dispatching his report to Hamilton, Shaw was thrown into a panic. "An express gave up the alarm," Shaw explained. "The whole city [of New Orleans] was convulsed, and the confusion which prevailed was general. . . . I have never before been witness to such general confusion and disarray."[58] Shaw's letter recorded the fallout of local diplomacy, or at least the sort of local diplomacy that Madison had hoped to practice. It was instead local diplomacy as practiced by frontier residents who intended to exploit diplomatic contingency to serve their own ends.

Surprised though Shaw was, there were scattered pieces of evidence that suggested the possibility of a slave revolt in Louisiana. The first signs of trouble came in the fall of 1810, when slaveowners reported a rash of runaways from the plantations outside New Orleans.[59] The elaborate system of patrols and deterrents collapsed in January 1811 on the German Coast. Located due west of New Orleans, the region had taken its name from the small German community that settled there in the mid-eighteenth century. By 1811, however, it was crowded with plantations, Creole planters, and slaves. Over 60 percent of the population was enslaved. Within twenty-four hours of the murder of a slaveholder on 8 January, a slave army took form in St. John the Baptist Parish and began to move east toward New Orleans. The size of that army was the subject of numerous estimates, but most white observers (the only remaining record) put the revolt at somewhere near 200 slaves.

The slaves' goals remain elusive, but their decision to strike directly at the heart of white authority suggests their intention to demand permanent changes in the racial regime. So too did their timing and their organization. Some of those very slaves who filled the ranks of the 1811 revolt had come from Saint Domingue, and the revolt as a whole modeled its organization on that of the Caribbean revolutionaries. Even white commentators, who often described slave violence as little more than mindless blood-lust, acknowledged something far more organized (and to them far more sinister) in the revolt. Divided into distinct units, the slaves reportedly created both uniforms and flags.[60]

The slaves also could not have chosen a better moment to strike, and most likely they knew it. In the winter of 1810–11 the slaves would have noticed a sudden change in the government. The bulk of the soldiers, militiamen, and territorial leaders who together sustained white supremacy were in West Florida. Yet the slaves' opportunity proved short-lived. Had they struck a few days earlier, they might well have reached New Orleans. But by the first week of January 1811 troops were on their way back from West Florida, with Claiborne at their head. General Wade Hampton, who had missed the annexation altogether as a result of numerous delays on his passage to the Southwest, conveniently reached New Orleans on 6 January. When the revolt began, Hampton confirmed Shaw's observation, concluding that "the confusion was great beyond description."[61] Hampton knew enough of the situation in Louisiana to reach the incorrect but nonetheless predictable American conclusion that the Spanish had somehow helped promote racial unrest. Hampton and Claiborne immediately reoriented American military strategy to launch what one observer called "the war" against the slaves.[62]

Nothing better indicated the slaves' goals than the direction in which they marched. Rather than heading for the territorial periphery, traditionally the place where slaves fled in pursuit of individual freedom, the slaves instead moved toward New Orleans, apparently intent on a more radical assault on the racial regime. As this army of resistance marched on the capital of racial supremacy, white authorities rushed to apply the institutions of exclusion. A combination of federal troops and Louisiana militiamen gathered at Jean Noël Destrehan's plantation. The slave army clashed with white forces on 11 January. Armed mostly with field implements, the slaves had little chance against the swords and firearms of the soldiers and militiamen. By the end of the day the slaves were fleeing into the countryside, abandoning military insurrection for the more common form of resistance: escape.[63]

In the aftermath of the revolt, the extended systems of racial control created by the mature territorial system combined to prevent any further threats to white supremacy. The same public institutions that were supposed to deter slave revolt — whether military, paramilitary, judicial, or legislative — now had to restore the peace. Soldiers in the U.S. Army, so recently extending federal sovereignty onto the Gulf Coast, again found themselves assigned to the more familiar assignment of protecting whites in Louisiana from slaves. The territorial militia, as disorganized and unreliable as militias throughout the United States, displayed a new vigilance, maintaining patrols throughout the territory. At the height of the revolt, members of the New Orleans City Council shared "the natural fear that communication existed between the rebels and the negroes of the City" and faced the "necessity [of] taking several extraordinary measures." Mather explained his own efforts, stating that "I considered myself as personally responsible for the safety of this City, so I immediately ordered the 25 supernumerary members of the City guard on duty, adding to abide thereby provided the number of good citizens applying to our posts to be on watch in the following night would be sufficient to save us the expense of commissioning a larger number of guards on regular pay for the same night." Apparently Claiborne did not consider this force adequate, because "the Governor notified me of the necessity of doubling the force of 60 guards at once, which he thought our force comprised at the time. And consequently by the following night, I had 101 men on duty. Friday morning, the Governor asked me at different times, to dispatch several small detachments of men which I complied with, one with 4 mounted guards and another with 9 men . . . and a third detachment of 12 men to escort the food supplies for the army." After diverting these men, Mather "determined . . . to replace them immediately with 25 more in order to be able to maintain the same amount of patrols last night as the night before." Mather did not have to explain himself. The council concurred with the mayor's measures.[64]

Once armed forces had contained the revolt, it was for the law and the legislature to prevent similar uprisings in the future. Less than five years old, the Black Code provided the structure for punishing the twenty-nine captured slaves accused of leading the revolt. Included was the alleged ringleader, a man named Charles who been hired to Andry and who was also accused of killing Andry's son. Charles's owner was the widow of Jean-Baptiste Deslondes, and in the absence of a last name for Charles, the uprising eventually became known as the Deslondes Revolt.

A hastily organized tribunal met at Jean Noël Destrehan's plantation, the site of the showdown between slaves and white troops. "In order to satisfy the common wish of the citizens of the Country," proclaimed the parish judge, Pierre St. Martin, "and to contribute as much as we can to the public welfare, I, the Judge, have constituted a tribunal." The five-man tribunal included Destrehan himself and operated under the provisions of the Black Code. In 1804 Destrehan had traveled to Washington with his fellow Creole, Pierre Sauve, and the French immigrant Pierre Derbigny to deliver the Remonstrance. Initially branded an enemy of the government by Claiborne, Destrehan had since emerged as a willing agent of the federal regime. Now he joined with other white Louisianians to preserve the racial order and the plantation system.[65] The court sentenced Charles and nineteen other slaves to death by firing squad.[66]

Convinced that racial revolt was a constant threat in Louisiana, white officials hoped to make an example of the convicted ringleaders. Samuel Hambleton, the naval agent in the Port of New Orleans, provided a grisly report of the aftermath. He wrote to his friend, David Porter, that four of the convicted slaves "were hung for the sake of their heads, which decorate our levee — They look like crows sitting on long poles." Whites reserved special attention for Charles, who "had his hands chopped off, then shot in one thigh and then in the other, until they were both broken — Then shot in the body and before he was expired was put into a bundle of straw and roasted!"[67]

For Porter, by then back in his home town of Chester, Pennsylvania, but still smarting from his experience in Louisiana, this news only confirmed his low opinion of white Louisianians. Porter was "shocked at the recital of the Barbarity of the planters — Shamefully depraved must be the minds that could commit such cruelties. Are these the men we would incorporate with us? Should we call them brothers? Shame on them."[68]

While Porter smirked from the East Coast, fear spread among whites throughout the Southwest. Officials in Mississippi prepared their own militia, "believing that there exists some grounds to apprehend that a similar attempt may possibly be made by the negroes in the lower part of this Territory."[69] Whites remained convinced that the conspiracy extended throughout the Southwest. Claiborne called on the legislature to restructure the legal and military systems to prevent any future uprisings. He concluded that recent arrivals from Saint Domingue and malcontent native-born slaves had been behind the revolt.

Of course, Louisiana's economy was too dependent on slavery for the revolt to generate any efforts to reduce white dependence on slave labor. For example, at the same meeting at which the New Orleans City Council contemplated how best to capture refugees from the revolt, Mayor James Mather lamented the shortage of slaves working at the city's meat market.[70] Yet for all the successes of the mature territorial system, the slave revolt had shown how people could exploit local diplomacy in ways contrary to the administration's objectives. This was most obviously the case with the slaves themselves, for whom the annexation of West Florida created unprecedented opportunities. But it was also the case for whites in Louisiana, who demanded that the institutional structures of territorial Louisiana be focused on preventing slave revolt, rather than on consolidating the hold on West Florida.[71]

"The Laws of This Territory Are in Force"

Incorporation always had certain fundamentally practical meanings. Incorporation required unquestioned American sovereignty over a Louisiana defined by the United States (as opposed to the definition imposed by Spain with its control of West Florida). Madison's vision of that process seemed to be settled. Although Spain did not formally recognize the American claim, the absence of any countermove by the beleaguered Spanish constituted a tacit acceptance. Yet it was not sufficient for the other nations to acknowledge American territorial claims. Incorporation required attachment. As had been the case with Louisiana in 1803, Madison had made only skeletal plans for the incorporation of West Florida in 1810. And they would use the experience of the past seven years to guide their actions.

Congress annexed West Florida to the Territory of Orleans, and the administration considered the matter complete. But as civil officials set about converting that edict into policymaking reality, they again reminded the administration how difficult incorporation could be. West Florida Conventioneers who had welcomed the end of Spanish rule now placed their own demands on the federal government. They wanted representation in the Orleans territorial legislature and resolution of disputed Spanish land claims.[72] A settler named James Neilson expressed the attitudes of many in West Florida when he reported to Madison that "although the Inhabitants of Florida are Generally warm friends to the Government of the United States — it can not be expected but they will look to be Secured in their Just rights and Property — let that be done, then there may be as much confidence placed in them as in any Such numerous branch of the United States."[73]

Convinced that American sovereignty remained insecure if white residents resented the annexation, the American officials assigned to take charge in West Florida advanced the agenda of Gulf Coast residents. They intended to curtail the "anarchy and confusion" that had followed the annexation, and advised the administration that all other objectives would have to wait. After traveling through West Florida to "reconcile the people" to annexation, for example, Mississippi territorial governor David Holmes informed Smith that the annexation "had occasioned a considerable degree of excitement: many seemed to think, that . . . the citizens had been treated with indignity by the United States, in taking possession of the Country without shewing to them the respect due to a people in the exercise of self government."[74] As they struggled to co-opt the new citizens, civil officials in the Southwest would not let the administration forget about West Florida. Public officials in the Territories of Orleans (which received direct jurisdiction over West Florida) and Mississippi persistently demanded time, money, and personnel from the federal leaders whose diplomatic decisions had created new administrative burdens.[75]

The administration again left local officials to their own devices, but now for reasons that had less to do with foreign distraction than with internal turmoil. Madison's doubts about Robert Smith's competence were only compounded by his belief that Smith and his family (a wealthy and influential force in Maryland) were actively undermining the president's support among Republicans. Madison also faced continued criticism from Monroe. Madison attempted to settle both these problems in April 1811 by replacing Smith with Monroe. This action removed Smith while stimulating a friendly collaboration between the two Virginians after a period of bitter dispute. The administrative changes were no less important than the political ones. After two years in which Madison assumed greater control over foreign affairs than had Jefferson because Madison distrusted his own secretary of state, Monroe restored to the State Department a level of authority that Madison had known in his own tenure under Jefferson.[76]

In the midst of these changes within the administration, officials in Louisiana continued their own efforts to settle the incorporation of West Florida in ways that would satisfy both domestic and foreign concerns. In an attempt to resolve the twin problems of local attachment and public administration, Claiborne returned to the tools he had used since 1803. Once again, he hoped to build a political kin through patronage. In the process, Claiborne would also show the extent to which ethnicity shaped the process of making public appointments. Selecting members of the Francophone and Hispanic populations of Louisiana had been a torturous process, with American officials worried at every step and Louisianians chafing at the limitations of this system. By contrast, Claiborne was quick to bestow public office on Anglophone West Floridians, but in ways that also showed his growing trust of white Louisianians.

As soon as the Orleans territorial legislature created new administrative and judicial districts in West Florida, Claiborne rushed to fill them with local residents and with white Louisianians from west of the Mississippi. In addition to the *administrative* demands of governance, Claiborne hoped to secure *political* goals by co-opting populations whose attachment was always at issue. One of his first appointments within the local population was John Rhea as a judge for Feliciana Parish, one of the four new parishes created by the legislature. But delivering news of the appointment and distributing copies of the *Civil Digest* went to a trusted Creole, Soniant Dufosat. This simple process of appointing a man and sending him the tools of his office told volumes about the use of public office. The co-optation of the West Floridian John Rhea provided the means to co-opt the Creole Dufosat. Claiborne was hard at work bringing Dufosat into the federal fold. In the spring of 1811 Claiborne secured a commission in the army for Dufosat's son, also named Soniant.[77] Meanwhile Rhea, the former president of the West Florida Convention, was soon addressing the mundane responsibilities of adjudicating local disputes and directing local administration, much as he had only a few months before as an alcalde serving the Spanish. He deferred to Claiborne on all matters. In 1812 Rhea fell ill and resigned from the bench. With the co-optation of Rhea complete, Claiborne now had a vacancy to use in delivering patronage to another deserving West Floridian.[78]

On 20 January 1811 Claiborne wrote a triumphant letter to Jefferson, informing the former president that "that the Laws of this Territory are in force in every part . . . [of West Florida] except a small District around the Town and Fort of Mobile." Territorial officials and federal leaders had begun a process of incorporation of West Florida that would serve national as well as regional objectives.[79]

The administration also provided tacit acceptance because public officials in the expanded Territory of Orleans were implementing policies that promoted diplomatic as well as domestic objectives. Four years after lamenting that Spanish possession of West Florida interfered with speedy correspondence, Postmaster General Gideon Granger could at last build his mail routes through West Florida without opposition from the Spanish, the threat of Indian raids, or the possibility of a lawless "banditti" of white troublemakers. Military engineers followed suit, eventually building a small network of roads connecting New Orleans to other strategic points in the Southwest.[80] Federal troops could more easily pursue runaway slaves fleeing the plantations of the Mississippi Valley or the white troublemakers who had eluded prosecution by traversing international borders.[81]

"A Strange Comedy"

Despite the benefits that seemed to be emerging from American possession of West Florida, Madison's decision to assert direct authority indicated the limitations of local diplomacy as the acquisition of new territory unleashed a host of demands on the federal government that, if not altogether unanticipated, were not eventualities for which the administration had adequately prepared. Nor were those problems limited to West Florida. The further adventures of George Mathews and Augustus Magee, who had seemed so useful in West Florida and on the Neutral Ground respectively, provided additional lessons.

In 1811, only months after issuing his West Florida proclamation, Madison received permission from Congress to seize East Florida in the event of foreign intervention or a local request for annexation. When Madison dispatched Mathews to observe the situation, Mathews instead attempted to revolutionize East Florida as a prelude to an American claim. Meanwhile, Magee had resigned from the army and settled in western Louisiana. In 1812 he joined a filibustering expedition designed to create an independent republic in east Texas that would include much of the Neutral Ground. Like his venture into the Neutral Ground, this expedition was a multinational affair, with Magee serving under the nominal leadership of Bernardo Gutierrez de Lara, a former Spanish officer.[82]

Mathews and Magee could easily see these ventures as in keeping with the traditions of local diplomacy. To Madison, however, the expeditions threatened to disrupt American relations with Spain and its new ally, Great Britain. Writing of the situation in East Florida, Madison complained to Jefferson that "Mathews has been playing a strange comedy, in the face of common sense, as well as of his instructions. His extravagances place us in the most distressing dilemma." Madison ordered a quick end to Mathews' activities, and Secretary of State Monroe sent a perfunctory letter informing Mathews that "you will, therefore, consider your powers as revoked." Madison and Monroe were equally relieved when Magee's separatist movement disintegrated.[83] The unpredictability of men like Mathews and Magee served to solidify the administration's trust in Claiborne, and goes a long way toward explaining why a man whom Jefferson and Madison had chosen with considerable reservations eventually won their praise for his ability to discern the administration's goals.[84]

Indeed, William C. C. Claiborne and George Mathews symbolized to the administration the possibilities and the limitations of local diplomacy. Whatever he might think of the practice, Madison had to acknowledge local diplomacy as a critical factor in his ongoing efforts to complete the incorporation of Louisiana. Public officials and private citizens in Louisiana had also become practiced at the art of soliciting support from Washington. In 1811 they were joined by residents of West Florida, who soon learned the ways in which foreign crisis and domestic unrest combined to drive policymaking. The convulsions of 1810–11 came in the midst of an important question: Should the Territory of Orleans live or die?

6

Polities

They came to New Orleans in the winter of 1811–12, forty-three men from throughout the Territory of Orleans. Jean Noël Destrehan was there, less than a year after presiding over the tribunal following the Deslondes Revolt. James Brown was there as well, almost four years after helping to write the *Civil Digest*. These men were treated with special courtesy. Three members of the territorial legislature had the honor (although some might have said "chore") of arranging housing for the visitors.[1] On 18 November the delegates gathered at Tremoulet's Hotel and set to work. They had come to New Orleans to write a state constitution, a responsibility that most had awaited for years.

Two months later the convention's president, Julien Poydras, composed a letter to James Madison. "The Representatives of the People of the Territory of Orleans . . . have the honour to submit . . . the Constitution or form of Government." It was a simple but momentous statement, and it could not have come a moment too soon for Poydras. The French-born Poydras, once a resident of Saint Domingue and for many years a resident of Louisiana, was among the federal government's first allies there, an influential figure who attempted to sustain local support for an often unpopular territorial regime. Poydras had once referred to Louisiana as "an adopted child of a great family." Not only did he consider himself and his fellow Louisianians entitled to statehood, but he worried that any further delay would undermine attachment in Louisiana.[2] With connections in the American, Creole, and Francophone immigrant communities, as well as connections in Washington acquired during two years as the territorial delegate to Congress, Poydras had built a career as one of a growing number of men who hoped to function as translators between the ethnic communities, between governments and private citizens, between the local and the national.

The Louisianians' efforts brought good results. In 1812 Congress created the state of Louisiana, an event that seemed to mark a milestone in the process of incorporation. And yet statehood was only the latest in a series of developments that would establish Louisiana's incorporation, and it would by no means be the last. The movement for statehood would also lead people to revisit issues they had discussed since 1803, often emphasizing that nationhood was both a means and an end. For white Louisianians, the language of nationhood would provide the means for political development, with statehood showing once and for all just why nationhood on American terms was so attractive. For American policymakers, nationhood of a particular form remained the only viable strategy to preserve the union. Regardless of their concerns or even their language, the men who debated statehood would always discuss Louisiana's fate in terms of attachment.

"The Attachment and Devotion of the Citizens"

Appeals for statehood were nothing new in Louisiana. When Louisianians first learned of Article III in the summer of 1803, many assumed that "incorporation" was synonymous with statehood. The federal government soon said otherwise, forcing Louisianians to accept the notion of incorporation as a process that included — but did not necessarily begin with — statehood. Congress settled the matter in the 1805 Governance Act, which required a free population of 60,000 before the federal government would even consider a request for statehood. From 1805 through 1812, people in Louisiana engaged in a series of activities that, if not explicitly designed to achieve statehood, nonetheless had the effect of creating in both Washington and Louisiana a climate that would support it. By exploiting the very crises that endangered Louisiana, by calling conspicuous attention to their own behavior, and especially by employing the terminology of nationhood, white Louisianians made the case for statehood. By invoking this strategy, and by eliciting a federal response on identical terms, Louisianians further solidified the principles of incorporation and attachment that defined American nationhood.

White Louisianians had learned with some difficulty that statehood re-

quired proof of incorporation at the same time that it would propel incorporation. So they set out to convince federal leaders that the twin projects of
building a republican policymaking apparatus and a republican political culture were well under way. The effort began in a clumsy way during the first
years after the Purchase, when Louisianians made their general statements of
loyalty and issued pointed statements of discontent. The fits and starts of
1803–1806 showed that general statements were insufficient and that complaints could do as much harm as good. From 1806 through 1812 the Louisianians developed more effective ways to convey their message, in large part
because the domestic and diplomatic controversies that consumed Louisiana
provided opportunities perfectly suited to the Louisianians' needs. In creating
a mature territorial system and in creating the means to call attention to the
attachment, Louisianians created the means to argue for statehood.

White Louisianians seized on the principle that loyalty to the United States,
republican government, and the Republican party (which to many Jeffersonians were almost indistinguishable) formed the basis of membership in the
national community. In response to American arguments, they claimed that
uniformity of political allegiance and diversity of local culture were not contradictory. They used a fusion of the two to construct a modified nationalism
that they effectively imposed on relations with the rest of the United States.

And the Louisianians had abundant opportunities in which to explain the
sort of relationship they sought between the local and the national. Even the
Batture controversy and the *Civil Digest,* which generated so much disagreement about which legal tradition should reign in Louisiana, provided Louisianians with crucial opportunities to establish themselves within a national
polity. After all, Louisianians were united with Thomas Jefferson in their
attempts to suppress Livingston's claim to the Batture, despite the fact that
both groups operated from different motives (Louisianians sought a defense of
local legal customs, Jefferson a defense of federal prerogatives). And while the
attempt to create a legal system in Louisiana did generate disputes, the resolution of that problem took the form of close collaboration between Louisianians and Americans, between local attorneys and federal leaders.

More than anything, however, it was the Burr Conspiracy that gave the
Louisianians the ammunition they needed. Nowhere else were the lines so
clearly drawn, and nowhere else did a local crisis provide such a specific test of
the Louisianians' national attachment. Americans of all political stripes predicted that Burr would find an army of ready allies in Louisiana.[3] Louisianians responded by going to extremes in their denunciation of the conspirators. When James Wilkinson wrote to the City Council that "an evil of greater
magnitude & more dangerous tendency is the influx of Strangers which I

understand has been remarkable for some time past," council members, most
of them Louisianians, responded by passing a "resolution relative to strangers" that granted municipal patrols with unprecedented powers to investigate and detain newcomers.[4] Like Wilkinson, Claiborne, and Jefferson,
they wanted to isolate anyone who would undermine American authority. At
the same time, by placing their suspicion at the feet of "strangers," they underscored their contention that the danger did not come from Louisianians
themselves.[5]

Throughout the winter of 1806–07 Louisianians found that the Burr crisis
created as many opportunities as threats. Here was the chance to prove their
loyalty to the United States. Here was the chance to show their attachment, in
contrast to the duplicity of Burr and his American cohorts. In 1807 an anonymous poet paid tribute to Wilkinson with the following lines:

> Haste, guardian Chief, to measure back the waves,
>   Thy quick return a grateful people craves,
> Grateful they think on all thy generous zeal,
>   And patriot labors for thy Country's weal,
> Malicious factions still that weal pursue,
>   And every anxious heart reverts to you.

The poet was one of the general's few defenders (others criticized him for
preserving the union with a heavy hand), but invoked a common incantation
for the Louisianians. By protecting the union, they claimed membership in it.
In the process, they reminded Americans that the union was more than a
geographic space. It was instead a people whose boundaries were coterminous
with national borders.[6] What made the Louisianians most unusual, indeed
almost un-American, was their rejection of separatism on a frontier where
separatism often appeared rampant. It was a confusing, potentially disorient-
ing situation for American observers, as the region that seemed the most
different in its history and customs established itself as the home of one of the
most loyal white populations.

On New Year's Day 1807 John Dickinson wrote Jefferson with one of the
most astute observations on conditions in Louisiana. Dickinson doubted reports he had heard "that the people settled in the Country ceded by France to
the United States, are universally dissatisfied with our Government." Instead,
Dickinson believed, "their dissatisfaction arises in some Measure, from their
not partaking as fully as they hoped, of Benefits from the Cession, and from
the expected difficulty of procuring slaves." Dickinson's solution: see to it that
"more Benefit can soon be conferred on them." Jefferson agreed, and blamed
the situation in Louisiana on familiar problems: the practical difficulties of

establishing sovereignty and Federalist schemes. Indeed, Jefferson assumed that the administration's enemies in Louisiana must be Federalists who had "been long endeavoring to batter down the Governor."[7]

In all these situations, controversy provided vital opportunities for nation-building. In the Batture controversy, the crafting of the *Civil Digest,* and the Burr crisis, Louisianians constructed narratives attesting to their loyalties and explaining their goals. A budding publishing industry enabled Louisianians to produce a growing number of pamphlets. All these documents addressed disputes particular to Louisiana. In each case, however, Louisianians called attention to their anger at any activity that threatened to undermine attachment in all its forms.[8]

The Louisianians' strategy of nationalizing their activities was particularly evident in a lengthy list of resolutions the Orleans territorial legislature dispatched to Congress. The first came less than three years after the angry tones of the Remonstrance. In 1807 a territorial legislature dominated by Creoles and émigrés from France and the French Caribbean swore to uncover any lingering Burrites. They wanted the rest of the nation to be "assured of the attachment and Devotion of the Citizens of this Territory to the Government of the United States."[9] Similar memorials became standard long after the Burr crisis subsided, striking a tone of collective loyalty to the United States and to the Republicans in Congress and the administration. The City Council expressed the same sentiments in its letter congratulating Madison on his election. In an 1810 memorial to Jefferson, the territorial House of Representatives explained that "the long, important & faithful service of Thomas Jefferson . . . entitle[s] him to the thanks of a grateful people." Louisiana legislators called special attention to Jefferson's "paternal protection" of the people of Orleans. The legislature included many of the same men who had decried American "tyranny" only a few years earlier. In all these proclamations, Louisianians claimed that they had repudiated European colonialism, Burr's separatism, Federalist partisans, and excessive localism. Reiterating a point first articulated in the Remonstrance, the Louisianians asserted that, like the thirteen original colonies, they too had evolved from tyranny to embrace liberty.[10]

The complex terms that Louisianians hoped to use in their dialogue with Americans shaped symbolically loaded public spectacles. The Fourth of July in particular became an opportunity for Americans to judge the sentiments of Louisianians and for Louisianians to present their own vision of nationality.[11] The Louisianians, like other Americans, conducted elaborate celebrations that combined local customs with thoroughly American rituals. After Louisianians attended high mass on 4 July 1806, for example, they performed a new play called *Washington, or the Liberty of the New World.* In a nation where the Protestant majority expressed often vicious anticatholicism, Louisianians struggled to make Catholic rituals fit within a rubric of acceptable American behavior.[12] In the 4 July 1810 issue of the *Louisiana Courier,* an editorial by "Americus" used the occasion to describe incorporation in very familiar terms: "The great anniversary of our national independence has again returned with its crowded blessings and attach[es] us more firmly to our native soil, and raise[s] our veneration for those illustrious worthies who planned our freedom, as well as support[ing] our cause in the cabinet by their counsels, and in the field by their valour."[13]

Another Fourth of July celebration in 1810 provided an opportunity for people to combine their celebration of attachment with attacks on disunion. After toasting the administration and the union, one gathering condemned Aaron Burr and Daniel Clark (a suspected conspirator and, by 1810, a pariah among Louisianians) as "twin brothers in villainy — their own confessions cover them with ignominy." The toast further lambasted other "conspirators, spies and intriguers: may they all meet the fate of burr and that which awaits his adherents." And at a time when the Spanish regime was faltering east of the Mississippi came a toast for "our neighbors in Florida: may they soon participate in all the blessings of independence."[14]

Gone was the indignation of the Remonstrance. Louisianians had recognized that their own efforts to secure attention, resources, and allies in Washington were most successful when they emphasized deferential loyalty to the American nation and to the Jeffersonian leadership. While annual events like the Fourth of July or Washington's birthday created regular moments to make such proclamations, political controversies — especially those in which Americans like Burr and Livingston were the villains — were even better.

When the territorial legislature finally, explicitly petitioned Congress for statehood in March 1810, officials in Louisiana laid claim to more than a population exceeding the threshold of 60,000. They even argued that Congress could ignore the 60,000-person requirement if other conditions made statehood both necessary and acceptable.[15] They proclaimed that they understood how to govern themselves in a Jeffersonian manner. They opened their appeal with the sentimental language of attachment: the residents of the territory "Bring you not testimony of their Discontent, but . . . the homage and fidelity which they again swear to the Constitution of the United States." The petitioners closed with the pragmatic lexicon of public administration. They acknowledged that Congress might have legitimate reasons for rejecting past appeals, but "things are now materially changed." They explained that "the System of Government which you have given [the residents of the Territory of

Orleans] . . . does not suit either their physical or political situation. . . . In almost all the measures which we attempt to take for the amelioration of the Government of the territory, the provisions of the [governance] ordinance shackle our efforts." Only statehood would resolve the tensions within Louisiana's legal and administrative apparatus.[16]

Claiborne actively endorsed petitions for statehood, hoping to accelerate the process by which Orleans would be brought "into the Bosom of the American family."[17] He had come a long way from 1803, when upon arrival in Louisiana he predicted a long period of incorporation and limited bonds of attachment. But incorporation remained a two-way street. The attachment of Louisianians was necessary but not sufficient to secure their incorporation. It was for the Americans to accept the Louisianians, in the process creating their own forms of attachment. The American interpretations of the Louisianians followed a shifting course that stood in marked contrast to the Louisianians' consistent desire to claim their own place within the national community. The fundamental change in American attitudes is therefore more difficult to locate or to explain. It was the product of internal as well as external causes ranging from human sociability to foreign relations.

The sociability occurred in subtle forms. As in so many other areas, Claiborne's experiences and comments distilled those of other Americans. His comment about the "American family" had a particular meaning to the governor in 1812, the year he married his third wife, this time a sixteen-year-old Francophone Creole named Cayetana Bosque.[18] Claiborne's experience was emblematic of the rapid growth in personal contact between Americans and Louisianians, contact that convinced many people in Louisiana that local residents were sincere in their pronouncements of attachment. Despite the remarriage, for example, Claiborne did not lose touch with Martin Duralde, father of Claiborne's second wife, nor did the political connections within this extended family dwindle.[19]

The extended kinship network of William Claiborne and the pronouncements of white Louisianians provided indications of the political maturity of the population. And by 1810 federal policymakers had other compelling evidence of their administrative maturity as well. Once again, the very controversies that created so much concern also created the ideal circumstances for officials in Louisiana to establish local diplomacy as proof of their ability to contribute to federal policymaking goals. Whether such a system would remain in place once state officials were released from the constitutional constraints of the territorial system remained to be seen, but officials in Washington proved ready to test the residents of Louisiana further by permitting them to craft a state constitution.

Besides, Claiborne and other American officials were convinced that the existing administrative structure delivered diminishing returns. "The Territorial Government was always difficult to administer," Claiborne admitted.[20] John Prevost agreed and informed his friend, Secretary of State James Monroe, that "the inefficiency of a territorial system heightened by the prospect of a change has sensibly diminished the authority of the laws, and so weakened the whole administration of justice that it has become an object with us all to hasten the moment of our Union." To this Prevost added that "no member of our community has more uniformly discovered a sincere attachment to the government of the UStates."[21]

The Louisianians' request in 1810 was familiar stuff to the administration and Congress. Territorial residents throughout the frontier had made the argument — with varying degrees of success — that statehood would enable them to put their administrative houses in order. For all their belief in the benefits of statehood, however, residents of Louisiana found that their request was low among congressional priorities, eclipsed primarily by the mounting diplomatic tensions between the United States and Great Britain. Congress barely considered the matter in 1810, and it was not until February 1811 that Congress authorized enabling legislation permitting a constitutional convention in Orleans.[22]

Seats at the convention were hot properties, generating spirited contests throughout the territory. Nowhere was this more the case than in New Orleans and the surrounding districts, home to many of Louisiana's most ambitious politicians. The victors included men representing the full range of Louisiana's elite. The delegates from the German Coast — James Brown, Jean Nöel Destrehan, and Alexandre La Branche — stand as a case in point of the diversity as well as the homogeneity of the convention. Brown was a newcomer who had built his career through an unwavering loyalty to the American regime. La Branche was a militia officer and one of those Creoles who entered public service under the Spanish, where the need for an inexpensive public officialdom created the opportunity for a commission in the militia but the restriction of high offices to Spaniards frustrated the ambitions of many Creoles. The Creole Destrehan had completed his transformation from Remonstrance-writing troublemaker to loyal advocate for an American government. Despite these differences, however, all men were members of the same elite in Louisiana that connected planters, lawyers, and merchants, an elite that had sought expanded political opportunities since 1803 with the same zeal it sought to contain restless whites and free people of color while preserving control over slaves. In fact only eight months before serving together at the constitutional convention, La Branche and Destrehan had done equally important work as members of the tribunal following the Deslondes Revolt.

Claiborne actively recruited Poydras to seek a seat from Pointe Coupée.[23] Poydras was more successful than Claiborne could have wished. Not only did he win handily in Pointe Coupée, but his selection as president of the convention gave him a powerful role in the proceedings. Yet for all his support of the territorial regime, Poydras treated the convention as an opportunity to lambaste territorial politics. "Let us hail our emancipation from that odious servitude which has cost us so dear," he said as he assumed the presidency of the convention.[24] Despite (or perhaps because of) his complicity in the territorial system, there was little else he could say given a political culture that condemned the quasi-colonial conditions of the territorial system. The language of politics in Louisiana might celebrate loyalty to the federal regime, but by 1811 it allowed little room for celebrating the territorial system itself.[25]

In the wake of these elections the territorial legislature made preparations for the convention delegates. Not only did a committee of the legislature need to arrange housing, but fifteen members of the convention were present or former members of the territorial legislature.[26] Although the convention had its share of squabbles driven by local political disputes, they never overshadowed the commitment to statehood. Objections to statehood were in fact few and far between.[27] On 26 January 1812 the convention unanimously approved the constitution. Allan Bowie Magruder and Eligius Fromentin soon left for Washington as the convention's official delegation to Congress. Like Brown and Moreau-Lislet writing the *Civil Digest* or the diverse group of men who composed the constitution itself, Magruder and Fromentin characterized the sort of collaborative arrangements that so many in Louisiana hoped to institutionalize. Cooperation in the public interest symbolized politics at its best, promoting harmony and creating circumstances that would overcome ethnic and historic differences.[28] At least that was the rosy portrait that Louisianians hoped to paint. The question was whether Congress would see things the same way.

"The Great Object Is to Make Us One People; to Make This Nation One"

If Louisianians wanted to discuss statehood in terms of attachment, members of Congress were only too happy to oblige. In 1810–11 (when Congress considered enabling legislation for the convention) and again in the winter of 1812 (when Congress debated statehood itself), members of both houses invoked the same principles of attachment and nationhood they had first tackled in 1803 and 1804, when they considered both the Purchase and the Governance Act. Members of Congress actually had little to say about the merits of the proposed state constitution itself. But if they were not concerned about constitutions, they were profoundly interested in nations.

Members of Congress laid out their assumption that attachment, whether individual or corporate, was the prerequisite for membership in the national community. They combined the local, national, and international terms that had always shaped discussions of Louisiana. Louisianians themselves had to feel an attachment to an American nation. Likewise, Louisiana had to be attached to the other states and to the federal government through political, administrative, and economic systems. Finally, Louisiana had to be attached in diplomatic terms, with American possession unchallenged by foreign powers. And these distinct forms of attachment served as a reminder of the ways that nationhood and incorporation served each other. Attachment was proof of incorporation, and would convince Americans that Louisiana was no longer foreign, in turn serving the Louisianians' objectives. At the same time, however, American policymakers who considered attachment a prerequisite for the union were equally eager for evidence of incorporation.

That the proposed constitution for a state of Louisiana was a fundamentally conformist act did not hurt the Louisianians either. In documents like the Remonstrance, white Louisianians had approached Congress with an adversarial tone. Now they acted on Congress' terms, a fact that many in Congress immediately took as evidence that Louisianians knew how to behave in an ideal American political manner.

Nathaniel Macon offered the most uncompromising claims that incorporation was successfully under way, attacking the notion that the Louisianians remained somehow foreign. In the process he also reasserted the absolute primacy of attachment for the viability of nation. "There are various political considerations which operate in favor of the formation of such a State," Macon explained. "A powerful State on the southern seacoast of the United States is an object of great magnitude in perpetuating the Union, which, for the happiness of the great American family, ought never to be dissolved." Indeed, the notion of an "American family," the very term that Poydras had used, was among the most common tropes that people used to describe the union. Statehood would overcome the geographic and cultural distances that separated Louisiana and its residents, respectively, from the rest of the nation. "There ought to be no question as to what stock they sprung from," he informed his House colleagues. Macon "was as willing now to make Orleans a State as he had been to make Ohio a State. The great object is to make us one people; to make this nation one."[29] This statement was less an assumption than an argument. The overtly nationalist language that Macon adopted was new in the rhetorical landscape. Americans had rarely made such unapologetic claims that the American people were in fact one people. But nationhood provided the ideal means — perhaps the *only* means — to argue for Louisiana statehood.

The Burr Conspiracy, so useful to the Louisianians since 1807, now provided members of Congress with the tools to make the case for statehood. "When some citizens of the old States forgot the love every honest heart owes to his country," Macon stated, the Louisianians "showed their attachment to the Union by the readiness with which they lent their aid to repel them. To make them a State would make the attachment still greater, and it was therefore advisable to act on the subject."[30] Macon's commentary rejected the conclusion of naval officers and civil officials who had often claimed that Louisianians were an impediment to public policy. By calling attention to the Louisianians' conspicuous service to the federal government at moments of crisis, Macon argued that a state of Louisiana would reinforce a national system of public administration.

Samuel Mitchill, who had spoken so effectively in defense of incorporation, was still in Washington in 1812, elevated to the Senate. He remained a quiet participant in the debate over Louisiana statehood. Macon borrowed from Samuel Mitchill's words in 1804, however, explaining that "they had already served a sufficient apprenticeship to the United States." Not only had people in Louisiana learned how to conduct themselves in a republican manner, but they had established themselves as members of the national community. It was now incumbent on Congress to do the same by making the federal structure reflect the reality of a single nation that spanned the Mississippi River.[31]

John Rhea of Tennessee (no relation to the former president of the West Florida Convention) shared not only Macon's conclusions but also his model of nationhood. He believed that the Louisianians' political incorporation to a union of states would reinforce the political incorporation of individual citizens. "It is with states as with individuals," Rhea explained. It was a telling statement, one that got to the core of nationhood. Like so many of his contemporaries, Rhea worried about the dynamics of union. And like so many others, he believed that a union among states worked by the same rules as a union of individuals. Both depended upon a harmony rooted in equality and attachment. The assumption that nationhood rested upon attachment rather than force had been so thoroughly assimilated into the American political lexicon that nobody proposed force as an effective means of unity.[32]

Opponents of statehood argued that the apprenticeship to liberty was far from over. They, too, believed that statehood required attachment and political socialization. The only difference was to use different theories of human behavior to reach fundamentally different conclusions about conditions in Louisiana. They argued that Louisianians had not in fact proved their true understanding of republican principles, nor had they abandoned their foreign attachments. Such an explanation made sense, however, only at a time when anything but republican principles was definitively foreign. "I was born in Virginia, sir," said New York congressman Jonathon Miller, "and I have not yet lost some of my Virginia feelings. . . . I cannot see why we should expect the people of Orleans to act and feel differently from other people, more particularly, when the French nation is towering so far above the other nations of the earth." Attachments were not so easily malleable, he argued. The result was a situation in which the Louisianians "will have a secret pride in their glory, they will have some attachments, to what extent I cannot say; but, inasmuch as we know that if we send Paddy to Paris, that Paddy he will come back, the idea is certainly not unworthy of our consideration."[33]

"The population of the Orleans Territory is not a French population," was Rhea's rejoinder. "Whatever the population was, before the treaty alluded to, it is now and for about seven years past has been a population composed of citizens, to a certain extent of the United States." Rhea turned Miller's argument on its head, claiming that social policy in Louisiana combined with a change of heart among the Louisianians had transformed them from foreigners into Americans. Granted, they had been citizens only "to a certain extent." Nonetheless, they were by law citizens and had to be treated as such. Not only had white Louisianians proved their own loyalty to the United States, but for policymakers to consider them foreigners undermined the entire concept of nationhood.[34]

Both Rhea and Miller discussed Louisianians in terms similar to those of William Plumer, or for that matter David Porter. In his private recollections of his meeting with the men who delivered the Remonstrance in 1804, Plumer explained that "I was much gratified with their company — they have little of French flippery with them — They resemble New England men more than the Virginians."[35] In his angry commentary on the difficulties he faced in the Port of New Orleans in 1810, Porter easily classified Louisianians as "Frenchmen." In all cases, it was more than language or history that made somebody "French" and, implicitly, foreign. Plumer described the Louisianians as Frenchman, despite knowing that two of his guests were Creoles, yet the absence of "French flippery," the similarity to New Englanders, and the specific dissimilarity to Virginians all combined to make Louisianians acceptable. For Porter, their Frenchness was inseparable from their resistance to federal law. Miller made similar assumptions, claiming that Frenchness was rooted in attachments to France more than in local forms of culture. Rhea made a similar claim, arguing that American attachments proved the Louisianians had long since ceased to be foreigners.

The change had been not in the methodology, but in the conclusion. In 1804, when Congress passed the Governance Act, a majority had concluded the Louisianians were still foreign, but that their conversion to Americans was possible. In 1812 a majority decided that Louisianians were no longer foreigners. The Republicans in particular were convinced that the territorial system had functioned as a means of mass naturalization, cultivating the Louisianians' attachment while instructing them in republican government. Such unanimity in Congress was hardly the result of a coordinated strategy. The debate over Louisiana statehood came at a high point in party division, with Republicans engaged in bitter disagreements over foreign and domestic policy. The party leadership was split, as was the cabinet. Madison himself was still engaged in a difficult battle to secure his own renomination, a dispute that had only heightened disagreements within Republican ranks.[36]

As in so many other instances, the partisan debate over Louisiana statehood was a product of developments in both Washington and Louisiana. Louisianians had quickly deduced the advantages of proving their loyalty to the Jeffersonian Republicans. As a result, Federalists and Republicans alike recognized that a state of Louisiana would deliver two Republican senators and a Republican congressman. That Federalists were more likely to consider Louisianians "foreign" while Republicans considered them "American" extended beyond the rhetorical demonization of political opponents. American policymakers saw only the thinnest line between *partisan* loyalty and *national* loyalty. The same understandings of partisanship and foreignness that would enable Federalists to consider the Louisianians "Frenchmen" because of their loyalty to the Republicans led Jefferson to condemn Federalists as "Anglomen" because he saw a Federalist "attachment" to Great Britain.[37]

The question was not whether individual attachment was a necessity in Louisiana (nobody doubted that), but whether by 1812 it was a reality. A majority in both houses sided with Nathaniel Macon, concluding that the Louisianians identified themselves as Americans. Through a combination of direct action, political mobilization, and publicity white Louisianians had convinced policymakers that they embraced a firm devotion to the United States. They had also proved their belief in the political principles of American nationhood. That similarity trumped other forms of difference. Nationhood served their broader goals of incorporation in the same way it provided Macon with an argument for statehood.

In the same way that the conformist behavior of elite Louisianians culminating in the crafting of the state constitution had assuaged fears in Congress, so too did behavior in Washington inform the way people in Louisiana could interpret the federal structure. After delivering the state constitution, Allan Magruder had remained in Washington to observe what followed. He soon reported that "the political friends of Louisiana are much more numerous here than I expected. They seem to be extremely anxious to bring that country into the Union." He proclaimed that politics had become a powerful sinew of nationhood, connecting Louisiana to the rest of the nation.[38]

Besides, what else could Magruder have written? As a member of the administration's political kinship network, he owed his own advancement to the patronage he enjoyed in Washington. Long before serving as a delegate to the constitutional convention, he had been one of Gallatin's land commissioners in Louisiana. As a pamphleteer in Kentucky, he had celebrated the benefits of unity under the Jeffersonian leadership. His own background notwithstanding, however, his report — and the state constitution's reception — provided a poignant reminder of events only seven years before, when Congress had dismissed both the Remonstrance and the emissaries who brought it. Those differences spoke volumes. Public officials were persistently suspicious of conventions to which they were not invited or which they had not approved. By contrast, the process of writing a constitution confirmed the Louisianians' commitment to nationhood. Virginia congressman Thomas Gholson decided that "if we examine the history of these people since their connexion with us, abundant testimony will be found, not only to exonerate them from the charge of disaffection, but to demonstrate their fidelity to the American Government." They were loyal not only to the American nation, but to its political principles as well.[39] Macon added that the Louisianians had shown their eagerness to "rally around the standard of the Constitution." They were loyal and they understood how to govern themselves. They were a mature political society that deserved statehood.[40]

Congress accepted the constitution and created the state of Louisiana on 8 April 1812. The legislation did not go into effect until 30 April, a nice touch that created a certain chronological symmetry between statehood and the Louisiana Purchase nine years earlier. But even the lack of controversy in April 1812 served the Louisianians' goals. Congress had yet to deny statehood to any territory, usually engaging in lengthy debate before a final acceptance of the new polities on frontier. Although Louisiana retained its differences, the similarity to frontier norms in Congress' treatment was itself an act of incorporation that white Louisianians had always sought.

When Congress authorized Louisiana statehood, it did not so much ignore differentiation as discriminate among its forms. As loyal whites who embraced republican politics, white Louisianians were welcome to the national community. Americans hardly forgot the differences in customs and manners that made white Louisianans unique. Nonetheless, that difference was over-whelmed by the reality of national attachment and the ability of statehood to promote incorporation.

Election and Selection

Congressional authorization by no means ended the transformation from territory to state. Not only did Louisiana voters need to populate the elective offices of the new state, but the elected leadership in turn needed to decide how public administration would be recreated for the new polity. As they fashioned the political and administrative institutions of the new state of Louisiana in the spring and summer of 1812, whites hoped to realize the goals they had articulated during the territorial period. They attempted to prove that Louisianans and Americans could participate in a republican political culture that would not give way to ethnic battles.

When news of statehood reached Louisiana, aspiring political elites hit the ground running. The election of 1812 was everything that boosters of state-hood had predicted: an invitation for people to politicize themselves in a republican manner. It was a relatively peaceful affair, notable mostly for the large number of candidates. One editorialist called on "every independent elector [to] come forward to the polls to day and give his vote in favor of *a change, a radical change* — the happiness of our State depends on a change of officers." This letter was an implicit attack on Claiborne and his allies. Yet it was also an appeal for widespread participation. How better to prove a repub-lican political culture than through a citizenry that voted in large numbers?[41]

Elections in the state of Louisiana began at 9:00 A.M. on 29 June 1812, when voters went to the polls to cast their ballots for the Louisiana General Assembly (the state's bicameral legislature consisting of a House of Represen-tatives and Senate), the governorship, and the U.S. House of Representatives. The tallying process proceeded without incident or objection. The results of the governor's race were clear: of 3,874 ballots, 2,757 were cast for William C. C. Claiborne, an overwhelming majority for a man who had faced such bitter criticism, especially during the early years of his tenure as territorial governor. His nearest challenger, with 943 votes, was Jacques Philippe Villeré, the man whom Claiborne had first selected in 1805 for high command in the territorial militia. The General Assembly convened in New Orleans on 27 July, and the first order of business was to conduct another set of elections. Legislators began by choosing officers for the state Senate and House of Representatives. As had been the case in so many political gatherings, Francophone migrants divided power with Creoles, enabling them to deny the very real disagreements among white Louisianians. Pierre St. Martin, born in New Orleans and a former judge of St. Charles Parish, served as speaker of the House of Representatives. (Martin was the judge who convened the tribunal following the Deslondes Revolt.) Meanwhile the French migrant Poydras assumed the presidency of the Senate with the same ease that had placed him in charge of the constitutional convention. No longer the appointed lackey on the Legislative Council, as an elected official Poydras could now assert himself as the legitimate representative of his fellow Louisianians.[42]

State legislators, many of whom had opposed Claiborne during the territorial period, sent a conciliatory message to the new governor, phrased in much the same language that he had used to describe his own earlier work. "For nine years you have safely directed a territorial government when the seeds of republican principles were to be sown, and whose inhabitants [were] unaccustomed to all the privileges of a wise and free people," they wrote. "With you we hail the arrival of that happy period, and we reiterate the sentiments of the people in declaring our approbation of your conduct and ours of your merits." Without changing the state executive, election by itself had redeemed the political process. In addition, by writing to the governor with terms of affection, members of the legislature could claim to have overcome old animosities, one of the surest signs of an effective political system.[43]

For their one congressional representative, Louisiana voters chose Thomas Bolling Robertson, since 1807 Claiborne's territorial secretary, and legislators selected Destrehan and Magruder for the Senate. For unknown reasons, both senators had brief tenures. Destrehan resigned before moving to Washington, while Magruder served for only a year before returning to Louisiana. The Senate replaced Destrehan and Magruder with Thomas Posey and Eligius Fromentin respectively. Posey, a Virginian and former Kentucky lieutenant governor, was replaced in 1813 by James Brown, a man with very similar credentials.

Meanwhile Claiborne set about populating the rest of the state government. Among Claiborne's first selections was Pierre Derbigny to serve on the Louisiana Supreme Court. For Derbigny, 1812 was emerging as a marvelous year. After years of exclusion from public office, he managed to enter both the legislature and the judiciary. Soon before his appointment to the bench he had won election to the General Assembly. Despite his change of heart regarding the Louisianians, Claiborne was entirely comfortable surrendering judicial control to them, even to his political foes. Joining Derbigny on the Supreme Court was George Mathews Jr., a territorial judge and son of the former

Georgia governor who was at that moment launching his escapades in East Florida.[44] Presiding over the three-member court was Dominick Hall, a former South Carolina legislator and chief judge of the Fifth U.S. Circuit Court who had come to Louisiana in 1804 to become a territorial judge. Hall left the court only five months later for a seat on the Federal District Court in Louisiana. For the next two years Mathews and Derbigny presided alone. In 1815 they were joined by François-Xavier Martin, whom Claiborne had selected two years earlier to serve as attorney general. Martin served on the court for thirty-one years, setting a record that still stands in the state of Louisiana. Martin also continued as the official reporter for the court, a task he had begun with the decisions of the territorial superior court.

The men selected for the Supreme Court were only the first in a lengthy series of appointments, some simply conferring state office on men who had served the territorial regime, others filling new offices. The state would have to shoulder many of the burdens that the federal government had carried during the territorial regime. The debate over statehood had shown that white Louisianians knew how to prove their attachment to the United States. Now the question was whether the state they had created could solidify the other principles of attachment: racial supremacy, national security, and a republican political culture.

State leaders were hard at work creating these structures of incorporation by the end of the summer of 1812. Although local elections and the distribution of patronage generated considerable anger among the people who felt themselves unjustifiably excluded from power, after years of condemnation nobody was in a position to lament the passing of the Territory of Orleans. But while the creation of the state of Louisiana may have been cause for celebration, it came in the midst of crisis. James Madison was certainly aware of this fact, for the initial request for statehood in 1810 had come just as the president began his efforts to settle affairs on the Gulf Coast. Now, the completion of the shift from territory to state came as Madison prepared for a different diplomatic crisis. The diplomatic context that had always shaped developments in Louisiana now commanded the agenda of the new state, for the first task facing the new government was to mobilize for war. Nor was that problem coincidental. Much as Louisianians might claim that statehood had come as the natural conclusion to the apprenticeship to liberty, they were forced to acknowledge that the mounting Anglo-American tension—rather than the more familiar Spanish-American tension that had been so crucial in Louisiana—helped their cause in the spring of 1812. Likewise, warfare between the United States and Great Britain would show that the apprenticeship to liberty was hardly complete. Louisianians may have made the compelling case for their collective attachment to American principles, but whether Louisiana itself could remain attached to the United States remained in doubt.

The chronology of statehood provides an indication of these events. The date for congressional approval of Louisiana statehood — 30 April — seemed to harken back to the moment, nine years before, when American and French diplomats had concluded the Louisiana Purchase. But events only a few weeks later were equally important. On 18 June the United States declared war on Great Britain. The Territory of Orleans, created and organized in the wake of one diplomatic development, now ceased to exist in preparation for another.

7

"The Din of War"

The Louisiana Supreme Court was nothing if not measured in its tones. It was a new institution created by statehood, and assumed a somber and authoritative meter in all its documents. The court showed how somber it could be in January 1815. Everybody else in New Orleans seemed on the verge of panic. With British troops encamped outside the city and British warships commanding the mouth of the Mississippi, people of all backgrounds predicted disaster. Public officials and private citizens wrote letters in the most anxious tones, their fear exaggerated to make certain that outside recipients understood the danger.

Not so the Supreme Court. In a masterful example of understatement, the record for the Louisiana Supreme Court reads: "The city of New Orleans being besieged by a British army on the first Monday of January 1815, the Court was not opened." The court felt some need to account for this absence, however, explaining that "the din of war prevent any business being done this term."[1] It was still a two-member court. Over a year after Chief Justice Dominick Hall's resignation, Pierre Derbigny and George Mathews Jr. shared the bench. François-Xavier Martin joined them later that year.

Despite the apparent calm of the Supreme Court, many in Louisiana panicked in much the same way they had the last time an army marched on New Orleans. Four years earlier, the Deslondes Revolt had approached a city in which, as Wade Hampton described it, "the confusion was great beyond description."[2] The slaves provided one of the greatest tests of the mature territorial system. The War of 1812 in turn tested a young state system. In the process, however, the war propelled the development of that state in crucial ways. Indeed, statehood alone was no more important than the international context that surrounded it, for the definitively international process of warmaking fueled the distinctly domestic process of statebuilding.

It was that moment in 1815 that has crystallized the image of war in Louisiana, a tale of British invasion and American victory. The final battle between British and American forces, on 8 January 1815, likewise appears in ironic terms, coming as it did two weeks after negotiators had signed the Treaty of Ghent. Yet there are more problems with the Battle of New Orleans than its dubious strategic importance. The British invasion constituted only the briefest portion of the War of 1812, following more than two years of intense activity in Louisiana that, though propelled by the conflict with Great Britain, had little to do with the British.

The invasion was also hardly the apex of unity that a narrative focusing on American resistance to the British would suggest. There were in fact three Battles of New Orleans in the winter of 1814–15. The first is the most familiar: a confrontation between American and British armies on the morning of 8 January 1815. The second Battle of New Orleans was a racial contest that lasted considerably longer. It began when the British invasion force arrived in the winter of 1814 and continued after the battle of 8 January as whites struggled to preserve their vision of exclusion against slaves and Indians intent on subverting white supremacy. The third Battle of New Orleans pitted whites in Louisiana against one another as Louisianians demanded that Andrew Jackson end martial law. The losers varied, but in each case white Louisianians claimed victory in one form or another.

As much as any event, the War of 1812 revealed the contours of incorporation, where racial supremacy, attachment in all its forms, and public administration overlapped. Each of these three battles also encapsulated one of the three themes of incorporation that dominated public life in Louisiana during the War of 1812: preserving Louisiana against foreign threats, reinforcing racial supremacy, and securing the sentimental attachment of whites. In the process, the War of 1812 further shaped the structure of policymaking in the state of Louisiana in ways no less profound than the state constitution itself.

In Louisiana the War of 1812 was primarily a conflict among old adversaries on the southern borderlands. The United States exploited these newest international crises to finally realize its territorial goals on the Gulf Coast. The residents of Louisiana were no different, for the War of 1812 presented only the latest opportunity to make use of diplomatic contingency to claim membership in the national community. These local circumstances eventually combined with the British invasion to challenge the new administrative apparatus that advocates of statehood had trumpeted as the great benefit of ending the territorial system. The British invasion of 1814–15 was hardly a singular moment, but rather the crescendo to a lengthy series of tests for the structures of incorporation.

War

When James Madison dispatched a message to Congress on 1 June 1812 seeking a declaration of war against Great Britain, a battle on the southwestern frontier was the last thing on his mind. Madison instead sought a quick conflict on a small geographic scale that would serve highly specific goals. Madison's strategic outlook in 1812 deserves some retelling. Not only do his reasons for declaring war help clarify his reasons for purchasing Louisiana, but those two actions together help make sense of American expansion in the early republic. The Louisiana Purchase and the War of 1812 also produced two of the most challenging tests of policymaking within the political and constitutional structures of the early American republic.

The linkages between the Louisiana Purchase and the War of 1812 are all the more important because the two events together have generated a scholarly paper trail that does more to obfuscate than to clarify. The Louisiana Purchase and the War of 1812 have often functioned as part of the familiar story of American expansionism. In this narrative, the Louisiana Purchase was the result of an American quest to acquire new territory for white settlers, and the War of 1812 was the product of pressure by war hawks who, driven more by pique than by principle, forced the United States into war in order to add Canada to the national domain and to defend national honor. These narratives make a certain sense. The United States *did* successfully double its size in 1803, and the United States *did* unsuccessfully attempt to invade Canada in 1812. And yet the simple focus on expansionism does not wear well. American policymakers made clear their own commitment to limited territorial acquisition in 1803, as well as their ambivalence toward the considerable land and population they acquired. Meanwhile the warhawk explanation does not withstand close scrutiny, for members of Congress were often following the Madison administration's lead, invoking the language of honor to make the case for a war based on more tangible goals. Indeed, Madison emerges as the key player in these two moments of expansion realized and expansion frustrated, rather than the passive follower overwhelmed by the expansionist onslaught.[3]

Madison approached the invasion of Canada in much the same way he had originally conceived of a Louisiana Purchase. Madison's policies toward Spain and Great Britain, as well as his initiatives on the southwestern frontier in 1803 and on the northeastern frontier in 1812, emerged from the same strategic vision of promoting the union by safeguarding political economy that had consumed his attention since the 1780s. Within that rubric, his territorial aspirations remained limited while his diplomatic objectives remained ambitious. These concerns guided his reactions to the Jay Treaty in 1794 and the Treaty of San Lorenzo in 1795. In 1803 he had sought a treaty with Spain that would cede New Orleans and West Florida in order to secure commercial prosperity in the West. In 1812 he sought a war that would force Great Britain to agree to a treaty that would remove almost three decades of restrictions on American trade. After advocating commercial discrimination as a congressman and embargo as secretary of state, Madison became convinced as president that only war would enable the United States to coerce a change in British policy. Well aware that Canadian ports served as a nexus for British trade in the Atlantic and that Canadian forests provided the timber for the British fleet, he attempted to pursue a brief war in which the United States would seize the Canadian maritime provinces in exchange for a new treaty with Great Britain that guaranteed American commercial rights.[4]

The similarities in 1803 were in fact striking. Not only did Madison show no serious desire for wholesale expansion in his Mississippi and Canada policies, but in both cases the federal government was ill prepared for the ramifications of his plans. Since 1803 the terms of the Louisiana Purchase had tested every facet of the federal system. Likewise, in 1812 Madison lacked the domestic structure to prosecute a war successfully on the U.S.-Canadian frontier. The problems were, in part, constitutional, as state leaders refused to assist the federal war effort. But the problems were also administrative, as Madison and his advisors overestimated their ability to organize an army and to select competent generals to lead it. Conditions in Louisiana may well have fueled the administration's unrealistic expectations. The creation of an effective territorial regime and the successes of local diplomacy seemed to indicate that the government could extend its reach with relative ease. Territorial officials had shown themselves compliant instruments of administration policy. In contrast to these relationships within the federal government after 1803, state and federal leaders were soon at odds over war policy in 1812.[5]

"Insurrection, Invasion, or Eminent Danger of Invasion"

As the war on the U.S.-Canadian border began to spin out of control, people throughout Louisiana concluded that the Anglo-American conflict had a direct impact on their own lives. They reached this conclusion in a characteristic way: by understanding foreign affairs in a wholly local context. Could the government preserve authority over slaves and Indians in a time of war? Would white Louisianians face new suspicions about their loyalty? Could local officials preserve the tenuous peace in the Southwest even as they went to war with Spain's new ally, Great Britain? They joined with people throughout Louisiana in asking a more far-reaching question: How would war affect incorporation?

The War of 1812 provided rough lessons for federal policymakers, who learned that they lacked the fiscal resources, constitutional authority, and administrative structures to prosecute a war on the North American mainland. Men in Louisiana, however, reached a different conclusion. Warfare fueled the resolution of diplomatic and racial problems. Meanwhile, white residents of Louisiana would find that warfare provided novel opportunities for nationhood. From 1812 through 1814 federal leaders were also pleased by the outcome of American military ventures against Spanish and Indian forces in the South.

From the administration's perspective, war with Great Britain enabled the United States to finally realize its territorial goals in the Southeast. In the spring of 1813, Americans received erroneous reports that Spain had sold East Florida to the British, a decision that placed the southern frontier in tremendous jeopardy. Monroe concluded that the United States now had to seize East Florida, explaining, "That is a question settled."[6] The danger was obvious: East Florida could form a local base for a British invasion of the Deep South. With the United States firmly established in the western half of West Florida, and the Spanish able to defend everything to the east but incapable of ejecting the United States, the situation in the Floridas had been at a stalemate for over two years. Vicente Folch, still infuriated with Madison's annexation of October 1810, continued to keep southern Alabama and Mississippi isolated through his control of the tributaries along the Gulf Coast.

Monroe had support from his territorial officials, but as usual their concerns were not only more localized but also slightly different from the administration's, focusing less on security than on political economy. Officials in both Louisiana and in the Mississippi Territory lamented the ability of Spanish officials to restrict trade through Mobile and the surrounding waterways. In the summer of 1811 Claiborne had even attempted to force the issue when Folch refused to let American merchantmen pass through Mobile, hoping to cause the sort of crisis that had precipitated the annexation of West Florida.[7] No sooner did the United States declare war on Great Britain than David Holmes, Mississippi's territorial governor, concluded that the United States should seize Mobile. "I am well convinced that the safety & Interest of an important portion of this Territory would be greatly advanced by having possession of the Town & Fort of Mobile," Holmes wrote in October 1812. "Nay, the interest of the United States under existing circumstances requires that measure should be taken without delay to remove this obstacle to the complete exercise of sovereignty within the declared limits of the territory."[8] The matter was of particular concern to Holmes because it was merchants from his territory who were unable to pass Mobile en route to the Gulf Coast.

Madison and Monroe, who were already seeing the limitations of local diplomacy, were quick to act without any of the subterfuge they had employed so disastrously with George Mathews. Their instrument was James Wilkinson, who led a quick assault on the Gulf Coast, seizing Mobile in April 1813 and consolidating the American hold on West Florida. That Wilkinson was in the area at all was a marvel in survival. After his departure from command of western forces in 1810, Wilkinson had endured both a court-martial for his incompetence at Terre aux Boeufs and an inquiry into his complicity in the Burr Conspiracy. Somehow, Wilkinson not only weathered these trials but retained a reputation as an effective military leader. When the United States went to war against Great Britain, Wilkinson was again in command of the troops in the Southwest, just as had been the case when he arrived in New Orleans almost a decade before.[9]

In the end, it was not Wilkinson but Andrew Jackson who would reap the greatest political rewards of military service in the South. A year after Wilkinson's Mobile campaign, the War of 1812 created yet another crisis in the South as well as another opportunity to realize American security on the southern borderlands. In 1814 Jackson precipitated a war with the Creeks. The aggression was not entirely on the American side, for militant Creeks had hoped an alliance with the British and the strains of war on the United States would put Indians at an advantage.[10] When the Spanish provided shelter for Creek Indians as well as British soldiers, Jackson explained the situation in characteristically personal terms. "Insult, upon insult to my government, and the greatest disrespect for myself," he wrote to the Spanish governor, Gonzales Manrique. "You have thrown the gauntlet, and I take it up." Jackson immediately seized the Spanish fort at Pensacola. The irascible Tennessean decided to punish the Spaniard by seizing his outpost. He quickly drove out the Spanish and destroyed their fortress. Jackson just as quickly abandoned Pensacola, but the Spanish had neither the manpower nor the finances to rebuild. Equally important, Jackson could complete his rout of the Creeks. Although Pensacola never came under Louisiana's jurisdiction, its capture was important to Louisiana's diplomatic and racial incorporation, further eroding both Spanish and

Indian power in the region surrounding Louisiana. Americans admitted as much during the Creek War, repeatedly claiming that militant Creeks directly endangered Louisiana.[11]

With these opportunities came threats, however, and while the administration took pleasure in developments on the Gulf Coast, people in Louisiana were more circumspect. As Claiborne wrote to an anonymous correspondent in 1813, "insurrection, invasion, or eminent danger of invasion" were all likely in wartime Louisiana.[12] Public officials responded accordingly. They rushed to shore up alliances with the Caddo and to prevent other Indians from taking sides against the United States. The intersection of racial control, international war, and regional security became abundantly clear in September 1813, when Claiborne wrote to his militia colonels that "the War with the Creek Indians assumes a serious aspect; A Fort twenty five Miles distant from Mobile, has been taken, & 350 Men, Women, & children cruelly masacred." Worse still, there were dangers of slave revolt. "It is confidently reported that many slaves have escaped from their Masters and joined the Indians, and it is feared, the Chactaws if they have not already will soon become hostile."[13] The prospect of Indian unity or an Indian-slave alliance had always been a fear (and occasionally a reality) in Louisiana, but those fears seemed particularly well founded in 1813 given the confluence of war with Great Britain and the pan-Indian movements throughout North America.[14]

In September 1814 Claiborne and New Orleans mayor Nicholas Girod met to discuss what seemed a tripartite threat to Louisiana from slaves, Indians, and Great Britain. Claiborne later informed the City Council that he "had every reason to believe that there are among them, agents of the enemy who are strongly occupied in exciting our slaves to insurrections." He called on the council to respond as it had before, by passing new rules for the regulation of slaves and strangers. Council members were only too happy to oblige.[15]

Two days later the City Council's chambers became the site of a remarkable meeting. State and federal judges, justices of the peace, Louisiana secretary of state Louis Macarty, and General Jean Baptiste Labatut of the state militia joined Girod and the City Council to determine specific policies that would preserve New Orleans against the racial revolt and foreign invasion that together threatened the city. Council members staked their own claim as foreign and domestic policymakers, explaining "the interest and duty of the authorities and the citizens to combine their efforts to forestalle the dangers we have to fear from our enemies from within as well as from without."[16]

As state and municipal officials collaborated to control, expel, or kill non-whites, only the Caddo seemed immune. The combination of a neutral stance and the American decision not to press its claims on the Texas-Louisiana borderlands served the Caddo well. Unlike the Creeks — or for that matter many of the other Indians in the eastern half of North America — the Caddo emerged from the War of 1812 unscathed. Their success was not entirely the result of their own policy. The militant movements of the Eastern Woodlands and the Gulf Coast failed in large part because the United States was able to gather large numbers of troops under particularly aggressive commanders who felt no external limitations on their activities. Men like William Henry Harrison in the Old Northwest, William Clark in Missouri, and Andrew Jackson in the Deep South successfully crushed pan-Indian movements. By contrast, the Neutral Ground continued to deliver specific benefits that Claiborne did not want to lose.[17]

But the Caddo were the exception that proved the rule. From 1812 to 1814, war with Great Britain provided the pretext for the federal and state governments to take an aggressive stance toward Spaniards, Indians, and slaves. Meanwhile, the belief in both Washington and New Orleans that nonwhites posed a threat to security in its broadest definition meant that public officials at the state and local levels sustained the cooperation that had characterized local diplomacy even after the federal government surrendered direct authority over local affairs with the passing of the territorial regime.

Citizens of Louisiana

The threats to incorporation were hardly limited to foreign powers or to nonwhites. To the contrary, incorporation had always rested on the sentimental attachment of white citizens. As had been the case since 1803, those whites — like Indians and slaves — continued to conceive of nationhood in highly pragmatic terms. The confluence of war and statehood provided a new context in which people could press their own agendas. Whether defining themselves as citizens or not, people in Louisiana reinforced the clear boundaries of nationhood. They intended to establish once and for all the line between the foreign and the American.

With the declaration of war, newcomers to Louisiana faced new challenges. Federal law mandated that during wartime, foreigners would be classified as "alien enemies" (subjects of countries with which the United States was at war) or "alien friends" (subjects of neutrals). Both friends and enemies faced restrictions; it was only a matter of degree.[18] The status of immigrants created problems throughout the United States, but it was most complicated in Louisiana. The nebulous status of white Louisianians who had become citizens by virtue of the Louisiana Purchase, the influx of immigrants and refugees after 1803, and even statehood itself combined to make citizenship a confusing thing. This was in no small part a result of the fact that constitution writers (in Louisiana in 1811–12 or, for that matter, in Philadelphia in 1787) had paid scant attention to the relation between state and federal citizenship.[19] It was instead left for newcomers to Louisiana to advance their own definitions of citizenship. The convergence of war and the novelty of the state apparatus created the ideal circumstances for people to successfully join the national community or sustain their status as foreigners.

That was certainly the case with Jean Baptiste Desbois, a white Saint Domingue refugee who settled in the Territory of Orleans in 1806. Desbois failed to report his arrival to federal officials, and as a result did not begin the naturalization process. With the declaration of war, Desbois suddenly faced potential legal restrictions or persecution as an alien, even an "alien friend."[20] Only the recent transition from territory to state gave him the means to bypass the naturalization process.

Desbois claimed that by providing state citizenship for all residents, the Louisiana constitution automatically conferred federal citizenship, even for those who had not completed the mandatory period of naturalization. The Louisiana Supreme Court agreed in terms that reverberated with concerns Louisianians had stated since 1803. In its decision, the court stated: "He admits he has no claim of citizenship by birth, nor by naturalization, under the acts of congress to establish an uniform rule of naturalization. . . . He contends, however, that natural birth, and a compliance with the formalities of these laws, are not the only modes of acquiring the citizenship of the United States, that the constitution itself has provided a third, viz. the admission in to the Union, of a state of which one is a citizen."

The court further explained that "every alien, coming to the United States in time of peace, therefore, acquires an inchoate right under the constitution to become a citizen." Otherwise, a resident alien would be "thrown away, an outcast upon the world." *Desbois' Case* (the official title for the decision) reaffirmed the linkages between attachment and nationality that had been on the table in the United States since the Declaration of Independence and in Louisiana since the 1768 revolt. The court made similar decisions in following years, erring on the side of generosity when it came to claims of immigrants seeking classification as citizens.[21]

Desbois' Case also marked an important moment for the Louisiana Supreme Court. In its first session, the court showed no hesitancy about issuing expansive statements on the broadest questions of nationhood. Derbigny, Mathews, and Chief Justice Dominick Hall echoed the principles Nathaniel Macon had expressed only a few months before when, during the debate over Louisiana statehood, he said, "the great object is to make us one people; to make this nation one." The court also extended Congressman John Rhea's own assertion during the Louisiana statehood debate that "it is with states as with individuals." In the same way that Louisianians had assaulted the nebulous status of unincorporated territories, the court used the same logic to condemn the liminal status of unnaturalized aliens. But in making this claim, the court drew on intellectual roots much older than the Louisiana Purchase. The court only clarified what American nationalists had argued since 1776: that a nation could not survive with a large population of permanently alienated whites. If the national community expanded to match the geographic expansion of 1803, then it must continue to expand as immigrants reached American shores.

Because Congress did not pass any laws for the direct administration of alien enemies, officials in Louisiana maintained the prerogative to manage immigration policy that they had assumed for years. One of these local policies—an ordinance requiring enemy aliens to keep clear of the Mississippi River—set the stage for other newcomers to exploit the reasoning in *Desbois' Case*.[22] In 1813 Pierre Duplessis, the federal marshal in New Orleans, ordered an Irishman known only as Laverty to move the requisite forty miles from the river. Laverty claimed that, like Desbois, he had become an American citizen when he became a state citizen. The district court agreed, and when Duplessis took the case to the Louisiana Supreme Court, Derbigny and Mathews refused to hear the case, upholding the district court's decision. Although Laverty's victory came through constitutional technicalities (the Louisiana Supreme Court claimed that it lacked jurisdiction over the case), Laverty, like Desbois, nonetheless found that war provided the necessity of citizenship, while statehood provided the means.[23]

In these cases, people in Louisiana—whether immigrants like Desbois and Laverty or Louisiana jurists—created a legal and constitutional framework for the intellectual construction of nationhood. They extended the Jeffersonian principles that had served them so well in their appeals for incorporation during the territorial period. While they continued to claim membership in an undifferentiated nation of white men sharing a single republican identity, they still believed that their manners and customs made them unique.[24]

Did this mean that all residents of the Territory of Orleans became citizens of both the state of Louisiana and the United States in 1812? Neither the state government nor the Supreme Court ever made a public statement on the matter again. Nor did Louisianians later invoke *Desbois' Case* or *Laverty v. Duplessis*. But the Foreign French certainly seem to have been treated as citizens.[25]

Except, of course, for those migrants who asked to be considered aliens, and during the War of 1812, they had reason to do so. In 1813 male refugees from Saint Domingue began to realize that with U.S. citizenship came the requirement of wartime militia service. Louis Toussard, the French consul, acknowledged that "the strangers who have settled . . . no doubt, owe . . . their service, and thereby contribute to the safety of the place where they receive hospitality and protection. But when . . . they are called by draft . . . should these strangers be included in this order?" His choice of words could not have been better. Public officials in Louisiana had always used "stranger" as a colloquial reference for "foreigner." They usually did so to brand people whom they considered public enemies. Now Toussard used it to defend Frenchmen, arguing that so long as these men had not completed American naturalization, they "have not lost their title of French citizens." Worse still, he added that French law would strip these men of their citizenship once they became *"affiliated with a strange military corporation."* Toussard lamented this status in much the same way the Louisiana Supreme Court worried that men without formal nationality would become "thrown away, an outcast upon the world."[26]

By January 1814, seventy-five men claimed they were Frenchmen. They were not the metaphorical Frenchmen of American critics, who concluded that white Louisianians, despite their U.S. citizenship, seemed more French than American. These men claimed that they were French citizens and needed to be treated as such. In his defense of these claims, Toussard presented arguments similar to those in the decision of *Desbois' Case,* explaining that to force unnaturalized immigrants to lose their French citizenship before they could acquire American citizenship would create a throng of the very "outcasts upon the world" that the court hoped to prevent. Claiborne had little choice but to agree. The refugees won their case, and Claiborne excused them from militia service. By 1814 newcomers to Louisiana had imposed their own terms on the naturalization process. While their goals diverged, their means as well as their impact were the same. A clear distinction between foreigners and Americans was best for all concerned.

Claiborne and other Louisiana officials found Toussard and the foreign French so irritating because their own efforts to create an effective militia were meeting with no end of difficulty. Claiborne certainly had high hopes that the state apparatus would finally give him the means to create an effective militia system.[27] And the need certainly seemed pressing. When Indian war and racial revolt seemed likely in 1813, for example, Claiborne rushed a letter to Philemon Thomas, a militia general headquartered in Baton Rouge. "We are surrounded by dangers," he informed Thomas, "and we must unite our best efforts to place the Militia of the State on the best possible footing."[28] Public officials in New Orleans were equally eager for an enlarged militia that would supplement the City Guard. Like state leaders, municipal officials were convinced that the war might lead to internal revolt.[29]

Claiborne's partner in these efforts was Jacques Villeré, who, despite losing to Claiborne in the 1812 gubernatorial contest, maintained an effective working relationship during the war. That Villeré owed his own selection as major general commanding the first division of Louisiana's state militia to Claiborne's patronage may well have helped the situation. But reorganizing the militia proved a difficult task for both men. It was not until 1813 that Claiborne, Villeré, and state legislators could agree on general militia provisions.[30] And when Claiborne finally called out the militia in 1813, white Louisianians showed just how much they had learned about the language of American political culture. They took the lead in charging the governor with appointing unfamiliar officers to command them, and warned the governor against plans to make them serve in other states.[31] Left with little choice, the state relaxed its militia requirements. It was a strange moment for Claiborne, marking the first time he faced substantial resistance from anybody other than the white elites, slaves, or Indians whom he had always considered the primary threats to incorporation. But it marked an important moment for the militiamen, who made a statement about citizenship and participation that was no less powerful than the ruling in *Desbois' Case* or the status of the foreign French.[32]

Claiborne and Villeré were only the latest to encounter the difficult lesson that the militia, for all its political appeal, never seemed capable of realizing its potential as a policymaking instrument. Since 1776, leaders of the United States had made the state militias a crucial part of military planning, political economy, and national self-creation, only to find that state leaders and private citizens were loath to report for military service.[33] Madison learned this lesson the hard way during the War of 1812. The most acute and irritating conflicts came in the Northeast, where state officials — whether they opposed the administration's wartime strategy, feared the consolidation of centralized power, or simply hoped to obstruct the Republican administration in order to advance Federal goals — refused to grant federal authority over state militias. In most states, however, problems with the militia were more mundane, often amounting to the simple refusal of private citizens to report for military service. Militia affairs remained, appropriately enough, local affairs. This was certainly true in Louisiana, where the successes and failures of mobilizing the militia were a direct result of questions about politics, citizenship, and race in a place where officials were still struggling to determine how a state polity would operate.

For all the problems that militiamen created for military planning, their particular mobilization was part of a broader movement during the War of

1812 to define not only who could be a citizen, but also how those citizens would behave. The war and statehood remained both the catalyst of and the excuse for this kind of activity. Whites in Louisiana had been struggling for years to establish clear lines of citizenship that would create an undifferentiated American national community premised on republican political participation. Now they had the means to do so. If Claiborne and his fellow elites were upset, they nonetheless shared the same goals.

"Evidence the Like Patriotism"

The militia's resistance was unusual. Throughout the War of 1812, white Louisianians engaged in the familiar acts of immigrants and minority groups. Faced with long-term suspicions about their loyalty, they found that external threats only magnified the sense of foreignness. But wartime would provide new means for proving their attachment, and the very militia that created so many problems would also provide Claiborne with continued means to use patronage as his own tool of incorporation. As a result, war planning would prove crucial to the thoroughly domestic acts of statebuilding and networkbuilding.

The simplest story of Louisianians during the War of 1812 is one of loyalty proven. The war served as the last—and the greatest—test of the Louisianians' loyalty. This test was a long time coming. Since 1803 Americans had predicted that war might lead western settlers to form separate alliances with foreign powers. Separatism seemed all the more likely in Louisiana, where national attachment seemed less secure. The depths of national loyalty were obvious to observers throughout the United States when white Louisianians rejected British appeals.

Louisianians started the project of using the war for their own purposes long before the British arrived or for that matter before Congress even declared war, often expressing their intentions in subtle forms. In October 1811, for example, people in Louisiana condemned the British. "Although Great Britain has not issued a *formal declaration of war* against the United States," wrote one newspaper commentator, "yet she is in as actual a state of hostility, as if the declaration had been presented to the world in the usual form."[34] In January 1812 the *Louisiana Gazette* echoed the militant language of Madison's annual message the previous month, claiming: "We must abandon commerce, or it must be fought for."[35] Similar statements followed during the winter and spring of 1811–12. Madison had made clear that he was mobilizing the nation for war. People in Louisiana also made clear that they were resolute in their support for the administration.[36]

People in Louisiana had practical reasons for supporting a hard line against Great Britain from 1803 to 1812. The commercial economy of the Lower Mississippi Valley had suffered as a result of British restrictions on international commerce. Yet these same people soon recognized that with international crisis came possibilities to reform their administrative infrastructure and to advance their political ambitions. The timing could not have been more important. Members of Congress were at that very moment considering the case of Louisiana statehood. That these statements of national attachment would be made public in newspapers made particular sense given the limitations imposed by territorial status. Without voting representation in Congress and with only a single nonvoting voice in either House, people in the Territory of Orleans used newspapers to announce their sentiments.[37]

Louisianians only intensified their efforts once statehood increased Louisiana's presence in Washington. A particularly obvious attempt to use the British invasion to validate the Louisianians' attachment came in September 1814, when a militia officer named P. Allard informed Villeré that "nobody is more convinced than I in realizing that the safety of Louisiana lies in the most vigorous defense if attacked, and that the inhabitants' only hope of survival for their own person and property is in the firmest adhesion to the Government of the United States." Attachment would deliver Louisiana from the numerous threats it faced just as the deliverance of Louisiana would offer proof of the Louisianians' attachment.[38]

Even as the war provided Louisianians with an opportunity to incorporate themselves nationally, it created new offices locally. Wartime mobilization vastly expanded patronage, especially in the state militia and the U.S. military. These appointments enabled local residents to realize their own advancement and Claiborne to continue his campaign to co-opt white Louisianians, whether Francophone Louisianians or Anglo-Americans from West Florida.[39] By 1813 West Floridians had convinced Claiborne that they were "disposed to rally, *at the first call,* among the standard of their Country, and I shall be disappointed if the people of the Western parishes, (whom I mean also to visit) do not feel and evidence the like patriotism."[40] Three years after Philemon Thomas commanded the short-lived army of the Republic of West Florida, he was a major general of the Louisiana State Militia.[41] Even former officers of the Spanish regime in West Florida secured office during the war, and war planning connected them to senior officials at the state and federal levels.[42]

Most revealing was the activity of free men of color, who recognized that the War of 1812 provided the ideal means to reassert their own claims to membership in a national community of masculine public service. Years earlier the territorial legislature had refused to fund the militia detachment of free men of color created by the Spanish. When the United States went to war in 1812 and the new state of Louisiana attempted to mobilize against possible invasion, the reorganized militia included "certain free men of colour." By the end of the year free men of color were once again donning military uniforms and marching in patriotic celebrations. Claiborne was soon dispatching them to guard against the prospect of Indian revolt. Free men of color still faced the legal restrictions of the Black Code, but the war had created renewed opportunities to proclaim their own membership in the polity.[43]

Invasion

People in Louisiana could focus on extending the federal reach into the Floridas, suppressing revolts by slaves or Indians, and securing the attachment of white Louisianians because the British were nowhere on the horizon, either literally or figuratively. Things changed in 1814, when the war with Great Britain reached Louisiana. Yet in the winter of 1814–15 a series of battles in Louisiana would show how policymaking responded to the same priorities that had been in place since 1803. The War of 1812 was only a more intense version of business as usual.

In the fall of 1814 news reached Washington that a British armada was on its way to the Gulf of Mexico. Monroe, serving a brief and unprecedented tenure as both secretary of state and secretary of war, rushed orders to Andrew Jackson. Monroe assumed that the British had arrived "with the connivance of the Spanish authorities there, and at Havana." Indeed, he worried that the Spanish—whether royalists or Bonapartists he did not say—would send troops through the Nacogdoches-Natchitoches corridor on the Texas-Louisiana borderlands. Monroe added: "It is known that the regular troops are distributed into many posts, and that the militia of Louisiana will be less efficient for general purposes from the dread of domestic insurection, so that on the militia of Tennessee your principal reliance must be." Jackson's freshly minted commission as major general in the U.S. Army was not just a reward for his victories against the Creeks but a mandate that subordinated the general to the federal structure.[44]

Monroe need not have worried. Reports had already reached the Southwest of the approaching British armada. Long before receiving Monroe's orders, Jackson concluded that Louisiana was in imminent danger and immediately took his army west. On 16 December 1814, fifteen days after Jackson reached New Orleans and two days before Monroe actually ordered Jackson to Louisiana, the bulk of the British troops set foot on the marshy soil of Louisiana. Expressing far greater concern than the Louisiana Supreme Court used in its description of conditions in the state capital, New Orleans mayor Nicholas Girod wrote that "the State of Louisiana and New Orleans are in a time of crisis."[45] James Brown, by then a U.S. senator, believed that if "New Orleans [is] saved, everything else can be regained even if lost"; on the other hand, the city's capture would inevitably lead to the utter devastation of Louisiana.[46]

Since 1803 policymakers had feared that a malevolent force of some kind would descend on the Lower Mississippi Valley, stripping the United States of the thoroughfare that connected the western provinces to the eastern seaboard. That leviathan had emerged in forms—both real and imagined— varying from the intransigent Spanish of the Mississippi Crisis to a reestablished Napoleonic empire to insurrectionary slaves to Burr's separatists to Indian warriors. Although the British had occasionally been on this list, they were the last enemy whom members of the Jefferson and Madison administration considered likely to destroy the process of incorporation in Louisiana. Nonetheless, they were also the most dangerous threat to the whole of the United States. It was an imposing force indeed, consisting of almost 10,000 soldiers and sailors transported aboard a large fleet of British warships.

Jackson attempted to assume overall command, but eventually found himself part of a tripartite arrangement with Claiborne and Villeré. British troops made an easy passage to the outskirts of New Orleans, soon concluding that Villeré's own plantation would constitute a logical camp. Villeré's son, René Gabriel, whose commission as a major in the militia reflected the growing forms of political kinship in American Louisiana, had been assigned to defend the plantation as a strategic outpost. The British had little trouble seizing the Villeré estate, and René barely avoided capture as he fled his own home.

This anxiety and anticipation in New Orleans form part of a familiar story of the invasion, with urgency giving way to celebration after 8 January 1815, when the British army marched to its own destruction at the hands of Jackson's volunteers, Louisiana militiamen (whites and free men of color), and scattered Indians who allied themselves with the United States. Close to 2,400 of the 7,500 British soldiers were killed or wounded. The British commander, General Sir Edward Pakenham, died in the assault. The remnants of his army were preparing to evacuate when news of the Treaty of Ghent reached Louisiana in February, and veterans of the battle marveled at the irony that this most remarkable of American victories had occurred after both sides had come to terms.

So ends the story that lends itself to dramatic retelling in both scholarly monographs and popular fiction. The battle has been a favorite for Jackson biographers and Louisiana boosters alike. More recently it has often been described as something of a "multicultural moment," a crisis in which white

Louisianians and white Americans, free people of color and Indians, law-abiding elites and ruthless pirates united in defense of the Southwest.

Yet scholars have shown that the ability of Americans to mobilize a military force (or their failure to do so) was a product of political, cultural, and social forces.[47] That was certainly the case in Louisiana in the winter of 1814–15, and the outcome of the British invasion makes sense only in the context of incorporation. The fact that the British faced any force at all is particularly telling. In 1803 most Americans would have agreed that a defense of Louisiana would be almost impossible given the disloyalty of local citizens, the abundance of potentially insurrectionary slaves, the corrupt local government, and the scarcity of federal troops. The standard way to account for the errors in these predictions has been to emphasize the patriotism of the Louisianians.

A better way to understand the British invasion is through the lens of incorporation. That was certainly how people in Louisiana saw things. Indeed, the most revealing aspects of the first Battle of New Orleans have little to do with the battlefield itself, or for that matter with Americans and Louisianians. Instead, it is the British perspective that proves so illuminating, for in their misinterpretation of Louisiana the British brought the realities of incorporation into broad relief. The British predicted an easy victory in Louisiana. They saw a potentially fractious society, and they attempted to exploit those divisions to their advantage.

Understanding the British expectations — and in turn their strategy — means stepping back almost two years and shifting focus an ocean away. In March 1813 a Royal Navy captain named James Sterling wrote a lengthy memorandum to Lord Melville, the first lord of the admiralty, arguing for the necessity as well as the ease of an invasion of the Gulf Coast. Sterling possessed a keen grasp of Louisiana's strategic value, explaining that control of the Mississippi was "of the utmost importance to the Interior States." He also understood how the river fitted into American political economy, for western states "shut out from the Ports of the Eastern Coast of America as they are by the almost impassible chain of the Allegany Mountains, can alone participate in foreign commerce by committing their produce to the Rivers which fall into the Ohio & Mississippi on its progress to New Orleans, the Capital of Louisiana, from whence it is distributed over the World." Sterling further hoped to capitalize on racial conflict. Jackson's recent campaign against the Creeks made Gulf Coast Indians seem likely allies. Sterling was also aware of the Deslondes Revolt, adding that "the Blacks who exceed the white Inhabitants in number have of late been very troublesome." Finally, Sterling predicted that the white residents themselves would be Britain's unwitting allies. He saw specific opportunities among the foreign French, who he believed contributed to a

"Population . . . made up chiefly of Emigrants from all Nations, unconnected by blood or long fellowships with the other States of America, [that] might be brought to follow any plan favorable to their interest. At present the Country is in a very unsettled State from difference of Political opinions, and there can be no doubt but a considerable party might be formed in favor of a separation from the United States." Sterling concluded that internal dissent would at least prevent coordinated defense, and at best might provide Britain with allies from within the local population.[48]

In his portrait of Louisiana's history and population in 1813, Sterling got everything right. In his predictions of local behavior, he could not have been more wrong. Sterling's conclusions about the white residents might have been more appropriate ten years earlier, when racial and ethnic conflict seemed likely to prevent Louisiana's permanent incorporation. He did not know that white Louisianians dissented because they felt excluded from the national community, not because they resented their transfer of nationality. Nor was Sterling aware of the fundamentally pragmatic forms of national attachment in Louisiana. White Louisianians might indeed believe that they were "unconnected by blood or long fellowships," but they saw considerable advantages to membership in an American national community, advantages that far outweighed affiliation with European empires or the isolation that would come from separatism. Finally, Sterling did not grasp that sources of conflict could neutralize each other. Slave revolt and Indian unrest might provide the British with potential allies, but they also stimulated white solidarity. Nothing settled disagreement among whites as quickly as the threat of slave revolt, and nothing made white Louisianians more angry with the British than attempts to undermine the racial regime.

But men in London had no evidence to the contrary, and they attempted to follow Sterling's advice. They began their efforts to foment unrest before the main British invasion force actually reached Louisiana. When the British formed an alliance with the Creek Indians in the summer of 1814, Lieutenant Colonel Edward Nicholls circulated a broadside in Louisiana stating: "Spaniards, Frenchmen, Italians and British, whether settled, or residing for a time in Louisiana, on you also I call to aid me in this Just cause. The american *usurpation in this country,* must be abolished, and the lawful owners of the soil, put in possession." Like Sterling, Nicholls failed to appreciate the power of white solidarity and the popularity of American nationhood. "I am at the head of a large body of Indians, well armed, disciplined and Commanded by British officers."[49] If Nicholls thought this statement would frighten the Louisianians into switching sides, he was sorely mistaken.

Meanwhile Nicholls attempted to exploit other potential sources of resistance within Louisiana. In the summer of 1814 he contacted Jean Lafitte, the nominal leader of the Baratarian pirates, explaining that in exchange for their assistance the pirates would receive "lands in His *Majestys Colonies in America*."[50] For years the pirates had infuriated public officials. Operating from a stronghold on Barataria Bay (a swampy inlet just west of the Mississippi River), they did more than raid merchantmen or injure innocent American citizens; they subverted public administration itself, defying the structures of governance that were supposed to deliver law and order to American Louisiana. The Baratarians had one more reason to sign on with the British: on the eve of the invasion, the state government, the U.S. Army, and the U.S. Navy had launched a coordinated attack on the pirates' stronghold.

Yet here, too, the British failed to appreciate local circumstances. The Baratarian pirates had no love for Louisiana's public officialdom, but they saw no reason to sign on with the British. Perhaps the Baratarians doubted the chances of British success and recognized that they were more likely to incur attack as agents of a foreign enemy than as domestic lawbreakers. They may also have recognized that the war provided an opportunity to secure their own futures within the United States by exploiting exactly the sort of circumstances the British provided. Instead of accepting British offers, the Baratarians provided vital information to American forces. By siding with the United States, the pirates hoped to secure a long-term debt of gratitude from the federal government.[51]

The British outlook from 1813 through 1815 goes a long way toward explaining their defeat in the first Battle of New Orleans. Those tactics are usually the focus of military historians, who have studied the Louisiana campaign in greatest detail. That they came to New Orleans at all, however, was no less important. The basis of that broader strategy lies not in the standard realm of military history, but in the particulars of incorporation and the American vision of nationhood.

"The Excesses [of] the Army under Your Command"

When their bid to secure an alliance with the Baratarians failed, the British turned to Louisiana slaves, this time with greater success. As they had learned during the Revolutionary War, offering freedom to slaves in exchange for their services could throw an American army into chaos. As slaves fled plantations along the banks of the Mississippi in pursuit of their freedom, Louisianians demanded that militiamen abandon their defenses against the British to search for slaves or protect white slaveholders. Villeré and other senior militia officers were only too happy to oblige, for they too were slaveholders who feared the loss of property or the possibility of insurrection. The second Battle of New Orleans was under way as whites struggled to preserve slavery, a goal they had always considered a necessary component of incorporation. The second Battle of New Orleans actually started before and outlasted the rather brief battle that occurred on 8 January.[52]

Slaves ran away as soon as the British arrived and continued to do so long after. Even as the British attempted to negotiate their evacuation from Louisiana, American commanders pressed them to undo the damage they had caused to the racial regime. Two weeks after American forces defeated the British, Villeré wrote to General John Lambert, who had inherited the unpleasant title of defeated commander from the late General Pakenham. "I stayed calm when I witnessed the excesses the army under your command are guilty of. I was not even astonished at the kidnapping of my negroes knowing the conduct of the English in the rest of the Union," Villeré explained, writing in terms that could easily have expressed the anger of many other white slaveholders. He charged the British with theft as well as with inciting a race war. He cast the situation in highly personal terms, explaining that "I was grieved when my son, whose inexperience you abused, presented me with the sum of $490 which one of the commissaries of your army gave him, according to your orders, for the payment of my cattle, furniture and other objects. I shuddered with indignation from such an outrage of which I had no conception."[53]

Jackson was similarly outraged by the British policy of inciting slaves to run away, and demanded their return in no uncertain terms. Although the crime was clear, Jackson had difficulty putting his anger into words. "I can only repeat what I have already told you," he informed Claiborne when the governor suggested sending a delegation to negotiate for the slaves' return, "that such a mission for such a purpose is wholly unprecedented in the history of warfare. . . . Would it not be degradation of that national character of which we boast, to condescend to solicit the restoration of stolen property from an enemy who avows plunder & burning to be legitimate modes of warfare?"[54]

While American commanders negotiated with the defeated army for the return of runaways, the public apparatus of Louisiana attempted to preserve the racial regime. The situation tested the capacities of the state government as much as the invasion itself. In many ways, it was a test that public officials had expected, because they had always assumed that invasion would threaten the power of masters over slaves. For the first time since 1811, when the territorial regime marshaled its resources to prevent any renewed insurrection after the Deslondes Revolt, the state government initiated a wholesale campaign of slave control. Public officials ordered additional patrols to uncover any potential slave revolt that might take advantage of white distraction just as members of the Deslondes Revolt benefited from the annexation of West Florida.[55] The New Orleans City Council concluded that it was "advisable for the mainte- nance of order and the City's safety, that some measures of police relative to slaves and free colored persons should be taken." The council imposed a 7:00 P.M. curfew on all slaves, punishable with thirty lashes for slaves traveling without written permission from their masters. Likewise, the council required all free people of color to register with the municipal government and to carry a "safety pass" to prove they were not runaway slaves.[56]

The American forces that gathered in Louisiana in the winter of 1814–15 fulfilled missions that had been in place since 1803: an armed force to defend against both foreign powers and internal insurrection while providing the means for whites to prove their attachment. And once the British were in retreat, military leaders considered it their responsibility to recover those slaves who had successfully crossed the lines. It was not simply that slaves bold enough to flee their masters might yet foment insurrection. The government's task was to preserve individual property, even when that property had been seized by a foreign army. From 1806 to 1808 the territorial government had crafted texts designed to establish ownership over landed and human property as well as civil and paramilitary institutions that would enforce those rules. In 1814–15 those same institutions—together with the U.S. Army—continued the job.[57]

Slaves were more successful than the British or the Indians of the Gulf Coast. Some did indeed achieve their freedom, either by reaching the British or by fleeing into the hinterland. Yet the same white soldiers and militiamen who defeated the armies of Great Britain or the Indians of the Gulf Coast could also claim victory over their slaves. They contained the threat of insurrection. Meanwhile American negotiators secured the return of runaway slaves who had found their way to the British. The second Battle of New Orleans ended much as that of 8 January, with white Americans defeating their nation's enemies. Both battles enabled white Louisianians to delineate the boundaries of that "nation," a community in which they claimed membership and from which they excluded the British, slaves, and Indians against whom they fought.

"My Encampment"

By February 1815 white Louisianians concluded that even if some slaves had escaped, the foreign threats to Louisiana—whether British troops, slaves, or Indians—were thoroughly vanquished. With two battles behind them, white Louisianians felt victorious if not altogether secure. If the first two battles had shown the benefits of the institutional structures designed to protect against the threats of foreign powers and nonwhites, the third Battle of New Orleans raised the old specter that Americans might not welcome Louisianians into the national community.

Jackson's willingness to join in the search for runaway slaves did not mean he agreed with Louisianians on all matters of race. Nor did his vicious war against the Creeks prevent him from enlisting Indians against the British. He eagerly deployed free men of color serving in the militia, dismissing the complaints of white Louisianians who feared the prospect of free men of color gathered en masse and armed, or the protests of white militiamen who considered the free black militia an affront to their own honor. Jackson's reply was quick and indignant. "Be pleased to keep to yourself your opinions," he informed a paymaster who questioned whether he should pay the free men of color. Jackson ordered that all militiamen receive pay "without inquiring whether the troops are white, Black, or red." Free men of color, eager to advance their own incorporation locally, applauded Jackson's decision.[58]

Jackson's decision to pay free black militiamen was a simple one. Pragmatic to a fault, Jackson welcomed whatever support was available. Jackson was equally pragmatic in his belief that short-term concessions to free men of color or to Indians did not mean any long-term commitment to those groups. But Louisianians had no way of knowing that Jackson shared their vision of white supremacy. Likewise, Jackson failed to grasp just how important the exclusion of nonwhites was to the status of white Louisianians.

These initial tensions set the stage for the third Battle of New Orleans. On 16 December 1814 Jackson had imposed martial law in New Orleans and suspended habeas corpus. He encountered limited resistance from whites, who accepted these actions as necessary in time of war. But Jackson's decision did not age well. As the foreign threat vanished following news of peace and the departure of British forces, white Louisianians felt sufficiently comfortable flexing their own political muscle to challenge Andrew Jackson. Indeed, the invasion had enabled them to equate "foreign" with the British. Now they once again asserted that they were not foreigners and should not be treated as such. They also demanded what they saw as the political liberties they associated with American citizenship. Louisiana militiamen, always an independent-minded group, began demanding their release from military service. In 1813 they had successfully resisted Claiborne's attempts at mobilization. Jackson was less forgiving. Not only did he ignore their requests, but he also attempted to prevent New Orleans newspapers from publishing articles in their favor.[59]

Even Claiborne, who welcomed Jackson's arrival, agreed with the militiamen that Jackson was overstepping the bounds of his authority. The state constitution identified the governor as commander-in-chief of the militia, and although he saw no reason to usurp direct authority from trusted subordinates like Villeré, Claiborne was "unwilling to acknowledge any other officer either of the Regular army or of the Militia, on duty in *this Station,* as my military superior."[60] Claiborne was only the latest in a series of governors during the War of 1812 to challenge federal power over state militias. In Louisiana, however, the question of state prerogative was a particularly potent issue.

Claiborne, by 1815 well attuned to Louisiana politics, attempted to restore civil government and dismiss the militia, explaining that "applications being hourly addressed to me by the Militia officers . . . I take the liberty to ask whether in your Judgement the services of the . . . Militia . . . can be disposed and with at what period."[61] Jackson scorned Claiborne's efforts and went several steps further. On 28 February he ordered all French subjects to leave the city. His application of the criterion "French" was highly specific. He aimed this order at Louis Toussard, the French consul, and the immigrants who had used their French citizenship to avoid militia duty. Jackson rationalized his decision in terms of security, claiming that if they were not citizens then they might constitute a threat. They had explicitly rejected their attachment to the United States by establishing themselves as foreigners. Besides, as aliens they did not enjoy the civil liberties of American citizens. But it was clear that the general also issued the order to punish men whom he considered unwilling to shoulder the burdens of citizenship.[62]

Jackson's aide-de-camp throughout this period was none other than Edward Livingston. Livingston was still hard at work trying to restore his good name among both American officials and white Louisianians. In 1813 he had helped write the rules for the Louisiana Supreme Court. In 1814 he chaired the New Orleans Committee on Public Safety. When Jackson arrived, Livingston eagerly served the general (in 1813 Livingston had even asked to serve Jackson without pay as the general's aide-de-camp and proxy in Louisiana). Now Livingston's two constituencies — the local elite and the federal leadership — came into conflict. Livingston supported Jackson, and Jackson continued to sustain martial law.[63]

White Louisianians were infuriated, and Jackson's decision only fueled opposition to martial law. Jackson finally stepped over the line when he ordered the arrest of Louis Louaillier, a French-born member of the state House of Representatives, for writing an anonymous newspaper editorial condemning the general's actions. Now Jackson expanded his definition of dangerous foreigners to include white Louisianians who opposed his rule, and in this action he touched a raw nerve after a decade in which white Louisianians had argued so loudly that they were *not* foreigners. When Jackson learned that Dominick Hall, judge of the U.S. District Court and the former chief justice of the

Louisiana Supreme Court, was preparing to issue a writ of habeas corpus ordering Louaillier's release, Jackson had Hall arrested as well. Next Jackson incarcerated Louisiana district court judge Joshua Lewis for good measure. Jackson did eventually receive a writ, but it bore the signature of district court clerk Richard Claiborne, the only member of the judiciary whom Jackson had not imprisoned. Rather than arrest the governor's kin, Jackson simply ignored the order.

Meanwhile Jackson convened a court-martial for Louaillier. When the trial ended in acquittal, Jackson rejected the verdict and kept Louaillier in prison. He also ordered Hall to leave New Orleans, which Jackson referred to as "my encampment." Two days later, on 13 March, Jackson received news of the ratification of the Treaty of Ghent, which he considered a prerequisite for a true end to hostilities. He released Louaillier and permitted both Hall and Toussard to return to the city. Hall and Jackson suddenly found their circumstances reversed; the judge issued an order demanding Jackson to show why he should not be held in contempt of the court. In the case that followed, *United States v. Major General Andrew Jackson,* Hall imposed a $1,000 fine on Jackson. It was a matter of pride to the general that he paid the fine himself, refusing a subscription from local residents.[64]

Jackson's decision to maintain martial law and to suppress his local adversaries unleashed painful memories for Louisianians, who resented any restraints on political expression and mobilization. They had reacted similarly to the Governance Act of 1804. The events of 1815 also bore a particular similarity to the last time an imperious general had taken charge in Louisiana. In 1807 James Wilkinson had used the military to suppress the separatism of Aaron Burr (and to distance himself from the former vice president). Like Jackson, Wilkinson had shut down the political process. Whether Jackson appreciated just how much Louisianians resented limitations on political mobilization remains in question. What is clear, however, is that Louisianians considered resisting martial law no less important than resisting British appeals. And to mobilize peacefully against martial law provided yet another opportunity for Louisianians to show their loyalty not only to the United States, but to the principles of the Revolution that they had always interpreted as the bedrock of nationality.

Jackson encountered a rough education in Louisiana. At each step he tripped yet another landmine of race, politics, and public administration. What accounts for this resistance? The general's stubbornness and authoritarianism were legendary, but they are insufficient to account for the resistance he encountered in Louisiana. The best way to understand Jackson is to see him as an outsider who misinterpreted the Louisianians like so many other observers.

Like Captain James Sterling of the Royal Navy, Jackson either did not grasp or actively ignored the way white Louisianians had sought proof that the United States welcomed them into the national community.

Jackson had yet to learn about the rules of public life in Louisiana just as he had to learn about the Louisianians themselves. Jackson's pronouncements after the 8 January showdown with the British are the most famous. In these comments the general thanked the people of Louisiana for their assistance and praised their loyalty. Yet throughout the invasion, Jackson vacillated between complimenting and condemning the Louisianians. While he might compliment Louisianians for their "patriotic zeal" or for the "spirit of unanimity . . . [that has] been exhibited . . . accompanied with such ardent patriotism," he was just as quick to express his suspicions.⁶⁵ When British troops landed, for example, he wrote *"I fear the enemy obtained,* their foothold through the treachery of the guard."⁶⁶ Exactly whom he blamed was uncertain, but Jackson was nonetheless quick to suspect the loyalty of the Louisianians. He believed Louisianians might yet abandon American nationality for Spanish rule, an opinion that made him perhaps the only senior American official to consider separatism a viable threat in 1814.⁶⁷ White Louisianians in turn saw Jackson as they had seen other Americans who came blustering into the Southwest delivering orders without considering the political aspirations or the racial fears of local residents.

Jackson's inflexibility only reinforced the prevailing attitude among American policymakers that co-opting the Louisianians was infinitely preferable to confrontation. Claiborne certainly believed as much, and this attitude earned him Jackson's scorn. Madison himself shared Claiborne's opinion. Although Madison initially avoided public involvement in the affair, Alexander Dallas, Monroe's successor as secretary of war, explained to Jackson that "the President views the subject, in its present aspect, with surprize and solicitude." Speaking through Dallas, Madison offered one piece of advice for Jackson: "a conciliatory deportment may be observed towards the state authorities, and the citizens of New Orleans."⁶⁸ But Madison acquired that wisdom the hard way during the War of 1812. He was still bitter toward state officials whose interpretation of state sovereignty had, he believed, jeopardized American operations during the war. Yet unlike Jackson, Madison was also acutely aware of conditions in Louisiana. From 1803 to 1809 documents had flooded Madison's State Department office reporting the Louisianians' revulsion at any limitations on their desire to expand the polity.

Jackson left New Orleans in April 1815, reveling in his victory over the British but smarting from the local resistance he received at the hands of Louisianians and Americans alike. As he prepared to depart, Jackson presented a farewell address that was as much a command as it was a compliment. "I shall soon leave you, my fellow-citizens," he wrote. "Defend your constitution and your country, as you have done, against all open attacks in war, and when peace returns, support the civil authority by an exact obedience of decree." To be called "fellow-citizens" was all the Louisianians claimed they wanted. The next sentence provided exactly the sort of political definition of nationhood that Louisianians had embraced since 1803. But it was also a list of behaviors that Louisianians already believed they obeyed in full.[69]

Jackson's ambivalence toward the Louisianians stemmed from the fact that at a certain level he never grasped the nature of the opposition. At no point did he seem to appreciate the resentment that Louisianians felt toward policies which they believed denied their membership in the national community, and which by definition denied incorporation. He attributed his problems instead to "a few Traitors — Tories and foreign emisaries amongst whom may be included, Colo Toussard the French consul — with the aid of the Feeble Governor W. C. C. in petto — Toussard is a wicked and dangerous man and ought to be removed from the U States as consul."[70]

The third Battle of New Orleans left wounds that outlasted Jackson's tenure in Louisiana. His defenders, many of them members of his staff, found themselves engaged in a lengthy political dispute with men whom Jackson had imprisoned or white Louisianians who had condemned the general's actions. Many of these men had tied their futures to Jackson, most notably Livingston.[71]

The internal disputes became so vicious that they overshadow more subtle, less controversial, but in the end more important developments during the war. If Andrew Jackson's deep imprint eventually showed that Louisiana's political landscape remained contentious, the War of 1812 had also proved that the government of the state of Louisiana was capable of preserving domestic order against foreign threats in all their forms. In addition, white Louisianians had shown conspicuous attachment throughout this period. In fact the invasion could not have offered a more complete refutation of the specific dangers that American policymakers had foreseen in 1803. White Louisianians had shown their willingness to fight all the threats to incorporation, whether foreign powers, nonwhites, or their own lack of sentimental attachment to the republic and their grasp of republican principles.

Proof of the Louisianians' success was not long in coming. On 22 February 1815 members of Congress thanked the various constituencies responsible for the victory at New Orleans. One resolution thanked the sailors and marines serving in the naval detachment on the Mississippi and the Gulf Coast; a second thanked the troops serving under Jackson. The third resolution (actually the first passed) was addressed directly "to the people of Louisiana and of

New Orleans." The resolution explained that members of Congress "entertain a high sense of the patriotism, fidelity, zeal and courage with which the people of the state of Louisiana promptly and unanimously stepped forth under circumstances of imminent danger from a powerful invading army." The resolution added that "Congress declare and proclaim that the brave Louisianians deserve well of the whole people of the United States."[72]

The document could not have been more satisfactory had the Louisianians drafted it themselves. There was more to this proclamation than mere compliments. It was the wording of those compliments that mattered, for they were entirely in keeping with the means that Louisianians had attempted to incorporate themselves. By announcing that the Louisianians "deserve well of the whole people of the United States," Congress dissolved the distinctions within the national community that Louisianians had condemned as artificial and unnecessary. Louisianians had articulated that principle most powerfully when they asked in the Remonstrance whether "political axioms on the Atlantic become problems when transferred to the shores of the Mississippi." And the basis of that unity was to be found in the Louisianians' sentiments, in their "patriotism, fidelity, zeal and courage," or, as Louisianians and Americans alike defined it, their attachment.

The two other congressional resolutions also provided a vital context for the first, together establishing a vision of nationhood that merged the local with the national. The message to the Louisianians celebrated a people who, in defense of their locality, contributed to the defense of the nation. The message to the navy celebrated those men who had served the federal regime directly through their enlistment in the federal military. Finally, the message to Jackson's troops celebrated the ability of the United States to combine local and federal resources, identifying "the officers and soldiers of the regular army, of the militia, and of the volunteers . . . the great proportion of which troops consisted of militia and volunteers."[73]

The resolutions described things as men like Madison believed things ought to work for the military in particular and with governance in general. Throughout the war, Madison's greatest frustrations had come from the very constitutional structure he had helped devise, one that undermined his ability to combine state and federal forces to realize his objectives, in this case the prosecution of military campaigns. In Louisiana, however, that system had worked. Despite Claiborne's problems with the militia and Jackson's squabbles with the Louisianians, during the invasion itself the United States proved able to effectively coordinate its military force. Once again, Louisiana had proven itself anomalous. In 1803 the anomalies had been ethnic and historical. Since then, however, Louisiana had proven most anomalous for the absence there of separatist activity and resistance to federal authority. Evidence that Louisiana would remain a stable part of the union had appeared sporadically throughout the territorial period. Not only did it come in abundance during the War of 1812, but it stood in marked contrast to events in the Northeast.

It is tempting to explain the regional differences in the War of 1812 in strictly partisan terms. Madison did indeed face greater opposition to his wartime strategy from northeastern Federalists than from southern or western Republicans. Yet the war reinforced political alliances as much as it reflected them. Throughout the West, local dynamics and national war policy intersected to convince western observers that the conflict was in fact a great victory. On the western and southern frontiers, white residents proved eager to join the fight so long as military strategy also fulfilled other objectives that included the preservation of the slave regime and the control or elimination of Indians.[74]

If the War of 1812 propelled the incorporation of Louisiana, peace in 1815 seemed even more promising. Since 1803, international conflict had always threatened incorporation, whether through the ambitions of foreign powers, the ability of nonwhites to exploit diplomatic contingency, or the consumption of resources that public officials would have preferred to devote to other projects. Since 1809 international conflict had overshadowed the construction of the mature territorial system and then the creation of the state of Louisiana. In 1815 the conflicts in Europe and the Americas came to end. The question was whether the transformation from a world at war to one at peace would provide the context for completing the process of incorporation.

PART IV

Attachment
(1812–1820)

8

"The State of LOUISIANA Now Has Her Voice"

Eligius Fromentin took a stand. In 1815 and again in 1816, the junior senator from Louisiana rose before his colleagues in the U.S. Senate to speak on behalf of his constituents in the Southwest. It marked something of a breakthrough for Fromentin, who had been almost silent since coming to Washington in 1813. His passivity was all the more striking given the intimate nature of the Senate, which even with the new additions from Louisiana consisted of only thirty-six men.

The residue from the War of 1812 had not altogether faded when Fromentin's first opportunity came on the morning of 14 December 1815. He reached the Senate chamber with a stack of petitions from his constituents and instructions from the Louisiana General Assembly to seek reimbursement for property lost and damaged during the Battle of New Orleans.[1] Four months later, on 19 March 1816, Fromentin spoke out again, this time to attack a proposed constitutional amendment that would have opened the selection of president and vice president to a popular vote.[2]

United States senator was a far cry from the French priest that Eligius Fromentin had once been. In three decades he underwent a professional and geographic transformation that began when he realized that his religious training and affluent background would be a detriment in Revolutionary France. He crossed the Atlantic, eventually settling in Maryland. Like those other prominent French Louisianians, Pierre Derbigny and François-Xavier Martin, Fromentin became an attorney, financing his legal education by working as a teacher. Also like Derbigny and Martin, Fromentin eventually opted for New Orleans, where the combination of Francophone culture and Old World privileges (both social and religious) seemed to offer the best of all possible worlds. Fromentin became an American citizen by default in 1803 when the United States acquired Louisiana. He also emerged as something of a scribe in territorial politics, serving first as clerk of the territorial House of Representatives and later as secretary of the constitutional convention. In 1813 he returned to the East Coast as a senator from the new state of Louisiana, filling the seat that Allan Bowie Magruder had occupied from October 1812 until his resignation only six months later.[3]

Eligius Fromentin was also an agent of incorporation. From 1812 to 1820 he and other people in Louisiana set out to build a state polity that would govern public affairs within the state and connect it to the rest of the nation. Much of this work included the effort of white Louisianians to consolidate power locally and establish influence nationally. But these final steps also included the extension of the state's political system over West Florida, for the incorporation of West Florida within Louisiana's polity was no less important than the Madison administration's acquisition of territory by force from Spain. Throughout this process, the political incorporation of Louisiana remained both a means and an end, just as it had been during the territorial period. Whites throughout the United States continued to believe that incorporation was critical to the preservation of the union and of the republican system of government that stood as its foundation. At the same time, people continued to find that the language of incorporation provided the means for their own advancement. Incorporation as end and as means remained the essential combination that made nationhood seem possible as well as attractive. The end for many in Louisiana was to create a political system that would deliver both local opportunities and national connections. The means was the rapid adoption of the tropes and vocabulary that had come to define the political culture of the Jeffersonian Republicans. It was a language that Louisianians learned fast.

"A Gentleman of Talents and Respectability Will Not Demean Himself"

With statehood came a question: How would politics operate in the absence of a territorial system? To a certain degree, the answer went on hold as a result of Claiborne's easy rise to state governor and the demands created by the War of 1812. But even before peace or the end of Claiborne's tenure in office, some things were becoming clear. Through the Louisiana constitution of 1812 and in the political order that took form in its wake, elite Louisianians finally achieved what they had sought for generations: an expansive political system that delivered new opportunities throughout the polity while also reinforcing their own authority.

In 1812, constitution writers in Louisiana began with the assumption that public officials needed considerable distance from their constituencies. They found their inspiration not in the new states of the American frontier, but in older polities. Whereas western states like Tennessee and Ohio (which preceded Louisiana) or Illinois and Indiana (which achieved statehood later in the 1810s) were home to an unprecedented number of elected offices and low property requirements either for suffrage or to hold office, the Louisiana constitution of 1812 promised to make Louisiana one of the least democratic states in the union. If there was one state that provided a model for Louisiana, it was Kentucky, no surprise given the fact that two of the men who served on the committee that drafted the constitution—James Brown and Allan Bowie Magruder—were themselves transplants from Kentucky. Brown himself had also helped write the Kentucky constitution of 1799, a document that circumscribed the political ambitions of western settlers, preserving power within an elite of planters and attorneys.[4]

The appeal of Kentucky to the Americans was obvious. Many of those who were not Kentuckians were Virginians, and Virginia Republicans had made something of an art of celebrating Kentucky as a state that had distilled the essence of Virginia's political culture, stripped of its worst characteristics and transferred to the western frontier. But it was equally attractive to the Louisianians on the convention. They, too, were members of an elite which worried that Louisiana would spin out of control without their guidance.

Delegates to the constitutional convention made their vision of the entire polity clear in their plan for the governorship, at no time more so than in their deliberations on 14 January 1812, as they searched for a middle ground between popular control and popular exclusion. According to reports in the *Louisiana Gazette*, popular election was never an option. "Virginia, New Jersey and other states, who elect by the joint vote of the General Assembly, always have good governors." The commentator compared the situation with that of states with direct election, claiming that they "cannot boast of their recent governors; beside the disgraceful tumult it raises in a state, it almost universally gives you the worst governor." And yet it would be unrepublican to remove all popular participation in selecting a governor.[5]

Delegates to the convention eventually settled on a dual system in which voters could cast their ballot for any candidate, but the legislature would select from the two candidates with the highest number of votes. As the constitution eventually explained, "votes shall be returned by the persons presiding over the elections to the seat of government addressed to the president of the Senate, and on the second day the general assembly, the members of the two houses shall meet in the House of Representatives, and immediately after the two candidates who shall have obtained the greatest number of votes, shall be ballotted for and the one having a majority of votes shall be governor."[6]

At first glance, the constitution weakened gubernatorial power, especially in comparison to the authority Claiborne had known under the territorial regime. The constitution limited the governor to a single four-year term. The state senate enjoyed oversight for gubernatorial appointments. And yet the Louisiana constitution of 1812 provided for one of the most powerful governors in the United States by giving him undisputed control over the state bureaucracy. Everyone from justice of the supreme court to justice of the peace owed his office to the governor's patronage. If the governor himself was now subject to the voters, his delegates were not. Statehood had done nothing to change the systems of appointment that had shaped the policymaking structure under territorial rule.

Executive control over the public workforce made Louisiana an anomaly in national and especially in regional terms. Public officials in most states, especially new states created on the frontier, had to undergo some form of election, whether they were county officials elected by their neighbors or state officials nominated by the governor and confirmed by the legislature. In Louisiana the government remained the governor's tool, which he was free to use and to populate as he chose.[7]

The governor, state legislators, and member of the U.S. House of Representatives were the only officials selected directly by the voters of Louisiana, and even that list overstates the electorate's power given the legislature's potential veto over gubernatorial selection. This remained the case despite the fact that the same Louisianians who attended the convention had for years complained about the limited number of elective offices. Their concern seemed to be at the highest levels of government rather than at the level of local office. In addition, consolidating power in the governor also consolidated power in New Orleans, the goal for so many of the planters, merchants, and attorneys who had crafted the constitution. The one exception to the governor's power was New Orleans itself, where the City Council remained a semiautonomous body of elected aldermen. Outside the Crescent City, however, daily governance would be the exclusive preserve of an officialdom appointed by the governor.

Much like their counterparts in other states (or, for that matter, at Philadelphia in 1787), Louisiana's white elite hoped to establish a government at once responsive to yet distinct from the public will.[8] They only carried that principle to a greater extreme. Creating this system enabled constitution writers in Louisiana to remain both Jeffersonian and elitist, Democratic-Republicans who believed the people had an ample public voice.[9] They pre-empted the sort of democratic system that they believed would corrupt Louisiana's political culture. During the convention Jean Blanque (a French migrant who had come to Louisiana as part of Pierre Clément Laussat's entourage during the brief period of French rule in the winter of 1803 but who chose to remain after the departure of French rule) spoke for many when he expressed his pleasure with a system in which "a gentleman of talents and respectability will not demean himself to stoop to the little dirty *whisky-drinking* principles that our modern demagogues adopt."[10]

Although slaves had repeatedly attacked the structure of Louisiana politics, moments of popular resistance to elite rule by white Louisianians—like the effective resistance of militiamen to mobilization during the War of 1812— were few and far between. Louisiana statehood initiated a form of entrenched power for the local elite that had been impossible under the territorial and colonial systems. Validated by forms of popular participation unprecedented in the history of white settlement in the Lower Mississippi Valley, liberated from the rule of outside appointees, elite Louisianians finally had what they had wanted for so long: political power that seemed rational and beneficial for the entire polity. These developments did not make a sham of political reform. Widespread white male suffrage, an impossibility under colonial rule, marked a momentous change in public life. Those same elites were also delivering white supremacy, either by attacking the status of free people of color or by organizing the defense against slave revolt. Nonetheless, statehood was striking for how *little* the state elite changed.[11]

Conditions in Louisiana seem all the more extraordinary given the prevailing historiographical vision of the frontiers of the United States as places characterized by political opportunity and contingency, where settlers of modest means deployed democratic rhetoric to establish themselves in the political arena. While Louisiana politics was similar to other states in so many ways, it differed on these matters of class. And that distinction is instructive. Louisiana was *not* like other frontier states and territories. This difference was less the product of Louisiana's ethnic or historical distinctiveness than the product of a social and economic structure that shared more with South Carolina and Virginia than with Missouri or Illinois. Its stable social order, its complex economy, its plantation agriculture, its cosmopolitan center in New Orleans, and, above all, its powerful, ambitious elite made Louisiana seem quite familiar to visitors from the southeastern United States. Those characteristics go a long way toward explaining why Louisiana was such a political anomaly on the overwhelmingly democratic frontier.

Representatives

This constitutional order established the system over which William C. C. Claiborne ruled from 1812 to 1816. And that rule would have to end, for the state constitution limited governors to a single term, the only substantial hindrance imposed on Louisiana's chief executive. Although he navigated Louisiana politics with increasing deftness, Claiborne never threw himself entirely into state politics in the way that other Americans or white Louisianians did. Indeed, the state constitutional structure proved quite comfortable to Claiborne. Meanwhile, the men surrounding him were scrambling to convert that constitutional structure into political practice. And as they built a boisterous political culture in Louisiana, these men reinforced the principle that ethnicity would not determine political outcomes.

Gubernatorial contests showed how this system would work. As Claiborne prepared to surrender power after a thirteen-year tenure as governor of both territory and state, his opponent from 1812, Jacques Villeré, was eager to take his place.[12] A half-dozen other candidates joined the fray, but it soon became evident that the real contest was between Villeré and Judge Joshua Lewis.[13] Lewis was a classic product of Thomas Jefferson's political kinship network. A Virginian, he had arrived in Louisiana in 1807 to assume an appointment on the territorial court, a post he kept as a member of the state judiciary. Nor was Lewis without local bona fides. Only a year before the election, Andrew Jackson had imprisoned Lewis for attempting to secure the release of Louis Louaillier. In 1816 Lewis attempted to convert Republican patronage into local electoral success.

It was a close race, with Villeré receiving 2,314 votes against Lewis' 2,145. The General Assembly upheld Villeré's popular victory by a vote of thirty-three to one (the identity of the dissenter remains unknown).[14] Villeré's election had a powerful appeal to Louisianians, especially to Creoles. It marked the first time that Louisiana was governed by a Creole. The 1816 gubernatorial election provided a particularly appropriate counterpoint to the Louisianians' colonial history. Villeré's own father had died under mysterious circumstances after being imprisoned for participating in the 1768 revolt. Family lore maintained that the Spanish had murdered him.[15] Whether true or not, the narratives of father and son seemed to constitute the fulfillment of the Louisianians' aspirations for local political power and broader political influence.

The election itself was never a moment of high drama. Instead, the 1816 gubernatorial contest delivered a quiet assurance to white Louisianians that they could take charge of the state polity.

If the 1816 gubernatorial race displayed the advantages of election, the 1820 contest reminded people of its pitfalls. It was a vicious contest, nowhere more so than among two former allies. As they squared off in the 1820 contest for governor, Pierre Derbigny and Jean Nöel Destrehan had come a long way since they carried the Remonstrance to Washington. They had initially joined forces in opposition to the federal government's restriction on electoral offices in the newly created Territory of Orleans. Both men eventually assumed public offices under the territorial government, but whereas Destrehan became increasingly comfortable working with the American territorial regime, Derbigny maintained his opposition to that system. His estrangement from Claiborne continued even when the governor appointed him to the state supreme court in 1813.

Destrehan was no doubt confident as the election approached. He had placed third in the 1812 and 1816 contests despite poorly managed campaigns.[16] He had powerful connections within rural planter society as well as in cosmopolitan New Orleans. When Destrehan's allies wrote in his favor, they could point to a record of service that embodied the story of Louisiana's recent political history. "We do not think that you have so soon forgotten the honorable mission with which he was entrusted, in 1804," stated a letter in support of Destrehan's candidacy, referring to his trip to Washington with the Remonstrance, "nor his services as member of the Legislative Council, then as a member of the Territorial Legislature, and, finally of the *Convention* to which we owe that Constitution." Destrehan joined the scramble for state office in 1812, holding a seat in the state senate from 1812 to 1817. In fifteen years his public career provided a narrative to match that of Louisiana itself. Destrehan had risen from extrainstitutional resistance to appointed power to participation in the coveted act of crafting a state polity and finally to elected office.[17]

By comparison, Derbigny seemed the embodiment of the ambitious newcomers who so often irritated Louisiana Creoles. Nonetheless, a suggestion of Derbigny's future came in 1803, when he secured work as a translator, a job that, among other things, placed his name alongside Claiborne's on the 23 December 1803 regulations for the Port of New Orleans. He grasped that title with a vengeance. He tried to position himself as the Louisianians' interpreter, speaking on their behalf to Americans who seemed unable to understand local concerns. At the first celebration of the Fourth of July in 1804, for example, Derbigny translated for New Orleans mayor James Watkins, attempting to convert Watkins' explanation of American political principles into terms Louisianians could understand. This activity on behalf of the American-imposed government came at the same moment that Derbigny and other white Louisianians hoped the Remonstrance would prove their understanding of those principles.[18]

Derbigny also hoped to make himself the interpreter among the Francophone population, and it was here that his most impressive piece of translation occurred. He attempted to forge a unified political interest that would pacify the often tense relations among Creoles, French Caribbean migrants, and Frenchmen like himself, whether he was helping craft the Remonstrance, representing the city of New Orleans against Edward Livingston's claim on the Batture, or even when he defended the French vessel *Duc de Montebello* against what critics called the high-handed activities of the U.S. Navy.[19] By 1820 Derbigny was ready to test that coalition. The question was not whether Louisianians would unite behind a Creole, as they had done in 1816. The real unknown was whether Derbigny could make that relationship work the other way around in his contest with Destrehan. Would Creoles support a foreign-born Louisianian over one of their own?

It was never close. Derbigny outpaced Destrehan throughout the state, including heavily Creole districts. The immigrant received 1,187 votes compared with the Creole's 627. What Derbigny could not know was that his intellectual construction would be his own undoing; for when the dust settled, it was another newcomer to Louisiana, Thomas Bolling Robertson, who had received the largest margin of victory yet in a gubernatorial election. Claiborne's secretary during the final years of territorial rule and a three-term congressman after statehood, Robertson enjoyed a 716-vote margin over Derbigny, and the General Assembly quickly confirmed his election. Robertson was only the latest transplanted Virginian to assume high office in Louisiana. Even in defeat, however, Derbigny had shown that one need not be a Creole to be a Louisianian. Pierre Derbigny would not be denied. He eventually won the gubernatorial race in 1828, only to die the following year after being thrown from his carriage.[20]

By the time Derbigny became governor, Louisiana politics was becoming the site of bitter ethnic disputes. But those conditions were not in place in early national Louisiana. Creoles, Frenchmen, Saint Domingue migrants, and Americans might form distinct cultural communities, but they created porous political communities. Membership and allegiance shifted according to circumstance.[21] Although the 1816 gubernatorial vote did show signs of ethnic polarization, this result may also have reflected the candidates' geographic constituencies, since Villeré's political career had been in the original Territory of Orleans, while Lewis emerged from the distinct parishes of West Florida.[22] This was hardly the world of diehard ethnic political communities described by generations of later scholars.

Consider as well the almost uniformly American face of Louisiana's congressional delegation. For unknown reasons, Louisiana's first two senators — Jean Nöel Destrehan and Allan Bowie Magruder — had the briefest of terms. Destrehan resigned before moving to Washington, while Magruder served only six months before returning to Louisiana. The state senate replaced Destrehan and Magruder with Thomas Posey and Eligius Fromentin, respectively. Posey, a Virginian and former Kentucky lieutenant governor, served through the end of an abbreviated term only to be replaced in 1813 by James Brown, a man of similar geographic background and even greater political clout. Meanwhile, William C. C. Claiborne was hardly prepared to retire altogether after leaving the governorship. Instead, he sought one last election that would finally return him to the East Coast. In the spring of 1817 the Louisiana General Assembly selected Claiborne for the U.S. Senate. Yet another Virginian, Henry Johnson, rounded out the list of five Americans (all born in Virginia) to serve Louisiana in the U.S. Senate between 1812 and 1820. Virginian Thomas Bolling Robertson also ensconced himself in the state's one seat in the House of Representatives from 1812 through 1818 (when poor health precipitated a sudden resignation), to be succeeded by Thomas Butler, a Pennsylvania native who finally broke the Virginians' monopoly. Robertson apparently made a complete recovery, for two years later he was ready to run for governor.[23]

From 1812 through 1820 Louisiana sent only one Louisianian (and a Frenchman, at that) to serve a full term in either house of Congress. Nor was that Louisianian, Eligius Fromentin, a permanent fixture. He did not seek reelection in 1818, preferring to return to Louisiana and creating a vacancy that presented James Brown with the opportunity of returning to the Senate in his place. Aside from a brief stint as a federal judge in the Florida Territory in the 1820s, where he endured the considerable animosity of territorial governor Andrew Jackson, Fromentin remained in Louisiana.[24]

This state of affairs was hardly the result of ethnic voting. After all, Louisianians commanded majorities in the popular vote as well as in the General Assembly. They could easily have chosen Louisianians for either the House or the Senate. Of course, many Louisianians demurred at serving in the federal legislature, since it would mean leaving the businesses they had struggled to build at home. Yet state legislators had other reasons for dispatching Americans as their representatives, reasons that stemmed from their observations of American politics. For all the resentment that some Louisianians may have harbored toward the agents of the territorial regime, they recognized that the benefits of statehood rested on influence, and newcomers had a hard time accruing influence. By contrast, Louisianians had every reason to believe that the Virginians would arrive in Washington with their influence already established. Political kinship could work both ways. Not only did it extend the administration's influence to Louisiana, but it might also provide the new state with power in Washington. Robertson came from a wealthy Virginia family that enjoyed contacts with the state and federal elite (often one and same under the Jeffersonian Republicans); friendship and kinship connected Brown to House Speaker Henry Clay as well as to the Breckinridges; Claiborne corresponded with presidents.[25] Louisiana dispatched men who seemed prepositioned to establish the new state's influence. The trip to Washington was as much a homecoming for these men as it was a departure. The Virginians from Louisiana participated in a circulation of political power on a national scale as public office and commercial opportunity transported men from East to West and back East again.[26]

For the one representative of Louisiana who did not come from Virginia, reaching Washington meant beginning the difficult process of establishing contact and influence from scratch. No sooner did Fromentin join the Senate in 1813 than he made tentative steps toward building the sort of connections that the Louisiana congressional delegation seemed to possess in abundance. This networking occurred in numerous, often subtle forms. In 1818, for example, he joined John Crittenden and John Williams (senators from Kentucky and Tennessee, respectively) in writing to Secretary of War John C. Calhoun to recommend a candidate for judge advocate of the army. Combining the testimonials of personal acquaintance and professional skill that had always formed the basis of recommendations for patronage in the early republic, they explained that "we are influenced . . . not more by . . . personal friendship . . . than from a conviction of his eminent abilities to discharge all the duties of that station." But this act entailed more than a solicitation for patronage. By writing to Calhoun, Fromentin attempted to build Louisiana's influence within the administration. By joining forces with senators from Kentucky and Tennessee, Fromentin joined a political network that might bind the nation's southwestern states. So at the same time that Fromentin publicly demanded that the Senate pay attention to Louisiana's concerns—whether seeking reimbursement for outstanding costs in 1815 or opposing constitutional amendments in 1816—he was working privately to cultivate the influence that would prove crucial if Congress or the administration was to listen.[27]

By delivering resources or by expressing local sentiments at the centers of power, Louisiana's senators and congressmen were supposed to overcome the sense of peripheral neglect that so many Louisianians associated with the territorial period, or for that matter with European colonialism. In the decade since Derbigny, Destrehan, and Sauve had delivered the Remonstrance, Louisianians had assumed that their own isolation was merely the artificial product of external policy. Fromentin reached Washington with the same vision. He carried the Louisianians' nationalist outlook as he embraced the belief that effective politics would overcome both distance and difference. With the impediments of colonialism and the territorial system finally removed, Louisianians intended to participate fully in national politics.

The fear of peripheral irrelevance continued to shape the position Louisiana's congressional delegation took on national affairs and party operations. When Republicans adopted the caucus system (an innovation fashioned by the Federalists) to choose their presidential nominee in 1816, for example, Robertson dispatched an alarming message to his constituents. "I dislike caucusing under every view that I can take of it—I never will sanction . . . so vile an usurpation," he wrote. "The election of President will, I fear, depend hereafter on the nomination of the members of congress: the intrigue and corruption that will grow out of it, I leave you to conceive." An anonymous editorial used less diplomatic terms: "Now, his [the caucus'] power and prowess being known, every ambitious demagogue strives to mount him."[28]

The caucus seemed to remove politics from the public arena and from the local elites who were still consolidating their power in Louisiana. Worse still, after a lengthy struggle to establish election as the basis of authority, the caucus threatened to restore arbitrary forms of power restricted to a distant and detached center. It would reverse the work of the state's congressional delegation and promise a return to the isolation of the colonial era. Louisianians eventually reached yet another pragmatic accommodation on caucusing. When the system showed no signs of abating, Louisiana politicians set out to build influence within the caucus.

"This New-Orleans Washingtoninan"

In 1812 an editorialist for the *Louisiana Gazette* had written that "this Territory heretofore had little to do with the general politics of the nation. Our interest led us to keep well with the rulers." Things had changed, however, and his comments served notice that Louisiana was eager to engage itself in national politics.[29] The activities of Louisiana officials provided a powerful lesson in the functional realities of American federalism. The struggle to secure relevance, let alone influence, in Washington was the final test of American politics. If election was supposed to facilitate good government within Louisiana, than it also had to deliver the same in Washington. Nationbuilding did not occur exclusively in the selection of Virginians for Congress or the activities of Fromentin. In a broad range of circumstances, Louisianians attempted to make nationhood a reality by creating new contexts within which Louisianians could exploit ongoing fears about the union to continue the old task of proving their attachment.

"In producing this great good, the state of LOUISIANA now has her voice," wrote one commentator in 1812. "She will have two Senators and one Representative on the floor of Congress, and three votes in the choice of the next *President*."[30] No sooner did Congress authorize statehood than Eligius Fromentin rose to the challenge. As one of Louisiana's presidential electors he campaigned vigorously on Madison's behalf. He published a pamphlet critical of DeWitt Clinton, claiming "it is high time" for frontier electors to participate. Clinton's allies were quick to respond. A Pittsburgh pamphleteer wrote sneeringly, "Let us hear, once more, this New-Orleans Washingtoninan." His condescending tone resuscitated old claims that the Louisianians exceeded their limited political knowledge. What the pamphleteer did not mention (or perhaps did not realize) was that this sort of debate was exactly what white Louisianians wanted. With each exchange Louisiana became a more entrenched participant in the national political dialogue. This development was entirely consistent with the activities of other new states, where an effective congressional delegation meant more than federal resources. A vigorous debate in Washington, with westerners as participants, would prove the benefits of membership in a national community. It would also prove that a nation did in fact exist.[31]

Exactly how frontier residents established themselves in a national political community is a story of the subtle appropriation of national issues. But it was hardly new to the Louisianians. Since 1803 they had exploited domestic and foreign threats — especially threats of disunion — to realize their immediate goals and to build long-term contacts. The seemingly imminent possibility of a British invasion throughout the War of 1812 (a nightmare that came true in 1814) provided fertile soil for efforts by the state legislature to conduct business in Washington. By reinforcing the administrative connections that were supposed to advance the war effort, Louisiana built political connections. A political structure that delivered resources to the defense of the Southwest against slave revolt and British invasion would reinforce the contractual relationship promising the Louisianians national identity in exchange for full membership in a national community.[32]

The Federalists were no less dangerous or less useful. The General Assembly and Louisiana's congressional delegation opposed Federalist policies as loudly as possible, especially when those policies reflected long-standing Federalist antipathy toward the rapid integration of westerners or foreigners.[33] Federalists provided the ideal foil for the Louisianians, creating the leverage they needed to secure a permanent place in national politics. After all, the Federalists outlasted those other dangerous American cabals like the Burr Conspiracy or the West Florida Convention or even the Napoleonic Wars. Partisan battle enabled Louisianians to join a united front that extended beyond the particular issues of the Southwest. Louisianians could claim that the Federalists, and not themselves, were the foreigners. Federalists espoused policies that were alien to a republican government and a free society, while Louisianians had proved their loyalty to American principles. Louisianans had imposed their own legal definition of citizenship since 1803, merging Article III with American rhetoric about national attachment to establish their equality with people born in the United States or naturalized through lengthy immigration procedures. Federalists may have enjoyed the legal status of citizen, but their identity with foreign principles made them aliens, much as Loyalists had been a generation before. Federalists were also enemies of nationhood itself, as Robertson claimed in an 1813 broadside claiming "our enemy counts on factious opposition to government, to disunion."[34] The most damning occasion of Federalist opposition to nationhood seemed to come in the winter of 1814–1815, when Federalists gathered in Hartford. Although the New Englanders who led the party felt increasingly isolated, they rejected any calls for separatism. Nonetheless, the secretive gathering with its regionally specific appeal provided ample evidence for outside observers to conclude that it was prelude to separatism. Coming so soon before the Battles of New Orleans, the Hartford Convention confirmed everything white Louisianians had said about the real sources of attachment and disunion. That many leading Republicans misread the Hartford Convention only made things better. The administration was so concerned about the fate of the union that it was quick to see separatism coming from any corner.[35]

There was more to this action than condemning a political opposition or building political coalitions with other Republicans. Jefferson may have argued that "we are all republicans—we are all federalists," but the rhetoric from Louisiana was less forgiving. Louisianians had established their nationality by convincing others of their belief in republican principles and their loyalty to the Republican party. Now they carried that argument to its logical end, attempting to cast the Federalists outside the national community. And they did so with tremendous consistency. Six months after statehood, for example, Louisiana voted for James Madison, beginning a quadrennial ritual of loyalty to the Jeffersonian Republicans that continued until the Jeffersonians themselves disintegrated.

As Louisiana compared itself to other places and as Louisianians compared themselves to other people, public events increasingly provided moments for thinly veiled apocryphal statements of attachment. The public celebrations that had been so important before, especially in the argument for statehood, retained their potency into the 1810s. Celebrations of the Fourth of July, which had been so important in the movement for statehood, remained important after 1812. In later years, commemorations of George Washington's birthday and the Louisiana Purchase became equally important moments of public display. After 1815 the Battle of New Orleans provided Louisianians with the chance to demonstrate a particular relationship between local custom and national affiliation. Louisianians portrayed the battle as a moment when they displayed their unique loyalty to the United States. The battle showed the advantages that came from a national system that respected the concerns of frontier residents. Louisianians claimed that the assistance of federal soldiers, sailors, and volunteers from other states was evidence of the attention and protection that had been absent under French and Spanish colonial rule. Nonetheless, they repeatedly claimed that the battle had been won through their own hard work and sacrifice. This military heroism had proved they were Americans.[36] In the ultimate fusion of nationalizing moments, a Louisianian named Renault organized a fireworks display for 4 July 1817 that also celebrated Washington and the Battle of New Orleans.[37]

Louisianians also attempted to use these moments of public display to prove that their customs did not compete with national identity. By linking religious services to the Fourth of July or the Battle of New Orleans, they argued that loyalty to the Catholic Church did not indicate disloyalty to the United States.[38] By holding masked balls or street carnivals on Washington's Birthday, they tried to normalize and nationalize activities that predated the Louisiana Purchase. In all of these circumstances, they attempted to realize their own vision of the rights and responsibilities of American citizens.[39]

"You Have the Honor to be a Louisianan"

While white Louisianians were struggling to join the national polity, white men in West Florida attempted to incorporate themselves into the state polity. West Floridians proved no less pragmatic in their efforts to build influence in broader polities. In the immediate aftermath of the annexation, they had manipulated diplomatic tensions (and the anxieties of American officials like Claiborne and Holmes) to demand time and resources that the administration would have preferred to direct elsewhere. In the years that followed, the same pragmatism proved equally important in West Florida.

West Floridians began developing their political voice before Louisiana even became a state by successfully demanding that they be included in the Territory of Orleans and not in the Mississippi Territory. There were strategic reasons to do so, for Orleans was a prosperous territory on the verge of statehood, unlike the sparsely populated Territory of Mississippi, which lacked a commercial center like New Orleans. In the process of defending Louisiana's territorial pretensions, however, they also incorporated themselves into Louisiana politics.[40] White Louisianians were infinitely pleased by this state of affairs. "In particular," explained the Louisiana legislature in 1812, "they felicitate ... in the passage of the resolution annexing a large portion of West Florida to the state of Louisiana. They are convinced of the political value of this acquisition, and they deeply appreciate the strict attention and regard which the general government has thus manifest to this section of the union."[41]

In August 1812 the Louisiana General Assembly completed this acquisition by extending legislative apportionment to encompass West Florida.[42] West Floridians immediately rushed to build their own political influence. The West Floridian Joshua Lewis was a close second to Villeré in the 1816 gubernatorial election. When Thomas Bolling Robertson surrendered his seat in the House of Representatives in 1818, Thomas Butler, who had moved to West Florida from Kentucky soon after the 1810 annexation, defeated a slate of aspiring Louisiana politicians. After his brief stint as president of the Republic of West Florida, Fulwar Skipwith soon ran for more humble office in the state of Louisiana. Although he was unsuccessful in an 1816 run for Congress, by 1814 he was the president of the Louisiana Senate.

James Sterrett believed the incorporation of West Florida was already under way when he wrote a letter to his friend, Nathaniel Evans, in May 1814. The two men were old friends who had been separated by political boundaries. Sterrett lived on the west side of the Mississippi, Evans on the east. Both men considered themselves Americans, but Evans' decision to settle in West Florida made him a Spanish subject. In 1810 Evans found his nationality restored through the annexation of West Florida. "As you have the honor to be a Louisianan I address you on the approaching election," Sterrett wrote to Evans in 1814, and in this brief statement he told volumes about Louisiana's incorporation and its future.[43] West Floridians were indeed reinventing themselves as citizens of Louisiana and in the process rehabilitated themselves, years after they had left the United States for Spanish West Florida. While they continued to distinguish themselves from the Francophone Louisianians who constituted the majority of the population, they nonetheless believed that West Florida was a permanent fixture within Louisiana.

Representation and Corruption

As Louisiana's politicians created networks that reached to Washington or throughout West Florida, they were also busy completing Louisiana's local incorporation into the standards of an emerging American political culture. Before 1812 the territorial system itself and its advocates had always been easy targets, since the absence of public accountability in the form of election was the logical basis for corruption. After 1812 people in Louisiana reconfigured their definitions of virtue and corruption to accommodate statehood. They also shifted their focus away from debating the limitations of the territorial system and toward the individual character of politicians. Both strategies called conspicuous attention to the way in which Louisiana had become home to an American political language that combined republican and democratic concepts.

Election itself created new tools for political debate. First among these was the assumption that electioneering immediately threatened corruption. In every election cycle, newspapers, broadsides, and letters made assertions typical of what one observer wrote of the 1818 elections: "never perhaps was an election marked with so much low intrigue, as that which commences this day." Maybe so, but in protesting so loudly about corruption, politically active white Louisianians could show their attachment to an honest—what they called "American"—political system.[44]

Likewise, when Villeré thanked the legislature for its approbation in his 1816 inaugural, the *Louisiana Gazette* (which had endorsed Lewis) immediately reported: "All his excellency's gratitude, it would seem is due to the 'general assembly.' He begins pretty early to shew his contempt for the *swinish multitude,* his own and his 'general assembly's' *legitimate masters.*"[45] These accusations in 1816 touched a raw nerve, and not only with Villeré. Robertson acknowledged as much in his December 1820 inaugural address: "Government is not that mysterious difficulty which, for bad purposes it has been represented to be: it is not so far above the powers of ordinary capacity as art and cunning would make us believe." His strenuous assertions about how people should conceive of politics also acknowledged a world in which people assumed that politics itself fueled corruption.[46]

These accusations seem particularly appropriate given the corruption that later came to define Louisiana politics in the American consciousness. But the accusations of the 1810s were little different from what people were saying throughout the United States. Louisiana seemed no more corrupt than most other states. Instead, whites had completed the process of incorporating the tropes of political debate.

Accusations of corruption are all the more striking given the absence of any public conversation about the French and English languages. That the Francophone and Anglophone communities had communication problems was abundantly clear, yet only a certain form of that miscommunication became fodder for the political arena. Commentators rarely accused their opponents of failing to speak the French language of Louisiana's majority or the English that was the standard of American public discourse. Rather, it was the failure of officials to communicate their intentions clearly or to reflect their constituencies honestly that commanded public debate. A candidate who spoke only one language was merely limited. A candidate who misrepresented himself—a candidate who was not candid—was corrupt. A candidate who did not understand the principles of republican politics or who lacked loyalty to the Jeffersonian Republicans was un-American.[47]

The General Assembly responded to the ongoing fears about political corruption with legislation designed to sustain order and virtue in the political process. In 1813 the General Assembly passed an act "to regulate the politics of the town of St. Francis." In 1819 the Assembly altered election procedures in order "to support the privilege of free suffrage in election, to prohibit all undue influence thereon, and to prescribe the manner of determining contested elections." Legislators struggled to reinforce a stable political system based on public expression and electoral representation.[48]

Louisiana politicians deployed all the threats to the new political order when it came to one Pierre Dormenon. Immediately after the first statewide elections, residents of Pointe Coupée rushed a petition asking the legislature not to seat Dormenon. They complained of everything from insecure ballot boxes to nonresident voters. The accusations expressed a profound fear that Louisiana's newfound electoral system was in danger of corruption.[49]

When the state legislature eventually decided to expel Pierre Dormenon, it was for a crime far worse than rigging an election. A special committee concluded that he "headed, aided and assisted the negroes of St. Domingo in the horrible massacres and other outrages against the whites." Dormenon had been a civil official in Saint Domingue in 1793, which his accusers claimed was a front for his command of "an army of 1500 assassins." Other critics attempted to have him disbarred. So the legislature banished Dormenon, expelling him from the legislature explicitly for the chicanery of his electioneering and implicitly for his conspiracy across racial lines. To whites this result was only appropriate, for Dormenon had already placed himself outside the political arena. Whether by his campaign tactics or his activities in Saint Domingue, he had rejected republican politics. A crusade to disbar him was equally appropriate, for the law was supposed to establish the rules of civil behavior that Dormenon had ignored. Only when evidence subsequently absolved Dormenon of participation in the revolt did the Louisiana Supreme Court order his reinstatement.[50]

The Dormenon episode gave legislators the opportunity to restate their principles. Their reaction showed how much dissenters of all races helped define politics for whites even as those dissenters proposed models of their own. The challenge for public officials was to preserve their system and make it work in a way that balanced political freedom with public order.

So if statehood brought with it a reinforced elite, an unelected bureaucracy, and restrictions on participation by nonwhites, then what were the boundaries of democracy in Louisiana? Democratic rhetoric, rather than democracy itself, proved to be the greatest winner. This rhetoric established the foundation for a wholesale critique of the territorial regime and colonial rule. After statehood it became a standard device for condemning political adversaries. And yet Louisiana elites felt no need to change the arrangement of power. There was no move for constitutional amendment after the 1816 and 1820 elections led worried politicos to criticize legislative approval for the popular vote. New western states like Missouri, Ohio, and Tennessee were home to vigorous democratic movements against entrenched elites. Though never altogether successful, the attack on established power did provide opportunities for aspiring politicians of modest background. No such conditions existed in Louisiana.[51]

The emerging system of state politics became particularly clear in Louisiana's reception of two national figures. Both Henry Clay and Andrew Jackson visited New Orleans in 1819. For Clay, this trip had been long in coming. For Jackson, it was a cautious return. Both men enjoyed a warm welcome.[52] Not only had many Louisianians forgiven the general for his excesses, but why would Louisianians do anything else than welcome Jackson in such nationalizing terms?[53] In their resistance to the British and to Jackson himself, white Louisianians had found yet another means to call conspicuous attention to their attachments to the United States and to free government. Now, Jackson's return presented a similar opportunity. Once again nationhood would serve the purpose of incorporation, for in their claims to attachment Louisianians demanded membership in a broader national community.[54]

The celebrations of Clay and Jackson turned into conflict during the heated presidential campaigns of the 1820s.[55] But that reverence should not be understood in exclusively ironic terms. To the contrary, it made perfect sense, especially in marked contrast to comments about Jefferson, Madison, and Monroe. The three Virginia presidents occupied a special place in the celebratory politics of Louisiana. With their intimate connections to the Louisiana Purchase, Jefferson, Madison, and Monroe were the unchallenged leaders of republican (and Republican) America. Loyalty to them often served as a way for Louisianians to measure each other's political sentiments. But they were distant figures whose political connections to Louisiana seemed more sentimental than manifest. Whatever Clay and Jackson's own disagreements on national policy, Louisianians saw them together as part of a regional interest that would solidify Louisiana's place in national politics.

9

Louisiana

The ships came and went in ever-increasing numbers. It was as everybody had expected. When the Spanish restricted American trade through New Orleans in 1802, Jefferson and Madison had worried about foreign efforts to bottle up the flow of trade goods from the West. As civil and military officials in Louisiana had battled over commercial policy in 1809 and 1810, they debated how best to foster trade at a moment of increasingly complex international tensions. In 1812 the United States had gone to war against Great Britain to remove foreign restrictions on trade. And after 1815 it seemed that diplomatic changes would finally bring about the booming domestic economy that so many had predicted.

If Auguste Macarty had his way, the government would see to it that New Orleans prospered from this trade. Macarty was elected mayor in September 1815 after brief service in the New Orleans City Council, and began work just as the diplomatic conflicts that were so important to life in the Crescent City came to an end. In January 1818 he attempted to exploit the political connections that Louisianians hoped they had established in Washington. So he wrote to his congressman. In a letter to Thomas Bolling Robertson on behalf of the City Council, Macarty pleaded for federal money to construct a new quay for the Port of New Orleans to handle the additional maritime traffic. Council members concluded that this action alone was not sufficient. Joseph

Rouffignac, Ferdinand Percy, and Zénon Cavélier decided "to call in a body on Mr. Henry Johnson, the newly elected Senator from the State of Louisiana . . . to hand him a copy of the petition."[1]

This was more than a political test. It was an administrative necessity. At the same time that white men in Louisiana were building a raucous state political system with an elaborate set of national political connections, they were also attempting to realize their goals in public policy. Some of their concerns were the same: to connect the local to the national, to create rational systems of power, to solidify the prerogatives of the local elite. Politics and administration had proceeded on overlapping trajectories. And as a system of state politics solidified, so too did a system of state administration. At the same time, politics and public policy in the state of Louisiana had important distinctions, just as they had had during the territorial period.

The Monroe administration in Washington and the Villeré administration in Louisiana oversaw the final stages of administrative incorporation, a process that would emerge through the relationship between federal and state governments. And just as foreign and domestic policymaking intersected under the territorial regime, the final administrative incorporation of Louisiana included changes to domestic as well as foreign policy. But while Louisiana's political system became an increasingly insular collection of elite white men, nonwhites and nonelites remained vital players in the administrative processes, even as the very system of public administration they served was specifically designed to promote the exclusion of nonwhites. In the 1810s policymaking and institutional practice completed the process of incorporation.

The question after 1812 was not only whether a state could fill the shoes of the territorial government, but also what kind of relationship would exist between state and federal regimes. After years of chafing under federal rule, whites in Louisiana were only the latest in a long line of westerners to conclude that their administrative future depended upon the federal government. In the process of completing institutional incorporation, white Louisianians polished their language of nationhood. Meanwhile, in the process of completing administrative incorporation, federal policymaking continued their education in governance.

"The Exercise of Their Barbarous Custom"

As they set out to complete the revisions to the Louisiana Purchase, policymakers finally abandoned local diplomacy. The problems had been evident for years. Whether it was the unpredictability of men like George Mathews, the troublesome activities of filibusterers like Augustus Magee, or the nagging autonomy of Indians like the Caddo, members of the administration had been frustrated by what they saw as the occasional dangers of diplomatic latitude. Previously, the considerable advantages of an extended system of governance that seemed capable of handling diplomatic concerns had offset those dangers. But those advantages had stemmed primarily from the exigencies of international conflict. After 1815 a combination of diplomatic changes in the transatlantic community and generational changes in the American political leadership combined to weaken the support in Washington that had always been necessary for local diplomacy. These changes in distant capitals brought immediate consequences to people in Louisiana.

American policymakers began to change the rules because they considered 1815 a watershed. With Napoleon permanently exiled to St. Helena, two decades of European warfare finally came to an end. With the monarchist regime restored in Spain, the United States once again had an acceptable negotiating partner. And with the royalist political organizations that emerged in Spanish America during the Napoleonic invasion changing into independence movements, the Spanish were eager to reach an accord with the United States. The administration was eager to capitalize on this state of affairs. In February 1815 Monroe reported to the Senate Military Committee that "with Spain our affairs are yet unsettled." Nonetheless, with peace restored in Europe and the Americas, and with Spain reeling from dissent within the empire, Monroe believed that "the period is perhaps arrived when it may be practicable to settle on just and honorable conditions."[2] In December 1815 Monroe continued to believe that the British might attempt to interfere in Louisiana. But as he informed John Quincy Adams, then serving as American minister to Great Britain, "as well might the British Government send an army to Philadelphia or to Charlestown." Louisiana was so thoroughly incorporated that its strategic vulnerability was finally fading.[3]

The changes to the federal policymaking structure were dramatic. Madison himself took steps to rein in the international activities of southwestern officials during his last two years in office.[4] Monroe likewise asserted his control over the State Department employees who remained in the state of Louisiana. After more than a decade in which port officials had enjoyed relative independence, for example, Monroe dispatched a terse letter to Pierre Duplessis, the latest in a long line of New Orleans marshals at the center of diplomatic controversy. Duplessis had made his mark in 1813, when his order for the Irishman Laverty to move forty miles from the Mississippi River precipitated the Louisiana Supreme Court case that upheld the principles of citizenship first established in *Desbois' Case*. In November 1815 Monroe learned that Duplessis had issued "certificates of citizenship to American Seamen, men of color, distinct from those which you give to other seamen of the United States." He explained that "it is not known that this practice is prescribed by Law, or by any regulation founded on it." In short, Duplessis should toe the federal line and employ a strict observance of the law. This case was particularly telling. Since 1803 officials in Louisiana had asserted their autonomy in matters of citizenship and race. Although Monroe had no particular sympathy for African Americans, in the interest of reinforcing the administration's authority he unintentionally undermined the campaign for white supremacy.[5]

Monroe carried these administrative and diplomatic lessons with him into the presidency. He continued the effort to suppress filibusters, control acts of local diplomacy, and catalyze border negotiations with Spain.[6] Far from welcoming Andrew Jackson's incursions into the Florida peninsula in 1817, for example, Monroe feared that these operations would upset negotiations in Europe.[7]

Perhaps it was fitting that James Monroe also directed the final construction of a Louisiana Purchase consistent with American goals. The treaty he had signed in Paris had frustrated Monroe since 1803. He focused his energies as a diplomat and later as secretary of state on rewriting the contested boundaries of Louisiana. In his first annual message as president, issued in November 1817, Monroe happily reported that after considerable delays "a disposition has been lately shown by the Spanish Government to move in the negotiation, which has been met by this Government, and should the conciliatory and friendly policy which has invariably guided our councils be reciprocated, a just and satisfactory arrangement may be expected."[8] A final resolution arrived in 1819, when diplomats signed the Transcontinental Treaty. The treaty did not so much rewrite the Louisiana Purchase as fill in the gaps. Where the Purchase referred to a vaguely defined political entity (the Louisiana that Spain retroceded to France in 1800), the Transcontinental Treaty employed specific points of reference. Those references were generally in accord with what American policymakers wanted. The Spanish surrendered any residual claim to the Floridas, while the United States abandoned its claims to lands west of the Sabine River. Where the Louisiana Purchase provided for an awkward transfer of power and the departure of French and Spanish officials, the Transcontinental Treaty preserved the boundary between foreign and domestic by mandating that all Spanish troops would be off the American soil defined by the treaty within six months. Such language was vital to American officials who remembered just how long it had taken Spanish troops to depart New Orleans after the Purchase.[9]

The Transcontintal Treaty was an agreement of the sort the United States had wanted in 1803. Not only was the United States finally able to press its terms on the Europeans, but the wording of the Transcontinental Treaty was more in keeping with the draft document that Madison had dispatched with Monroe in March 1803. Replacing the vagaries of Article III in the Louisiana Purchase was Article VI in the Transcontintal Treaty, which was both more thorough and more specific. "The Inhabitants of the territories which His Catholic Majesty cedes to the United States by this Treaty, shall be incorporated in the Union of the United States, as soon as may be consistent with the principles of the Federal Constitution, and admitted to the enjoyment of all the privileges, rights and immunities of the citizens of the United States." The treaty still did not specify race, but the administration had made clear that its interpretation of "Inhabitants" referred only to whites.[10]

Ratified by the Senate in 1821, the Transcontinental Treaty marked an end to the troublesome, explosive arguments about the nation's southwestern border. That Monroe's own secretary of state, John Quincy Adams, showed little interest in local diplomacy was equally appropriate. By the time Adams joined the cabinet, the system that had reigned in Louisiana for the fifteen years following the Purchase had outlived its utility. Adams had been instrumental in negotiating the Transcontinental Treaty, but he rarely involved himself in the life of the people who lived on the borderlands.

John Quincy Adams enjoys a special reverence from historians, whether for the breadth of his public service, the thoughtfulness of his political commentary, or the power of his arguments against slavery. But a primary reason diplomatic historians have celebrated Adams as secretary of state was his effort to reorganize and consolidate authority within the State Department. In other words, Adams seems "modern" in his bureaucratic methodology. Such a scholarly approach makes sense, given the difficulty most historians have shown in seeing beyond the Progressive lens through which they interpret American public administration. But Adams' reforms in State Department policy constituted far more than a call for greater efficiency. They constituted a fundamental *redefinition* of efficiency. Disconnected from the realities of territorial governance and the benefits that his predecessors saw in a distributed system of federal power in the first years following the Louisiana Purchase, Adams began the process of centralizing foreign policymaking in Washington. These changes did indeed bring benefits to diplomatic operations, but they also indicated Adams' unwillingness to fully engage people beyond a particular community of elites. And that inability to distribute power or to co-opt elites on distant frontiers cost Adams dearly during his presidency.[11]

Adams was also not alone in seeking these sorts of changes. The War of 1812 led Madison, Monroe, and especially an emerging generation of younger political leaders to reconceptualize their definition of an effective government.

Local diplomacy lent itself to the sort of diffuse system of governance which many had endorsed since 1776, and which the Republicans attempted to implement once Jefferson assumed the presidency. After 1815, however, these men decided that decentralizing diplomatic and military affairs did more to undermine efficiency than to promote it.[12]

The possibilities and dangers that Monroe, Adams, and other American policymakers saw on the horizon after 1815 help account for the rapid decline of local diplomacy in the years that followed. Yet this change was also the result of local developments in the southwestern borderlands, and rightly so. Local diplomacy had always taken form in an intersection of diplomatic policymaking in Washington and Louisiana. Now events in Europe and throughout the Americas would dictate just how much the administration would be able to curtail diplomatic latitude. Local diplomacy may have ceased to shape the outcome of international affairs, but local officials continued to assume certain diplomatic prerogatives. And the contours of this new set of circumstances had less to do with priorities within the administration than with the realities of governing a large republic with distinct political constituencies and multiracial frontiers.

Since 1803 the strategic situation in the Southwest had enabled the Caddo to position themselves as a polity entitled to diplomatic engagement and political autonomy. With the Spanish removed from the equation in 1821, first by the Transcontinental Treaty and then by Mexican independence, the U.S. government could treat the Caddo as domestic dependents rather than independent actors. The Caddo suffered accordingly. Secretary of War John C. Calhoun expressed the administration's goals in no uncertain terms in an 1818 letter to John Jamison. He informed the Indian agent assigned to western Louisiana that "the Indians must be made to yield the exercise of their barbarous custom of retaliation upon murderers, to the milder influence of our laws."[13]

In 1820 Jamison's successor, George Gray, concluded that Dehahuit still "has more influence with those small tribes residing on Red River and the Province of Texas than any Indian within the limits of the Agency. In fact they are controlled by him entirely."[14] But if Dehahuit's power among the Caddo remained intact, his influence outside the Indian world was crumbling. By settling the boundaries between the United States and Spanish America, the Transcontinental Treaty also eliminated the Neutral Ground. The United States first forced the Caddo off American soil. The Caddo chose east Texas, only to find themselves forcibly removed to Oklahoma following the annexation of Texas by the United States. There they joined the Choctaw, for whom American control east of the Mississippi had also meant forced relocation on the Trail of Tears.[15]

In much the same way that local diplomacy emerged both in New Orleans and on the western borderlands, so too did it collapse in those two locales, but with different outcomes. While the Indians of the borderlands lamented the state of diplomatic affairs, white officials in New Orleans reaped new benefits. For years council members had complained that the navy's facilities restricted the city's commercial prospects. It was these concerns which led Auguste Macarty to contact Robertson on behalf of the City Council in 1818, but as early as 1812 they had concluded that additional space had become "indispensable for the loading and unloading of the ships whose number increases each day and is already disproportionate with the small extent which the said Port offers."[16] In 1815, when peace in both Europe and the United States ended decades of maritime warfare, the council reported that "many vessels are expected in the port."[17] Council members decided that the city could risk neither delay nor capitulation to naval officers who wanted to control precious dock space. Failure to increase port facilities might close the window of opportunity for commercial growth. With the federal strings removed by statehood, peace with Britain restored by the Treaty of Ghent, and the Napoleonic contest settled, the City Council decided it was time to take charge of the port.

"Since its incorporation into the American union," the council wrote to Congress in 1815, "New Orleans having rapidly increased, and being destined to become the great emporium of the Western part of the United States of America," it was essential that the federal government remove any obstacles to local prosperity. Incorporation would be a reality only so long as council members could sustain political linkages in Washington, and so long as Washington contributed to a political economy that promoted regional prosperity.[18]

Their foil was Daniel Patterson, commander of the New Orleans Naval Station. Patterson was no neophyte to Louisiana politics, nor was he a troublemaker like David Porter. Patterson had in fact enjoyed a rather amicable relationship with civil officials. He had arrived in New Orleans as a junior officer, and was thoroughly familiar with the area before succeeding Captain John Shaw during the War of 1812. Soon after coordinating naval defenses against the British invasion of 1814–15, however, Patterson faced an even more resourceful opponent in the City Council. Without Britain as a unifying enemy, the conflicts between the various public agencies in New Orleans that had been so common in the late territorial period exploded.

Hoping to exploit the commercial prosperity that seemed just over the horizon, the council expanded berthing facilities with little regard for the navy's protests. Patterson objected to these initiatives but found little support in Washington. By 1815 Secretary of the Navy Benjamin Crowninshield had already decided that the navy had to respect civilian jurisdiction. He informed Patterson that he should "endeavour to restrain the Commanders of Gun

Boats and other vessels from committing any unnecessary violence upon the rights of others." Crowninshield believed that naval officers had a tendency "to harass those vessels whose objects and pursuits appear to be honest & lawful." The courts and not the navy should take charge of local law enforcement. Crowninshield made the strategic decision to focus the navy's activities on the Gulf of Mexico, where his men could pursue pirates and smugglers while staying free of any municipal entanglements. This letter bore Madison's stamp, for the president had drafted specific orders to Crowninshield that limited the navy's domestic involvement as well as its institutional freedom.[19]

Crowninshield's statement seemed a long time coming for municipal officials who had chafed at the navy's heavy-handed policy. The new orders from the secretary of the navy finally created the opportunity council members needed to take charge of the port. The council expelled the navy from much of its dockyard space, ignoring Patterson's objections. In 1818 the council expanded the port further to create a separate facility for steamboats, eager to give those newfangled and often dangerous vessels a wide berth. Patterson was still in New Orleans in 1820, but he had been thoroughly subdued.[20] On 15 April 1819, for example, the council expressed concern "that there is a great quantity of gun powder aboard the pontoon and on another boat on the right bank of the river in front of the City." The council resolved that "a Committee shall be appointed to interview the Commodore and obtain from him the assurances that he will order the removal of said ships to a safe distance . . . should these ships be under his orders." No negotiation, no allowance for diplomatic contingency; the council confidently assumed that Patterson would do as it wished.[21]

The conflict between the New Orleans City Council and the U.S. Navy was more than a power struggle between institutions with a long history of antagonism. It was part of a broader effort to determine the distribution of power as well as the very purposes of public administration. Council members were committed to expanding commercial opportunity (hardly surprising, since the private fortunes of most members were in some way dependent on the city's trade). According to the City Council, commercial regulation was supposed to be an economic stimulus. By contrast, naval officers had persistently treated commercial regulation in the port as a police function to be performed by the navy. Their task was to intercept smugglers, slave traders, and privateers. If trade suffered or if Louisianians lost the profits of their illicit commerce, that was not the navy's concern. Louisianians would have to learn the cost of law enforcement. Naval officers considered this lesson all the more important because the City Council had a notorious record of laxness with regard to smuggling and piracy.[22]

Of course, illicit trade continued in Louisiana, and members of the City Council varied in the tacit endorsement and public condemnation of that trade. The tale of pirates and smugglers remains an engaging one, and with a personality as colorful as Jean Lafitte at center stage, why should it be anything else? Yet a discussion of commerce in New Orleans that focuses exclusively on smuggling and privacy obscures the very real battle to determine what role commercial regulation would serve and which agency of government — municipal, state, or federal — would determine the rules.

The battle between the City Council and the U.S. Navy constituted a tentative attempt to determine the boundaries of federal authority. Yet the showdown should not be taken as evidence of inevitable conflict between local and federal agencies. On the contrary, relations between the state and federal leadership remained generally cordial. The governor and the legislature welcomed the federal government's commitment to military defense and internal improvements. They demanded that the navy institute a more aggressive campaign against pirates in the Gulf of Mexico even as the New Orleans City Council constricted naval operations. The General Assembly resolved that Villeré "be required to solicit the President of the United States, to order that a sufficient Naval force be stationed on our coast, to protect us against the depredations of pirates which desolate them, and which impede our communications with Vera Cruz, and other Spanish ports in the Gulf of Mexico."[23] Officials in the state of Louisiana continued to embrace common priorities of regional development and racial supremacy. Any clashes with federal officials had less to do with constitutional principles or foreign policy than with political economy.

"They May Be Employed for Everything"

The very adoption of political tropes that had secured Louisiana's political incorporation left the state government with few options when it came to the practicalities of funding a government. In 1816, for example, the *Louisiana Courier* reminded its readers of Jefferson's own adage "A wise and frugal government shall not take from the mouth of labor the bread it has earned." An editorial three weeks later condemned "These internal taxes, *covering our land with officers, and opening our doors to their intrusion.*"[24] With political rhetoric validating private revulsion to taxation, public officials had to find some means of creating an effective political economy within the confines of a small state apparatus. State leaders sought a solution through an active partnership with the federal government. Their political economy eventually called on the resources of public and private, state and federal, slave and free.

Even as they celebrated the end of territorial rule, state leaders never attempted to expel the federal government. Weaned on a territorial system in which the federal government *was* the government, they considered federal activities essential to their security and prosperity. While the federal government delivered little in the way of direct funding for local projects, it nonetheless absorbed the cost of services that the state needed but could not afford. Each federal department was in some way vital to sustaining a government in Louisiana long after statehood supposedly removed federal influence.

In various areas of public policy, the federal government had to settle the threats to attachment that lingered from 1803. By the 1810s the landmark acts of governance passed from 1805 to 1808—the Land Title Act, the Black Code, and the *Civil Digest*—were having their effect. Not only did they create rules of conduct for private individuals, but they provided public officials with the guidelines they wanted. But implementing those key pieces of legislation would continue to shape the workings of government.

The trying process of settling land claims continued at a slow pace, connecting the territorial period to statehood in a single narrative of frustration and delay. The problems outlasted even Gallatin's lengthy tenure at the Treasury Department.[25] State officials were no less eager to settle the land-claim issue than their federal counterparts, in part because many of them owned questionable claims. They worried that this policy "arrests the hand of improvement, and weakens the energies of enterprise and industry, which flourish in their natural vigor on a soil where the title thereof is indisputable."[26] And while claims were never settled in accord with the ambitious goals of the Land Act of 1805, the *Civil Digest* provided rules that governed how people used land once they had established title. The successful definition of property was all the more important since it provided an intellectual foundation for denying the property of some in Louisiana and, equally important, defining others in Louisiana *as* property. This vision applied on both a local and an international scale. At the same time that state and federal officials worked in concert to establish legal claims throughout Louisiana, American negotiators worked on the biggest land claim of all: the Louisiana Purchase itself. The deed that completed the federal claim to that land—the Transcontinental Treaty—provided the United States with the means to invalidate Caddo sovereignty.

As in so many aspects of public life, federal, state, and local officials never forgot that one mission trumped any institutional disagreements. Public officials at all levels remained committed to racial supremacy. Exclusion—the campaign to keep nonwhites outside the national community and the national polity—could only promote incorporation. The mutually reinforcing principles of racial supremacy and economic development came together in daily governance. Evicting Indians from desirable land created new opportunities for settlement. Preserving slavery intact ensured an ample labor source for the difficult task of working crops in Louisiana's unforgiving climate.

That unfree labor was essential to the American economy is obvious. That unfree labor in particular — and nonwhites in general — could be essential to public policymaking is another matter altogether. Yet even as the structures of governance created new forms of exclusion for slaves, Indians, and free people of color, the needs of public policymaking sustained the seemingly contradictory reality of a multiracial workforce that helped keep public expenditures to a minimum. Beginning in 1813, for example, the New Orleans City Council commissioned free people of color to plant trees in the Place d'Armes. In much the same way that the free black militia provided a vital supplement to the state's defense, so too did these free black artisans provide the means for the municipality to save on public expenses.[27] Likewise, the efforts of the City Council to manage prisoners in the city jail ideally combined these principles of racial policymaking and political economy. Located only a few blocks from the Place d'Armes, the city jail was home to a chain gang of slaves imprisoned for various crimes. The City Council created the chain gang in 1805 to recoup the costs of imprisoning slaves, but soon found that this labor force offered numerous possibilities.[28] In 1812 Mayor James Mather reported that the chain gang "may be employed for everything inc. service of the prison, the clearing of the meat market, of the levee, of the banks of the river, the crossing-bridges is generally done by them and the rest of the hands is used for the works directed by the two overseers." The benefits were obvious, and the chain gang emerged as the municipality's all-purpose public workforce.[29]

The chain gang enabled the council to build or repair public works that would otherwise have been prohibitively expensive. In the process, the chain gang also made an aggressive city government more palatable. Council members could compel slaves to do work that whites would consider demeaning for themselves or that would otherwise be prohibitively expensive. Only on rare occasions did the council decide that its needs exceeded the chain gang's capabilities, in which case it chose to hire slaves rather than pay the higher price of free labor.[30]

The City Council became more dependent on the chain gang with each passing year. In 1811 the city began providing chain-gang slaves for various tasks at the College of Orleans, a public boarding school.[31] Two years later chain gangs cleaned roads, cleared ditches, and scrubbed the city market. By 1817 they were at work for the public gravedigger (a misnomer, given the distinctive above-ground sarcophagi necessitated by the swampy soil of New Orleans). Soon after the Mississippi River flooded New Orleans in June 1819, council members observed that "the rapid falling of said river leaves . . . bodies of dead animals and an accumulation of filth whose pestilential effluvia may be prejudicial to public health." The council immediately called on Mayor Auguste Macarty to have the chain gang dispatched to clear the waterways, work that included removing the carcasses.[32]

The racialized principles that shaped political economy at the municipal level were equally important in state and federal policymaking, where slave labor connected public policy to private enterprise. In 1820 Secretary of War John C. Calhoun decided to tear down an aging fort outside New Orleans. Although the fort was federal property, Calhoun believed that the demolition project should be a local affair. Villeré, nearing the end of his term as governor, was apparently happy to oblige. He hired a local contractor to do the job, who in turn hired white laborers. When the fort remained stubbornly intact, Villeré and Calhoun concurred that white labor was neither efficient nor cost effective. Under pressure from state and federal officials, the contractor agreed to lease slaves. That Calhoun and Villeré reached such quick accord on the matter made perfect sense. The secretary of war and the Louisiana governor shared a planter's vision of political economy that overcame any difference in national origin. They saw no reason to use expensive free labor when slave labor would do.[33]

Yet there was more to this story than the common principles that connected slaveholders. Considered in structural terms, the correspondence between Villeré and Calhoun indicated a fusion of state and federal resources. While states and localities certainly came to blows with the federal government, the story of governance in the early republic is more than one of the struggle over states' rights.

The situation in New Orleans showed that a policy of increasingly restrictive racial laws could coexist with a multiracial workforce, for nonwhites were critical to almost every aspect of public administration. While white soldiers patrolled the borderlands, Indian leaders remained an unpaid, unappointed, and often unrecognized extension of Louisiana's public officialdom. In 1814 Andrew Jackson dispatched a simple but foreboding message that captured the not-so-subtle clues that Indians provided. "This morning I was presented with a new British musket," Jackson wrote Claiborne, "given to a friendly Indian by those of Apalachicola Bay."[34] Whether this was in fact part of the arsenal of the British invasion force is a matter of conjecture. But Jackson certainly interpreted the gift in very clear terms: the British had arrived. State and federal governments found that the Caddo provided a cheap, effective auxiliary to police both the eastern states and western peripheries. Even as they coveted the Neutral Ground and made plans to undermine the Indians' power, federal officials nonetheless continued to see the Caddo as a necessary source of information and order. There was more than Caddo pragmatism at work here. Dehahuit's own vision of American federalism, one in which Indians were a distinct constituency, rationalized his decision to work with white officials and soldiers. In keeping with his attempt to establish himself as the true ruler of the western border of the United States, Dehahuit dispatched his own scouts to gather information for the federal government. Dehahuit also offered to provide information on Spanish efforts to preserve imperial authority in Texas.[35]

These relationships began during the War of 1812, but they continued after peace between the United States and Great Britain because public officials in Louisiana believed they still faced racial threats. In 1818, for example, an Indian agent in Louisiana named William Trimble reported that both "a friendly Indian and . . . a negro" who had deserted from the Spanish had provided news that the Spanish were amassing a force for their own assault on the Appalachicola River. Thus federal officials acknowledged that regional security depended on intelligence networks that included nonwhite sources.[36]

Indians, like the chain-gang slaves, hardly considered themselves civil servants. White officials certainly did not. Nonetheless, these nonwhites proved vital to government operations. The chain gang reduced the strain on the City Council's resources. Free people of color provided a cheap source of skilled labor. Indians provided information that white soldiers could not obtain. That this assistance came at the very moment when state and federal leaders were attempting to crush the autonomy of Indians and Afro-Louisianians was not simply ironic. It was entirely consistent with their visions of racial supremacy, foreign policy, and political economy.[37]

Calhoun might recognize the usefulness of slave labor to public projects, but he was not going to accept Indian autonomy at any cost. Andrew Jackson may have become Calhoun's nemesis in the 1830s, but in the 1810s both men struggled to assert white supremacy at the same time they were dependent on a nonwhite workforce. At the same time that Secretary of State John Quincy Adams was struggling to determine once and for all what was domestic and what was foreign through a diplomatic settlement, Secretary of War Calhoun and General Jackson intended to pursue strategies that would consolidate the federal government's authority over the Indians on the nation's frontiers. For Jackson and Calhoun, this move would mean abandoning the centuries-old system of Indian alliances that had been so important to white officials. But that change conformed not only with the administration's new power on the borderlands, but also with a vision of nationhood that left no room for alliances with nonwhites.

All this activity provides a picture of a less familiar John C. Calhoun and Andrew Jackson. This is not the young congressman Calhoun attempting to bolster the union through legislative and constitutional means or the old dissenter who assaulted federal power, but rather the secretary of war who, like other members of the cabinet, struggled for the practical means to realize the administration's ends. In the cosmopolitan center of Louisiana (a realm of slaves and free people of color) and on the state's periphery (a realm of Indians), the secretary of war attempted to consolidate white supremacy in a way that was consistent with the administration's fiscal resources. Likewise, in these activities we see not Andrew Jackson the general and politician, but Jackson the civil administrator. Finally, this is not the familiar political dynamic that would eventually bring Calhoun, Jackson, and Adams into conflict. Although all three men recognized that their political ambitions and their visions of the republic were in conflict, in the 1810s they sought the same goal: the incorporation of Louisiana.

These principles of public administration extended beyond their application in Louisiana. The way that federal officials governed *locally* was essential to the way they conceived of government *nationally*. Most members of Congress and the administration came to Washington with experience in state office. Historians have often considered that background the blueprint for the federal structure, and indeed most federal leaders drew from the lessons they had learned at the state level. Yet governing the frontiers of the union was equally instructive. It kept presidents, cabinet members, and congressmen directly connected to the complexities of local governance long after leaving state office. Louisiana residents did the same, basing their vision of state government on their experiences under federal rule.

The conflicts and collaborations that joined the state of Louisiana to the federal government reaffirmed one simple fact about the American federal structure: when it came to the realities of public administration or the relationship between the nation's peripheries and its center, tension was more often assumed than manifest. For decades Americans had wrestled with the pressures that came with a system of government that Madison first defined decades earlier in *Federalist* No. 39 as "partly federal and partly national." Their concerns were not groundless. States repeatedly clashed with the federal government. Yet in Louisiana state and federal officials found ways to satisfy each other's objectives.

Institutions

Men like Adams, Calhoun, and Jackson were only the latest in a series of federal officials to focus on Louisiana. And those federal leaders concluded that their work was, by and large, successful. Of a more dubious outcome was the local task of institutionbuilding. Since its creation, the government in the Territory of Orleans had concluded that it was responsible for building civic institutions that would provide necessary services while inculcating republican political principles in white Louisianians. By the 1810s, leaders in the state of Louisiana had surrendered that responsibility to private entrepreneurs. The language of incorporation that infused the world of politics was equally pervasive in the schools, churches, and philanthropic organizations that together constituted Louisiana's growing number of private and quasi-private institutions. For entrepreneurs and philanthropists alike, incorporation and nationhood provided both an end and means. This was hardly a planned effort by public officials, most of whom remain committed to the government's institutional role. Instead, the problems of political economy that limited the scope of institutionbuilding provided the means for private individuals to seize the initiative.

The shift in institutionbuilding and its nationalizing content was most evident in education. As the effort to create public schools — begun under the territorial regime and continued by the state government — languished through a lack of funds or public interest, the number of religious schools and private academies grew at a rapid pace. Not only did the formation of new Protestant congregations lead to the creation of new religious schools, but individual instructors created a host of small private academies. Many were one-room affairs in the homes of individual teachers or tutors, an arrangement in keeping with nationwide educational trends as well as the history of education in colonial Louisiana.[38]

As education became the preserve of private and religious entrepreneurship, a growing number of philanthropic organizations in the 1810s connected private individuals to public affairs. Whether it was the Female Orphan Society, the Louisiana Medical Society, or various library societies, these institutions flourished after 1815.[39] The growth of voluntary associations in Louisiana was consistent with conditions throughout the United States. But this development is more often associated with the North and with the second quarter of the nineteenth century. The case of Louisiana suggests a different geography and a different timetable. Region seemed less important than demography. It was the cosmopolitan center of New Orleans that fueled female philanthropy, an urban landscape in which women could meet with an ease that was impossible in the rest of Louisiana, an almost townless landscape dominated by farms and plantations.

Philanthropy grew as Louisiana's economy flourished, a development due in no small part to growth in that other essential institution: banking. The banking system of Louisiana, fostered by both the state and federal governments, became the incubator of capital and entrepreneurship. Louisiana had the most advanced banking system in the Southwest, with New Orleans functioning as a financial island that shared more with New York, Philadelphia, and Boston than with settlements in neighboring states and territories.[40] State banks joined a growing number of private banks. The banks funneled both private and public money through New Orleans.[41]

Economic integration was no small affair. To many Louisianians, it was a matter of paramount importance. Their very conception of nationhood, certainly their understanding of its benefits, rested on the assumption that membership in the American national community brought with it access to commercial networks that spanned the eastern half of the continent. Banking also provided a final example of the institutional policymaking that took form in Louisiana. The vaunted ambitions of public officials rapidly gave way to competing notions of development, often based more on private entrepreneurship than on government direction.

The very limitations of government resources created the opportunities for private and quasi-private organizations to exploit incorporation to advance their particular goals. Religious institutions likewise laid claim to their role as agents of incorporation. They began the process by incorporating themselves legally. Each church parish, regardless of denomination, came under the administration of church wardens whose activities mirrored the representative system of a republican government. Individual parishioners who might never hold public office would nonetheless engage in public service by serving as wardens. This objective was evident when the territorial legislature incorporated the small Catholic parish of St. Michael's in Acadia County, proclaiming that every "white catholic individual . . . and their successors, be and they are hereby created and made one body politic and corporate."[42]

For Protestants, it was an easy task to convince the Protestant majority in the United States that new churches would undermine Catholic power. Conversely, proving their contributions to civic life was a hard sell for Catholic organizations. But the same language of nationhood that had enabled Louisianians to claim a political role for themselves would also enable the Catholic church to define itself as an agent of incorporation. The first to do so successfully were the Ursuline nuns of New Orleans, who convinced federal officials that the United States "cannot but acquire honour in fostering & protecting" their activities, that they would advance the "moral climate" of the local population.[43] As proprietors of one of the few boarding schools for girls in the Southwest, the nuns claimed to bring together pupils from the neighboring territories of Mississippi and Orleans.[44]

Whether they knew it or not, the nuns had a receptive audience at the White

House. Jefferson had entrusted the education of his daughters to Catholic nuns during his tenure in Paris, and Madison dispatched his stepson, Payne Todd, to a Catholic school in Maryland.[45] The nuns soon found they could express themselves without arousing the suspicion that Americans felt toward Louisiana's male political or clerical elite.[46] Many observers felt that they promoted order and harmony. There was no schism within the female religious community. As sponsors of philanthropic activities ranging from education to public health to poor relief, the nuns actively contributed to institutional development. In return, the Ursuline nuns enjoyed both influence and favorable treatment by state and federal officials alike.[47]

While the Ursuline nuns made the case for their own public contributions, John Carroll was building an argument that even male clergy might contribute to incorporation. His increasingly strong assertions that Catholicism need not undermine nationhood were part of a broader effort on his part to normalize Catholicism in a republic governed by Protestants. As early as 1806 he had argued that any priest he dispatched to Louisiana would be "a clergyman . . . whose attachment to the U. States was unequivocal & who at the same time would be acceptable to the original inhabitants of Louisiana and keep them well affected to our government & their fellow citizens."[48]

The Catholic church also resolved its jurisdictional disputes in ways that church leaders tied to incorporation. In 1812 Carroll appointed Louis William DuBourg as Louisiana's "apostolic administrator." A Saint Domingue native, he seemed ideally qualified to work with white Louisianians. A former head of Saint Mary's College, where his students included none other than Payne Todd, he seemed equally likely to please the administration. But DuBourg met immediate resistance, in part because white Louisianians found him too heavy-handed, but in larger part because he still was not what they wanted: a bishop.[49] When the Vatican finally created a diocese for American Louisiana in 1815 with DuBourg as bishop, his experience in New Orleans had been so unpleasant that he settled in St. Louis. Although many American Protestants would remain staunchly anticatholic, their worst fears never materialized, in large part because the Catholic use of the language of incorporation left Americans with no room for maneuver.[50]

Divisions, Connections

Public officials could easily accommodate themselves to this state of affairs. Private institutionbuilding saved public revenue, and the language of incorporation rationalized innumerable activities. More troubling was the absence of a resolution on defining who could be an American. The incorporation of Louisiana and American nationhood depended on a clear line between the American and the foreign, and those terms were still up for grabs. Not only did citizenship still lack certain critical forms of definition, but many in Louisiana ignored the provisions of racial exclusion. Indeed, the latter made the former all the more important.

Try as they might, white officials were never able to construct an impervious barrier between white citizens and nonwhite aliens. Whites as well as non-whites ignored the new racial structure that came in the wake of the Louisiana Purchase. These relationships predated and outlasted legal and administrative reform, and remained no less entrenched than the laws and procedures that were supposed to prevent them. A decade after the uncertainty of 1803–1806, people in Louisiana were still cavorting with one another in ways that ignored the laws enacted in the intervening years.

At the very moment that Catholic leaders were making the case for their ability to aid incorporation, the church remained the site of linkages that crossed racial lines.[51] Free people of color likewise also maintained social and economic ties with whites. This was a strategy that free people of color pursued throughout the United States, but one that continued to generate particular prosperity and interracial contact in Louisiana. The fact that so many free people of color were of mixed-race parentage both sustained and explains this state of affairs.[52]

These social realities continued to defy every institutional mechanism designed to use race to establish clear lines between American and foreign. Likewise, *Desbois' Case* and *Laverty v. Duplessis* — the landmark Louisiana Supreme Court decisions that equated state and federal citizenship — may have opened new avenues to citizenship, but they did not entirely resolve the question of who was an American. That task remained incomplete on the national level, and Louisiana was the logical polity to tackle it. At stake were some big questions. Who could be an American? How could nations construct clear lines in which the boundaries between peoples were coterminous with the boundaries between polities? And finally, how could answers emerge within the particular structures of the federal system? In their efforts to settle this matter, people in Louisiana returned to the central principles that had shaped incorporation since 1803.

It therefore made sense that a congressman from Louisiana, Thomas Bolling Robertson, proposed the first bill to establish rules for expatriation. In 1818 he introduced a bill that provided for the easy transfer of nationality *away* from the United States. As Robertson explained, "the question which had arisen during the late war made a decision necessary." He specifically referred to the case of British immigrants who had served in the U.S. Army and, after capture by Great Britain, faced the danger of trial for treason. But the problem of citizenship had exploded in numerous forms in Robertson's Louisiana. Once an individual laid claim to foreign allegiance, that person could easily surrender any legal attachment to the United States. Robertson's bill received considerable support from leading Republicans, including House Speaker Henry Clay, but eventually disappeared in a lengthy debate over amendments.[53]

Robertson's efforts formed a natural counterpart to a Louisiana state law of 1816 that standardized the most minor procedures of transferring nationality, removing exactly the sort of ambiguity that had created so many problems in the years immediately following the Purchase, when the nationality of Louisiana's residents was the subject of unending dispute. Among other things, the Louisiana act stated that only citizens could vouch for immigrants. At the same time that it preserved the Republicans' quest for easy access to American citizenship, it upheld the principle that membership in the national community required an immigrant's attachment and participation as well as the community's acceptance. Louisiana's state citizenship act of 1816 and Robertson's efforts to create a federal expatriation law in 1818 constituted a joint effort to streamline a disparate set of regulations. They reasserted the notion that citizenship had to be rooted in individual attachment. They also denied the reality of continuing contact across racial lines.[54]

Clear rules for expatriation were no less important than rules for naturalization. Membership in a national community had to be uniform and clear. White Louisianians had been able to impose their own vision of citizenship on the United States, reasserting the concept that citizenship and alienation were in polar opposition without any shades of gray. They were successful in large part because they worked within a framework of existing principles of loyalty and nationality. Likewise, they could reach a consensus on the language of citizenship only once Americans relaxed their fears that local customs conflicted with national identity.

The national importance that Louisianians attributed to their actions was more than mere pretension. They were vocal participants in the successful campaign by territorial residents to press their claims for a system that acknowledged them as American citizens. They were also crucial to the ongoing argument about how individuals and corporate entities related in an American polity. In 1805 the U.S. Supreme Court decided that territorial residents existed outside the realm of constitutional protections, which were reserved to the states. Fifteen years later Chief Justice John Marshall wrote that the United States "is composed of States and territories," expanding the national community to include all individuals regardless of the polities in which they lived. Marshall only reiterated an argument the Louisianians had made throughout the territorial period and sharpened after statehood. The national community had to be coterminous with national boundaries. Statehood might be essential to full citizenship, but it was not a precondition. Louisiana had played no small role in establishing that the territorial frontier not only *could* be, but *had* to be fully incorporated in all the meanings of that word. Any other configuration was intellectually untenable and corrosive to the bonds of unity that had to connect both a collection of states and a national community of individual citizens.[55]

By the time the Supreme Court issued this decision in 1820, the critical question of the Louisianians' attachment to the United States had been settled. American nationalism proved to be a robust, resilient theory that corresponded well with the practical effort to construct a stable nation, in large part because it was able to contain demographic as well as geographic expansion. The notion that loyalty and sentimental attachment formed the basis of national existence forced policymakers to develop a supple, flexible apparatus that would mitigate internal tensions without depending on force. The principle that any white person could be a national citizen bolstered the strengths of the federal system, eliminating the constitutional fissures of European empires. Attachment had also rationalized new forms of racial supremacy, and the administrative structures of the federal system combined state and federal resources to preserve that racial order. These systems of attachment and exclusion had faced their greatest test in Louisiana, where the principle of ideological unity collided with the fact of ethnic and cultural diversity and where the goal of racial supremacy faced its greatest threats. The loyalty of white Louisianians and the control over nonwhites validated the concepts of American nationalism.

Policymakers in Washington did not believe the transformation of Louisianians into Americans happened by itself. Though aware and appreciative of the Louisianians' loyalty, they congratulated themselves for creating an apparatus that transformed these foreigners despite the absence of normal naturalization procedures. Looking forward in 1803 and looking back in 1820, Americans focused on institutions to evaluate the Louisianians' progress. Likewise, those institutions would serve as the yardstick that Louisianians used to determine their own relationship with the rest of the nation.

Meanwhile, the emerging cadre of policymakers within Louisiana's white elite were equally impressed with themselves. They tended to see their own lives as parables of Louisiana's progress. Men in Washington had done the same thing as well, claiming that it was a prudent policy that had overcome the apparent divisions separating people on both sides of the Mississippi. These people found in Louisiana a comfortable narrative of a passage from danger to stability, from potential isolation to national incorporation.

Conclusion

The two events that provide the capstone to the story of incorporation are an odd pair: a wedding and a lawsuit.

On Monday, 4 October 1819, a man named Jean Baptiste Desbois married "the amiable miss Malila Dreur."[1] Seven years earlier, Desbois had made history. In 1812 Desbois' demand to be considered an American citizen led the Louisiana Supreme Court to issue a landmark decision on citizenship. It was one of the rare occasions on which Desbois' name appeared in print. Like so many women, Malila Dreur left an even smaller imprint on the documentary record. Not so for Father Antonio de Sedella, who presided over the wedding. Sedella was the most famous — and infamous — priest in Louisiana. He had defended slaves and free people of color. He was rumored to have a long-running romantic relationship with his slave housekeeper that had produced a son who worked for the St. Louis parish. He had also generated dissent within Catholic parishes and the ire of civil officials.[2]

Sedella provided the linkage between the wedding and the lawsuit. Seven years before marrying Desbois and Dreuer, he had performed another wedding, but by 1819 the bride was a widow and was taking a case to the Louisiana Supreme Court. The 1819 lawsuit left a bigger paper trail, as lawsuits normally do. The widow's case concerned a dispute from May 1816, when a flood broke through one of the levees guarding New Orleans. Her husband used his own money to pay for men and equipment to seal the "crevasse," as the break in the levee became known. The man died the following year, and in 1819 the General Assembly passed legislation to reimburse his family. The legislature required Orleans Parish to provide part of the funding, but the parish police jury refused to do so. The widow sued the jury, demanding that it carry out the General Assembly's mandate. When the Louisiana District Court upheld her request, requiring the police jury to impose a special tax to raise the funds, the jury in turn appealed to the Louisiana Supreme Court.

Arguments in this case marked a gathering of ambitious Louisianians. Representing Orleans Parish was Louis Moreau-Lislet, the coauthor of the *Civil Digest* who had just completed two years as Louisiana's attorney general. Representing the widow was Abner Duncan, a successful attorney who had been one of Andrew Jackson's lawyers in *United States v. Major General Andrew Jackson* and was preparing to run for governor in 1820. Pierre Derbigny, who delivered the court's opinion, may already have been making plans for his own 1820 gubernatorial bid. In the end, the court decided that "the imposition of the tax . . . would be an act purely legislative." It was beyond the purview of the judiciary to compel legislative action. So the state supreme court could take no action except to annul the district court's decision. It would be for the General Assembly and Orleans Parish to settle between themselves how to reimburse the widow.[3]

The widow came to court with considerable political connections of her own. Martin Duralde and John Clay served as tutor and subtutor, respectively, for her stepson, the child of her late husband's previous marriage.[4] The widow had been born Cayetana Bosque, although she was often called Susana. Her lineage exemplified the numerous backgrounds of Louisiana's residents. Her father came from Mallorca; her mother was the Creole child of a Creole mother and a French father. And in 1812, when she was sixteen years old, she had married William C. C. Claiborne, a man twenty-one years her senior.

The wedding and the lawsuit each connected numerous facets of incorporation. And rightly so, for incorporation always entailed intertwined goals and challenges. For example, Sedella's presence served as a reminder of the Catholic church's complicated role in public affairs. Nobody represented the church's capacity to upset external systems of power — whether civil or ecclesiastical — better than Sedella. And yet his ability to preside over Desbois and Claiborne's wedding reflected the church's ability to establish itself as a nationalizing institution alongside the citizenship process that was so important for Desbois and the policymaking structure that was so important for Claiborne.

Then there is Claiborne himself, whose vision of a civil polity of white supremacy seemed borne out by the calm proceedings at Desbois' wedding and at his widow's day in court. Though one of the most important figures in the process of incorporation, he was hardly alone. His death serves its own narrative role, not only for concluding the story of early national Louisiana, but also for putting his own role in context.

Claiborne had already outlived two wives, the Tennessean Eliza Lewis Claiborne, who came with him to the Southwest in 1801 and died during her first winter in New Orleans; and the Creole Clarissa Duralde, who married Claiborne in 1806 but died of illness three years later. Claiborne's third marriage was a rushed affair. Susana was apparently pregnant at the time, for references to a daughter, Sophronia, appeared only a few months after the November 1812 wedding. A second child was born within the year but died after only a few days.[5]

Claiborne's death is a story of irony and bad fortune, but also a reminder of the networks that connected the frontier to the centers of power. When his term as governor ended in 1816, the General Assembly elected Claiborne to replace James Brown in the U.S. Senate. The trip to Washington that Claiborne planned to make in 1817 had been a long time coming. Since he arrived in Mississippi as territorial governor in 1801, Claiborne's only departure from the southwestern frontier had been his visit east in 1810, a trip cut short by the annexation of West Florida. As for so many western officials, the return to Washington in 1817 would complete a circle in which a lengthy sojourn on the frontier enabled Claiborne to realize his ambitions.[6] Claiborne would also leave behind an extensive political network that would make its mark on Louisiana and Mississippi well into the twentieth century.[7]

Claiborne took his time leaving, and his movements in 1817 are almost impossible to ascertain. Since 1801 he had preserved detailed letterbooks chronicling his every act as territorial and state governor. Those letterbooks remain among the most useful sources for studying Louisiana during the turbulent years following the Louisiana Purchase. Once Claiborne left office, however, that chronicle stopped. In what may have been his last letter, Claiborne wrote on 26 September 1817 to his sister-in-law, Magdalene Claiborne, of his imminent departure for Washington.[8] Perhaps Claiborne waited too long. On 24 November the *Louisiana Courier* included a brief article reporting: "Died last night, at half past eight o'clock, the honorable WILLIAM CHARLES COLE CLAIBORNE, formerly Governor of this State, and when he died, Senator in the Congress of the U.S. His funeral will proceed from the Government House this day at 4 o'clock P.M." Typically for the time, doctors could not identify an exact cause of death. They referred to a "liver ailment," a vague term often used to describe unexplained deaths.[9]

What followed were rituals characteristic for the death of public officials throughout the United States and characteristic for a Louisiana intent on making public displays of its national attachment. The General Assembly and the City Council shut down so members could attend the funeral. A local church erected a statue to the former governor. Public notices celebrated Claiborne, but also used his life to remind people of how white Louisianians had transformed themselves into Americans. The death and funeral of Claiborne provided yet another opportunity for Louisianians (including Claiborne's most public critics) to voice their appreciation, if not of the former governor then of the American nation that had embraced them. One published statement used Claiborne to reassert the narrative of incorporation that so many white Louisianians had hoped to make a reality: "He exerted his influence in propagating that inviolable attachment which he bore to republican institutions."[10]

So why not end the story of incorporation with Claiborne's death? The timing is certainly convenient, coming so soon after statehood and the Battle of New Orleans. Yet incorporation was not completed by the Battle of New Orleans, nor was it complete by the time Claiborne died. The United States had yet to reach a final accord with Spain on the boundaries of Louisiana. White Louisianians had just begun the process of establishing political influence on a national scale, shifting from the nationalizing politics of complaint (their only means to create moments when they might speak in a national venue) that characterized the territorial period to the process of building more subtle and lasting forms of influence. Some free people of color continued to build durable inroads into white society despite the increasingly industrious efforts to create new systems of exclusion. So if there is a corollary to be found between Claiborne and the process of incorporation, it stems from the fact that Claiborne's public presence, or at least his private accounts, did not end with his death in 1817. The case of *Claiborne v. Police Jury* and the wedding of Jean Baptiste Desbois signaled the completion of incorporation more effectively than Claiborne's death.

For example, the emerging rules of public administration became clear in the state supreme court's decision, as did the equally complicated relationship between public administration and politics. In one of its lengthier decisions, the court felt compelled to reassert two principles of American political belief. "The first fundamental principle of our constitutions is that the powers of the government are divided into three departments, ever to be kept distinct, to wit, the legislative, the executive, and the judiciary." The court further explained that "in a deliberative body, the majority rules the minority."[11] Both statements were as much ideal as reality, for power in Louisiana remained concentrated in an elite minority, while local governance never allowed for such clear separation of powers.

Then there was the flood itself, the event that eventually precipitated the case. The response to the flood of 1816 brought into broad relief the political, racial, and institutional mechanisms in Louisiana. As the waters rose, the City Council rushed to dispatch the chain-gang slaves in a vain attempt to keep the levee intact. The waters eventually consumed the major cemetery in New Orleans, leaving behind a grisly trail of overturned and occasionally opened caskets. Public officials and church officials immediately created a temporary cemetery, which was itself overrun by the rising waters. Catholic leaders, eager to claim their role as a civic institution that promoted regional development, directed work on the cemetery and used public funds to oversee its eventual repair. Meanwhile, the City Council that considered itself so important to Louisiana's political economy provided direct aid to whites whose homes had been destroyed.[12]

The flood of 1816 and the case of *Claiborne v. Police Jury* seemed to prove that Louisiana was a stable and permanent member of an American nation, at once unique in its local activities yet undeniably incorporated. Interlocking systems of diplomacy, citizenship, institutional development, race, public administration, and politics had built powerful bonds between Louisiana and the United States. Meanwhile, Desbois' ability to establish his own membership in both local and national communities showed how people navigated that world of contingency.

Even the case's timing proved important. *Claiborne v. Police Jury* came in the same year that Spanish and American negotiators crafted the Transcontinental Treaty and finally drew a map of Louisiana with borders acceptable to both sides. No sooner were these residual acts of incorporation complete than Louisiana underwent changes that transformed the state's cultural and political landscape. These changes came about as the United States underwent its own transformations.

The first of those changes was demographic. The Panic of 1819, together with the scarcity of fertile or unclaimed land in eastern states, led Americans by the thousands to seek their fortunes in the Southwest. Louisiana itself underwent few of the economic convulsions that came with the Panic of 1819, but its very insulation guaranteed that it would be an attractive spot for migrants from the East. The result was an ethnic shift in Louisiana, not only through the arrival of Anglo-American whites but also from the forced migration of Anglophone slaves.[13]

That this demographic transformation occurred *after* 1820 is essential to understanding incorporation. In 1803 Kentucky senator John Breckinridge predicted that Louisiana "will, beyond all question, be settled fully at a period not very remote. It is equally certain, that it will be settled by americans."[14] Perhaps so, but not any time in the immediate future. His cousin James Brown admitted as much in 1810, when he lamented the paucity of American migrants and the abundance of Saint Domingue immigrants.[15] The incorporation of Louisiana did not happen through the dilution of the local population or through some amorphous "Americanization" of local institutions. The objects of incorporation — the permanent American claim to Louisiana, the affection of the local population, the creation of effective administrative and political structures, and the preservation of white authority — were all in place by 1820 despite the fact that Louisiana remained a legal, demographic, and cultural anomaly.

The second change in Louisiana after 1820 was political. As Americans battled over whether to admit Missouri as a free or slave state, Louisianians exchanged regionalism for sectionalism. Louisiana sided with other slave states, and in the process shifted from an odd periphery in the multiethnic West to a solid member of the slaveholding South. In becoming southern, Louisianians also became American.

Ironically, the ability of Louisiana to resituate itself was in no small part a result of the Louisiana Purchase. It was the debate over whether slavery could extend into new territories carved from the Louisiana Purchase that fueled the sectional divide in the antebellum era. But that argument would rest on profoundly different questions of union and attachment from the concerns that brought so much attention to Louisiana during the early republic.

Louisiana's internal politics underwent its own transformation. The interethnic coalitions that had been the goal and often the achievement of America and Louisiana began to disintegrate, giving way to the sort of ethnic polarization that historians would later apply to the entire period following the Louisiana Purchase. Americans, Creoles, and the Foreign French divided into political communities during the antebellum period that had never been so stable or clearly delineated during the early republic.[16]

Many of the old coalitions from early national Louisiana collapsed, and some of the most unlikely figures emerged as political leaders. After all, Pierre Derbigny finally overcame his setback in 1820 to win the gubernatorial race eight years later. It was a brief victory, however, ending less than a year later when he died after being thrown from his carriage. Meanwhile Edward Livingston executed a more remarkable comeback. In 1819 he joined with Derbigny and Etienne Masureau (Louisiana's secretary of state and former attorney general) to compose both French and English translations of *Las siete partidas*, a tome of Spanish jurisprudence that had guided Louisiana law throughout much of the forty-year Spanish reign.[17] Livingston later helped revise the *Civil Digest* and emerged as the leading figure in Louisiana's legal community.[18] For Livingston, this administrative task would lead to political rebirth. He might be a legal pest, but in the process he had shown that he was an extremely capable attorney.[19] In 1820 Livingston won election to the state House of Representatives. Members of the General Assembly challenged his election victory, and only after an extensive debate did the House of Representatives vote twenty-two to twelve to admit Livingston.[20] In 1822 Livingston left Louisiana, first returning to the U.S. House of Representatives and later joining the Senate. In 1831, sixteen years after serving as General Jackson's aide-de-camp, Livingston became President Jackson's secretary of state. In 1833 Livingston went to Europe as American minister to France, the office his older brother had held when negotiating the Louisiana Purchase. In 1835, his reputation thoroughly restored, Livingston came home to New York, where he died the following year.[21]

Derbigny and Livingston benefited from shifts in Louisiana's political culture that were in no small part a result of the influx of Americans and the growing political aspirations of Creoles. But those changes were possible only because the old fears of internal disunion and external assault had faded to the point that ethnic squabbles no longer appeared like a battle between the American and the foreign. That one era sets the stage for the next is obvious. The causal linkages of change separating the first quarter of the nineteenth century from the second were, however, more direct in Louisiana. Louisiana became an attractive location for white migrants only because of unquestioned American title and a stable racial regime. Likewise, Louisianians were able to exploit the Missouri Crisis to their advantage because they had learned how American politics worked and had already convinced many Americans of their commitment to membership in a national community. In Louisiana as much as in any other state in the union, the passage from the early republic to the antebellum era was a dramatic one.

As was so common on American frontiers, the story of Louisiana in the years following the Purchase is as much a tale of opportunities lost as of opportunities realized. For Indians, slaves, and free people of color, Louisiana's frontier status and its European colonial heritage created unique possibilities that they struggled to realize with varying degrees of success. For white Louisianians, the imminent fear of frontier disunion provided the context in which they were able to ingratiate themselves nationally while still wielding the threat of disunion to make their own demands.

The task of incorporating Louisiana convinced many Americans of the necessity of nationhood, for nationhood offered the only means to preserve their hold on the distant province of Louisiana. The uncertainty (as well as the possibility) that abounded in frontier Louisiana was gone by the 1820s. Americans and Louisianians could also disagree so loudly because the principles on which they had agreed were so thoroughly ingrained in Louisiana's political culture as to be almost invisible. A social system of white supremacy, an economic system connecting East and West, and a political system guaranteeing elite white rule were all firmly in place. But perhaps most important, everybody knew what was foreign and what was American. The incorporation of Louisiana had defined an American nation.

Abbreviations

Acts Passed	*Acts Passed at the Legislature of the Territory of Orleans,* 6 vols. (New Orleans: Bradford and Anderson, 1806–12); *Acts Passed at the General Assembly of the State of Louisiana* (New Orleans: Thierry, Baird and Wagner; Peter K. Wagner; J. C. de St. Romes, 1812–20)
Annals of Congress	*Debates and Proceedings of the Congress of the United States,* 42 vols. (Washington, D.C.: Gales and Seaton, 1834–56)
ASP	*American State Papers: Documents, Legislative and Executive, of the Congress of the United States,* 38 vols. (Washington, D.C.: Gales and Seaton, 1832–61). Series abbreviations: FR (Foreign Relations), Misc (Miscellaneous), PL (Public Lands).
Boyd	*The Papers of Thomas Jefferson,* ed. Julian Boyd et al., 29 vols. to date (Princeton: Princeton University Press, 1950–)

Calhoun Papers	*The Papers of John C. Calhoun,* ed. Robert L. Meriwether et al., 28 vols. to date (Columbia: University of South Carolina Press, 1959–)
Carter	*The Territorial Papers of the United States,* ed. Clarence Edward Carter, 28 vols. (Washington, D.C.: Government Printing Office, 1934–75)
Claiborne Letterbooks	*The Letter Books of William C. C. Claiborne, 1801–1816,* ed. Dunbar Rowland, 6 vols. (Jackson: Mississippi State Library and Archive, 1917)
Clay Papers	*The Papers of Henry Clay,* ed. James F. Hopkins et al., 10 vols. (Lexington: University of Kentucky Press, 1959–91)
DLB	*Dictionary of Literary Biography.* 289 vols. to date. (Detroit: Gale Research, 1978–)
Domestic Letters	Domestic Letters of the Department of State, Record Group 59, Microfilm Copy M-40, National Archives
Ford	*The Works of Thomas Jefferson,* ed. Paul Leicester Ford, 10 vols. (New York: G. P. Putnam's Sons, 1904–05)
HNO	Historic New Orleans Collection, New Orleans
House Journal	*Journal of the House of Representatives of the State of Louisiana* (New Orleans: Thierry, Baird and Wagner; Peter K. Wagner; J. C. de St. Romes, 1812–20)
Jackson Papers	*The Papers of Andrew Jackson,* ed. Sam B. Smith et al., 6 vols. to date (Knoxville: University of Tennessee Press, 1980–)
JAH	*Journal of American History*
Jefferson Papers	Thomas Jefferson Papers, Microfilm Collection, Library of Congress
JER	*Journal of the Early Republic*
LAH	*Louisiana History*
LC	Library of Congress, Washington, D.C.
LCDV	Letters, Petitions, and Reports Received by the Conseil de Ville, New Orleans Public Library
Letters Received, Registered Series	Letters Received by the Secretary of War: Registered Series, Record Group 107, Microfilm Copy M22, National Archives

Letters to Officers	Letters Sent by the Secretary of the Navy to Officers, Record Group 45, Microfilm Copy 149, National Archives
Territorial Papers	Territorial Papers of the United States, Record Group 59, Microfilm Copy M116 (Florida), T260 (Orleans), National Archives
LHQ	*Louisiana Historical Quarterly*
LSU	Special Collections, Hill Memorial Library, Louisiana State University
Madison Papers	James Madison Papers, Microfilm Collection, Library of Congress
Madison Writings	*The Writings of James Madison: Comprising His Public Papers and His Private Correspondence, Including Numerous Letters and Documents Now for the First Time Printed*, ed. Gaillard Hunt, 9 vols. (New York: G. P. Putnam's Sons, 1900–10)
Martin	François-Xavier Martin, *Reports of Cases Argued and Determined in the Supreme Court of Louisiana and in the Superior Court of the Territory of Orleans* (St. Paul: West Publishing, 1913). All references are to the old series, covering 1809–24, unless cited as "Martin NS" for "New Series."
Miscellaneous Letters	Miscellaneous Letters of the Department of State, Record Group 59, Microfilm Copy M179, National Archives
MMCDV	Messages from the Mayor to the Conseil de Ville, New Orleans Public Library
Monroe Papers	James Monroe Papers, Microfilm Collection, Library of Congress
Monroe Writings	*The Writings of James Monroe*, ed. Stanislaus Murray Hamilton, 7 vols. (New York: G. P. Putnam's Sons, 1898–1903)
NA	National Archives, Washington, D.C.
NOPL	New Orleans Public Library
PCDV	Proceedings of the Conseil de Ville, New Orleans Public Library

PJM	*The Papers of James Madison,* ed. William T. Hutchison et al., 17 vols. (Charlottesville and Chicago: University Press of Virginia and University of Chicago Press, 1962–91)
PJM-PS	*The Papers of James Madison: Presidential Series,* ed. Robert A. Rutland et al., 4 vols. to date (Charlottesville: University Press of Virginia, 1986–)
PJM-SS	*The Papers of James Madison: Secretary of State Series,* ed. Robert J. Brugger et al., 6 vols. to date (Charlottesville: University Press of Virginia, 1986–)
RASP	*Records of Ante-bellum Southern Plantations,* ed. Kenneth M. Stampp et al. (Bethesda: University Publications of America, 1985–)
Senate Executive Journal	*Journal of the Executive Proceedings of the Senate of the United States of America,* 36 vols. (New York: Johnson Reprint, 1969)
Statutes at Large	*The Public Statutes at Large of the United States of America,* 8 vols. (Boston: Charles C. Little and James Brown, 1845)
TUL	Special Collections, Howard-Tilton Memorial Library, Tulane University
UVA	Special Collections, Alderman Library, University of Virginia
WMQ	*William and Mary Quarterly*
WSL	Special Collections, Olin Library, Washington University, St. Louis, Missouri

Notes

Introduction

1. Villasana Haggard, "The Neutral Ground between Louisiana and Texas, 1806–1821," *LHQ* 28 (1945): 1001–1128; F. Todd Smith, "The Kadohadacho Indians and the Louisiana-Texas Frontier, 1686–1870," *Southwestern Historical Quarterly* 95 (1991): 177–205.

2. Gregory H. Nobles, *American Frontiers: Cultural Encounters and Continental Conquest* (New York: Hill and Wang, 1997), xii, 3–16; Jeremy Adelman and Stephen Aron, "From Borderlands to Borders: Empires, Nation-States, and the Peoples in Between in North American History," *American Historical Review* 104 (1999): 814–41.

3. James Madison to Thomas Jefferson, 27 November 1806, in *The Republic of Letters: The Correspondence between Thomas Jefferson and James Madison*, ed. James Norton Smith, 3 vols. (New York: Norton, 1995), 3: 1460–61.

4. Madison to Robert R. Livingston and James Monroe, 2 March 1803, *PJM-SS*, 4: 364–78.

5. Benedict Anderson, *Imagined Communities: Reflections on the Origin and Spread of Nationalism* (London: Verso, 1991); Craig Calhoun, *Critical Social Theory: Culture, History, and the Challenge of Difference* (Oxford: Oxford University Press, 1995); Eric Hobsbawm and Terence Ranger, eds., *The Invention of Tradition* (Cambridge: Cambridge University Press, 1993); David Waldstreicher, *In the Midst of Perpetual Fetes: The Making of American Nationalism, 1776–1820* (Chapel Hill: University of North Carolina Press, 1997).

6. Walker Connor, "The Politics of Ethnonationalism," *Journal of International Affairs* 27 (1973): 1–21; Philip D. Gleason, "American Identity and Americanization," in

The Harvard Encyclopedia of American Ethnic Groups, ed. Stephan Thernstrom (Cambridge: Belknap Press of Harvard University Press, 1980); idem, "Identifying Identity: A Semantic History," *JAH* 69 (1983): 910–31; Richard Handler, "Is 'Identity' a Useful Cross-Cultural Concept?" in *Commemorations: The Politics of National Identity,* ed. John R. Gillis (Princeton: Princeton University Press, 1996), 27–40; idem, "On Sociocultural Discontinuity: Nationalism and Cultural Objectification in Quebec," *Current Anthropology* 25 (1984): 55–71; Daniel Segal and Richard Handler, "How European Is Nationalism?" *Social Analysis* 32 (1992): 1–15.

7. For studies in nationalism and national identity, see Liah Greenfeld, *Nationalism: Five Roads to Modernity* (Cambridge: Harvard University Press, 1992), 399–484; David G. Hackett, "The Social Origins of Nationalism: Albany, New York, 1754–1835," *Journal of Social History* 21 (1987–88): 659–81; E. J. Hobsbawm, *Nations and Nationalism since 1780* (Cambridge: Cambridge University Press, 1990); Elie Kedourie, *Nationalism* (London: Hutchinson, 1960); Hans Kohn, *Nationalism: Its Meaning and History* (New York: D. Van Nostrand, 1965); idem, *American Nationalism: An Interpretive Essay* (New York: Macmillan, 1957); idem, *Prelude to Nation-States: The French and German Experience, 1789–1815* (Princeton: D. Van Nostrand, 1967); Clinton Rossiter, *The American Quest, 1790–1860: An Emerging Nation in Search of Identity, Unity, and Modernity* (New York: Harcourt Brace Jovanovich, 1971); Waldstreicher, *In the Midst of Perpetual Fetes;* Yhoshua Ariela, *Individualism and Nationalism in American Ideology* (Cambridge: Harvard University Press, 1964); Guido Zernatto, "Nation: The History of a Word," *Review of Politics* 6 (1944): 351–66.

8. Hans W. Baade, "The Law of Slavery in Spanish Luisiana," in *Louisiana's Legal Heritage,* ed. Edward F. Haas Jr. (Pensacola: Perdido Bay Press, 1983), 51–70; Ira Berlin, "From Creole to African: Atlantic Creoles and the Origins of African-American Society in Mainland North America," *WMQ,* 3d ser., 53 (1996): 251–88; David C. Rankin, "The Tannenbaum Thesis Reconsidered: Slavery and Race Relations in Antebellum Louisiana," *Southern Studies* 18 (1979): 5–31; Frank Tannenbaum, *Slave and Citizen: The Negro in the Americas* (New York: Knopf, 1947); David J. Weber, *The Spanish Frontier in North America* (New Haven: Yale University Press, 1992), 177–79, 327–28, 343; Stephen Webre, "The Problem of Indian Slavery in Spanish Louisiana, 1769–1803," *LAH* 25 (1984): 117–35; Richard White, *The Middle Ground: Indians, Empires, and Republics in the Great Lakes Region, 1650–1815* (Cambridge: Cambridge University Press, 1991), 382–84, 417–19.

9. For the linkages between slavery, freedom, and equality in Revolutionary America, see Edmund S. Morgan, "Slavery and Freedom: The American Paradox," *JAH* 59 (1972): 5–29.

10. Joseph G. Tregle, "Creoles and Americans," in *Creole New Orleans: Race and Americanization,* ed. Arnold R. Hirsch and Joseph Logsdon (Baton Rouge: Louisiana State University Press, 1992), 131–85, 132–34.

11. Carl A. Brasseaux, *Acadian to Cajun: Transformation of a People, 1803–1877* (Jackson: University Press of Mississippi, 1992); Gwendolyn Midlo Hall, *Africans in Colonial Louisiana: The Development of Afro-Creole Culture in the Eighteenth Century* (Baton Rouge: Louisiana State University Press, 1992); Richard Holcombe Kilbourne Jr., *Debt, Investment, Slaves: Credit Relations in East Feliciana Parish, Louisiana, 1825–*

1885 (Tuscaloosa: University of Alabama Press, 1995); Daniel H. Usner Jr., *Indians, Settlers, and Slaves in a Frontier Exchange Economy: The Lower Mississippi Valley before 1783* (Chapel Hill: University of North Carolina Press, 1992).

12. Alexander DeConde, *This Affair of Louisiana* (New York: Charles Scribner's Sons, 1976); Thomas R. Hietala, *Manifest Design: Anxious Aggrandizement in Late Jacksonian America* (Ithaca: Cornell University Press, 1985); Reginald Horsman, *Expansion and American Foreign Policy* (East Lansing: Michigan State University Press, 1967); idem, *Race and Manifest Destiny: The Origins of American Racial Anglo-Saxonism* (Cambridge: Harvard University Press, 1981); Patricia Nelson Limerick, *The Legacy of Conquest: The Unbroken Past of the American West* (New York: Norton, 1987), 121–26, 196–208; Frank Lawrence Owsley Jr. and Gene A. Smith, *Filibusters and Expansionists: Jeffersonian Manifest Destiny, 1800–1821* (Tuscaloosa: University of Alabama Press, 1997); Reginald C. Stuart, *United States Expansionism and British North America, 1775–1871* (Chapel Hill: University of North Carolina Press, 1988), 255; Weber, *Spanish Frontier in North America,* 274.

13. Stephen Aron, *How the West Was Lost: The Transformation of Kentucky from Daniel Boone to Henry Clay* (Baltimore: Johns Hopkins University Press, 1996); Michael A. Bellesiles, *Revolutionary Outlaws: Ethan Allen and the Struggle for Independence on the Early American Frontier* (Charlottesville: University Press of Virginia, 1993); Andrew R. L. Cayton, *The Frontier Republic: Ideology and Politics in the Ohio Country* (Kent: Kent State University Press, 1986); Rachel N. Klein, *Unification of a Slave State: The Rise of the Planter Class in the South Carolina Backcountry, 1760–1808* (Chapel Hill: University of North Carolina Press, 1990); Peter S. Onuf, *Statehood and Union: A History of the Northwest Ordinance* (Bloomington: Indiana University Press, 1987); Alan Taylor, *William Cooper's Town: Power and Persuasion on the Frontier of the Early American Republic* (New York: Norton, 1995).

14. Bernard Bailyn, *The Ideological Origins of the American Revolution* (Cambridge: Belknap Press of Harvard University Press, 1992); Jack P. Greene, *Peripheries and Center: Constitutional Development in the Extended Polities of the British Empire and the United States* (New York: Norton, 1986); Peter S. Onuf, *Jefferson's Empire: The Language of American Nationhood* (Charlottesville: University Press of Virginia, 2000); Jack N. Rakove, *The Beginnings of National Politics: An Interpretive History of the Continental Congress* (New York: Knopf, 1979); idem, *Original Meanings: Politics and Ideas in the Making of the Constitution* (New York: Vintage, 1997); Gordon S. Wood, *The Creation of the American Republic, 1776–1787* (New York: Norton, 1969). For a survey of debates in the political history of the early republic, see Daniel T. Rodgers, "Republicanism: The Career of a Concept," *JAH* 79 (1992): 11–38.

15. Alan Taylor, *Liberty Men and Great Proprietors: The Revolutionary Settlement on the Maine Frontier, 1760–1820* (Chapel Hill: University of North Carolina Press, 1990); Taylor, *William Cooper's Town;* Waldstreicher, *In the Midst of Perpetual Fetes.*

16. For examples, see Lawrence S. Kaplan, *Thomas Jefferson: Westward the Course of Empire* (Wilmington: SR Books, 1999); Drew R. McCoy, *The Elusive Republic: Political Economy in Jeffersonian America* (New York: Norton, 1980); Noble E. Cunningham, *The Jeffersonian Republicans in Power: Party Operations, 1801–1809* (Chapel Hill: University of North Carolina Press, 1963).

17. For considerations of American nationhood focusing on constitutional relationships, see Terence Ball and J. G. A. Pocock, eds., *Conceptual Change and the Constitution* (Lawrence: University Press of Kansas, 1988); Richard Beeman, Stephen Botein, and Edward C. Carter II, eds., *Beyond Confederation: Origins of the Constitution and American National Identity* (Chapel Hill: University of North Carolina Press, 1987).

18. The most thorough analysis of the early American bureaucracy remains Leonard White, *The Federalists: A Study in Administrative History* (New York: Macmillan, 1948); idem, *The Jeffersonians: A Study in Administrative History, 1801–1829* (New York: Macmillan, 1951). See also Richard R. John, "Leonard D. White and the Invention of American Administrative History," *Reviews in American History* 24 (1996): 344–60; Matthew A. Crenson, *The Federal Machine: Beginnings of Bureaucracy in Jacksonian America* (Baltimore: Johns Hopkins University Press, 1975); Cunningham, *The Jeffersonian Republicans in Power,* 23–24, 30–70, 96.

19. This sort of logic reveals a convenient circular reasoning. Historians and political science have established a definition of a "state" apparatus (whether actually at the state or the federal level) comporting with the bureaucratic systems that took form during the Progressive era. The government of the early republic does not fit that definition; therefore, it is not a state. In his definition of "nineteenth-century government," for example, Wallace Farnham focused on the period 1862–1873 to the exclusion of almost a century of governing since independence. See Wallace D. Farnham, " 'The Weakened Spring of Government': A Study in Nineteenth-Century American History," *American Historical Review* 68 (1963): 662–80. For other examples of recent work on the history of the American bureaucratic apparatus, see Peter B. Evans et al., eds., *Bringing the State Back In* (Cambridge: Cambridge University Press, 1985); Theda Skocpol, *Protecting Soldiers and Mothers: The Political Origins of Social Policy in the United States* (Cambridge: Belknap Press, 1992); Stephen Skowronek, *Building a New American State: The Expansion of National Administrative Capacities, 1877–1920* (Cambridge: Cambridge University Press, 1982).

20. Bradford Perkins, *The First Rapprochement: England and the United States, 1795–1805* (Philadelphia: University of Pennsylvania Press, 1955), 146–70. For exceptions, see DeConde, *This Affair of Louisiana;* Lawrence S. Kaplan, *Entangling Alliances with None: American Foreign Policy in the Age of Jefferson* (Kent: Kent State University Press, 1987); James E. Lewis Jr., *The American Union and the Problem of Neighborhood: The United States and the Collapse of the Spanish Empire, 1783–1829* (Chapel Hill: University of North Carolina Press, 1998); Peter S. Onuf and Nicholas G. Onuf, *Federal Union, Modern World: The Law of Nations in an Age of Revolutions, 1776–1814* (Madison, Wis.: Madison House, 1993), 144–54.

21. McCoy, *The Elusive Republic,* 195–208; Gordon S. Wood, *The Radicalism of the American Revolution* (New York: Knopf, 1992), 310.

22. The greatest interest in Louisiana and American public affairs came in the first decades of the twentieth century, when studies of the Southwest proliferated on the heels of scholarly interest in the American frontier and the centennial of the Louisiana Purchase. For examples of the chronological breadth of diplomatic studies of the Louisiana Purchase, see Everett S. Brown, *The Constitutional History of the Louisiana Purchase* (Clifton, N.J.: Augustus M. Kelley, 1972).

23. Charles E. A. Gayarré, *History of Louisiana*, 4 vols. (New Orleans: F. F. Hansell and Bro., 1903), 4: 1. See also Earl Noland Saucier, "Charles Gayarré, the Creole Historian" (Ph.D. diss., George Peabody College for Teachers, 1935); Edward M. Socola, "Charles Gayarré: A Biography" (Ph.D. diss., University of Pennsylvania, 1954). Much of Gayarré's material is housed in the Charles E. A. Gayarré Collection, LSU. See François-Xavier Martin, *The History of Louisiana* (New Orleans: J. A. Gresham, 1882). See also Alcée Fortier, *A History of Louisiana*, 4 vols. (New York: Manzi, Joyan, 1904), vol. 3.

24. Joseph G. Tregle Jr., "Louisiana in the Age of Jackson: A Study in Ego-Politics" (Ph.D. diss., University of Pennsylvania, 1954); idem, *Louisiana in the Age of Jackson: A Clash of Cultures and Personalities* (Baton Rouge: Louisiana State University Press, 1999). For Cable's appeal to literary critics, see Violet Bryan, *The Myth of New Orleans in Literature: Dialogues of Race and Gender* (Knoxville: University of Tennessee Press, 1993); Barbara Ladd, *Nationalism and the Color Line in George W. Cable, Mark Twain, and William Faulkner* (Baton Rouge: Louisiana State University Press, 1996), xiv–xv, 38–40.

25. Judith Kelleher Schafer, *Slavery, the Civil Law, and the Supreme Court of Louisiana* (Baton Rouge: Louisiana State University Press, 1994), xiv.

26. Joseph G. Tregle, "Political Reinforcement of Ethnic Dominance in Louisiana, 1812–1845," in *The Americanization of the Gulf Coast, 1803–1850*, ed. Lucius F. Ellsworth (Pensacola: Historic Pensacola Preservation Board, 1972); Lewis William Newton, *The Americanization of French Louisiana: A Study of the Process of Adjustment between the French and Anglo-American Populations of Louisiana, 1803–1860* (New York: Arno, 1980); idem, "Creoles and Anglo-Americans in Old Louisiana: A Study in Cultural Conflicts," *Southwestern Social Science Quarterly* 14 (1933): 21–48; John Wilds, Charles L. Dufour, and Walter G. Cowan, *Louisiana, Yesterday and Today: A Historical Guide to the State* (Baton Rouge: Louisiana State University Press, 1996), 19–22.

27. Madison to Monroe, 13 February 1819, *Letters and Other Writings of James Madison*, 4 vols. (New York: R. Worthington, 1884), 3: 117.

28. Jacques Philippe Villeré to the Louisiana State Legislature, 6 January 1819, *Journal of the Senate of the State of Louisiana* (New Orleans: Thierry; Baird and Wagner; Peter K. Wagner; J. C. de St. Romes, 1812–1820), (1819), 5.

Chapter 1. America

1. John Kukla, ed., *A Guide to the Papers of Pierre Clément Laussat: Napoleon's Prefect for the Colony of Louisiana and of General Claude Perrin Victor at the Historic New Orleans Collection* (New Orleans: Historic New Orleans Collection, 1993), 1–2, 8–9.

2. *National Intelligencer*, 28 December 1803.

3. T. H. Breen, "Ideology and Nationalism on the Eve of the American Revolution: Revisions *Once More* in Need of Revising," *JAH* 84 (1997): 31, 36; Jack P. Greene, *Peripheries and Center: Constitutional Development in the Extended Polities of the British Empire and the United States* (New York: Norton, 1986), 79–87; Rogers M. Smith,

Civic Ideals: Conflicting Visions of Citizenship in U.S. History (New Haven: Yale University Press, 1997).

4. Boyd, 1: 429–32; Pauline Maier, *American Scripture: Making the Declaration of Independence* (New York: Knopf, 1997), 86.

5. David Waldstreicher, *In the Midst of Perpetual Fetes: The Making of American Nationalism, 1776–1820* (Chapel Hill: University of North Carolina Press, 1997), 34–36, 43–48; Peter S. Onuf, *The Origins of the Federal Republic: Jurisdictional Controversies in the United States, 1775–1787* (Philadelphia: University of Pennsylvania Press, 1983), 103–45.

6. For studies examining the linkages between nations and national identity, see Eric Hobsbawm and Terence Ranger, eds., *The Invention of Tradition* (Cambridge: Cambridge University Press, 1993); Claudia Hilb, "Equality at the Limit of Liberty," in *The Making of Political Identities,* ed. Ernesto Laclau (New York: Verso, 1994), 103–12; Maurizio Viroli, *For Love of Country: An Essay on Patriotism and Nationalism* (New York: Oxford University Press, 1995).

7. Lance Banning, *The Sacred Fire of Liberty: James Madison and the Founding of the Federal Republic* (Cornell: Cornell University Press, 1995), 295–8; Greene, *Peripheries and Center,* 163–64; William T. Hutchinson, "Unite to Divide; Divide to United: The Shaping of American Federalism," *Mississippi Valley Historical Review* 66 (1959): 3–18.

8. For the political foundation of American nationalism, see Andrew W. Robertson, " 'Look on This Picture . . . and on This!': Nationalism, Localism, and Partisan Images of Otherness in the United States, 1787–1820," *American Historical Review* 106 (2001): 1263–80.

9. For studies in nationalism, see Liah Greenfeld, *Nationalism: Five Roads to Modernity* (Cambridge: Harvard University Press, 1992); David G. Hackett, "The Social Origins of Nationalism: Albany, New York, 1754–1835," *Journal of Social History* 21 (1987–88): 659–81; Richard Handler, *Nationalism and the Politics of Culture in Quebec* (Madison: University of Wisconsin Press, 1988); E. J. Hobsbawm, *Nations and Nationalism since 1780* (Cambridge: Cambridge University Press, 1990); Hans Kohn, *Prelude to Nation-States: The French and German Experience, 1789–1815* (Princeton: D. Van Nostrand, 1967); John M. Murrin, "A Roof without Walls: The Dilemma of American National Identity," in *Beyond Confederation: Origins of the Constitution and American National Identity,* ed. Richard Beeman, Stephen Botein, and Edward C. Carter II (Chapel Hill: University of North Carolina Press, 1987), 333–48; Yhoshua Ariela, *Individualism and Nationalism in American Ideology* (Cambridge: Harvard University Press, 1964); Guido Zernatto, " 'Nation': The History of a Word," *Review of Politics* 6 (1944): 351.

10. James H. Kettner, *The Development of American Citizenship, 1608–1870* (Chapel Hill: University of North Carolina Press, 1978), 173–209; Smith, *Civic Ideals,* 167–96; Waldstreicher, *In the Midst of Perpetual Fetes,* 124–25, 129. Perhaps it was appropriate that the product of another British colony, New Zealander John Salmond, first investigated the linkages between contractualism and modern citizenship almost a century ago with reference to the British empire of Queen Victoria. See John Salmond, "Citizenship and Allegiance," *Law Quarterly Review* 17 (1901): 270–391 and 18 (1902): 49–363.

11. Marylin C. Baseler, *"Asylum for Mankind": America, 1607–1800* (Ithaca: Cornell University Press, 1998), 143–44, 199–208; Kettner, *The Development of American Cit-*

izenship, 173–209; Robert F. Oaks, "Philadelphians in Exile: The Problem of Loyalty during the American Revolution," *Pennsylvania Magazine of History and Biography* 96 (1972): 298–325; Charles Royster, *A Revolutionary People at War: The Continental Army and American Character, 1775–1783* (New York: Norton, 1979), 262–64, 276–82; Henry J. Young, "Treason and Its Punishment in Revolutionary Pennsylvania," *Pennsylvania Magazine of History and Biography* 90 (1966): 287–313.

12. Ira Berlin, *Slaves without Masters: The Free Negro in the Antebellum South* (New York: New Press, 1974), 79–107; David Brion Davis, *The Problem of Slavery in the Age of Revolution* (Ithaca: Cornell University Press, 1975); Paul Finkleman, *An Imperfect Union: Slavery, Federalism, and Comity* (Chapel Hill: University of North Carolina Press, 1981), 33–45; Edmund S. Morgan, "Slavery and Freedom: The American Paradox," *JAH* 59 (1972): 5–29; Peter S. Onuf, " 'To Declare Them a Free and Independent People': Race, Slavery, and National Identity in Jefferson's Thought," *JER* 18 (1998): 1–46. For a broader approach on the linkages between homogeneity and citizenship, see Jeff Spinner, *The Boundaries of Citizenship: Race, Ethnicity, and Nationality in the Liberal State* (Baltimore: Johns Hopkins University Press, 1994). I refer to the absence of a "middle ground" for a specific reason. It was this system of nationhood that made American conceptions of race so different from those of Europeans and Indians, systems that allowed for the vague differentiations within a polity or a community. See Richard White, *The Middle Ground: Indians, Empires, and Republics in the Great Lakes Region, 1650–1815* (Cambridge: Cambridge University Press, 1991).

13. Linda K. Kerber, *No Constitutional Right to Be Ladies: Women and the Obligations of Citizenship* (New York: Hill and Wang, 1998); idem, *Women of the Republic: Intellect and Ideology in Revolutionary America* (Chapel Hill: University of North Carolina Press, 1980), 120–36. For the nationalist activities of women in the years following independence, see Waldstreicher, *In the Midst of Perpetual Fetes,* 81–84, 233–35.

14. Smith, *Civic Ideals,* 98–101. For the rights and responsibilities of federal citizenship, see Akhil Reed Amar, "The Bill of Rights as a Constitution," *Yale Law Journal* 100 (1991): 1131–1210.

15. Smith, *Civic Ideals,* 4–9.

16. The most succinct analysis of American inequality remains Morgan, "Slavery and Freedom."

17. Amar, "Bill of Rights as Constitution," 1134–37; Kettner, *The Development of American Citizenship,* 75–80, 193. State legislatures only followed the lead of their colonial predecessors, which had enacted their own laws on naturalization and citizenship in the mid-1700s. See Ronald Beiner, ed., *Theorizing Citizenship* (New York: State University of New York Press, 1995); Rogers Brubaker, *Citizenship and Nationhood in France and Germany* (Cambridge: Harvard University Press, 1992); Bernard Murchland, "The Rigors of Citizenship," *Review of Politics* 59 (1997): 127–34; Peter Sahlins, *Boundaries: The Making of France and Spain in the Pyrenees* (Berkeley: University of California Press, 1989).

18. James Madison to Edmund Randolph, 27 August 1782, *PJM,* 5: 86; James Madison, *Notes of the Debates in the Federal Convention of 1787,* ed. Max Farrand (New York: Norton, 1987), 128; Kettner, *The Development of American Citizenship,* 224–32.

19. Finkleman, *An Imperfect Union,* 30–34; Greene, *Peripheries and Center,* 182;

Kettner, *The Development of American Citizenship,* 222; Peter S. Onuf and Nicholas G. Onuf, *Federal Union, Modern World: The Law of Nations in an Age of Revolutions, 1776–1814* (Madison, Wis.: Madison House, 1993), 54–58.

20. Merle E. Curti, *The Roots of American Loyalty* (New York: Columbia University Press, 1946); Onuf and Onuf, *Federal Union, Modern World,* 137; Smith, *Civic Ideals,* 137–64. For debate over the Alien and Sedition Acts, see Lance Banning, *The Jeffersonian Persuasion: Evolution of a Party Ideology* (Ithaca: Cornell University Press, 1978), 255–57, 277; Banning, *The Sacred Fire of Liberty,* 385–87; Baseler, *"Asylum for Mankind,"* 269–85; James Morton Smith, *Freedom's Fetters: The Alien and Sedition Laws and American Civil Liberties* (Ithaca: Cornell University Press, 1956). For territorial governance, see Robert F. Berkhofer Jr., "The Northwest Ordinance and the Principle of Territorial Evolution," in *The American Territorial System,* ed. John Porter Bloom (Athens: Ohio University Press, 1969), 45–55; John Wunder, "American Law and Order Comes to the Mississippi Territory: The Making of Sargent's Code, 1798–1800," *Journal of Mississippi History* 38 (1976): 131–55.

21. Michael A. Bellesiles, *Revolutionary Outlaws: Ethan Allen and the Struggle for Independence on the Early American Frontier* (Charlottesville: University Press of Virginia, 1993); Andrew R. L. Cayton, *Frontier Indiana* (Bloomington: Indiana University Press, 1996); idem, *The Frontier Republic: Ideology and Politics in the Ohio Country* (Kent: Kent State University Press, 1986), 68–75; Peter S. Onuf, *Statehood and Union: A History of the Northwest Ordinance* (Bloomington: Indiana University Press, 1987), 71–72, 85–87.

22. Jefferson, First Inaugural Address, 4 March 1801, in *Jefferson: Public and Private Papers,* ed. Merrill D. Peterson (New York: Library of America, 1990), 167. Wilson quoted in Smith, *Civic Ideals,* 151.

23. Jay Gitlin, "On the Boundaries of Empire: Connecting the West to Its Imperial Past," in *Under an Open Sky: Rethinking America's Western Past,* ed. William Cronon, George Miles, and Jay Gitlin (New York: Norton, 1992), 80–3; idem, "Children of Empire or Concitoyens? Louisiana's French Inhabitants," in *The Louisiana Purchase: Emergence of an American Nation,* ed. Peter J. Kastor (Washington, D.C.: CQ Press, 2002), 23–37, 22–37; Peggy K. Liss, "Creoles, the North American Example and the Spanish Imperial Economy," in *The North American Role in the Spanish Imperial Economy, 1760–1819,* ed. Jaques A. Barbier and Allen Kuethe (Manchester: Manchester University Press, 1984), 12–25. The Louisiana colonists left no lengthy intellectual paper trail as did the British colonists in North America during the 1770s, or the Spanish colonists in Central and South America almost a half-century later.

24. For a succinct review of the byzantine territorial transfers of the 1760s–1780s, see David J. Weber, *The Spanish Frontier in North America* (New Haven: Yale University Press, 1992), 267–76.

25. Daniel H. Usner Jr., *Indians, Settlers, and Slaves in a Frontier Exchange Economy: The Lower Mississippi Valley before 1783* (Chapel Hill: University of North Carolina Press, 1992), 122–30; Ira Berlin, *Many Thousands Gone: The First Two Centuries of Slavery in North America* (Cambridge: Belknap Press of Harvard University Press, 1999), 77–92, 195–215.

26. Gilbert C. Din and John E. Harkins, *The New Orleans Cabildo: Colonial Louisi-*

ana's *First City Government, 1769–1803* (Baton Rouge: Louisiana State University Press, 1996), 84–85; Jerah Johnson, "Colonial New Orleans: A Fragment of the Eighteenth-Century French Ethos," in *Creole New Orleans: Race and Americanization,* ed. Arnold R. Hirsch and Joseph Logsdon (Baton Rouge: Louisiana State University Press, 1992), 44–57; John Preston Moore, *Revolt in Louisiana: The Spanish Occupation, 1766–1770* (Baton Rouge: Louisiana State University Press, 1976), 39–45.

27. Carl A. Brasseaux, *Denis-Nicolas Foucault and the New Orleans Rebellion of 1768* (Ruston: Louisiana Tech University, 1987); Moore, *Revolt in Louisiana,* 143–64, 185–215; Sidney Louis Villeré, *Jacques Philippe Villeré, First Native-Born Governor of Louisiana, 1816–1820* (New Orleans: Historic New Orleans Collection, 1981), 13–18.

28. Brasseaux, *Denis-Nicolas Foucault;* Moore, *Revolt in Louisiana,* 84–142; Reinhart Kondert, "The German Involvement in the Rebellion of 1768," *LAH* 26 (1985): 385–97; Usner, *Indians, Settlers, and Slaves,* 116–18.

29. Charles E. A. Gayarré, *History of Louisiana,* 4 vols. (New Orleans: F. F. Hansell and Bro., 1903), 3: 97–98; Peggy K. Liss, *Atlantic Empires: The Network of Trade and Revolution, 1713–1826* (Baltimore: Johns Hopkins University Press, 1983), 95.

30. Gilbert C. Din, *Francisco Bouligny: A Bourbon Soldier in Spanish Louisiana* (Baton Rouge: Louisiana State University Press, 1993), 140; William E. Foley, *The Genesis of Missouri: From Wilderness Outpost to Statehood* (Columbia: University of Missouri Press, 1989), 32–47.

31. Carl A. Brasseaux and Glenn L. Conrad, eds., *The Road to Louisiana: The Saint-Domingue Refugees, 1792–1809* (Lafayette: University of Southwestern Louisiana, 1992).

32. Nicholas Canny and Anthony Pagden, eds., *Colonial Identity in the Atlantic World, 1500–1800* (Princeton: Princeton University Press).

33. C. Richard Arena, "Philadelphia–Spanish New Orleans Trade in the 1790s," *LAH* 2 (1961): 429–45; Liss, *Atlantic Empires,* 142–44; François-Xavier Martin, *The History of Louisiana* (New Orleans: J. A. Gresham, 1882), 267; Jesús Lorente Miguel, "Commercial Relations between New Orleans and the United States, 1783–1803," in *The North American Role in the Spanish Imperial Economy, 1760–1819,* ed. Jacques A. Barbier and Allan J. Kuethe (Manchester: Manchester University Press, 1984), 177–91, 177–91.

34. Din, *Francisco Bouligny,* 110–12, 199–200; Din and Harkins, *The New Orleans Cabildo,* 83–89; Johnson, "Colonial New Orleans," 18, 46–57.

35. Gwendolyn Midlo Hall, *Africans in Colonial Louisiana: The Development of Afro-Creole Culture in the Eighteenth Century* (Baton Rouge: Louisiana State University Press, 1992); Paul F. Lachance, "The Politics of Fear: French Louisianans and the Slave Trade, 1786–1809," *Plantation Society* 1 (1979): 162–97. For general studies of the American Revolution in Spanish Louisiana, see Jack D. L. Holmes, "The Historiography of the American Revolution in Louisiana," *LAH* 19 (1978): 309–25.

36. Din, *Francisco Bouligny,* 142–43.

37. For the development of nationhood in France and Spain, see Sahlins, *Boundaries.*

38. The discussion of Louisiana slavery in a comparative context is a lengthy paper trail. For particularly useful considerations, see Laura Foner, "The Free People of Color in Louisiana and St. Domingue: A Comparative Portrait of Two Three-Caste Slave Societies," *Journal of Social History* 3 (1970): 404–30; Thomas N. Ingersoll, "Free Blacks

in a Slave Society: New Orleans, 1718–1812," *WMQ,* 3d ser., 48 (1991): 173–200; Lachance, "The Politics of Fear"; David C. Rankin, "The Tannenbaum Thesis Reconsidered: Slavery and Race Relations in Antebellum Louisiana," *Southern Studies* 18 (1979): 5–31; Paul F. Lachance, "The Formation of a Three-Caste Society: Evidence from Wills in Antebellum New Orleans," *Social Science History* 18 (1994): 211–42; Judith Kelleher Schafer, *Slavery, the Civil Law, and the Supreme Court of Louisiana* (Baton Rouge: Louisiana State University Press, 1994), xiii–xv; Frank Tannenbaum, *Slave and Citizen: The Negro in the Americas* (New York: Knopf, 1947); Stephen Webre, "The Problem of Indian Slavery in Spanish Louisiana, 1769–1803," *LAH* 25 (1984): 117–35.

39. Berlin, *Many Thousands Gone,* 195–215; G. M. Hall, *Africans in Colonial Louisiana;* Usner, *Indians, Settlers, and Slaves,* 31–34, 40; Webre, "The Problem of Indian Slavery."

40. *An Account of Louisiana, Being an Abstract of Documents, in the Offices of the Departments of State, and of the Treasury* (Washington, D.C.: Duane, 1803), lxxxv–lxxxvii. Demographic data for Louisiana at the time of the Purchase are spotty. The only statistics from 1803 are divided by Spanish administrative districts. These figures correspond roughly to the Territory of Orleans, but some districts included land that straddled the border with the Louisiana District and Spanish West Florida. Most of the Louisiana slaves not included in the Territory of Orleans lived in the Upper Louisiana settlements of St. Louis and Ste. Genevieve. Complicating matters is the fact that close to 10,000 refugees from Saint Domingue settled in Louisiana between the collection of these data and the creation of the Territory of Orleans.

41. Hans W. Baade, "The Law of Slavery in Spanish Luisiana," in *Louisiana's Legal Heritage,* ed. Edward F. Haas Jr. (Pensacola: Perdido Bay Press, 1983), 51–70; G. M. Hall, *Africans in Colonial Louisiana,* 304–06; Kimberly S. Hanger, *Bounded Lives, Bounded Places: Free Black Society in Colonial New Orleans, 1769–1803* (Durham, N.C.: Duke University Press, 1997).

42. Hanger, *Bounded Lives, Bounded Places;* Caryn Cossé Bell, *Revolution, Romanticism, and the Afro-Creole Protest Tradition in Louisiana, 1718–1868* (Baton Rouge: Louisiana State University Press, 1997), 9–40.

43. Berlin, *Slaves without Masters;* Gary B. Nash, *Forging Freedom: The Formation of Philadelphia's Black Community, 1720–1840* (Cambridge: Harvard University Press, 1988); Shane White, *Somewhat More Independent: The End of Slavery in New York City, 1770–1810* (Athens: University of Georgia Press, 1991).

44. Hanger, *Bounded Lives, Bounded Places.*

45. Usner, *Indians, Settlers, and Slaves,* 278–86.

46. Berlin, *Many Thousands Gone,* 199; G. M. Hall, *Africans in Colonial Louisiana,* 277–315.

47. G. M. Hall, *Africans in Colonial Louisiana,* 373–74; Jack D. L. Holmes, "The Abortive Slave Revolt at Pointe Coupée, Louisiana, 1795," *LAH* 11 (1970): 341–62.

48. Hanger, *Bounded Lives, Bounded Places,* 152.

49. Kimberly S. Hanger, "Conflicting Loyalties: The French Revolution and Free People of Color in Spanish Louisiana," *LAH* 34 (1993): 5–34; Lester Langley, *The Americas in the Age of Revolution* (New Haven: Yale University Press, 1996), 107–10.

50. Berlin, *Many Thousands Gone,* 88–89; F. Todd Smith, *The Caddo Indians: Tribes at the Convergence of Empires, 1542–1854* (College Station: Texas A&M Press, 1995),

87–88; Usner, *Indians, Settlers, and Slaves,* 81–84, 88–92; Richard White, *The Roots of Dependency: Subsistence, Environment, and Social Change among the Choctaws, Pawnees, and Navajos* (Lincoln: University of Nebraska Press, 1983), 95–96.

51. F. T. Smith, *The Caddo Indians.*

52. Gregory Dowd, *A Spirited Resistance: The North American Indian Struggle for Unity* (Baltimore: Johns Hopkins University Press, 1992); R. White, *The Middle Ground,* 413–68. See also Jay Gitlin, "Private Diplomacy to Private Property: States, Tribes, and Nations in the Early National Period," *Diplomatic History* 22 (1998): 87–99; Tanis C. Thorne, *The Many Hands of My Relations: French and Indians on the Lower Missouri* (Columbia: University of Missouri Press, 1996).

Chapter 2. Acquisition

1. Jefferson to Thomas Mann Randolph, 5 July 1803, Jefferson Papers, reel 46.

2. Reginald Horsman, "The Dimensions of an 'Empire for Liberty': Expansion and Republicanism, 1775–1825," *JER* 9 (1989): 1–20; Cathy D. Matson and Peter S. Onuf, *A Union of Interests: Political and Economic Thought in Revolutionary America* (Lawrence: University Press of Kansas, 1990); James E. Lewis Jr., *The American Union and the Problem of Neighborhood: The United States and the Collapse of the Spanish Empire, 1783–1829* (Chapel Hill: University of North Carolina Press, 1998), 23; Drew R. McCoy, *The Elusive Republic: Political Economy in Jeffersonian America* (New York: Norton, 1980), 121–23, 196–205; Peter S. Onuf, "The Expanding Union," in *Devising Liberty: Preserving and Creating Freedom in the New American Republic,* ed. David T. Konig (Stanford: Stanford University Press, 1995), 50–80; Peter S. Onuf and Nicholas G. Onuf, *Federal Union, Modern World: The Law of Nations in an Age of Revolutions, 1776–1814* (Madison, Wis.: Madison House, 1993), 124.

3. Charles E. Bevans, ed., *Treaties and Other International Agreements of the United States of America, 1776–1949,* 13 vols. (Washington, D.C.: Government Printing Office, 1968–76), 11: 516–35; Daniel Clark to Madison, 22 March 1802, *PJM-SS,* 3: 59; Samuel Flagg Bemis, *Jay's Treaty: A Study in Commerce and Diplomacy* (New Haven: Yale University Press, 1962); Robert W. Tucker and David C. Hendrickson, *Empire of Liberty: The Statecraft of Thomas Jefferson* (New York: Oxford University Press, 1990), 64.

4. Rufus King to Madison, 29 March 1801, *PJM-SS,* 1: 55. See also William C. C. Claiborne to Madison, 3 January 1803, *PJM-SS,* 4: 237; Onuf and Onuf, *Federal Union, Modern World,* 147–53; Tucker and Hendrickson, *Empire of Liberty,* 96–100.

5. Jefferson to Livingston, 18 April 1802, Ford, 8: 143; Livingston to Madison, 10 November 1802, *PJM-SS,* 4: 110–11; Peter P. Hill, *French Perceptions of the Early American Republic, 1783–1793* (Philadelphia: American Philosophical Society, 1988); Lawrence S. Kaplan, *Entangling Alliances with None: American Foreign Policy in the Age of Jefferson* (Kent: Kent State University Press, 1987), 24–34, 99–161.

6. Fulwar Skipwith to Madison, 20 November 1802, Consular Dispatches, Paris, reel 1.

7. Madison to William Hulings, 18 October 1802, *PJM-SS,* 4: 30; Claiborne to Jefferson, 29 October 1802, Jefferson Papers, reel 43; Madison to William Jarvis, 17 December 1802, *PJM-SS,* 4: 197.

8. Madison to Livingston, 28 September 1801, *PJM-SS,* 2: 142–47.

9. Madison to Livingston, 17 January 1803, *PJM-SS,* 4: 198; Albert Gallatin to Madison, 27 February 1803, *PJM-SS,* 4: 350.

10. Madison to Livingston and Monroe, 2 March 1803, *PJM-SS,* 4: 364–78.

11. Madison to Livingston and Monroe, 2 March 1803, *PJM-SS,* 4: 364–78. See also Madison to Pinckney and Monroe, 2 March 1803, *PJM-SS,* 4: 381–82.

12. For the most recent example of this conclusion, see Lawrence Owsley Jr. and Gene A. Smith, *Filibusters and Expansionists: Jeffersonian Manifest Destiny, 1800–1821* (Tuscaloosa: University of Alabama Press, 1997). Alexander DeConde, who has written the most thorough analysis of the negotiations for Louisiana, displayed a certain ambivalence toward this issue in *This Affair of Louisiana.* DeConde chronicles both the administration's limited ambitions and Napoleon Bonaparte's role as arbiter of the final shape of Louisiana, yet nonetheless situates the Louisiana Purchase within a history of unquestionable American hunger for new land. Drew McCoy reached similar conclusions in *The Elusive Republic.* See DeConde, *This Affair of Louisiana* (New York: Charles Scribner's Sons, 1976), 241–55; Richard Drinnon, "The Metaphysics of Empire-Building: American Imperialism in the Age of Jefferson and Monroe," *Massachusetts Review* 16 (1975): 666–89; McCoy, *The Elusive Republic,* 204–05; Tucker and Hendrickson, *Empire of Liberty,* 102–04. The most popular treatment of Louisiana, Stephen Ambrose's study of the Lewis and Clark expedition, also reveals the excesses that constitute a logical extension of reading Manifest Destiny back to 1803. See Stephen A. Ambrose, *Undaunted Courage: Meriwether Lewis, Thomas Jefferson, and the Opening of the American West* (New York: Simon and Schuster, 1996), 56.

13. DeConde, *This Affair of Louisiana,* 147–75; Tim Matthewson, "Thomas Jefferson and Haiti," *Journal of Southern History* 61 (1995): 209–49.

14. E. Wilson Lyon, *The Man Who Sold Louisiana: The Career of François Barbé-Marbois* (Norman: University of Oklahoma Press, 1942), 118–19.

15. Madison to Livingston and Monroe, 2 March 1803, *PJM-SS,* 4: 365–66; King to Madison, 5 March 1802, *PJM-SS,* 3: 3–4; Livingston to Madison, 10 November 1802, *PJM-SS,* 4: 110–11.

16. Bevans, *Treaties and Other International Agreements,* 7: 812–13. The Louisiana Purchase consisted of three documents: the treaty ceding Louisiana to the United States and two conventions detailing payments and debt forgiveness. For a detailed description of the events surrounding the negotiations, see E. Wilson Lyon, *Louisiana in French Diplomacy* (Norman: University of Oklahoma Press, 1934), 118–30.

17. Livingston and Monroe to Madison, 13 May 1803, *PJM-SS,* 4: 601–06. See also Livingston to Madison, 12 May 1803, *PJM-SS,* 4: 590–94; Monroe to Jefferson, 18 May 1803, Jefferson Papers, reel 45.

18. Samuel Brazer, *Address, Pronounced at Worcester, on May 12th: 1804 in commemoration of the cession of Louisiana to the United States* (Worcester, Mass.: Sewall Goodridge, 1804); Allan Bowie Magruder, *Political, Commercial, and Moral Reflections on the Late Cession of Louisiana to the United States* (Lexington, Ky.: D. Bradford, 1803); Charles Brockden Brown, *An Address to the Government of the United States, on the Cession of Louisiana to the French and on the Late Breach of Treaty by the Spaniards,* (Philadelphia: John Conrad, 1803); Orasmus Cook Merrill, *The Happiness of America: An Oration Delivered at Shaftsbury, on the Fourth of July* (Bennington, Vt.: Anthony

Haswell, 1804); David Ramsay, *An Oration on the Cession of Louisiana to the United States...* (Charleston: W. P. Young, 1804); St. George Tucker, *Reflections on the Cession of Louisiana to the United States* (Washington, D.C.: Samuel Harrison Smith, 1803); Isabelle Claxton Deen, "Public Response to the Louisiana Purchase: A Survey of American Press and Pamphlets, 1801–1804" (Master's thesis, University of Virginia, 1972); Betty Houchin Winfield, "Public Perception and Public Events: The Louisiana Purchase and the American Partisan Press," in *The Louisiana Purchase: Emergence of an American Nation,* ed. Peter J. Kastor (Washington, D.C.: CQ Press, 2002), 38–50.

19. Vicente Folch, "Reflections on Louisiana" (1804), in *Louisiana under the Rule of Spain, France, and the United States, 1785–1807,* ed. James A. Robertson, 3 vols. (Cleveland: Arthur H. Clark, 1911), 2: 323–47; Abraham Nasatir, *Borderland in Retreat: From Spanish Louisiana to the Far Southwest* (Albuquerque: University of New Mexico Press, 1976), 128–29; David J. Weber, *The Spanish Frontier in North America* (New Haven: Yale University Press, 1992), 291–92. Historians of the North American borderlands have tended to see things the same way, constructing a synthesis of unchecked and unwavering American expansionism.

20. John Breckinridge to Jefferson, 10 September 1803, Jefferson Papers, reel 47. For a thoughtful analysis of the Louisiana Purchase and expansion during the early republic, see Horsman, "Dimensions of an 'Empire for Liberty,' " 6–8.

21. Bevans, *Treaties and Other International Agreements,* 8: 813. The cache of documents recording the negotiations for Louisiana does not provide any evidence to suggest why and how Article VII became Article III. Monroe and Livingston, concerned primarily with the costs and boundaries of Louisiana, left no indication of their role in drafting such language. The French had their own reasons for seeking Article III. They wanted to establish some guarantees for their former citizens. In addition, by eliminating the conditional tone, they probably hoped to make certain that the United States would never be able to sell Louisiana to another European power, namely Spain or Great Britain. This was not an unreasonable concern. Although American posturing had shown how much Jefferson and Madison wanted to guarantee permanent American control over the mouth of the Mississippi, Article III would make it impossible for the United States to cede Upper Louisiana, which the United States had never requested.

22. Madison to Livingston and Monroe, 2 March 1802, *PJM-SS,* 4: 371.

23. Ibid., 376.

24. *Statutes at Large,* 2: 153; Marylin C. Baseler, *"Asylum for Mankind": America, 1607–1800* (Ithaca: Cornell University Press, 1998), 264–68; James H. Kettner, *The Development of American Citizenship, 1608–1870* (Chapel Hill: University of North Carolina Press, 1978), 240–44.

25. Jack P. Greene, *Peripheries and Center: Constitutional Development in the Extended Polities of the British Empire and the United States* (New York: Norton, 1986), 197–211; Onuf and Onuf, *Federal Union, Modern World,* 135–37.

26. James E. Scanlon, "A Sudden Conceit: Jefferson and the Louisiana Government Bill of 1804," *LAH* 9 (1968): 141–45.

27. John Pintard to Gallatin, 14 September 1803, Carter, 9: 50; Berquin-Duvallon, *Travels in Louisiana and the Floridas in the Year 1802* (New York: I. Riley, 1807); James Pitot, *Observations on the Colony of Louisiana from 1796 to 1802* (Baton Rouge:

Louisiana State University Press, 1979). For similar newspaper commentary, see *Charleston* (S.C.) *Courier*, 11 January 1804.

28. William Plumer, *William Plumer's Memorandum of Proceedings in the United States Senate, 1803–1807*, ed. Everett Somerville Brown (New York: Macmillan, 1923), 6. See also *Annals of Congress*, 8th Cong., 1st sess. (1803–04), 33–34; Everett S. Brown, *The Constitutional History of the Louisiana Purchase* (Clifton, N.J.: Augustus M. Kelley, 1972), 14–83; Adolfo Arriaga Weiss, "The Domestic Opposition to the Louisiana Purchase: Anti-Expansionism and Republican Thought" (Ph.D. diss., University of Virginia, 1993).

29. Charles Francis Adams, ed., *Memoirs of John Quincy Adams, Comprising Portions of His Diary from 1795 to 1848* (Philadelphia: J. B. Lippincott, 1874), 278; Scanlon, "A Sudden Conceit," 145.

30. McCoy, *The Elusive Republic*, 195–208; Onuf, "The Expanding Union," 50–80; Gordon S. Wood, *The Radicalism of the American Revolution* (New York: Knopf, 1992), 310.

31. Aaron Burr to Joseph Alston, 18 January 1804, *Political Correspondence and Public Papers of Aaron Burr*, ed. Mary-Jo Kline, 2 vols. (Princeton: Princeton University Press, 1983), 2: 818.

32. Partisan affiliation in the first party system is extremely difficult to discriminate. Candidates clearly identified themselves with Republican and Federalist policies, but did not formally identify themselves by party when they entered office. As a result, the only list of party membership comes from John H. Hoadley's statistical analysis of voting behavior by representatives and senators in *Origins of American Political Parties, 1789–1803* (Lexington: University of Kentucky Press, 1986), 199–219. Hoadley's study ends with the Seventh Congress. Although the majority of members returned for the Eighth Congress, which debated the governance bill, it is impossible to be absolutely certain about the aggregate party alignment on this piece of legislation.

33. *Alexandria* (Va.) *Advertiser*, 23 November 1803. See also Plumer, *Memorandum of Proceedings in Senate*, 135.

34. Plumer, *Memorandum of Proceedings in Senate*, 111.

35. Andrew R. L. Cayton, *The Frontier Republic: Ideology and Politics in the Ohio Country* (Kent: Kent State University Press, 1986), 16, 69–70; Peter S. Onuf, *Statehood and Union: A History of the Northwest Ordinance* (Bloomington: Indiana University Press, 1987), 69–72.

36. *Annals of Congress*, 8th Cong., 1st sess. (1803–04), 2.

37. Ibid., 463.

38. Plumer, *Memorandum of Proceedings in Senate*, 111.

39. Adams, *Memoirs of John Quincy Adams*, 276–77, 278.

40. *Annals of Congress*, 8th Cong., 1st sess. (1803–04), 1061. Lucas had the chance to make his own mark on Louisiana, serving as both a territorial judge and a land claims commissioner in St. Louis. See *Biographical Directory of the United States Congress, 1774–1989* (Washington, D.C.: Government Printing Office, 1989), 1397.

41. *Annals of Congress*, 8th Cong., 2d sess. (1804–05), 477–80; Alan David Aberbach, *In Search of an American Identity: Samuel Latham Mitchill, Jeffersonian Nationalist* (New York: Peter Lang, 1988), 64–69.

42. *Annals of Congress,* 8th Cong., 1st sess. (1803–04), 43–44.

43. Ibid., 480.

44. Madison to Livingston, 7 February 1804, Madison Papers, reel 8. Madison repeated these sentiments in a letter of 10 February 1804 to Daniel Clark, ibid.

45. Madison to Claiborne, 6 February 1804, Carter, 9: 176–77. See also Madison to Livingston, 7 February 1804, Madison Papers, reel 8; Madison to Clark, 10 February 1804, Consular Dispatches, New Orleans, reel 1. Albert Gallatin was surprisingly silent on this matter considering his own personal experience in such matters. In 1793 the Senate had refused to seat him, despite an electoral victory in Pennsylvania, because he had not met the statutory residency requirement for senators. Gallatin in turn endorsed short residency requirements and objected to all efforts to postpone naturalization.

46. *Statutes at Large,* 2: 283–89. For a review of the debate over the Governance Act, see Scanlon, "A Sudden Conceit," 139–62.

47. David Brion Davis, *The Problem of Slavery in the Age of Revolution* (Ithaca: Cornell University Press, 1975), 156–57; Winthrop Jordan, *White over Black: American Attitudes toward the Negro, 1550–1812* (Chapel Hill: University of North Carolina Press, 1968), 321–22; Onuf, *Statehood and Union,* 110–13.

48. Magruder, *Political, Commercial, and Moral Reflections,* 148–50. For general analyses of diffusion, see McCoy, *The Elusive Republic,* 251–52. Magruder and other contemporary commentators suggested Upper Louisiana as the site for an independent nation of freed slaves. This plan proved short-lived, however, when it became obvious to white officials that the fertile land of the eastern plains would attract white settlers.

49. Brazer, *Address, Pronounced at Worcester;* Magruder, *Political, Commercial, and Moral Reflections;* Brown, *An Address on the Cession;* Merrill, *The Happiness of America;* Ramsay, *An Oration on the Cession;* Tucker, *Reflections on the Cession;* Deen, "Public Response to Louisiana Purchase."

50. The pamphlets of late 1803 and 1804 have stood as the central evidence of many historians who interpret the Louisiana Purchase as the first step toward Manifest Destiny. See McCoy, *The Elusive Republic,* 198 n. 35, 204 n. 43; Thomas R. Hietala, *Manifest Design: Anxious Aggrandizement in Late Jacksonian America* (Ithaca: Cornell University Press, 1985), 109.

Chapter 3. *"Numerous and Troublesome Neighbors"*

1. Andrew R. L. Cayton, " 'Separate Interests' and the Nation-State: The Washington Administration and the Origins of Regionalism in the Trans-Appalachian West," *JAH* 79 (1993): 39–67; Francis Paul Prucha, *The Sword of the Republic: The United States Army on the Frontier, 1783–1846* (New York: Macmillan, 1969).

2. A second, more modest ceremony occurred in the small trading post of St. Louis on 9 March 1804, when Spain surrendered Upper Louisiana to the United States.

3. William C. C. Claiborne, *Port Regulations* (New Orleans, 1803), broadside, HNO.

4. "Remonstrance of the People of Louisiana against the Political System Adopted by Congress for Them," *ASP,* Misc, 1: 396.

5. *ASP,* Misc, 1: 399.

6. *ASP,* Misc, 1: 397, 402–04.

7. *ASP,* Misc, 1: 399. See also Robert Perry to James Brown, 6 April 1807, James Brown Papers, LSU.

8. *ASP,* Misc, 1: 399.

9. Pierre Derbigny (signed "Peter Derbigny") to Gallatin, 12 August 1803, Carter, 9: 12–13; Louisianias (Pierre Derbigny), *Esquisse de la situation politique et civile de la Louisiane . . .* (New Orleans, 1804). See Claiborne to James Pitot, 20 March 1804, LCDV, 1: 486; Hore Browse Trist to Gallatin, 1 April 1804, Carter, 9: 218.

10. Jefferson, Fourth Annual Message, 8 November 1804, *A Compilation of the Messages and Papers of the Presidents, 1789–1897,* ed. James D. Richardson, 16 vols. (Washington, D.C.: Government Printing Office, 1896–99), 1: 371. For details of the meeting between the delegation from Louisiana and Jefferson, see *Orleans Gazette,* 11 June 1805; William Plumer, *William Plumer's Memorandum of Proceedings in the United States Senate, 1803–1807,* ed. Everett Somerville Brown (New York: Macmillan, 1923), 223. Jefferson himself left no record of this meeting. The most detailed analysis of his reaction to the Remonstrance is Dumas Malone, *Jefferson the President: First Term, 1801–1805* (Boston: Little, Brown, 1970), 360–61.

11. Plumer, *Memorandum of Proceedings in Senate,* 222.

12. Ibid.

13. *Annals of Congress,* 8th Cong., 2d sess. (1804–05), 727–28.

14. Ibid., 1014–15.

15. *Orleans Gazette,* 11 June 1805. See also Claiborne to Madison, 18 March 1805, Carter, 9: 420–21.

16. *Orleans Gazette,* 11 June 1805; *Union* (New Orleans), 11 July 1804.

17. Antonio de Sedella to Patrick Walsh, 7 March 1805; Sedella to Marquis de Casa Calvo, 8 March 1805; Casa Calvo to Walsh, 9 March 1805; all in Antonio de Sedella Papers, TUL. See also Charles Edward O'Neil, "'A Quarter Marked by Sundry Peculiarities': New Orleans, Lay Trustees, and Père Antoine," *Catholic Historical Review* 76 (1990): 237–38. Sedella tendered his resignation as an act of protest when Walsh failed to resolve the differences between two of Sedella's assistant pastors.

18. Claiborne to Henry Hopkins, 29 May 1804, *Claiborne Letterbooks,* 2: 170; Claiborne to Hopkins, 28 July 1804, ibid., 275. Claiborne later singled out Hopkins for special commendation in his handling of the affair. See Claiborne to Madison, 12 December 1806, Carter, 9: 540.

19. It was almost two years after the transfer of power in December 1803 that Carroll finally received written authorization to take charge in Louisiana. See Propaganda Fide, 20 September 1805, in *United States Documents in the Propaganda Fide Archives,* ed. Finbar Kenneally, 7 vols. (Washington, D.C.: Academy of American Franciscan History, 1966–81), 3: 1365; Fide to Walsh, 21 September 1805, ibid., 1366; *Moniteur de la Louisiane* (New Orleans), 21 February 1807, ibid., 5: 1509; Annabelle M. Melville, "John Carroll and Louisiana, 1803–1815," *Catholic Historical Review* 64 (1978): 406. Carroll wrote to Pierre Clément Laussat, the last French governor, seeking his "advice" on Louisiana's ecclesiastical jurisdiction. See John Carroll to Pierre Clément Laussat, 1804, *The John Carroll Papers,* ed. Thomas O'Brien Hanley, 3 vols. (Notre Dame: University of Notre Dame Press, 1976), 2: 429.

20. Caryn Cossé Bell, *Revolution, Romanticism, and the Afro-Creole Protest Tradition in Louisiana, 1718–1868* (Baton Rouge: Louisiana State University Press, 1997), 32.

21. Address from the Free People of Color, January 1804, Carter, 9: 174.

22. PCDV, 1: 98.

23. Claiborne to Casa Calvo, 30 October 1804, *Claiborne Letterbooks,* 2: 382–83.

24. Claiborne to Madison, 5 October 1807, Carter, 9: 765.

25. Edward Turner to James Wilkinson, 15 October 1804, Letters Received, Registered Series, 2: W-466. See also Turner to Claiborne, 16 October 1804, *Claiborne Letterbooks,* 2: 386–88; Turner to Claiborne, 17 October 1804, ibid., 385–86; Claiborne to Turner, 3 November 1804, ibid., 389–90; Claiborne to Madison, 17 October 1807, ibid., 4: 135–36.

26. Thomas Rodney to unknown recipient, 30 September 1805, *Annals of Congress,* 9th Cong., 1st sess. (1805–06), 1201–02. See also John Graham to Claiborne, 16 September 1805, Carter, 9: 504–06. Similar circumstances were also evident in *Paul Macarty's Case,* 2 Martin 279 (La., 1812). See also James Dormon, "The Persistent Specter: Slave Rebellion in Territorial Louisiana," *LAH* 18 (1977): 389–92.

27. For works investigating the intersection of international relations and racial unrest, see Randolph Campbell, *An Empire for Slavery: The Peculiar Institution in Texas, 1821–1865* (Baton Rouge: Louisiana State University Press, 1989), 62–66, 180–81, 218; Woody Holton, "'Rebel against Rebel': Enslaved Virginians and the Coming of the American Revolution," *Virginia Magazine of History and Biography* 105 (1997): 157–92; Christopher Morris, *Becoming Southern: The Evolution of a Way of Life, Warren County and Vicksburg, Mississippi, 1770–1860* (New York: Oxford University Press, 1995).

28. Gwendolyn Midlo Hall, *Africans in Colonial Louisiana: The Development of Afro-Creole Culture in the Eighteenth Century* (Baton Rouge: Louisiana State University Press, 1992), 347–48; Robert L. Paquette, "Revolutionary Saint Domingue in the Making of Territorial Louisiana," in *A Turbulent Time: The French Revolution and the Greater Caribbean,* ed. David B. Gaspar and David Patrick Geggus (Bloomington: Indiana University Press, 1997), 204–25, 219–20.

29. Claiborne to Jean Etienne Boré, 10 August 1804, LCDV, 1: 519. See also Claiborne to Benjamin Butler, 8 November 1804, *Claiborne Letterbooks,* 3: 1; Claiborne to District Commanders, 8 November 1804, Carter, 9: 325–26; Casa Calvo to Claiborne, 10 November 1804, ibid., 329–32; Graham to Claiborne, 19 September 1805, ibid., 513.

30. Petition to Claiborne by inhabitants of Pointe Coupée, 9 November 1804, Carter, 9: 326. See also Claiborne to Civil Commandants, 8 November 1804, ibid., 325–26; Casa Calvo to Claiborne, 9 November 1804, ibid., 328–29; John Watkins to City Council, 14 March 1806, MMCDV, 2: 29–31.

31. Claiborne to Richard Butler, 8 November 1804, *Claiborne Letterbooks,* 3: 1.

32. Douglas R. Egerton, *Gabriel's Rebellion: The Virginia Slave Conspiracies of 1800 and 1802* (Chapel Hill: University of North Carolina Press, 1993); James Sidbury, *Ploughshares into Swords: Race, Rebellion, and Identity in Gabriel's Virginia, 1730–1810* (Cambridge: Cambridge University Press, 1997).

33. PCDV, 1: 132.

34. Watkins to Council, MMCDV, 1: 62.

35. PCDV, 2: 106–07.

36. PCDV, 3: 86. For more on the suspected revolt, see Watkins to Graham, 6 September 1805, Carter, 9: 500–04; Watkins to Council, 7 September 1805 (twice), MMCDV, 1: 58, 67.

37. Hans W. Baade, "The Law of Slavery in Spanish Luisiana," in *Louisiana's Legal Heritage,* ed. Edward F. Haas Jr. (Pensacola: Perdido Bay Press, 1983), 71.

38. PCDV, 2: 100.

39. John Sibley to Henry Dearborn, 1 May 1805, *Annals of Congress,* 9th Cong., 1st sess. (1805–06), 1205. Captain Edward Turner sent a similar report based on identical sources. See Turner to Wilkinson, 5 March 1805, ibid., 1206.

40. Claiborne address to Indians, 28 September 1806, *Claiborne Letterbooks,* 4: 21; Claiborne to John Collins, 28 September 1806, ibid.; Claiborne to Dearborn and Sibley (two letters), 25 July 1807, Letters Received, Registered Series, 5: C-317; Dearborn to Jefferson, 26 December 1807, Jefferson Papers, reel 60.

41. Henry Bry to Dearborn, 1 September 1807, Letters Received, Registered Series, 4: B-295.

42. Carlos Martinez de Yrujo to Pedro Cevallos, 2 December 1802, *Letters of the Lewis and Clark Expedition, with Related Documents, 1783–1854,* ed. Donald Jackson (Urbana: University of Illinois Press, 1978), 1: 4–6; Casa Calvo to Cevallos, 30 March 1804, ibid., 173–74; Carlos de Grand Pré to Daniel P. Hickey, 12 October 1806, Daniel P. Hickey Papers, LSU.

43. Dearborn to Wilkinson, 6 May 1806, Jefferson Papers, reel 57. See also Dearborn to Robert Williams, 8 May 1806, ibid.; J. L. Donaldson to William Stewart, 8 July 1806, ibid., reel 58; Claiborne to Constant Freeman, James Mather, and Richard Claiborne (three letters), 17 August 1806, *Claiborne Letterbooks,* 3: 377–81; Statement by James McKim, David Henson, and Thomas Teal, 26 September 1806, Letters Received, Registered Series, 14: W-190.

44. Villasana Haggard, "The Neutral Ground between Louisiana and Texas, 1806–1821," *LHQ* 28 (1945): 1028–47; Jack D. L. Holmes, "Showdown on the Sabine: General James Wilkinson vs. Lieutenant-Colonel Simón de Herrera," *Louisiana Studies* 3 (1964): 46–76; F. Todd Smith, "The Kadohadacho Indians and the Louisiana-Texas Frontier, 1686–1870," *Southwestern Historical Quarterly* 95 (1991): 192.

45. Wilkinson to Dearborn, 27 September 1806, Letters Received, Registered Series, 14: W-190.

46. Antonio Cordero y Bustamente to Wilkinson, 29 September 1806, ibid., W-191.

47. Cordero y Bustamente to Wilkinson, 29 September 1806, ibid.; Wilkinson to Dearborn, 17 October 1806, ibid., W-195; Wilkinson to General Smith, 23 October 1806, Jefferson Papers, reel 59.

48. Manuel Salcedo to Wilkinson, 18 September 1806, Letters Received, Registered Series, 14: W-195; Wilkinson to Cordero y Bustamente, 24 September 1806, ibid., W-190; Cordero y Bustamente to Wilkinson, 29 September 1806, ibid., W-191.

49. Dehahuit, speech to Claiborne, 5 September 1806, *Claiborne Letterbooks,* 3: 4.

50. Claiborne to Dearborn, 29 July 1806, ibid., 374–75.

51. Gideon Granger to Blaise Cenas, 30 March 1807, Carter, 9: 724–25. Granger's

complaints eventually appeared in the New Orleans press. See *Louisiana Gazette*, 5 January 1811. See also Claiborne to Madison, 21 April 1805, 29 April 1805, Carter, 9: 437–39, 445–46. Claiborne specifically shared Granger's lament about a road to Natchez in Claiborne to Granger, 7 November 1808, *Claiborne Letterbooks,* 4: 245.

52. Richard R. John, *Spreading the News: The American Postal System from Franklin to Morse* (Cambridge: Harvard University Press, 1995), 3–5; John Lauritz Larson, "Jefferson's Union and the Problem of Internal Improvements," in *Jeffersonian Legacies,* ed. Peter S. Onuf (Charlottesville: University Press of Virginia, 1993), 340–69; Drew R. McCoy, *The Last of the Fathers: James Madison and the Republican Legacy* (Cambridge: Cambridge University Press, 1988), 102.

53. Dearborn to Williams, 8 May 1806, Jefferson Papers, reel 57. See also Harry Toulmin to Claiborne, 6 July 1805, *Annals of Congress,* 9th Cong., 1st sess. (1805–06), 1186–87; Claiborne to Juan Ventura Morales, 22 October 1805, *Claiborne Letterbooks,* 3: 205–06; Toulmin to Madison, 6 July 1805, *Annals of Congress,* 9th Cong., 1st sess., 1187; Claiborne to Madison, 24 October 1805, ibid., 1186–87; Claiborne to Madison, 9 December 1805, Carter, 9: 542–43; Claiborne to Jefferson, 3 March 1806, Jefferson Papers, reel 57; Claiborne to Madison, 21 April 1807, *Claiborne Letterbooks,* 4: 124–25; *Annals of Congress,* 11th Cong., 2d sess. (1809–10), 1257, 1443, 1761.

54. Peter Joseph Hamilton, *Colonial Mobile: An Historical Study, Largely from Original Sources, of the Alabama-Tombigbee Basin from the Discovery of Mobile Bay in 1519 until the Demolition of Fort Charlotte in 1821* (Boston: Houghton Mifflin, 1897); Daniel H. Usner Jr., *Indians, Settlers, and Slaves in a Frontier Exchange Economy: The Lower Mississippi Valley before 1783* (Chapel Hill: University of North Carolina Press, 1992), 106–30; David J. Weber, *The Spanish Frontier in North America* (New Haven: Yale University Press, 1992), 265–70.

55. Isaac Cox, *The West Florida Controversy, 1798–1813: A Study in American Diplomacy* (Baltimore: Johns Hopkins Press, 1923), 158–68; Andrew McMichael, "Reluctant Revolutionaries: The West Florida Borderlands, 1785–1810" (Ph.D. diss., Vanderbilt University, 2000). For more general problems facing Spanish officials, see Cox, 139–87.

56. William Brown to James Brown, 31 July 1806, James Brown Papers; John Owings to David Porter, 20 August 1808, *Weekly Chronicle* (Natchez, Miss.), 27 August 1808; David F. Long, *Nothing to Daring: A Biography of Commodore David Porter, 1780–1843* (Annapolis: Naval Institute Press, 1970), 43–45.

57. William B. Hatcher, *Edward Livingston: Jeffersonian Republican and Jacksonian Democrat* (Baton Rouge: Louisiana State University Press, 1940), 93–98.

58. Ibid., 94.

59. PCDV, 4: 263–64.

60. PCDV, 4: 287; 5: 11. See also PCDV, 4: 263–66; 5: 14–18; *Examination of the Rights of the United States and the Claims of Mr. Edward Livingston on the Batture in Front of the Faubourg Ste. Marie* (New Orleans: Thierry, 1808).

61. Claiborne to Jefferson, 29 June 1804, Carter, 9: 245. See also Claiborne to Jefferson, 1 July 1804, Jefferson Papers, reel 43; William Dunbar to Jefferson, 15 October 1804, in *Life, Letters and Papers of William Dunbar,* ed. Eron Rowland (Jackson: Mississippi Historical Society, 1930), 160–62; Claiborne to Jefferson, 10 December 1804, Jefferson Papers, reel 51.

62. Clark to Claiborne, 24 May 1807, in Claiborne to Jefferson, 28 May 1807, Jefferson Papers, reel 62. For the events leading to the duel, see Joseph T. Hatfield, *William Claiborne: Jeffersonian Centurion in the American Southwest* (Lafayette: University of Southwestern Louisiana, 1976), 159–61.

63. Claiborne to Jefferson, 12 June 1807, Jefferson Papers, reel 62.

64. Wilkinson Deposition, 25 November 1806, *Annals of Congress,* 9th Cong., 2d sess. (1806–07), 1008. See also Jefferson to Claiborne, 29 December 1806, Jefferson Papers, reel 59.

65. Jefferson Proclamation, 27 November 1806; William Duane to Jefferson, September 1806; Jefferson to James Ferguson, 3 December 1806; Thomas Truxtun to Jefferson, 4 December 1806; Claiborne to Jefferson, 5 December 1806; Jefferson to George Langdon, 22 December 1806; all in Jefferson Papers, reel 59; Justus Bollman to Jefferson, 27 September 1806, *Annals of Congress,* 9th Cong., 2d sess. (1809–10), 1011–12; Joseph Browne to Madison, 12 November 1806, Carter, 9: 34; Wilkinson to Dearborn, 12 November 1806, Letters Received, Registered Series, 14, W-209; Andrew Jackson to Claiborne, *Jackson Papers,* 2: 116–17; Jackson to Jefferson, 24 November 1806, Jefferson Papers, reel 59; Jefferson to Jackson, 3 December 1806, *Jackson Papers,* 2: 121; Jackson to George Washington Campbell, 15 January 1807, ibid., 147–50, especially 148.

Chapter 4. Codes

1. Monroe to Madison, 10 January 1806, *Monroe Writings,* 4: 392.

2. Jefferson, "Chronological series of facts," 1803, Jefferson Papers, reel 47; idem, "An Examination into the Boundaries of Louisiana," 7 September 1803, ibid.; "An inquiry concerning the Northern Boundary of Canada and Louisiana," undated 1803 original from Madison to Monroe, Madison Papers, reel 8. For American diplomatic policies during these years, see Alexander DeConde, *This Affair of Louisiana* (New York: Charles Scribner's Sons, 1976), 213–25; Robert W. Tucker and David C. Hendrickson, *Empire of Liberty: The Statecraft of Thomas Jefferson* (New York: Oxford University Press, 1990), 136–44.

3. Grand Pré to Philip Hickey, 12 October 1806, Philip Hickey Papers, LSU.

4. Jefferson, Sixth Annual Message, 2 December 1806, *A Compilation of the Messages and Papers of the Presidents, 1789–1897,* ed. James D. Richardson, 16 vols. (Washington, D.C.: Government Printing Office, 1896–99), 1: 405–06.

5. Merrill D. Peterson, *Thomas Jefferson and the New Nation: A Biography* (Oxford: Oxford University Press, 1970), 810–18. See also Gallatin to Jefferson, Jefferson Papers, reel 59. An indication of the administration's concerns came almost a year before. See Albert Gallatin's notes of cabinet meeting, 4 April 1806, Jefferson Papers, reel 59.

6. Anthony Merry to Lord Hawkesbury, 19 March 1804, quoted in Tim Matthewson, "Thomas Jefferson and Haiti," *Journal of Southern History* 61 (1995): 233.

7. *Statutes at Large,* 2: 351–52. The exclusion was originally limited to one year, but in 1807 the United States extended the policy for a second year. See ibid., 421–22. For the broader influence of Haitian independence on American foreign and domestic policy, see Peter S. Onuf, " 'To Declare Them a Free and Independent People': Race, Slavery, and

National Identity in Jefferson's Thought," *JER* 18 (1998): 1–46; Robert L. Paquette, "Revolutionary Saint Domingue in the Making of Territorial Louisiana," in *A Turbulent Time: The French Revolution and the Greater Caribbean,* ed. David B. Gaspar and David Patrick Geggus (Bloomington: Indiana University Press, 1997), 204–05. Although Jefferson's policy toward Haiti has been the subject of considerable scholarly interest, Madison's policy has not. Historians of American foreign relations have situated revolutionary Saint Domingue within a context of Madison's plans for the acquisition of Louisiana, but few have considered the way Madison constructed a policy toward the independent Haiti. For examples, see Ralph Ketcham, *James Madison: A Biography* (Charlottesville: University Press of Virginia, 1990); Drew R. McCoy, *The Last of the Fathers: James Madison and the Republican Legacy* (Cambridge: Cambridge University Press, 1988).

8. Lester Langley, *The Americas in the Age of Revolution* (New Haven: Yale University Press, 1996), 140–41. In the 1820s President James Monroe and his secretary of state, John Quincy Adams, excluded Haiti from their efforts to build diplomatic ties throughout the Americas.

9. *Annals of Congress,* 8th Cong., 2d sess. (1804–05), 1016–17. For discussion of the revisions in Orleans governance, see ibid., 45–46, 68–69, 957, 1020–21, 1213, 1215.

10. *Statutes at Large,* 2: 322–23. Claiborne had already recognized that the creation of a congressional delegate might satisfy many of the Louisianians' complaints. See Claiborne to Madison, 22 October 1804, Madison Papers, reel 8. In addition to structural changes in the government of the Territory of Orleans, complaints from the District of Louisiana were equally effective. The Governance Act of 1805 also reconstituted the District of Louisiana in the Territory of Louisiana, separating it once and for all from the Indiana Territory. Jefferson soon appointed James Wilkinson the first territorial governor.

11. *Statutes at Large,* 2: 324–29; Harry Lewis Coles, *History of the Administration of Federal Land Policies and Land Tenure in Louisiana, 1803–1860* (New York: Arno, 1979), 10–13.

12. Edward T. Price, *Dividing the Land: Early American Beginnings of Our Private Property Mosaic* (Chicago: University of Chicago Press, 1995), 289–304.

13. Black Code, in François-Xavier Martin, *A General Digest of the Acts of the Legislatures of the Late Territory of Orleans, and the State of Louisiana . . .* (New Orleans: Peter K. Wagner, 1816), 616.

14. Ibid., 640–42.

15. Ibid., 614.

16. Virginia Domínguez, *White by Definition: Social Classification in Creole Louisiana* (New Brunswick, N.J.: Rutgers University Press, 1986).

17. *Acts Passed* (1806), 126. The 1806 law applied only to free *men* of color, not to women and children under fifteen, "who shall be supposed to have left the island above named, to fly from the horrors committed during its insurrection."

18. Much of the emerging literature on whiteness has argued that establishing whiteness was an attractive means for immigrants to claim what they saw as the benefits of life in the United States. In the process, they were quick to support racial supremacy. See Matthew Frye Jacobson, *Whiteness of a Different Color: European Immigrants and the Alchemy of Race* (Cambridge: Harvard University Press, 1998).

19. Stephen Aron, *How the West Was Lost: The Transformation of Kentucky from Daniel Boone to Henry Clay* (Baltimore: Johns Hopkins University Press, 1996); Gregory S. Alexander, *Commodity and Propriety: Competing Visions of Property in American Legal Thought, 1776–1970* (Chicago: University of Chicago Press, 1977), 26–88; Jennifer Nedelsky, *Private Property and the Limits of American Constitutionalism: The Madisonian Framework and Its Legacy* (Chicago: University of Chicago Press, 1990); John R. Nelson Jr., *Liberty and Property: Political Economy and Policymaking in the New Nation, 1789–1812* (Baltimore: Johns Hopkins University Press, 1987); Alan Taylor, "Land and Liberty on the Post-Revolutionary Frontier," in *Devising Liberty: Preserving and Creating Freedom in the New American Republic,* ed. David T. Konig (Stanford: Stanford University Press, 1995), 81–108.

20. James Brown and Louis Moreau-Lislet, *A Digest of the Civil Laws Now in Force in the Territory of Orleans ... Adapted to its Present System of Government* (New Orleans: Bradford and Anderson, 1808). Over two decades ago, George Dargo correctly admonished historians to refer to the 1808 document as a digest, not a civil code. The 1808 *Civil Digest* was just that—a compilation of existing legal principles. Not until 1825 did Louisiana enact a true civil code, a treatise that spelled out legal principles with far greater detail than the 1808 *Digest.*

21. Ira Berlin, "From Creole to African: Atlantic Creoles and the Origins of African-American Society in Mainland North America," *WMQ,* 3d ser., 53 (1996): 251–88; David C. Rankin, "The Tannenbaum Thesis Reconsidered: Slavery and Race Relations in Antebellum Louisiana," *Southern Studies* 18 (1979): 5–31; Judith Kelleher Schafer, *Slavery, the Civil Law, and the Supreme Court of Louisiana* (Baton Rouge: Louisiana State University Press, 1994); Frank Tannenbaum, *Slave and Citizen: The Negro in the Americas* (New York: Knopf, 1947).

22. Laura Foner, "The Free People of Color in Louisiana and St. Domingue: A Comparative Portrait of Two Three-Caste Slave Societies," *Journal of Social History* 3 (1970): 404–30; Thomas N. Ingersoll, "Free Blacks in a Slave Society: New Orleans, 1718–1812," *WMQ,* 3d ser., 48 (1991): 194–97; Paul F. Lachance, "The Formation of a Three-Caste Society: Evidence from Wills in Antebellum New Orleans," *Social Science History* 18 (1994): 212–13, 225–36; Rankin, "The Tannenbaum Thesis Reconsidered"; Schafer, *Slavery, Civil Law, and Supreme Court of Louisiana,* 6.

23. Claiborne to Madison, December 27, 1803, Madison Papers, reel 8. See also Claiborne to Madison, February 4, 1804, ibid.; Claiborne to Major Boré, February 8, 1804, *Claiborne Letterbooks,* 1: 8.

24. For Louisiana's colonial legal heritage, see George Dargo, *Jefferson's Louisiana: Politics and the Clash of Legal Traditions* (Cambridge: Harvard University Press, 1975); Mark F. Fernandez, "The Appellate Question: A Comparative Analysis of Supreme Courts of Appeal in Virginia and Louisiana, 1776–1840" (Ph.D. diss., College of William and Mary, 1991). For examples from Upper Louisiana, see Stuart Banner, "The Political Function of the Commons: Changing Conceptions of Property and Sovereignty in Missouri, 1750–1860," *American Journal of Legal History* 41 (1997): 61–93.

25. Claiborne to Madison, 15 June 1806, *Claiborne Letterbooks,* 3: 331–32; Warren M. Billings, "Origins of Criminal Law in Louisiana," *LAH* 32 (1991): 65; idem, "A Neglected Treaty: Lewis Kerr's Exposition and the Making of Criminal Law in Loui-

siana," *LAH* 38 (1997): 261–86; Mark F. Fernandez, "The Rules of the Courts of the Territory of Orleans," *LAH* 37 (1997): 63–86.

26. Petition to Congress by Lawyers of the Territory (no date), enclosed in Brown to Samuel Smith, 28 November 1805, Carter, 9: 539. See also Derbigny to Watkins, 24 January 1806, MMCDV, 1: 12–14; Fernandez, "The Appellate Question," 102.

27. Helen Tunncliff Catterall, ed., *Judicial Cases Concerning American Slavery and the Negro*, 5 vols. (Washington, D.C.: Carnegie Institution, 1932–37), 3: 1; Philip J. Schwartz, *Slave Laws in Virginia* (Athens: University of Georgia Press, 1996); Rowland Berthoff, "Conventional Mentality: Free Blacks, Women, and Business Corporations as Unequal Persons, 1820–1870," *JAH* 76 (1989): 753–84.

28. Laussat to Council, 11 December 1803, LCDV, 1: 462; PCDV, 1: 5–6; James Pitot, *Observations on the Colony of Louisiana from 1796 to 1802* (Baton Rouge: Louisiana State University Press, 1979), 30; Hans W. Baade, "The Law of Slavery in Spanish Louisiana," in *Louisiana's Legal Heritage,* ed. Edward F. Haas Jr. (Pensacola: Perdido Bay Press, 1983), 188–90, 195; Paul F. Lachance, "The Politics of Fear: French Louisianans and the Slave Trade, 1786–1809," *Plantation Society* 1 (1979): 177–84.

29. Coles, *Administration of Federal Land Policies,* 70–71; Edward F. Haas, "Odyssey of a Manuscript Collection: Records of the Surveyor General of Antebellum Louisiana," *LAH* 27 (1986): 5–19.

30. Gallatin to Joseph Anderson, 4 April 1806, Carter, 9: 624.

31. *Statutes at Large,* 2: 391–92. See also ibid., 324–29.

32. Lance Banning, *The Sacred Fire of Liberty: James Madison and the Founding of the Federal Republic* (Cornell: Cornell University Press, 1995), 184–91, 259–61; Jack N. Rakove, *Original Meanings: Politics and Ideas in the Making of the Constitution* (New York: Vintage, 1997), 280–87; Gordon S. Wood, *The Creation of the American Republic, 1776–1787* (New York: Norton, 1969), 545–53.

33. Matson and Onuf, *A Union of Interests;* Drew R. McCoy, *The Elusive Republic: Political Economy in Jeffersonian America* (New York: Norton, 1980), 5–10, 40–41; Herbert E. Sloan, *Principle and Interest: Thomas Jefferson and the Problem of Debt* (New York: Oxford University Press, 1995), 86–124.

34. Andrew R. L. Cayton, *The Frontier Republic: Ideology and Politics in the Ohio Country* (Kent: Kent State University Press, 1986), 21–32; idem, " 'Separate Interests' and the Nation-State: The Washington Administration and the Origins of Regionalism in the Trans-Appalachian West," *JAH* 79 (1993): 39–67; Richard H. Kohn, *Eagle and Sword: The Federalists and the Creation of the Military Establishment in America, 1783–1802* (New York: Free Press, 1975), 86–87, 183–89, 281–86; Matson and Onuf, *A Union of Interests,* 78–81, 95–97, 150. For the importance of economic development to the nation as a whole, see Joyce O. Appleby, *Capitalism and a New Social Order: The Republican Vision of the 1790s* (New York: New York University Press, 1984).

35. For Claiborne's early career, see Joseph T. Hatfield, *William Claiborne: Jeffersonian Centurion in the American Southwest* (Lafayette: University of Southwestern Louisiana, 1976), 1–95. For Claiborne's accumulation of power, see Marion Nelson Winship, "The Territorial Aspirations of William Charles Cole Claiborne: A Western Success Story from the Jeffersonian Empire," paper presented at the 1998 meeting of the Society for Historians of the Early American Republic.

36. Hatfield, *William Claiborne,* 207–08.

37. Claiborne to Jefferson, 29 September 1803, Jefferson Papers, reel 47. See also Claiborne to Madison, 2 January 1804, Madison Papers, reel 8.

38. Claiborne to the Territorial Legislature, 24 March 1806, *Claiborne Letterbooks,* 3: 274–79.

39. *Acts Passed* (1805), 44–73.

40. Ibid., 388–99; Billings, "Origins of Criminal Law in Louisiana," 63–76; Fernandez, "Rules of Courts of Territory of Orleans," 63–86.

41. *Acts Passed* (1805), 384–87; Alain A. Levasseur, *Louis Casimir Elisabeth Moreau-Lislet, Foster Father of Louisiana Civil Law* (Baton Rouge: Louisiana State University, 1996), 118–19. For similar conditions in other territories, see John Wunder, "American Law and Order Comes to the Mississippi Territory: The Making of Sargent's Code, 1798–1800," *Journal of Mississippi History* 38 (1976): 140–41; Kermit I. Hall, "Hacks and Derelicts Revisited: American Territorial Judiciary, 1789–1959," *Western Historical Quarterly* 12 (1981): 273–89. The latitude that territorial judges enjoyed was quite similar to that of the judiciary in Spanish America. See John R. Cutter, "The Administration of Law in Colonial New Mexico," *JER* 18 (1998): 99–115.

42. PCDV, 4: 6–8, 132.

43. Brian J. Cook, *Bureaucracy and Self-Government: Reconsidering the Role of Public Administration in American Politics* (Baltimore: Johns Hopkins University Press, 1996), 24–48; Leonard White, *The Federalists: A Study in Administrative History* (New York: Macmillan, 1948), 36.

44. Andrew R. L. Cayton, "Land, Power, and Reputation: The Cultural Dimension of Politics in the Ohio Country," *WMQ,* 3d ser., 47 (1990): 268; Jack Ericson Eblen, *The First and Second United States Empires: Governors and Territorial Government, 1784–1912* (Pittsburgh: University of Pittsburgh Press, 1968), 114–36; Richard Ellis, *The Jeffersonian Crisis: Courts and Politics in the Young Republic* (New York: Norton, 1971), 5–6; Robert M. Ireland, *The County Courts in Antebellum Kentucky* (Lexington: University Press of Kentucky, 1972); David Thomas Konig, "Jurisprudence and Social Policy in the New Republic," in *Devising Liberty: Preserving and Creating Freedom in the New American Republic,* ed. Konig (Stanford: Stanford University Press, 1995), 178–216.

45. Orders from Claiborne and J. Faurie, 22 September 1804, *Claiborne Letterbooks,* 2: 339–40; *Acts Passed* (1805), 98–103; Mary P. Adams, "Jefferson's Military Policy with Special Reference to the Frontier, 1805–1809" (Ph.D. diss., University of Virginia, 1958).

46. Deposition of Francis Whitmell, 28 November 1807, William C. C. Claiborne Papers, LSU; Charles Laveau Trudeau to Claiborne, 29 November 1811, Mayor's Minute Book, NOPL, 1: 49–50; Rosemarie Catherine McGrath, "The Issue of the Foreign Slave Trade in the Louisiana Territory, 1803–1810" (Master's thesis, University of Virginia, 1967).

47. PCDV, 2: 97. For local demands that the army defend New Orleans, see Watkins to Council, 1 August 1805, MMCDV, 1: 46; David Holmes to Thomas Cushing, 28 September 1810, Carter, 6: 121–22. See also Theodore J. Crackel, *Mr. Jefferson's Army: Political and Social Reform of the Military Establishment, 1801–1809* (New York: New York University Press, 1987), 104–10.

48. Watkins to Council, 29 September 1805, MMCDV, 1: 63; Claiborne to Jefferson, 6 November 1805, Jefferson Papers, reel 55; Watkins to Council, 4 January 1806, 14 February 1806, 1 March 1806, MMCDV, 2: 1, 21–24, 26–27; Mather to Council, 14 March 1807, 7 April 1807, 6 October 1807, 13 April 1808, 1 November 1809, 17 January 1810, MMCDV, 2: 29–31, 142–43, 198–200; 3: 31, 166–68; 4: 1–4. For relations between the Guard and militia, see Watkins to Council, 4 September 1805, MMCDV, 1: 57; PCDV, 2: 25–32, 92, 134, 144, 155–56, 165. For comparisons between the Guard and other urban police forces, see Dennis C. Rousey, *Policing the Southern City: New Orleans 1805–1889* (Baton Rouge: Louisiana State University Press, 1996), 16–18.

49. PCDV, 2: 30.

50. PCDV, 5: 232. For additional comments on the City Guard, see PCDV, 2: 107; 6: 1–2; 5: 182; 6: 269; 8: 239–40, 247; 10: 48–50; Watkins to Council, 7 September 1805, MMCDV, 1: 58.

51. Claiborne to Madison, 27 December 1803, Madison Papers, reel 8. See also Claiborne to Madison, 4 February 1804, ibid.; Claiborne to Major Boré, 8 February 1804, *Claiborne Letterbooks*, 1: 8.

52. Roland C. McConnell, *Negro Troops of Antebellum Louisiana: A History of the Battalion of Free Men of Color* (Baton Rouge: Louisiana State University Press, 1968), 41.

53. Claiborne to Madison, 27 December 1803, *Claiborne Letterbooks*, 1: 314.

54. Caryn Cossé Bell, *Revolution, Romanticism, and the Afro-Creole Protest Tradition in Louisiana, 1718–1868* (Baton Rouge: Louisiana State University Press, 1997), 41–45; McConnell, *Negro Troops of Antebellum Louisiana*, 43–54.

55. For studies of early American governance that employ these conceptions of efficiency and corruption, see Noble E. Cunningham, *The Jeffersonian Republicans in Power: Party Operations, 1801–1809* (Chapel Hill: University of North Carolina Press, 1963), 12–28, 30–70; L. White, *The Federalists*, 256–63; idem, *The Jeffersonians: A Study in Administrative History, 1801–1829* (New York: Macmillan, 1951), 151–56. In his multivolume study of American public administration, White called particular attention to the problems he associated with patronage.

56. Robert Gough, "Officering the American Army, 1798," WMQ, 3d ser., 43 (1986): 460–71; Christopher McKee, *A Gentlemanly and Honorable Profession: The Creation of the U.S. Naval Officer Corps, 1794–1815* (Annapolis: Naval Institute Press, 1991), xii–xiii, 43–48; L. White, *The Jeffersonians*, 151. Although presidents tended to keep in office men who had been appointed by their predecessors, they based their own appointments on partisan allegiance.

57. Brian W. Beltman, "Territorial Commands of the Army: The System Refined but Not Perfected," *JER* 11 (1991): 185–218; Richard White, *"It's Your Misfortune and None of My Own": A New History of the American West* (Norman: University of Oklahoma Press, 1991), 58.

58. Benjamin Morgan to Chandler Price, 11 August 1803, Carter, 9: 8. See also Claiborne to Jefferson, 16 January 1804, ibid., 161; Claiborne to Miguel Cantrell and Francis Connel (two letters), 3 May 1804, *Claiborne Letterbooks*, 2: 127–28; Claiborne to Jefferson, 27 October 1804, Jefferson Papers, reel 50.

59. While postal delivery did foster a nationalizing political culture, it was too slow to promote fundamental change in the American administrative culture. Correspondence had to coexist with personal networks that enabled officials to trust in the discretion of their subordinates. For the speed of postal delivery, see Richard R. John, *Spreading the News: The American Postal System from Franklin to Morse* (Cambridge: Harvard University Press, 1995), 1–63. For a comparison at the state level, see Peter J. Kastor, " 'Equitable Rights and Privileges': The Divided Loyalties of Washington County, Virginia, during the Franklin Separatist Crisis," *Virginia Magazine of History and Biography* 105 (1997): 198–201, 215–16.

60. Cayton, "Land, Power, and Reputation"; idem, " 'Separate Interests' "; Winship, "Territorial Aspirations of Claiborne."

61. For a full discussion of the candidates whom Jefferson considered for the office of governor, see Walter Prichard, ed., "Selecting a Governor for the Territory of Orleans," *LHQ* 31 (1948): 269–393.

62. Jefferson to Claiborne, 30 August 1804, Carter, 9: 281–82. Clarence Carter, the editor of *Territorial Papers of the United States,* claimed that Jefferson was referring to Lafayette.

63. Jefferson to John Dickinson, 13 January 1807, Ford, 9: 9.

64. Porter to Samuel Hambleton, 18 July 1810, David Dixon Porter Papers, LC; David F. Long, *Nothing too Daring: A Biography of Commodore David Porter, 1780–1843* (Annapolis: Naval Institute Press, 1970).

65. Claiborne wrote dozens of letters appointing or recommending men to public office. Many of these letters are clustered in groups. For an example, see *Claiborne Letterbooks,* 2: 78–80. Claiborne's authority became evident in 1807, when Jefferson asked him to find an appointment for J. Philip Reibelt; Jefferson to Claiborne, 3 May 1807, Jefferson Papers, reel 61.

66. Claiborne to Theodore Stark, 1 April 1805, Carter, 9: 431–32. Other officials also attempted to secure appointments. They did so by seeking favors from the administration, while Claiborne enjoyed an unquestioned right to act to select officials. See Trist to Gallatin, 1 April 1804, ibid., 218–19; Brown to Gallatin, 29 May 1807, ibid., 741–42.

67. Jefferson's numerous lists of nominees are contained in a box titled "Nominations," SEN 9B-A1-A2-A3, NA. For the debate over the constitutional controls for the federal workforce, see Cook, *Bureaucracy and Self-Government,* 1–20.

68. "Nominations"; Register of Civil Appointments in the Territory of Orleans, 13 February 1806, Carter, 9: 598–603; Graham to Madison, 8 May 1808, ibid., 631–40; List of Civil and Military Officers, 21 April 1809, ibid., 835–38. See Cayton, "Land, Power, and Reputation," 274–84; Winship, "Territorial Aspirations of Claiborne"; Marion Nelson Winship, "Enterprise in Motion in the Early American Republic: The Federal Government and the Making of Thomas Worthington," *Business and Economic History: The Journal of the Business History Conference* 23 (1994): 81–91.

69. Prevost's appointment was a long time coming. No sooner was Jefferson's victory in 1800 apparent than Prevost was asking Monroe to intercede on his behalf. See Harry Ammon, *James Monroe: The Search for National Identity* (Charlottesville: University Press of Virginia, 1990), 196.

70. Jefferson to Judge Lewis, 16 January 1807, Carter, 9: 703; Jefferson to Gallatin,

9 February 1807, Jefferson Papers, reel 61; John Prevost to Monroe, 3 February 1812, Miscellaneous Letters, reel 25; Claiborne to Seth Lewis, 19 October 1802, *Claiborne Letterbooks,* 1: 204; Jefferson to the United States Senate, 31 December 1806, "Nominations."

71. *Annals of Congress,* 9th Cong., 1st sess. (1805–06), 928.

72. For the story of Trist and his family, see *PJM-PS,* 2: 424–26; Gallatin to Jefferson, 12 November 1803, Jefferson Papers, reel 47; Gallatin to Trist, 14 November 1803, Carter, 9: 106–07; Trist to Gallatin, 5 December 1803, Albert Gallatin Papers, LC, reel 9. For Trist's experience before reaching Louisiana, see Trist to Jefferson, 17 October 1803, Jefferson Papers, reel 47. For his death, see Claiborne to Madison, 29 August 1804, Carter, 9: 279.

73. Gallatin to Jefferson, 12 November 1803, Jefferson Papers, reel 47; Gallatin to Trist, 14 November 1803, Carter, 9: 106–07; Claiborne to Madison, 29 August 1804, ibid., 279; John Gelston to Jefferson, 1 September 1804, ibid., 289–90; Barker to Nathaniel Evans, 1 September 1804, Nathaniel Evans Papers, LSU. The yellow fever epidemic of 1804 devastated southern Louisiana, and by September Claiborne estimated that five to eight people were dying every day. William Brown eventually disappeared with the port revenue, prompting a manhunt throughout Louisiana. When he was not found, Lieutenant Joseph Bainbridge, commanding the ketch *Etna,* scoured the Caribbean in the winter of 1809–10. Only after dropping anchor at Cuba, New Providence, Antigua, St. Kitts, and St. Bartholomew did Bainbridge, too, give up the search. See *PJM-PS,* 2: 424–25; Joseph Bainbridge to Paul Hamilton, 6 February 1810, Letters to Officers, 8: 80.

74. Crackel, *Mr. Jefferson's Army;* Cunningham, *The Jeffersonian Republicans in Power,* 15–29.

75. Robert V. Remini, *Henry Clay: Statesman for the Union* (New York: Norton, 1991), 18, 22, 29, 32–33. Brown's advocates in Kentucky initially hoped to secure an appointment for him as collector in New Orleans. See Thomas Sandford and others to Jefferson, 28 December 1803, Carter, 9: 154. For Brown's attitude as a client of federal patronage, see Brown to Claiborne, 24 August 1805, ibid., 494; Brown to Madison, 7 May 1805, ibid., 448–49.

76. "Some Letters of James Brown of Louisiana to Presidents of the United States," *LHQ* 20 (1937): 58–136; "Letters of James Brown to Henry Clay, 1804–1835," *LHQ* 24 (1941): 922–34.

77. Claiborne and Thomas B. Robertson to Porter, 6 May 1809, *Claiborne Letterbooks,* 4: 349. For similar examples of Clay's patronage, see Breckinridge to Henry Clay, 30 December 1803, *Clay Papers,* 1: 124–25; Clay to Caesar A. Rodney, 10 April 1810, ibid., 409; Clay to Rodney, 17 August 1811, ibid., 574–75.

78. Jefferson to Claiborne, 7 January 1805, Carter, 9: 363; Claiborne to Jefferson, 3 May 1807, ibid., 730. For Madison's opinion of Graham, see Madison to Pinckney, 9 June 1801, *PJM-SS,* 1: 279 and n. 8. Another relative, William Brent, moved to Louisiana sometime around 1809 to begin his own legal practice before serving as deputy attorney general for the western portion of the Territory of Orleans. William Brent was elected to Congress from Louisiana in 1823.

79. Claiborne to Jefferson, 3 May 1807, Carter, 9: 729.

80. Carroll to Daniel Brent, 3 March 1807, *The John Carroll Papers,* ed. Thomas O'Brien Hanley, 3 vols. (Notre Dame: University of Notre Dame Press, 1976), 3: 11–12.

81. Martin's most substantial publishing projects were François-Xavier Martin, ed., *A Treatise on the Powers and Duties of Executors and Administrators* . . . (New Bern, N.C.: Martin and Ogden, 1803) and *The Office and Authority of a Justice of the Peace* . . . (New Bern, N.C.: Martin and Ogden, 1804).

82. William Blackledge to Madison, 12 December 1808, Carter, 9: 811.

83. For the nationalizing role of the government and political networks, see John, *Spreading the News,* 52–53; David Waldstreicher, *In the Midst of Perpetual Fetes: The Making of American Nationalism, 1776–1820* (Chapel Hill: University of North Carolina Press, 1997), 280–81.

84. Jefferson to Claiborne, 17 April 1804, Carter, 9: 225.

85. Claiborne to Jefferson, 30 August 1804, ibid., 284–85; Jefferson to Dickinson, 13 January 1807, Ford, 9: 9.

86. Wilkinson to Jefferson, 1 July 1804, Carter, 9: 248–58.

87. For Claiborne's eagerness to appoint Louisianians, see Claiborne to Robert Smith, 30 May 1809, *Claiborne Letterbooks,* 4: 373.

88. Claiborne to Madison, 4 March 1810, *PJM-PS,* 2: 262. See also Claiborne to Jefferson, 13 November 1805, Jefferson Papers, reel 55; Jefferson to Claiborne, 10 February 1806, ibid.; Claiborne to Territorial House of Representatives, 26 March 1806, *Claiborne Letterbooks,* 3: 282; Claiborne to Jefferson, 3 April 1806, ibid., 283–84; Winship, "Territorial Aspirations of Claiborne."

89. Claiborne to Jefferson, 15 November 1805, Carter, 9: 525.

90. Julien Poydras, *A Speech by Mr. Poydras, President of the Legislative Council of Orleans* (New Orleans, 1804), 7–8; Claiborne to Richard Relf, 12 March 1805, Carter, 9: 416; Claiborne to John Alexander, 7 May 1805, *Claiborne Letterbooks,* 3: 42–43; Jefferson to Senate, 31 December 1806, "Nominations."

91. Frances Pirotte Zink, *Julien Poydras: Statesman, Philanthropist, Educator* (Lafayette: University of Southwestern Louisiana, 1968), 1–20.

92. Poydras, *A Speech by Mr. Poydras,* 7–8; Claiborne to Relf, 12 March 1805, Carter, 9: 416; Claiborne to Alexander, 7 May 1805, *Claiborne Letterbooks,* 3: 42–43; Jefferson to Senate, 31 December 1806, "Nominations."

93. Claiborne to Lewis, 19 October 1802, *Claiborne Letterbooks,* 1: 204. See also Claiborne to Dearborn, 9 June 1804, ibid., 2: 200; Claiborne to Dearborn, 22 June 1804, ibid., 217; Julien Poydras to Gallatin, 27 October 1803, Albert Gallatin Papers, reel 8; Oliver Pollock to Gallatin, 18 October 1803, ibid.; Claiborne to Manuel Andry, 9 July 1805, *Claiborne Letterbooks,* 3: 118; Claiborne to Jefferson, 16 October 1805, ibid., 204; Claiborne to Lewis Kerr, 14 November 1805, ibid., 232–33.

94. Sidney Louis Villeré, *Jacques Philippe Villeré, First Native-Born Governor of Louisiana, 1816–1820* (New Orleans: Historic New Orleans Collection, 1981), 36; list of militia officers, 8 May 1805, in Graham to Madison, 8 May 1805, Carter, 9: 635. Of the ten colonels in 1809, half were Louisianians. See list of civil and military officers, ibid., 838.

95. Wilkinson to Dearborn, 3 November 1804, Letters Received, Registered Series, 2: W-291; Wilkinson to Dearborn, 2 January 1805, ibid., W-312; *Senate Executive Journal,*

2: 91, 153, 201, 271, 405, 540; Crackel, *Mr. Jefferson's Army;* McKee, *A Gentlemanly and Honorable Profession,* 62–63. Michael Walsh prospered in the army, receiving regular promotions and weathering the considerable reduction in the officer corps that came in 1809, when the end of the Embargo and the imminent threat of war with Great Britain led the Madison administration to dismiss many of the officers who had been in the large expansion of the army that came only two years earlier. See *Senate Executive Journal,* 1: 480; 2: 52, 199.

96. Clay to Rodney, 17 August 1811, *Clay Papers,* 1: 575; John Clay to Clay, 31 October 1820, ibid., 2: 899; *DLB,* 1: 273.

97. Claiborne to Jefferson, 12 November 1806, Carter, 9: 687.

98. Claiborne and Robertson to Porter, 6 May 1809, *Claiborne Letterbooks,* 4: 349; Clay to Rodney, 17 August 1811, *Clay Papers,* 1: 574–75. See also Recommendation of Brown to Jefferson, 28 December 1803, Carter, 9: 154; Breckinridge to Clay, 30 December 1803, *Clay Papers,* 1: 124–25; Brown to Madison, 7 May 1805, Carter, 9: 448–49; Brown to Claiborne, 24 August 1805, ibid., 494. For a similar example of Clay's patronage, see Clay to Rodney, 10 April 1810, *Clay Papers,* 1: 409.

99. Claiborne to Smith, 1 June 1809, *Claiborne Letterbooks,* 4: 375; Hambleton to Porter, 25 January 1811, David Dixon Porter Papers; Claiborne to Martin Duralde, Lewis, and Thomas Oliver, 31 May 1811, William C. C. Claiborne Papers.

100. Claiborne to Duralde, 2 February 1811, *Claiborne Letterbooks,* 5: 143; *Louisiana Gazette,* 27 February 1811; *Senate Executive Journal,* 2: 123, 156. No sooner had Claiborne dispatched this letter than he learned that Martin Duralde Jr. had declined the appointment, citing poor health. See Claiborne to Monroe, 18 March 1811, *Claiborne Letterbooks,* 5: 183.

101. Claiborne to Duralde, 1 February 1811, *Claiborne Letterbooks,* 5: 142–43.

102. Claiborne to Dearborn, 5 July 1806, ibid., 3: 353–54.

103. Claiborne to Johnson, 26 May 1812, ibid., 6: 106–08.

104. Claiborne to Madison, 17 December 1809, Carter, 9: 859.

105. Claiborne to Lady Abyss of the Ursuline Convent, 28 December 1808, *Claiborne Letterbooks,* 4: 279. For Claiborne's increasingly collegial relations with the convent, see Claiborne to Convent, 3 April and 3 June 1811, ibid., 201, 260; Claiborne to Gallatin, 7 June 1811, ibid., 265.

106. Claiborne to Duralde, 1 February 1811, ibid., 5: 143.

Chapter 5. Local Diplomacy

1. Madison, First Annual Message, 23 May 1809, *PJM-PS,* 1: 199–200.
2. The standard study of the Embargo is Burton Spivak, *Jefferson's English Crisis: Commerce, Embargo, and the Republican Revolution* (Charlottesville: University Press of Virginia, 1979). See also Drew R. McCoy, *The Elusive Republic: Political Economy in Jeffersonian America* (New York: Norton, 1980), 215–35; Peter S. Onuf and Nicholas G. Onuf, *Federal Union, Modern World: The Law of Nations in an Age of Revolutions, 1776–1814* (Madison, Wis.: Madison House, 1993), 183–84; Bradford Perkins, *Prologue to War: England and the United States, 1805–1812* (Berkeley: University of California Press, 1968), 140–183.

3. Council to Madison, 10 June 1809, PCDV, 5: 71–72; Mather to Madison, 10 June 1810, *PJM-PS*, 1: 236–37.

4. Madison to Council, 23 July 1809, *PJM-PS*, 1: 297–98.

5. Historians have usually considered the State Department in terms either wholly foreign (the case with most scholars of American foreign relations) or exclusively domestic (the case for historians of the federal territories). Both diplomatic historians and historians of American domestic governance have tended to ignore the State Department's domestic role. Leonard White, whose work remains the point of reference for most studies of public administration, discussed the State Department in depth without once addressing territorial administration. See White, *The Jeffersonians: A Study in Administrative History, 1801–1829* (New York: Macmillan, 1951), 187–202.

6. *PJM-SS*, 1: xxiii; L. White, *The Jeffersonians*, 187.

7. James E. Lewis Jr., *The American Union and the Problem of Neighborhood: The United States and the Collapse of the Spanish Empire, 1783–1829* (Chapel Hill: University of North Carolina Press, 1998), 17, 218; Onuf and Onuf, *Federal Union, Modern World*.

8. Gallatin to Trist, 27 February 1804, Carter, 9: 192–94; Dearborn to Freeman, 23 April 1804, ibid., 229–30; Dearborn to Sibley, 13 December 1804, ibid., 352–53; Gallatin to Samuel Mitchill, 3 January 1805, Jefferson Papers, reel 51; Gallatin to Allan Bowie Magruder, Brown, and Felix Grundy, 8 July 1805, Carter, 9: 468–69. For studies examining dynamics within territorial administration, see also Brian W. Beltman, "Territorial Commands of the Army: The System Refined but Not Perfected," *JER* 11 (1991): 185–218; L. White, *The Jeffersonians;* John Wunder, "American Law and Order Comes to the Mississippi Territory: The Making of Sargent's Code, 1798–1800," *Journal of Mississippi History* 38 (1976): 131–55.

9. Carl A. Brasseaux and Glenn L. Conrad, eds., *The Road to Louisiana: The Saint-Domingue Refugees, 1792–1809* (Lafayette: University of Southwestern Louisiana, 1992).

10. Paul F. Lachance, "The Foreign French," in *Creole New Orleans: Race and Americanization,* ed. Arnold R. Hirsch and Joseph Logsdon (Baton Rouge: Louisiana State University Press, 1992), 105.

11. James Sterrett to Evans, 24 June 1809, Nathaniel Evans Papers, LSU, in *RASP,* H, reel 1, frame 315. See also anonymous to Hughes de la Vergne, 24 June 1803, de la Vergne Papers, TUL. For the general migration patterns of Saint Domingue refugees, see Brasseaux and Conrad, *The Road to Louisiana;* Lachance, "The Foreign French," 101–30; Paul F. Lachance, "The 1809 Immigration of Saint-Domingue Refugees to New Orleans: Reception, Integration and Impact," *LAH* 29 (1988): 109–41. For an account of mounting anti-French sentiment in Cuba, see *Weekly Chronicle,* 7 September 1808.

12. Mather to Council, 17 May 1809, MMCDV, 3: 132; Mather to Claiborne, 17 August 1809, *Claiborne Letterbooks,* 4: 404–08.

13. Claiborne to Michael Walsh, 12 May 1809, *Claiborne Letterbooks,* 4: 351; Claiborne to Smith, 15 May 1809, ibid., 354–55; Claiborne to Sam Davis and to the commander at Plaquemines (two letters), 16 May 1809, ibid., 355; Mather to Council, 17 May 1 and 7 June 1809, MMCDV, 1: 130–34, 138–39.

14. Gwendolyn Midlo Hall, *Africans in Colonial Louisiana: The Development of*

Afro-Creole Culture in the Eighteenth Century (Baton Rouge: Louisiana State University Press, 1992); Kimberly S. Hanger, "Conflicting Loyalties: The French Revolution and Free People of Color in Spanish Louisiana," *LAH* 34 (1993): 5–33; Paul F. Lachance, "The Politics of Fear: French Louisianans and the Slave Trade, 1786–1809," *Plantation Society* 1 (1979): 162–97.

15. Chevalier Lejeune Mahlerbe and others to Madison, 5 September 1809, *PJM-PS,* 1: 352–53; Tench Cox to Madison, 3 June 1809, *PJM-PS,* 1: 222–24 (see also n. 2); Lachance, "The 1809 Immigration," 118–19.

16. Rogers M. Smith, *Civic Ideals: Conflicting Visions of Citizenship in U.S. History* (New Haven: Yale University Press, 1997), 119–20, 161–62.

17. Claiborne to Smith, 15 May 1809, *Claiborne Letterbooks,* 4: 354–55; Claiborne to the commander at Plaquemines, 15 May 1809, ibid., 355; Claiborne to Captain Many, 18 May 1809 (four letters), ibid., 358–60. Claiborne had begun to institute his policy three days before seeking Smith's advice. See Claiborne to Walsh, 12 May 1809, ibid., 351. See also Claiborne to Michael Walsh, 12 May 1809, ibid., 351; Claiborne to Porter, 10 November 1809, ibid., 5: 6–7; Claiborne to Smith, 12 November 1809, ibid., 8–9.

18. Claiborne to William Savage, 10 November 1809, ibid., 5: 3–5.

19. Claiborne to Dearborn, 11 December 1807, Letters Received, Registered Series, 5: C-396; Gallatin to Jefferson, 23 December 1807, Jefferson Papers, reel 65; Claiborne to Madison, 17 February 1808 (two letters), *Claiborne Letterbooks,* 4: 155–57.

20. Porter to Hambleton, 18 July 1810 (incorrectly attributed in letterbook to 1809), David Dixon Porter Papers, LC; Hamilton to John Trippe, 20 July 1810, Letters to Officers, 9: 140; *National Intelligencer,* 23 July 1810; Hamilton to Madison, 3 August 1810, *PJM-PS,* 2: 458–59; *Louisiana Gazette,* 12 July 1811.

21. Porter to Hamilton, 1 January 1810, Letters Received by the Secretary of the Navy from Commanders, Record Group 45, Microfilm Copy M147, NA, 4: 1.

22. Porter to Madison, 21 September 1810, *PJM-PS,* 4: 621. See also Porter to Hamilton, 1 January and 10 March 1810, Letters Received from Commanders, 4: 1, 35; Porter to Hambleton, 18 July 1810, David Dixon Porter Papers.

23. Officers of the New Orleans naval station to Porter, 16 June 1810, *National Intelligencer,* 27 July 1810.

24. *Louisiana Gazette,* 28 June 1811.

25. Smith to Juan Baptiste Bernabue, 19 January 1810, Domestic Letters, 13: 406; Rodney to Smith, 4 April 1810, ibid., 433–34; Porter to Hambleton, 18 July 1810, David Dixon Porter Papers; Porter to Madison, 21 September 1810, *PJM-PS,* 4: 621.

26. Robertson to Smith, 8 April and 6 July 1810, Carter, 9: 881, 888; Robertson Circular, 6 September 1810, quoted in Charles E. A. Gayarré, *History of Louisiana,* 4 vols. (New Orleans: F. F. Hansell and Bro., 1903), 4: 228–29.

27. Lewis to the Sheriff of New Orleans, 26 March 1810, *Claiborne Letterbooks,* 5: 28; Petition of Pierre Derbigny, 26 March 1810, ibid., 26–28; Robertson to Smith, 8 April 1810, Carter, 9: 880–81.

28. Claiborne to Deforgues, 30 March 1810, *Claiborne Letterbooks,* 5: 28–29; Claiborne to Mather, 27 January 1810, ibid., 29–30. For a similar disagreement between Claiborne and Porter in 1808, see Claiborne to Porter, 21 October 1808, ibid., 4: 229.

29. Robertson to Smith, 8 July 1809, ibid., 4: 380; Mather to Council, 14 and 25 October 1809, MMCDV, 3: 161, 164.

30. For discussions of the relationship between political order and the activity of squatters, see Stephen Aron, *How the West Was Lost: The Transformation of Kentucky from Daniel Boone to Henry Clay* (Baltimore: Johns Hopkins University Press, 1996), 60–101; Rachel N. Klein, *Unification of a Slave State: The Rise of the Planter Class in the South Carolina Backcountry, 1760–1808* (Chapel Hill: University of North Carolina Press, 1990); Alan Taylor, *Liberty Men and Great Proprietors: The Revolutionary Settlement on the Maine Frontier, 1760–1820* (Chapel Hill: University of North Carolina Press, 1990).

31. Claiborne to Madison, 8 November 1808, *Claiborne Letterbooks,* 4: 245–46. Americans were well aware of the disorder in Texas that followed the French invasion of Spain. See Claiborne to Madison, 5 April 1804, Carter, 9: 332–33; Claiborne to Madison, 6 August 1805, *Claiborne Letterbooks,* 3: 152; Claiborne to Casa Calvo, 8 August 1805, ibid., 155.

32. Claiborne to the Orleans Territorial Legislature, 20 January 1809, *Claiborne Letterbooks,* 4: 306; Claiborne to Salcedo, 21 February 1809, ibid., 319; Claiborne to Madison, 22 February 1809, ibid., 320; Claiborne to John Carr, 26 March 1809, ibid., 306; *Acts Passed* (1805), 16–18. Salcedo's last action on the matter was to request mercy for the returned slaves. In the interest of humoring the Spanish official, Claiborne offered a general pardon. What individual masters did with their reunited slaves, however, remains a frightening mystery. See Claiborne to Parish Judges, 11 Mary 1809, *Claiborne Letterbooks,* 4: 350.

33. Cushing to William Eustis, 24 April 1810, Letters Received, Registered Series, 35: C-126.

34. Ibid. See also Thomas Wollstonecraft to Wade Hampton, 15 April 1810, ibid.; Wollstonecraft to Cushing, 12 June and 12 July 1810, ibid., C-191; Eustis to Cushing, 15 June 1810, Territorial Papers, 6: 70–71; Eustis to Madison, 7 September 1810, *PJM-PS,* 2: 531 and n. 2; Wollstonecraft to Cushing, 15 August 1810; Salcedo to Wollstonecraft, 17 August 1810; Wollstonecraft to Augustus Magee, 29 August 1810; Magee to Wollstonecraft, 4 September 1810; all in Letters Received, Registered Series, 35: C-217.

35. Wollstonecraft to Hampton, 15 April 1810, Letters Received, Registered Series, 35: C-126; Wollstonecraft to Cushing, 12 June and 12 July 1810, ibid., C-191; Eustis to Cushing, 15 June 1810, Territorial Papers, 6: 70–71; Eustis to Madison, 7 September 1810, *PJM-PS,* 2: 531 and n. 2; Wollstonecraft to Cushing, 15 August 1810; Salcedo to Wollstonecraft, 17 August 1810; Wollstonecraft to Magee, 29 August 1810; Magee to Wollstonecraft, 4 September 1810; all in Letters Received, Registered Series, 35: C-217; Villasana Haggard, "The Neutral Ground between Louisiana and Texas, 1806–1821," *LHQ* 28 (1945): 1062.

36. Wollstonecraft to Hampton, 16 April 1810; Wollstonecraft to Salcedo, 16 April 1810; Cushing to Wollstonecraft, 23 April 1810; all in Letters Received, Registered Series, 35: C-126.

37. James Ripley Jacobs, *Tarnished Warrior: Major-General James Wilkinson* (New York: Macmillan, 1938), 262–63.

38. Eustis to Hampton, 15 June 1810, Territorial Papers, 6: 70–71; Hampton to

Eustis, 22 August 1810, Letters Received, Registered Series, 5: H-181; Eustis to Madison, 7 September 1810, *PJM-PS*, 2: 531–32; Hampton to Eustis, 24 September 1810, Letters Received, Registered Series, 37: H-196; Hampton to Eustis, 3 November 1810, ibid., H-222; Hampton to Alexander Smyth, 15 December 1810, ibid., 40.

39. Eustis to Hampton, 15 June 1810, Territorial Papers, 6: 71; Hampton to Eustis, 22 August 1810, Letters Received, Registered Series, 5: H-181; Hampton to Eustis, 24 September 1810, ibid., 37: H-196; Hampton to Eustis, 3 November 1810, ibid., H-222; Hampton to Claiborne, 23 January and 14 February 1812, ibid., 44: H-170; Hampton to Zebulon Pike, 6 February 1812, and Pike to Hampton, 26 March 1812, both in ibid., 45: H-212; Claiborne to John Carr, 16 February 1812, *Claiborne Letterbooks,* 6: 56–57; William Henry Harrison to Eustis, 22 April 1812, Letters Received, Registered Series, 45: H-212.

40. Freeman to Hampton, 25 January 1810, Letters Received, Registered Series, 37: H-54; Hampton to Cushing, 5 April 1810, ibid., 35: C-117; Hampton to Eustis, 11 July 1810, ibid., 37: H-145.

41. The most thorough analysis of Madison's attitudes during the West Florida Crisis and the chronology of American decisionmaking is contained in a lengthy editorial note in *PJM-PS*, 2: 305–20.

42. Stanley C. Arthur, *The Story of the Kemper Brothers: Three Fighting Sons of a Baptist Preacher who fought for Freedom when Louisiana was Young* (St. Francisville, La.: St. Francisville Democrat, 1933), 8–11; Isaac Cox, *The West Florida Controversy, 1798–1813: A Study in American Diplomacy* (Baltimore: Johns Hopkins Press, 1923), 152–53.

43. Vicente Folch, "Reflections on Louisiana" (1804), in *Louisiana under the Rule of Spain, France, and the United States, 1785–1807,* ed. James A. Robertson, 3 vols. (Cleveland: Arthur H. Clark, 1911), 2: 327–35. For a letter expressing similar fears among Spanish officials that the United States would take West Florida by force, see Grand Pré to Hickey, 12 October 1806, Philip Hickey Papers, LSU; anonymous letter to Jefferson, 22 December 1807, Jefferson Papers, reel 65.

44. Folch to John McDonogh, 26 August 1809, John McDonogh Papers, LSU, in *RASP,* H, reel 4, frame 769. The wine was actually from Pensacola, and had recently arrived on a merchantman called the *Castor.* See Vincente de Adorgoritti to McDonough, 27 July 1809, ibid., 755–57. For similar attempts by Americans working for the firm of Panton-Leslie, see receipt list from Panton-Leslie, 31 October 1803, Henry Wilson Papers, LSU; Wilkinson to James Innerarity, 30 March 1813, ibid.

45. Frederick Kimball to Benjamin Wade, 24 May 1807, Frederick Kimball Papers, LSU. See also Kimball to Wade, 15 August 1806, ibid.

46. Kimball to Wade, 2 June and 7 November 1808, ibid.

47. Madison to Jefferson, 19 October 1810, *PJM-PS,* 2: 585; *National Intelligencer,* 26 February 1810; Andrew McMichael, "Slavery on the Southwestern Borderlands: Anglos, Slaves, and Receding Spaniards," paper presented at the 1999 meeting of the Society for Historians of the Early American Republic, Lexington, Ky.; idem, "Reluctant Revolutionaries: The West Florida Borderlands, 1785–1810" (Ph.D. diss., Vanderbilt University, 2000).

48. "The West Florida Revolution of 1810, as Told in the Letters of John Rhea, Fulwar

Skipwith, Reuben Kemper, and Others," *Louisiana Historical Quarterly* 21 (1938): 76–77.

49. Petition to Philip Hickey, 1 July 1810, Philip Hickey Papers.

50. Richard Sparks to Eustis, 12 July 1810, Carter, 6: 79–82.

51. Smith to William Wykoff, 20 June 1810, ibid., 9: 884. See also Smith to William Crawford, 20 June 1810, ibid., 885; Smith to Holmes, 12 July 1810, Domestic Letters, 13: 444; Madison to Smith, 17 July 1810, *PJM-PS*, 2: 419; Smith to Holmes, 21 July 1810, Domestic Letters, 13: 471; Holmes to Smith, 31 July 1810, Carter, 9: 889–91.

52. For the argument that these men were covert agents, see Stephen F. Knott, *Secret and Sanctioned: Covert Operations and the American Presidency.* New York, 1996, 61–115; Lawrence Owsley Jr. and Gene A. Smith, *Filibusters and Expansionists: Jeffersonian Manifest Destiny, 1800–1821* (Tuscaloosa: University of Alabama Press, 1997); Joseph Burkholder Smith, *The Plot to Steal Florida: James Madison's Phony War* (New York: Arbor House, 1983), 58–60.

53. Jefferson to Monroe, 8 January 1804, Jefferson Papers, reel 47.

54. Reuben Kemper to Cayetano Peréz and Joseph Kennedy, 3 November 1810, in "West Florida Revolution of 1810," 100.

55. Madison, Proclamation, 27 October 1810, *PJM-PS*, 2: 595.

56. Hamilton to John Read, 3 December 1810, Letters to Officers, 9: 238. See also Hampton to Eustis, 13 November 1810, Letters Received, Registered Series, 37: H-227.

57. John Shaw to Hamilton, 3 January 1811, Letters Received by the Secretary of the Navy from Captains, Record Group 45, Microfilm Copy M125, NA, 19: 6.

58. Shaw to Hamilton, 18 January 1811, ibid., 35. For the slave revolt, see Hampton to Eustis, 11 January 1811, Carter, 9: 917; *Louisiana Gazette,* 10 and 11 January 1811; *New York Evening Post,* 19 February 1811; *Aurora General Advertiser* (Philadelphia), 19 February 1811. For analysis of the slave revolt see James Dormon, "The Persistent Specter: Slave Rebellion in Territorial Louisiana," *LAH* 18 (1977): 394; Robert L. Paquette, "Revolutionary Saint Domingue in the Making of Territorial Louisiana," in *A Turbulent Time: The French Revolution and the Greater Caribbean,* ed. David B. Gaspar and David Patrick Geggus (Bloomington: Indiana University Press, 1997), 204–25.

59. *Louisiana Courier* (New Orleans), 21 March, 14 and 29 July 1810.

60. Dormon, "The Persistent Specter," 396–97.

61. Hampton to Eustis, 11 January 1811, Carter, 9: 917. See also Claiborne to Hampton, 7 January 1811, *Claiborne Letterbooks,* 5: 92; *Louisiana Courier,* 7 January 1811.

62. Hampton to Claiborne, 12 January 1811, Carter, 9: 916–17; Peter V. Ogden to Evans, 11 January 1811, Nathaniel Evans Papers. See also Claiborne to Hampton, 9 January 1811, *Claiborne Letterbooks,* 5: 94; Claiborne to Smith, 9 January 1811, ibid., 95–96; Claiborne to Michael St. Amant, 9 January 1811, ibid., 94; *Richmond* (Va.) *Enquirer,* 22 February 1811; *Aurora General Advertiser,* 19 February 1811.

63. Ogden to Evans, 20 January 1811, Nathaniel Evans Papers. See also Claiborne to Smith, 12 January 1811, *Claiborne Letterbooks,* 5: 97; Claiborne to Jefferson, 20 January 1811, Jefferson Papers, reel 74; Claiborne to Dr. Steele, 20 January 1811, *Claiborne Letterbooks,* 5: 112–13; *Louisiana Gazette,* 11 February 1811; *Charleston Courier,* 15 February 1811; *Moniteur de la Louisiane,* 19 February 1811; *Aurora General Advertiser,* 20 and 25 February 1811; *Richmond Courier,* 22 February 1811; PCDV, 6: 1;

Dormon, "The Persistent Specter," 394, 396–97; Thomas N. Ingersoll, "Free Blacks in a Slave Society: New Orleans, 1718–1812," *WMQ*, 3d ser., 48 (1991): 198.

64. Mather to Council, 12 January 1811, MMCDV, 4: 90–91; PCDV, 6: 1.

65. "Summary of Trial Proceedings of those Accused of Participating in the Slave Uprising of January 9, 1811," *LAH* 18 (1977).

66. For general proceedings following the revolt, see Claiborne to Louis Moreau-Lislet, 20 January 1811, *Claiborne Letterbooks*, 5: 112; Claiborne to Steele, 20 January 1811, ibid., 112–13; Claiborne to Cantrell, 4 April 1811, ibid., 203; Holmes to Butler, 18 January 1809, Thomas Butler and Family Papers, LSU; Claiborne to the Legislature, 19 April 1811, *Claiborne Letterbooks*, 5: 214; Claiborne to Bernard Genoie, 24 January 1811, ibid., 117; Claiborne to Hampton, 24 January 1811, ibid.; Hampton to William Eustis, 19 January 1811, Letters Received, Registered Series, 37: H-294; *Acts Passed* (1805), 196.

67. Hambleton to Porter, 25 January 1811, David Dixon Porter Papers.

68. Porter to Hambleton, 23 February 1811, ibid.

69. Holmes to Butler, 18 January 1811; Holmes to the commander of Ft. Adams, 19 January 1811; both in Thomas Butler and Family Papers.

70. PCDV, 6: 2.

71. Claiborne to William McRae, 23 December 1811, *Claiborne Letterbooks*, 6: 16–17; Claiborne to Michael Fortier, Andry, and Mather (three letters), 24 December 1811, ibid., 17–18; Holmes to David Pannell, 23 July 1812, Territorial Papers, 6: 301; Holmes to Wilkinson, 19 October 1812, ibid., 328–29; Auguste Macarty to Wollstonecraft, 26 October 1812, Secretary of State Letterbook, Charles E. A. Gayarré Collection, LSU; *Paul Macarty's Case*, 2 Martin 279 (La., 1812).

72. "Mr. Lee" to anonymous recipient, 24 December. 1810, *National Intelligencer*, 26 February 1810; *Annals of Congress*, 9th Cong., 1st sess. (1805–06), 41–42; Samuel C. Hyde Jr., *Pistols and Politics: The Dilemma of Democracy in Louisiana's Florida Parishes, 1810–1899* (Baton Rouge: Louisiana State University Press, 1996), 20–23.

73. James Neilson to Madison, 5 January 1811, *PJM-PS*, 3: 102. See also Pollock to Thomas Butler, 2 November 1810, Thomas Butler and Family Papers, box 2, folder 9; "Mr. Lee" to anonymous recipient, 24 December 1810, *National Intelligencer*, 26 February 1810; *Annals of Congress*, 11th Cong., 3d. sess. (1810–11), 41–42.

74. Holmes to Smith, 1 January 1811, Carter, 9: 909–10. See also Claiborne to Smith, 5 January 1811, *Claiborne Letterbooks*, 5: 81; Claiborne to William Flood, 5 January 1811, ibid., 82–84; Claiborne to Smith, 5 January 1811, ibid., 81; Claiborne to Eustis, 5 January 1811, Letters Received, Registered Series, 35: C-342; Claiborne to Bernard Genoie, 24 January 1811, *Claiborne Letterbooks*, 5: 117.

75. Toulmin to Madison, 28 November 1810, Carter, 6: 140–43; Claiborne Proclamation to the Territorial Legislature, 22 December 1810, *Claiborne Letterbooks*, 5: 64–65; John Pollock to Butler, 7 January 1811, Thomas Butler and Family Papers, box 2, folder 9; Toulmin to Madison, 10 January 1811, *PJM-PS*, 3: 110–16; *Aurora General Advertiser*, 30 January 1811; *Acts Passed* (1811), 3–5; *National Intelligencer*, 16 March 1811.

76. Harry Ammon, *James Monroe: The Search for National Identity* (Charlottesville: University Press of Virginia, 1990), 280–88; J. C. A. Stagg, "James Madison and the 'Malcontents': The Political Origins of the War of 1812," *WMQ*, 3d ser., 33 (1976): 569–78.

77. Claiborne to Eustis, 23 May 1811, *Claiborne Letterbooks,* 5: 250–51; Claiborne to Pierre Duplessis, 17 August 1811, ibid., 339; Claiborne to Shaw, 9 October 1811, ibid., 361; Claiborne to Eustis, 20 July 1812, ibid., 129–30; *Senate Executive Journal,* 201. Claiborne's opinion of the Dufosats became particularly evident when the young Soniant traveled to Europe in the summer of 1811. See Claiborne to the American Chargé des Affaires in Britain, 29 July 1811, *Claiborne Letterbooks,* 5: 318; Claiborne to James Maury, 1 August 1811, ibid., 322.

78. Kimball to Wade, 23 June 1811, Frederick Kimball Papers; Claiborne to Philip Grymes, 24 May 1811, *Claiborne Letterbooks,* 5: 256; Claiborne to John Rhea, 3 September 1811, ibid., 353–54; 1811 Orleans Territory Tax Record, HNO; Claiborne to Rhea, 20 December 1811 and 1 February 1812, Claiborne Letterbooks, 6: 47–48.

79. Claiborne to Jefferson, 20 January 1811, Jefferson Papers, reel 74.

80. Powell A. Casey, "Military Roads in the Florida Parishes of Louisiana," *LAH* 15 (1974): 229–40. For the ongoing problems of building an administrative apparatus in West Florida, see Hyde, *Pistols and Politics,* 23.

81. Claiborne to Hampton, 24 January 1811 (three letters), *Claiborne Letterbooks,* 5: 115–17; Claiborne to Bernard Genoie, 24 January 1811, ibid., 117; Hampton to Cushing, 24 January 1811, Letters Received, Registered Series, 35: C-362; Claiborne to the Legislature, 29 January 1811, *Claiborne Letterbooks,* 5: 126; Claiborne to Hampton, 8 February 1811, Letters Received, Registered Series, 35: C-362; Hampton to Cushing, 9 February 1811, ibid.; Toulmin to Madison, 27 February 1811, *PJM-PS,* 3: 192.

82. Smith to George Mathews, 11 January 1811, Domestic Letters, 13; Isaac J. Cox, "The Border Missions of General George Mathews," *Mississippi Valley Historical Review* 12 (1925): 309–33; Harry McCorry Henderson, "The Magee-Gutierrez Expedition," *Southwestern Historical Quarterly* 55 (1951): 43–48; Paul Kruse, "A Secret Agent in East Florida: George Mathews and the Patriot War," *Journal of Southern History* 18 (1952): 193–217; Rembert Patrick, *Florida Fiasco: Rampant Rebels on the Georgia-Florida Border, 1810–1815* (Athens: University of Georgia Press, 1954); Rufus Kay Wyllys, "The East Florida Revolution of 1812–1814," *Hispanic American Historical Review* 9 (1929): 415–45.

83. Monroe to Mathews, 4 April 1812, *ASP,* FR, 3: 572; Madison to Jefferson, 24 April 1812, *Madison Writings,* 8: 190; Lewis, *American Union and Neighborhood,* 32–40.

84. Jefferson to Claiborne, 30 August 1804, Carter, 9: 281–82; Jefferson to Madison, 23 March 1805, in *The Republic of Letters: The Correspondence between Thomas Jefferson and James Madison,* ed. James Norton Smith, vol. 3 (New York: Norton, 1995), 1367; Jefferson to John Dickinson, 13 January 1807, Ford, 9: 9.

Chapter 6. Polities

1. *Acts Passed* (1805), 124–30.

2. Poydras to Madison, 28 January 1812, in *Constitution or Form of Government of the State of Louisiana* (New Orleans: Jo. Bar. Baird, 1812).

3. Jefferson to Claiborne, 20 December 1806, Jefferson Papers, reel 59. See also Jefferson Proclamation, 19 December 1806; Jefferson to Thomas Leiper, 22 December

1806; Jefferson to Smith, 23 December 1806; all ibid.; Claiborne to Shaw, 1 January 1807, *Claiborne Letterbooks*, 4: 74–75; Annabelle M. Melville, "John Carroll and Louisiana, 1803–1815," *Catholic Historical Review* 64 (1978): 408.

4. Wilkinson to Council, 1 January 1807, LCDV, 1: 545. Wilkinson also forwarded Dearborn's wish to see tighter local control on strangers.

5. Watkins to Smith, 21 January 1807, MMCDV, 1: 122–23; Mather to Council, 12, 23, and 30 December 1807, MMCDV, 1: 223–24, 225, 231. The effort to control strangers predated the Burr crisis. See Watkins to Council, 4 January 1806, 12 February 1805, MMCDV, 1: 9–12, 19–20.

6. [Mrs. Soniant du Fossat], *The Invitation: A Poem Addressed to General Wilkinson, Commander in Chief of the United States Army* (Natchez: Andrew Marschalk, 1807).

7. Dickinson to Jefferson, 1 January 1807, Jefferson Papers, reel 59; Jefferson to Dickinson, 13 January 1807, Ford, 9: 9.

8. *Reflections on the Cause of the Louisianians Respectfully Submitted by Their Agents* (Washington, D.C., 1803); Louisianais (Pierre Derbigny), *Esquisse de la situation politique et civile de la Louisiane . . .* (New Orleans, 1804); Julien Poydras, *A Speech by Mr. Poydras, President of the Legislative Council of Orleans* (New Orleans, 1804); *Examination of the Rights of the United States and the Claims of Mr. Edward Livingston on the Batture in Front of the Faubourg Ste. Marie* (New Orleans: Thierry, 1808); *Instructions from the Inhabitants of the Territory of Orleans* (New Orleans, 1810). Other documents were published, appropriately enough, in Washington. See Louis Moreau-Lislet, *Examination of the Judgment Rendered in the Cause between Jean Gravier and the City of New Orleans* (Washington, D.C.: A. and G. Way, 1809); Julien Poydras, *A Defense of the Right of the Public to the Batture of New Orleans* (Washington, D.C.: Julien Poydras, 1809).

9. Resolution of the Orleans Territorial Legislature, 20 February 1807, Carter, 9: 707.

10. Representatives to Jefferson, 19 January 1810, Jefferson Papers, reel 74. See also Representatives to Jefferson, 29 March 1808, ibid., reel 66.

11. Clay to Clay, 7 July 1804, *Clay Papers*, 1: 139–41. See also Claiborne to Madison, 5 July 1804, *Claiborne Letterbooks*, 2: 236–38; *Louisiana Courier*, 9 July 1810.

12. For analysis of Fourth of July celebrations, see Philip F. Detweiler, "The Changing Reputation of the Declaration of Independence: The First Fifty Years," *WMQ*, 3d ser., 19 (1962): 557–74; Fletcher M. Green, "Listen to the Eagle Scream: One Hundred Years of the Fourth of July in North Carolina," in *Democracy in the Old South and Other Essays*, ed. J. Isaac Copeland (Nashville: Vanderbilt University Press, 1969), 111–56; Henry A. Hawker, *Trumpet of Glory: Fourth of July Orations, 1786–1861* (Granby, Conn.: Salmon Brook Historical Society, 1976); A. V. Huff Jr., "The Eagle and the Vulture: Changing Attitudes toward Nationalism in Fourth of July Orations Delivered in Charleston, 1788–1860," *South Atlantic Quarterly* 73 (1974): 10–22; Len Travers, *Celebrating the Fourth: Independence Day and the Rites of Nationalism in the Early Republic* (Amherst: University of Massachusetts Press, 1997). For public celebrations in Louisiana and their nationalist content, see David Waldstreicher, *In the Midst of Perpetual Fetes: The Making of American Nationalism, 1776–1820* (Chapel Hill: University of North Carolina Press, 1997), 281–82.

13. *Louisiana Courier*, 4 July 1810.

14. Ibid., 6 July 1810.

15. Although the Louisiana legislature made no direct reference to numbers, they implicitly did some fancy work with numbers. According to the 1810 census, the population of the Territory of Orleans consisted of 34,311 whites (44.82 percent), 7,585 free people of color (9.91 percent), and 34,660 slaves (45.27 percent). But these figures did not include the people acquired through the annexation of West Florida, a population that territorial legislators claimed as part of any state of Louisiana. Nor did the census include the recent refugees from Cuba.

16. Legislature to Congress, 12 March 1810, Carter, 9: 873–77.

17. Claiborne to Nathaniel Macon, 2 February 1812, *Claiborne Letterbooks,* 6: 51; Claiborne to George Morgan, 31 March 1812, ibid., 66.

18. The details surrounding these births are, not surprisingly, vague, albeit for different reasons. Suzette, as Claiborne's third wife was known, outlived her husband and resided for years in New York before returning to Louisiana, where she died in 1881. See Jane Lucas DeGrummond, "Cayetana Susana Bosque y Fanqui: 'A Notable Woman,'" *LAH* 22 (1982): 277–94.

19. For examples of these linkages outside New Orleans, see Sarah Russell, "Ethnicity, Commerce, and Community on Lower Louisiana's Plantation Frontier, 1803–1828," *LAH* 40 (1999): 389–405.

20. Claiborne to Gallatin, 3 May 1812, Carter, 9: 1019.

21. Prevost to Monroe, 3 February 1812, Miscellaneous Letters, reel 25. See also Edward Livingston to Monroe, 2 February 1812, ibid.

22. *PJM-PS,* 3: 480 n. 2; *Statutes at Large,* 2: 641–43.

23. Claiborne to Poydras, 18 July 1811, *Claiborne Letterbooks,* 5: 307–08.

24. Quoted in Charles E. A. Gayarré, *History of Louisiana,* 4 vols. (New Orleans: F. F. Hansell and Bro., 1903), 4: 270. For Poydras' election as president of the convention, see *Louisiana Gazette,* 19 November 1811.

25. Claiborne made reference to Poydras' comments but never expressed his opinion about them in writing. See Claiborne to Gallatin, 21 November 1811, Carter, 9: 956.

26. *The First Constitution of the State of Louisiana,* ed. Cecil Morgan (Baton Rouge: Louisiana State University Press, 1975), 15–16.

27. The convention itself is difficult to chronicle. In a region already marked by a paucity of extant correspondence, especial among Louisianians, comments about the proceedings in New Orleans are even more difficult to locate. Both the *Louisiana Courier* and the *Louisiana Gazette* provided some coverage, but much of the commentary is limited at best, frustratingly cryptic at worst. For a discussion of the source problems, see Warren M. Billings, "From This Seed: The State Constitution of 1812," in *In Search of Fundamental Law: Louisiana's Constitutions, 1812–1974,* ed. Warren M. Billings and Edward F. Haas (Lafayette: Center for Louisiana Studies, University of Southwestern Louisiana, 1993), 6–20 and n. 15. One of the criticisms of the constitution came from Destrehan. See *Louisiana Gazette,* 21 November 1811. Destrehan's comments eventually snowballed within the historiographical literature, creating a unified portrait of him as an opponent of statehood. These conclusions still rest on his 20 November comment opposing the wording of the congressional legislation authorizing a convention. There is no substantive evidence to support the notion that he or any member of the convention

expressed sustained opposition to statehood. Unlike in other states, local newspapers provided only limited coverage of the convention. Unlike the case of the framing of the federal Constitution of 1787, there was nobody like James Madison to record a detailed analysis of the daily proceedings. Despite these limitations, however, the documentation that has survived combined with the Louisiana constitution of 1812 itself provides a picture of people struggling to establish an effective administrative apparatus. These considerations existed alongside the desire to reconstitute Louisiana's political landscape. For one of the rare examples of opposition to statehood in any form, see *Louisiana Gazette,* 12 July 1811.

28. For Fromentin and Magruder's appointment, see *Louisiana Gazette,* 25 January 1812.

29. *Annals of Congress,* 11th Cong., 3d sess. (1810–11), 507, 485. For the congressional debate on Louisiana statehood, see ibid., 98–110, 484–577, 1103. See also Josiah Quincy, *Speech of Mr. Quincy . . . on the Bill Admitting the Territory of Orleans in to the Union* (Baltimore: Benjamin Edes, 1811).

30. *Annals of Congress,* 11th Cong., 3d sess. (1810–11), 485.

31. Ibid.

32. Ibid., 499.

33. Ibid., 496.

34. Ibid., 501.

35. William Plumer, *William Plumer's Memorandum of Proceedings in the United States Senate, 1803–1807,* ed. Everett Somerville Brown (New York: Macmillan, 1923), 222.

36. J. C. A. Stagg, "James Madison and the 'Malcontents': The Political Origins of the War of 1812," *WMQ,* 3d ser., 33 (1976): 569–71.

37. For references to Federalists as "Anglomen," see Jefferson to Thomas Lomax, 12 March 1799, in *Jefferson Writings,* ed. Merrill D. Peterson (New York: Library of America, 1984), 1063; Jefferson to John Langdon, 5 March 1810, ibid., 1219; Jefferson to the Marquis de Lafayette, 14 May 1817, ibid., 1407.

38. Magruder to anonymous recipient, 17 March 1812, *Louisiana Gazette,* 14 April 1812.

39. *Annals of Congress,* 11th Cong., 3d sess. (1810–11), 504.

40. Ibid., 506.

41. *Louisiana Gazette,* 30 June 1812.

42. *House Journal* (1812), 4, 2.

43. Louisiana House of Representatives to Claiborne, 12 August 1812, ibid., 31–32.

44. For the court's role in the construction of political kinship, see Donn M. Kurtz II, *Kinship and Politics: The Justices of the United States and Louisiana Supreme Courts* (Baton Rouge: Louisiana State University Press, 1997).

Chapter 7. "The Din of War"

1. 3 Martin 528–29 (1813).

2. Wade Hampton to William Eustis, 11 January 1811, Carter, 9: 917.

3. Ronald L. Hatzenbuehler and Robert L. Ivie, *Congress Declares War: Rhetoric,*

Leadership, and Partisanship in the Early Republic (Kent: Kent State University Press, 1983), 13–25; Ralph Ketcham, *James Madison: A Biography* (Charlottesville: University Press of Virginia, 1990), 530–31; J. C. A. Stagg, "James Madison and the Coercion of Great Britain: Canada, the West Indies, and the War of 1812," *WMQ,* 3d ser., 38 (1981): 3–34; idem, *Mr. Madison's War: Politics, Diplomacy, and Warfare in the Early American Republic, 1783–1830* (Princeton: Princeton University Press, 1983).

4. Stagg, "Madison and Coercion," 20–31; Richard Glover, "The French Fleet, 1807–1814: Britain's Problem and Madison's Opportunity," *Journal of Modern History* 39 (1967): 238.

5. Stagg, *Mr. Madison's War,* 3–34.

6. Monroe to Gallatin, 5 and 6 May 1813, *Monroe Writings,* 5: 252–54, 259.

7. Claiborne to Folch, 29 June 1811, *Claiborne Letterbooks,* 5: 281–82; Claiborne to Monroe, 29 June 1811, ibid., 282; Claiborne to Hamilton, 29 June 1811, ibid., 283; Claiborne to Leonard Covington, 28 July 1811, ibid., 316; John McKee to Monroe, 7 August 1811, Territorial Papers, reel 1; Claiborne to Folch, 9 September 1811, Carter, 9: 945–46; Claiborne to Hamilton, 14 September 1811, *Claiborne Letterbooks,* 5: 358–59.

8. Holmes to Wilkinson, 19 October 1812, Carter, 6: 328.

9. Lawrence Owsley Jr. and Gene A. Smith, *Filibusters and Expansionists: Jeffersonian Manifest Destiny, 1800–1821* (Tuscaloosa: University of Alabama Press, 1997), 91–92.

10. For the broad contours of Creek militancy and the American war on the Creeks, see Gregory Dowd, *A Spirited Resistance: The North American Indian Struggle for Unity* (Baltimore: Johns Hopkins University Press, 1992), 185–90; Claudio Saunt, *A New Order of Things: Property, Power, and the Transformation of the Creek Indians, 1733–1816* (Cambridge: Cambridge University Press, 1999), 237.

11. Jackson to Gonzales Manrique, 9 September 1814, *Jackson Papers,* 3: 130; Stagg, *Mr. Madison's War,* 490; *Louisiana Courier,* 4 August 1813. Americans had feared since 1811 that the Spanish would initiate a war by the Creeks. See Toulmin to Madison, 27 February 1811, *PJM-PS,* 3: 192.

12. Claiborne to recipient, 28 July 1813, *Claiborne Letterbooks,* 6: 248–49.

13. Claiborne to militia colonels, 8 September 1813, ibid., 265; Claiborne to Philemon Thomas, 10 September 1813, ibid., 266. See also Claiborne to Robertson, 4 September 1813, ibid., 264–65; Laneuville to Villeré, 30 August 1814, Jacques Philippe Villeré Papers, HNO. For Creek activities during the war, see Dowd, *A Spirited Resistance,* 185–90.

14. Claiborne to Fortier, 11 September 1813, de la Vergne Papers, TUL.

15. PCDV, 7: 244.

16. PCDV, 7: 245.

17. Dowd, *A Spirited Resistance,* 183–90; William E. Foley, *The Genesis of Missouri: From Wilderness Outpost to Statehood* (Columbia: University of Missouri Press, 1989), 227–37.

18. *Statutes at Large,* 1: 577.

19. Rogers M. Smith, *Civic Ideals: Conflicting Visions of Citizenship in U.S. History* (New Haven: Yale University Press, 1997), 159–64, 195–96.

20. For actions against aliens, see *Louisiana Courier,* 21 April 1813.

21. *Desbois' Case*, 2 Martin 185 (La., 1812). See also *Laverty v. Duplessis*, 3 Martin 42 (La., 1813); *Johnson v. Duncan et al.'s Syndics*, 3 Martin 530 (La., 1815); *United States v. Laverty*, 3 Martin 733 (La., 1815). For actions against aliens, see *Louisiana Courier*, 21 April 1813.

22. Claiborne also ordered the dismissal of any British citizens serving on the vessels at Balize, an anchorage south of New Orleans. See Claiborne to pilots, 10 June 1813, *Claiborne Letterbooks*, 6: 219–20; Claiborne to Shaw, 10 June 1813, ibid., 221–22.

23. *Laverty v. Duplessis; United States v. Laverty*.

24. James H. Kettner, *The Development of American Citizenship, 1608–1870* (Chapel Hill: University of North Carolina Press, 1978), 248.

25. The major studies of the foreign French do not consider when or how white migrants from Saint Domingue gained the legal status of citizens.

26. Louis Toussard to Claiborne, 30 December 1813, Louis Toussard Papers, TUL. See also Claiborne to Toussard, 13 October 1812, *Claiborne Letterbooks*, 6: 190; Toussard to Claiborne, 9 and 10 January 1814, both in William C. C. Claiborne Papers, LSU. The controversy began when Claiborne demanded that Toussard produce a list of all French nationals in Louisiana. See Claiborne to Toussard, 31 August 1812, *Claiborne Letterbooks*, 6: 169–70. Diego Morphy, the Spanish consul, made similar claims. See Diego Morphy to Jackson, 17 February 1815, *Jackson Papers*, 3: 283.

27. Claiborne, Inaugural Address, 27 July 1812, Secretary of State Letterbook, Charles E. A. Gayarré Collection, LSU; Claiborne to Louisiana General Assembly, 12 August 1812, *House Journal* (1812), 33.

28. Claiborne to Thomas, 10 September 1813, *Claiborne Letterbooks*, 6: 266.

29. Trudeau to Claiborne, 5 September 1812, Mayor's Minute Book, NOPL, 1: 78.

30. Claiborne to Assembly, 5 September 1812, *Claiborne Letterbooks*, 6: 174–75; *Acts Passed* (1812), 40–85. See also Sterrett to Skipwith, 8 September 1812, Fulwar Skipwith Papers, LSU; Claiborne to Wilkinson, 22 September 1812, *Claiborne Letterbooks*, 6: 180–81. For ongoing problems with the milita, see Claiborne to Fortier, 11 September 1813, de la Vergne Papers.

31. Claiborne to Thomas Flournoy, 6 December 1813, *Claiborne Letterbooks*, 6: 281; Claiborne to Brown, 11 December 1813, ibid., 281–82; Charles E. A. Gayarré, *History of Louisiana*, 4 vols. (New Orleans: F. F. Hansell and Bro., 1903), 4: 320–27. For the general problem of militia coordination during the War of 1812, see Lawrence Delbart Cress, *Citizens in Arms: The Army and the Militia in American Society to the War of 1812* (Chapel Hill: University of North Carolina Press, 1982); Stagg, *Mr. Madison's War*, 131–32, 241–47.

32. Stagg, *Mr. Madison's War*, 493.

33. Ibid., 138–40; Cress, *Citizens in Arms*.

34. *Louisiana Courier*, 25 October 1811.

35. *Louisiana Gazette*, 5 January 1812.

36. For similar attacks on Great Britain, see *Louisiana Courier*, 13 November 1811; *Louisiana Gazette*, 6 February and 8 April 1812.

37. For the role of newspapers and print culture in the circulation of nationalist sentiment, see David Waldstreicher, *In the Midst of Perpetual Fetes: The Making of American Nationalism, 1776–1820* (Chapel Hill: University of North Carolina Press, 1997).

38. P. Allard to Villeré, 20 September 1814, Jacques Philippe Villeré Papers.

39. Claiborne to unknown recipient, 15 December 1812, *Claiborne Letterbooks,* 6: 202–03; *Senate Executive Journal,* 2: 271. For a list of Louisianians serving in both the army and the militia, see War of 1812 Series, TUL. For examples of wartime appointments, see Claiborne to Brown, 27 July 1813, *Claiborne Letterbooks,* 6: 245–46.

40. Claiborne to Flournoy, 17 September 1813, *Claiborne Letterbooks,* 6: 269.

41. Louis Valentin Foelckel to Jackson, 8 January 1815, *Jackson Papers,* 3: 237–38.

42. Thomas Posey to Philip Hickey, 12 December 1812, Philip Hickey Papers, LSU; Claiborne to Philip Hickey, 13 March 1813, ibid.; *Louisiana Courier,* 26 February 1813. Posey served the shortest of tenures in the Senate. Selected by the General Assembly in October 1812, he reached Washington but resigned his office in February 1813.

43. *Acts Passed* (1812), 72; Claiborne to Fortier, 11 September 1813, de la Vergne Papers; Roland C. McConnell, *Negro Troops of Antebellum Louisiana: A History of the Battalion of Free Men of Color* (Baton Rouge: Louisiana State University Press, 1968), 43–54.

44. Monroe to Jackson, 27 September 1814, *Monroe Writings,* 5: 296–97.

45. Jackson to Claiborne, 31 October 1814, *Claiborne Letterbooks,* 6: 312; Claiborne to William McRae, 4 November 1814, ibid., 309–10; Monroe to Jackson, 7 December 1814, *Monroe Writings,* 5: 301; PCDV, 8: 28–29.

46. Brown to Jackson, 3 January 1815, *Jackson Papers,* 3: 229.

47. E. Wayne Carp, *To Starve the Army at Pleasure: Continental Army Administration and American Political Culture, 1775–1783* (Chapel Hill: University of North Carolina Press, 1984); Theodore J. Crackel, *Mr. Jefferson's Army: Political and Social Reform of the Military Establishment, 1801–1809* (New York: New York University Press, 1987); Cress, *Citizens in Arms;* Hans Kohn, *American Nationalism: An Interpretive Essay* (New York: Macmillan, 1957); Charles Royster, *A Revolutionary People at War: The Continental Army and American Character, 1775–1783* (New York: Norton, 1979); Stagg, *Mr. Madison's War.*

48. James Sterling Memorandum, 17 March 1813, HNO.

49. Edward Nicholls Broadside, 29 August 1814, Edward Nicholls and William H. Percy Letters, HNO.

50. William Percy, orders to unknown recipient, 30 August 1814, Nicholls and Percy Letters; John H. Nicholson to unknown recipient, 1 September 1814, ibid.

51. Jane Lucas DeGrummond, *The Baratarians and the Battle of New Orleans* (Baton Rouge: Louisiana State University Press, 1961); John Sugden, "Jean Lafitte and the British Offer of 1814," *LAH* 20 (1979): 159–67.

52. Letter to Villeré, 12 August 1814, Jacques Philippe Villeré Papers. See also Jackson to New Orleans Citizens and Soldiers, 15 December 1815, *Jackson Papers,* 3: 204–05; Jackson to the Assembly, 31 December 1814, ibid., 226–27; Butler to Villeré, 21 January 1815, Jacques Philippe Villeré Papers.

53. Villeré to John Lambert, 29 January 1815, Jacques Philippe Villeré Papers.

54. Jackson to Claiborne, 5 February 1815, *Jackson Papers,* 3: 270. See also David Morgan to Livingston, 16 January 1815, David Morgan Papers, LSU; Butler to Villeré, 21 January 1815, Jacques Philippe Villeré Papers; Claiborne to Jackson, 3 February 1815, *Jackson Papers,* 3: 268; Jackson to de la Vergne, 20 February 1815, ibid., 283.

55. Letter to Villeré, 12 August 1814, Jacques Philippe Villeré Papers; Claiborne to Thomas, 17 December 1814, *Claiborne Letterbooks*, 6: 323–24; *Acts Passed* (1812), 30–35.

56. PCDV, 8: 24–25. See also Claiborne to Choctaw Chief, August 1812, *Claiborne Letterbooks*, 6: 153–55; Holmes to Wilkinson, 7 September 1812, Carter, 6: 320–21; Claiborne to Brown, 27 July 1813, *Claiborne Letterbooks*, 6: 245–46.

57. Lambert to Jackson, 20 January 1815, *Jackson Papers*, 3: 253–54; Jackson to Claiborne, 5 February 1815, ibid., 270; Lambert to Jackson, 27 February 1815, ibid., 290.

58. Jackson to Waters Allen, 23 December 1814, ibid., 216.

59. Claiborne to Jackson, 24 February 1815, ibid., 286. For a general description of Jackson's activities, see Robert V. Remini, *Andrew Jackson and the Course of American Empire, 1767–1821* (New York: Harper and Row, 1977).

60. Claiborne to Monroe, 9 December 1814, *Claiborne Letterbooks*, 6: 322. For examples of Jackson's efforts to direct militia activities, see Jackson to Thomas, 22 December 1814, *Jackson Papers*, 3: 214.

61. Claiborne to Jackson, 31 January 1815, *Claiborne Letterbooks*, 6: 337; Claiborne to Etienne Masureau, 24 February 1815, ibid., 338–39.

62. Remini, *Andrew Jackson and American Empire*, 308–11.

63. William B. Hatcher, *Edward Livingston: Jeffersonian Republican and Jacksonian Democrat* (Baton Rouge: Louisiana State University Press, 1940), 212, 218–25.

64. Remini, *Andrew Jackson and American Empire*, 313–14.

65. PCDV, 7: 31; Jackson to Claiborne, 3 February 1815, *Jackson Papers*, 3: 266.

66. Jackson to Robert Hays, 26 December 1814, ibid., 221–22.

67. Thomas Butler Broadside, 15 December 1814, HNO.

68. Alexander Dallas to Jackson, 12 April 1815, *Jackson Papers*, 3: 345–46.

69. Jackson to the Citizens and Soldiers of New Orleans, 31 March 1815, ibid., 337.

70. Jackson to Dallas and Monroe, 28 April 1815, ibid., 349.

71. Joseph G. Tregle, "Andrew Jackson and the Continuing Battle of New Orleans," *JER* 1 (1981): 373–92. For a general overview of Jackson's activities following the American victory against the British, see Remini, *Andrew Jackson and American Empire*, 308–18.

72. *Statutes at Large*, 3: 248.

73. Ibid., 249.

74. Dowd, *A Spirited Resistance*, 170–72, 181–90; Foley, *The Genesis of Missouri*, 225–33; Remini, *Andrew Jackson and American Empire*, 191–245; Stagg, *Mr. Madison's War*, 177–269, 304–47; Reginald C. Stuart, "Special Interests and National Authority in Foreign Policy: American-British Provincial Links during the Embargo and the War of 1812," *Diplomatic History* 8 (1984): 311–28.

Chapter 8. *"The State of LOUISIANA Now Has Her Voice"*

1. *Louisiana Courier*, 17 January 1816. For related discussions, see John C. Calhoun to Crawford, 28 May 1818, *Calhoun Papers*, 2: 314. Whether Fromentin succeeded is something of a mystery. Neither the *Annals of Congress* nor the *Senate Executive Journal* makes any reference to his activities on the Senate floor. If he did receive any resources

from Congress, however, they must have been limited, for people in Louisiana continued to complain about unreimbursed costs.

2. *Annals of Congress,* 14th Cong., 1st sess. (1815–16), 224. The proposed amendment would have established that the president and vice president be selected by the same electors qualified to vote for "the most numerous branch of the State Legislature." See ibid., 214.

3. *DLB,* 1: 327. Andrew Jackson was not so kind to Fromentin. In 1821 Fromentin was appointed a judge in the Florida Territory, where Jackson was serving as governor. Jackson claimed that "Mr. Fromentin . . . has no standing here or at New Orleans, as a Lawyer or as a moral man." He accused Fromentin of everything from adultery to theft of public funds to desecrating his priestly training by marrying a woman from Maryland after which he "left his wife — took up with a base woman." See Jackson to Calhoun, 29 July 1821, *Calhoun Papers,* 6: 293.

4. Stephen Aron, *How the West Was Lost: The Transformation of Kentucky from Daniel Boone to Henry Clay* (Baltimore: Johns Hopkins University Press, 1996), 82–95.

5. *Louisiana Gazette,* 15 January 1812.

6. Francis Newton Thorpe, ed., *The Federal and State Constitutions, Colonial Charters, and Other Organic Laws of the States, Territories, and Colonies Now or Heretofore Forming the United States of America,* 7 vols. (Washington, D.C.: Government Printing Office, 1909), 3: 1384.

7. For comparisons, see ibid., 1: 104–07, 573, 542; 2: 797–802, 976–78, 1063; 3: 1281, 1657, 1693–95; 4: 2040–41, 2158–59, 2482; 5: 2904–08, 3098, 3263, 3420, 3766; Mark Kruman, *Between Authority and Liberty: State Constitution Making in Revolutionary America* (Chapel Hill: University of North Carolina Press, 1997).

8. The question of the framers' attitude toward democratization has left a considerable scholarly paper trail. See Lance Banning, *The Sacred Fire of Liberty: James Madison and the Founding of the Federal Republic* (Cornell: Cornell University Press, 1995), 203–08, 372–73; Jack N. Rakove, *Original Meanings: Politics and Ideas in the Making of the Constitution* (New York: Vintage, 1997), 49–53; Gordon S. Wood, *The Creation of the American Republic, 1776–1787* (New York: Norton, 1969), 554–58, 563–64.

9. *Louisiana Gazette,* 31 November 1811. Most historians of the 1812 convention focus on the territorial context to the exclusion of all other factors. They emphasize debate on the governor's powers, with particular attention to efforts at eliminating the prerogatives Claiborne enjoyed under the territorial regime. Historians of other states, especially those studying constitutions of the 1770s and 1780s, have examined questions of class and power that have important corollaries in Louisiana.

10. *Louisiana Gazette,* 15 January 1815.

11. Samuel C. Hyde Jr., *Pistols and Politics: The Dilemma of Democracy in Louisiana's Florida Parishes, 1810–1899* (Baton Rouge: Louisiana State University Press, 1996), 35–36, 47.

12. *Louisiana Courier,* 10 May 1816. See also ibid., 24 June 1816.

13. Ibid., 24 June, 5 and 8 July 1816; *Louisiana Gazette,* 3, 7, and 10 July 1816.

14. *House Journal* (1812), 4–5.

15. Sidney Louis Villeré, *Jacques Philippe Villeré, First Native-Born Governor of Louisiana, 1816–1820* (New Orleans: Historic New Orleans Collection, 1981), 13–18.

16. Destrehan apparently failed to make people aware that he was even running for governor in 1812, and his allies were forced to print a last-minute announcement informing the people of Louisiana that he was a candidate. See *Louisiana Gazette,* 30 June 1812.

17. *Louisiana Courier,* 10 May 1820. For Destrehan's career, see *DLB,* 1: 242.

18. John Clay to Henry Clay, 7 July 1804, *Clay Papers,* 1: 139–41.

19. George Dargo, *Jefferson's Louisiana: Politics and the Clash of Legal Traditions* (Cambridge: Harvard University Press, 1975), 77–83.

20. *Louisiana Gazette,* 27 November 1820.

21. For the subsequent development of more cohesive — and more combative — ethnic communities, see Joseph G. Tregle, "Creoles and Americans," in *Creole New Orleans: Race and Americanization,* ed. Arnold R. Hirsch and Joseph Logsdon (Baton Rouge: Louisiana State University Press, 1992), 131–85; idem, *Louisiana in the Age of Jackson: A Clash of Cultures and Personalities* (Baton Rouge: Louisiana State University Press, 1999).

22. *House Journal* (1812), 4–5. Villeré did not receive a single vote in Catahoula, Concordia, and Feliciana Parishes. The first two were in northeastern Louisiana, home to a growing number of migrants from Kentucky, Mississippi, and Tennessee. Villeré's strongest majorities were in the small but densely populated parishes along the Mississippi north and west of New Orleans.

23. Louisiana Congressional Election Papers, LSU; Sterrett to Skipwith, 8 September 1812, Fulwar Skipwith Papers, LSU; *Louisiana Gazette,* 21 July 1818. See also ibid., 6 August 1818.

24. Claiborne to Posey, 25 January 1813, *Claiborne Letterbooks,* 6: 209–10 (incorrectly attributed to 1812); *Biographical Directory of the United States Congress, 1774–1989* (Washington, D.C.: Government Printing Office, 1989), 934, 1062, 1434, 1679.

25. All these men had close relatives in Congress. In addition to Brown's extensive connections, Robertson's younger brother, John, was Virginia's attorney general before representing Virginia in Congress from 1834 to 1838. Claiborne's brother, Nathaniel, also served in Virginia's congressional delegation from 1825 to 1837. Even dissent within the local government could serve as the basis of a political network. Robertson and Claiborne had their own disagreements, and Robertson's decision to complain about the governor by writing directly to Secretary of State Monroe constituted an early attempt to build his own political network in Washington. The colonial and territorial regimes had taught Louisianians the importance of kinship, both literal and political, and they used those relationships to guarantee an effective congressional delegation. See Robertson to Monroe, 20 December 1811, Carter, 9: 962–63. Meanwhile other Americans were attempting to build their own connections to Clay. See Woodson Wrenn to Clay, 12 September 1812, *Clay Papers,* 1: 726; Robert Miller to Claiborne, 13 September 1816, "Three Letters from Robert Miller to Richard Claiborne, 1813–1817," *Louisiana Historical Quarterly* 24 (1941): 736–38; Clay to Thomas Butler, 19 July 1819, *Clay Papers,* 2: 698.

26. Claiborne to Magruder, 25 January 1813, *Claiborne Letterbooks,* 6: 208–09; Marion Nelson Winship, "The Territorial Aspirations of William Charles Cole Claiborne: A Western Success Story from the Jeffersonian Empire," paper presented at the

1998 meeting of the Society for Historians of the Early American Republic. Graham's cousins, the Brents, were a similar case in point. William Brent established a law practice in Louisiana, secured appointment under the territorial regime, and represented Louisiana in Congress during the 1820s.

27. John Crittenden, Elegius Fromentin, and John Williams to Calhoun, 29 January 1818, *Calhoun Papers*, 2: 101. Other members of the Louisiana delegation followed suit. See Henry Johnson to Calhoun, 12 April 1818, ibid., 242; Robertson to Calhoun, 9 March 1818, ibid., 183; Robertson to Calhoun, 24 April 1820, ibid., 5: 74.

28. *Louisiana Gazette,* 20 and 29 April 1816. For the history of the caucus system, see James M. Banner Jr., *To the Hartford Convention: The Federalists and the Origins of Party Politics in Massachusetts, 1789–1815* (New York: Knopf, 1970), 227–67.

29. *Louisiana Gazette,* 6 May 1812.

30. Ibid.

31. *The Election of a President* (Pittsburgh, 1812).

32. Robertson to Villeré, 25 December 1813, Jacques Philippe Villeré Papers, HNO; anonymous letter to Fromentin, 19 October 1814, ibid.

33. *Acts Passed* (1812), 170–72; *Annals of Congress,* 13th Cong., 2d sess. (1813–14), 324; Banner, *To the Hartford Convention,* 31, 323; J. C. A. Stagg, *Mr. Madison's War: Politics, Diplomacy, and Warfare in the Early American Republic, 1783–1830* (Princeton: Princeton University Press, 1983), 252–56, 305–07.

34. Thomas B. Robertson Broadside, 1813, HNO; *Louisiana Courier,* 5 January 1816. See also *Louisiana Gazette,* 26 December 1811. The notion of the Federalists as "foreign" was hardly an invention of the Louisianians. Jefferson often characterized Federalists as "Anglomen," proclaiming them foreign by virtue of their political beliefs. See Jefferson to Lomax, 12 March 1799, in *Jefferson Writings,* ed. Merrill D. Peterson (New York: Library of America, 1984), 1063; Jefferson to Langdon, 5 March 1810, ibid., 1219; Jefferson to the Marquis de Lafayette, 14 May 1817, ibid., 1407.

35. Banner, *To the Hartford Convention,* 333–35, 234–35.

36. Mather to Council, 18 February 1808, MMCDV, 1: 110; Claiborne to Lieutenant Colonel Croghan, 20 December 1815, *Claiborne Letterbooks,* 6: 397; *Louisiana Courier,* 1 January and 2 July 1817. For celebrations of the battle of New Orleans in eastern cities, see Len Travers, *Celebrating the Fourth: Independence Day and the Rites of Nationalism in the Early Republic* (Amherst: University of Massachusetts Press, 1997), 199, 202. For an analysis of nationalizing politics in Louisiana that focuses on the public sphere, see David Waldstreicher, "Rites of Rebellion, Rites of Assent: Celebrations, Print Culture, and the Origins of American Nationalism," *JAH* 82 (1995): 37–61.

37. *Louisiana Courier,* 2 July 1817. For similar moments of conspicuous national celebration, see ibid., 6 July 1810, 19 August 1811, 22 July and 19 August 1816, 7 July 1817, 12 June 1818, 29 March and 21 May 1819, 10 January 1820.

38. Ibid., 5 July 1813, 10 January 1816, 10 January 1820.

39. For studies of the political roles of public activities, see Waldstreicher, "Rites of Rebellion, Rites of Assent," 37–61.

40. Mississippi Territorial Legislature to Congress, 27 December 1811, Carter, 6: 253–57; Claiborne to George Poindexter, 6 January 1812, *Claiborne Letterbooks,* 6: 30–31; Claiborne to John Dawson, 1 January 1812, ibid., 24; *Annals of Congress,* 11th Cong.,

3d sess. (1810–11), 482; John Ballinger to Monroe, 26 December 1811, Miscellaneous Letters, reel 24; Claiborne to Rhea, 24 February 1812, *Claiborne Letterbooks,* 6: 60–61.

41. *House Journal* (1812), 32–33.

42. *Acts Passed* (1812), 8–12.

43. Sterrett to Evans, 20 May 1814, Nathaniel Evans Papers, LSU, in *RASP,* H, reel 4, frame 374.

44. *Louisiana Gazette,* 6 July 1818.

45. Ibid., 18 December 1816.

46. Sidney J. Romero, *"My Fellow Citizens . . .": The Inaugural Addresses of Louisiana's Governors* (Lafayette: University of Southwestern Louisiana, 1980), 34.

47. For discussions of political language and political sensibility, see Jay Fliegelman, *Declaring Independence: Jefferson, Natural Language, and the Culture of Performance* (Stanford: Stanford University Press, 1993), 125–32; Joanne B. Freeman, "Slander, Poison, Whispers, and Fame: Jefferson's 'Anas' and Political Gossip in the Early Republic," *JER* 15 (1995): 26–31.

48. *Acts Passed* (1812), 130–33. For similar efforts to regulate local politics, administration, and development, see ibid., 32–35, 96–105.

49. *House Journal* (1812), 9–11.

50. Ibid., app. 2, ii–iii. See also *Dormenon's Case,* 1 Martin 129 (La., 1812).

51. Andrew R. L. Cayton, *The Frontier Republic: Ideology and Politics in the Ohio Country* (Kent: Kent State University Press, 1986), 110–25; Gordon S. Wood, *The Radicalism of the American Revolution* (New York: Knopf, 1992), 310–11.

52. *Louisiana Courier,* 21 May 1819; Clay, Speech at New Orleans, 19 May 1819, *Clay Papers,* 2: 692–93. See also *Louisiana Courier,* 5 and 19 May 1819; Lewis to Clay, 18 May 1819, *Clay Papers,* 2: 690; Tregle, "Jackson and Battle of New Orleans," 377–79.

53. Tregle, "Jackson and Battle of New Orleans," 377–79.

54. For the near-obsessive coverage of Jackson's movements, see Livingston to Jackson, 4 January 1816, *Jackson Papers,* 4: 419; *Louisiana Gazette,* 23 January 1816, 3 February 1816, 26 March 1816, 4 and 16 April 1816, 19 and 28 August 1816, 16 October 1816; *Louisiana Courier,* 19 May 1819.

55. For antebellum political disputes in Louisiana, see Tregle, *Louisiana in the Age of Jackson.*

Chapter 9. Louisiana

1. PCDV, 10: 106; Macarty to Robertson, 15 January 1818, MMCDV, 1: 159. For Macarty's election as mayor, see PCDV, 8: 87–88.

2. Monroe to Senate Military Committee, 22 February 1815, Monroe Writings, 5: 323–24; Madison to Crawford, 23 September 1816, Hunt, 8: 366. See also Monroe to John Quincy Adams, 10 December 1815, *Monroe Writings,* 5: 380–81. For the changing Spanish-American relationship in the 1810s, see James E. Lewis Jr., *The American Union and the Problem of Neighborhood: The United States and the Collapse of the Spanish Empire, 1783–1829* (Chapel Hill: University of North Carolina Press, 1998), 115–25.

3. Monroe to Adams, 10 December 1815, *Monroe Writings,* 5: 380–81.

4. Madison, "Instructions prepared for the Navy Department," 1815 or 1816, *Letters and Other Writings of James Madison,* 4 vols. (New York: R. Worthington, 1884), 3: 10–11.

5. Monroe to Duplessis, 15 November 1815, Domestic Letters, 14: 267. Duplessis himself had benefited from the active patronage of William C. C. Claiborne. See Claiborne to Gallatin, 3 May 1812, Carter, 9: 1019.

6. Monroe, First Annual Message, 2 December 1817, *Monroe Writings,* 6: 33–44; Monroe to Madison, 22 December 1817, 13 February and 10 July 1818, Madison Papers, reel 68; Calhoun to William A. Trimble, 26 January 1818, *Calhoun Papers,* 2: 94; Monroe to Jackson, 19 July and 20 October 1818, *Monroe Writings,* 6: 55–61, 74–75; Monroe, Second Annual Message, 16 December 1818, ibid., 75–83; Lewis, *American Union and Neighborhood,* 32–40, 80–84, 92–94.

7. Lewis, *American Union and Neighborhood,* 121.

8. Monroe, First Annual Message, 2 December 1817, *Monroe Writings,* 6: 34.

9. Charles E. Bevans, ed., *Treaties and Other International Agreements of the United States of America, 1776–1949,* 13 vols. (Washington, D.C.: Government Printing Office, 1971), 11: 530.

10. Ibid.

11. Samuel Flagg Bemis, *John Quincy Adams and the Union* (New York: Knopf, 1956), 1: 257–77; Lynn H. Parsons, *John Quincy Adams* (Madison, Wis.: Madison House, 1998), 134–35; Leonard White, *The Jeffersonians: A Study in Administrative History, 1801–1829* (New York: Macmillan, 1951), 194.

12. Lewis, *American Union and Neighborhood,* 48–50, 58, 120–24.

13. Calhoun to John Jamison, 8 January 1818, *Calhoun Papers,* 3: 476. See also Jamison to Calhoun, 26 May and 16 June 1819, ibid., 4: 75–76, 110; Calhoun to Jamison, 5 July 1819, ibid., 149–52.

14. George Gray to Calhoun, 14 October 1820, J. Fair Hardin Collection, LSU.

15. F. Todd Smith, *The Caddo Indians: Tribes at the Convergence of Empires, 1542–1854* (College Station: Texas A&M Press, 1995), 103–16; Richard White, *The Roots of Dependency: Subsistence, Environment, and Social Change among the Choctaws, Pawnees, and Navajos* (Lincoln: University of Nebraska Press, 1983), 94–146. For the changes in perspective that came with the resolution of boundary disputes among white nations, see Jeremy Adelman and Stephen Aron, "From Borderlands to Borders: Empires, Nation-States, and the Peoples in Between in North American History," *American Historical Review* 104 (1999): 814–41.

16. PCDV, 6: 179–80; 7: 42–43. See also PCDV, 7: 113–14; 8: 62, 68, 70–74. As early as 1809 the City Council attempted to eject the navy yard, but Secretary of the Navy Paul Hamilton convinced the administration to reject this plan. With the federal government's control over all branches of the territorial regime, there was little the council could do. See PCDV, 5: 45.

17. PCDV, 8: 42.

18. PCDV, 8: 70. See also PCDV, 8: 57, 64, 70–74, 147–51; 9: 155–56, 90.

19. Benjamin Crowninshield to Daniel Patterson, 8 December 1815, Letters to Officers, reel 12, frame 233. See also Crowninshield to Patterson, 8 September 1815, ibid., 200; Madison, "Instructions prepared for the Navy Department," 1815 or 1816 (exact

date unknown), in *Madison Writings*, 3: 10–11; Crowninshield to Patterson, 7 March 1817, Letters to Officers, reel 12, frame 465.

20. PCDV, 9: 111; 10: 75, 185, 196; 11: 225; Crowninshield to Patterson, 27 June 1815, Letters to Officers, reel 12, frame 159.

21. PCDV, 11: 48. See also see PCDV, 10: 190–91.

22. Claiborne Proclamation, 24 November 1813, *Claiborne Letterbooks*, 6: 279–80; Claiborne to John Dick, 11 February 1815, ibid., 338; Claiborne to Patterson, 5 April 1815, ibid., 355.

23. *Acts Passed* (1812), 134–35; *Louisiana Gazette*, 31 May 1820.

24. *Louisiana Courier*, 9 and 25 January 1816. For the Republican aversion to taxation, see Herbert E. Sloan, *Principle and Interest: Thomas Jefferson and the Problem of Debt* (New York: Oxford University Press, 1995), 95–98, 182–84.

25. Gallatin to Congress, 9 June 1813, *ASP, PL*, 744. Gallatin enclosed a list of surveyed claims totaling 128 pages. In 1814 Congress passed another act extending the deadline for submitting land claims, again stating that this would be the last opportunity. But this was no more successful than previous acts. See *Statutes at Large*, 3: 121–23, 528–32, 573–75. See also Crawford to Monroe, 8 December 1818, *ASP, PL*, 3.

26. Resolution to Congress, 23 February 1820, *ASP, PL*, 3: 379–81.

27. PCDV, 6: 125, 132; 7: 50. White resentment of free black competition was hardly limited to Louisiana. See Ira Berlin, *Slaves without Masters: The Free Negro in the Antebellum South* (New York: New Press, 1974), 229–31; Gary B. Nash, *Forging Freedom: The Formation of Philadelphia's Black Community, 1720–1840* (Cambridge: Harvard University Press, 1988).

28. PCDV, 2: 33. The Orleans Parish Police Jury also saw the advantages of using slave labor for public projects. See *Louisiana Courier*, 22 August 1810.

29. Mather to Council, 25 April 1812, MMCDV, 5: 26.

30. PCDV, 8: 141; 9: 179.

31. PCDV, 6: 91.

32. PCDV, 11: 85. For similar work collecting animal carcasses, see PCDV, 8: 99. For other tasks, see PCDV, 4: 154–55, 299–300; 5: 58; 6: 22, 116, 174; 7: 129, 149, 153, 157; 8: 55, 92, 116; 9: 40–44, 84; 10: 196–97. The city initially provided compensation for the owners of slaves on the chain gang, a policy it annulled in 1814 after deciding that the city already absorbed the cost of housing, feeding, and supervising the slaves during their incarceration. See PCDV, 7: 251; 8: 90.

33. Calhoun to Villeré, 25 November 1820, *Calhoun Papers*, 5: 453. Andrew Jackson made liberal use of slave labor in preparing the defense of New Orleans during the British invasion of 1814–15. See Jackson to Villeré, 19 December 1814, *Jackson Papers*, 3: 210; Claiborne to Jackson, 3 February 1815, ibid., 267.

34. Jackson to Claiborne, 2 July 1814, *Jackson Papers*, 3: 91. See also Jackson to Monroe, 26 October 1814, ibid., 173–75; McKee to Jackson, 30 November 1814, ibid., 479.

35. Sibley to Eustis, 18 May 1812, J. Fair Hardin Collection. See also Claiborne to Dehahuit, 18 October 1813, *Claiborne Letterbooks*, 6: 274–77. For white efforts to exploit the Caddo authority in the western borderlands, see Gray to Calhoun, 14 October 1820, J. Fair Hardin Collection.

36. Trimble to Calhoun, 8 February 1818, *Calhoun Papers,* 3: 126.

37. Jane Landers, *Black Society in Spanish Florida* (Urbana: University of Illinois Press, 1999), 231–35. For a similar fort in Spanish America, see idem, "Gracia Real de Santa Teresa de Mose: A Free Black Town in Spanish Colonial Florida," *American Historical Review* 95 (1990): 9–30.

38. Philander Chase, *Bishop Chase's Reminiscences* (Boston: J. B. Dow, 1848), 99–100; Georgia Fairbanks Taylor, "The Early History of the Episcopal Church in New Orleans, 1805–1840," *LHQ* 22 (1939): 443–44.

39. For the Female Orphan Society, see *Acts Passed* (1812), 192–95. For library societies, see *Acts Passed* (1805), 322–35; *Acts Passed* (1812), 50–57, 76–77; PCDV, 9: 56, 58, 66, 115–16; 10: 99; 11: 59, 179; *Louisiana Courier,* 29 December 1817. For the Medical Society, see ibid., 29 August 1817, 16 September 1818; *Acts Passed* (1812), 20–25.

40. George D. Green, *Finance and Economic Development in the Old South: Louisiana Banking, 1804–1861* (Stanford: Stanford University Press, 1972), 52–54.

41. Calhoun to Henry Sherburne, 10 September 1818, *Calhoun Papers,* 3: 118; Calhoun to Crawford, 8 October 1818, ibid., 191; Calhoun to Eleazer W. Ripley, 8 October 1818, ibid., 194.

42. *Acts Passed* (1805), 20–26. For other examples, see ibid., 88–95; *Acts Passed* (1812), 10–15.

43. Ursuline Nuns to Jefferson, 23 April 1804, Jefferson Papers, reel 30.

44. For an example of Americans studying at the convent, see Edith Buhler Devall to Margaret Buhler, 22 May 1805, Buhler Family Papers, LSU.

45. Dumas Malone, *Jefferson and the Rights of Man* (Boston: Little, Brown, 1951), 131–32.

46. Claiborne to Pitot, 24 June 1806, *Claiborne Letterbooks,* 3: 344; Claiborne to Convent, 8 March 1809, 14 March 1809, *Claiborne Letterbooks,* 4: 329; Claiborne to Madison, 20 March 1809, Madison Papers, reel 11; Claiborne to Gallatin, 4 April and 7 June 1811, *Claiborne Letterbooks,* 5: 132–33, 160–62; Claiborne to Convent, 19 February and 24 March 1812, ibid., 6: 62.

47. Claiborne to Madison, 8 November 1808, *Claiborne Letterbooks,* 4: 246. For similar references, see Claiborne to Gallatin, 4 April 1811, ibid., 5: 203; Claiborne to Dawson, 11 December 1811, ibid., 400.

48. Carroll to Madison, 17 November 1806, in *The John Carroll Papers,* ed. Thomas O'Brien Hanley, 3 vols. (Notre Dame: University of Notre Dame Press, 1976), 2: 534–35.

49. Annabelle M. Melville, *Louis William DuBourg, Bishop of Louisiana and the Floridas, Bishop of Montauban, and Archbishop of Besançon, 1766–1833* (Chicago: Loyala University Press, 1986), 281–305; Charles Edward O'Neil, " 'A Quarter Marked by Sundry Peculiarities': New Orleans, Lay Trustees, and Père Antoine," *Catholic Historical Review* 76 (1990): 253–54.

50. Louis DuBourg to the Prefect of the Fide, 12 July 1815, in *United States Documents in the Propaganda Fide Archives,* ed. Finbar Kenneally, 7 vols. (Washington, D.C.: Academy of American Franciscan History, 1966–81), 1: 201; DuBourg to Pope Pius VII, 4 September 1815, ibid., 5: 1488; Notes from the General Congregation, 11 December 1815, ibid., 3: 1485; The Fide to Carroll, 23 December 1815, ibid., 1400; DuBourg to

A. Dugnani, 11 April 1816, ibid., 1: 219; DuBourg to the Fide, 5 September 1822, ibid., 5: 1735; DuBourg to the Fide, 24 June 1816, ibid., 1: 221; The Fide to DuBourg, 2 June 1821, ibid., 3: 1589; O'Neil, "'A Quarter Marked by Sundry Peculiarities,'" 273–75.

51. *Marie v. Avart,* 6 Martin 731 (La., 1819); *Bazzi v. Rose and Her Child,* 8 Martin 149 (La., 1820); Caryn Cossé Bell, *Revolution, Romanticism, and the Afro-Creole Protest Tradition in Louisiana, 1718–1868* (Baton Rouge: Louisiana State University Press, 1997), 70–71. See also Julia Huston Nguyen, "Worldly Rites: The Social and Political Significance of Religious Services in Louisiana, 1803–1865" (Ph.D. diss., Louisiana State University, 2001), 15.

52. *Doubrere v. Grilier's Syndics,* 2 NS Martin 171 (La., 1824). For a similar case, see petition from J. A. Demarchi, Lanoix, Peychaud, Jean Pugeel, Sainet, Qauntin, and L. Tainturier, 30 July 1804, LCDV, 1. See also *Tonnelier v. Maurin,* 2 Martin 206 (La., 1812); *Cloutier v. Lecomte,* 3 Martin 481 (La., 1814); *Bore's Executors v. Quirry's Executors,* 3 Martin 545 (La., 1816); *Cuffy v. Castillon,* 5 Martin 1818 (La., 1818); *Marie v. Avart;* Carl A. Brasseaux, Keith P. Fontenot, and Claude F. Oubre, *Creoles of Color in the Bayou Country* (Jackson: University of Mississippi Press, 1994); Gary Mills, *The Forgotten People: Cane River's Creoles of Color* (Baton Rouge: Louisiana State University Press, 1977), 49; Jennifer M. Spear, "The Louisiana Purchase and the Gens de Couleur Libre in New Orleans," paper presented at the 2002 meeting of the Society for Historians of the Early American Republic, Berkeley, Calif. For a comparison from the colonial era indicating the resilience of these networks, see Kimberly S. Hanger, "Conflicting Loyalties: The French Revolution and Free People of Color in Spanish Louisiana," *LAH* 34 (1993): 15–18, 29–30.

53. *Annals of Congress,* 15th Cong., 2d sess. (1818–19), 448, 1030; Rogers M. Smith, *Civic Ideals: Conflicting Visions of Citizenship in U.S. History* (New Haven: Yale University Press, 1997), 169–70.

54. *Acts Passed* (1812), 26–29.

55. *Hepburn v. Ellzey,* 2 Cranch 445 (U.S., 1805); *Loughborough v. Blake,* 18 Wheaton 317 (U.S., 1820).

Conclusion

1. *Louisiana Courier,* 6 October 1819.

2. Caryn Cossé Bell, *Revolution, Romanticism, and the Afro-Creole Protest Tradition in Louisiana, 1718–1868* (Baton Rouge: Louisiana State University Press, 1997), 71.

3. For the Crevasse and the battle over reimbursement, see *Claiborne v. Police Jury of Orleans,* 4 Martin (La., 1819); *Acts Passed* (1812), 4–5; *Louisiana Gazette,* 8, 10, and 17 May 1816; PCDV, 9: 2–19.

4. Jane Lucas DeGrummond, "Cayetana Susana Bosque y Fanqui: 'A Notable Woman'," *LAH* 22 (1982): 286.

5. Ibid., 277–84.

6. Marion Nelson Winship, "The Territorial Aspirations of William Charles Cole Claiborne: A Western Success Story from the Jeffersonian Empire," paper presented at the 1998 meeting of the Society for Historians of the Early American Republic.

7. Claiborne's brother, Ferdinand, sired his own political dynasty, first in Mississippi

and eventually in Louisiana. Ferdinand's son, John Francis Hamtramck Claiborne, represented Mississippi in the House of Representatives from 1835 to 1837. His Louisiana descendants included Louisiana representative Thomas Hale Boggs, who was succeeded by his wife, Lindy Boggs. Another branch of the family eventually moved to the Northeast, a branch that included Herbert Claiborne Pell, a congressman from New York, and his son, Rhode Island senator Claiborne Pell.

8. Claiborne to Magdalene Claiborne, 26 September 1817, Magdalene Claiborne Papers, Southern Historical Collection, University of North Carolina–Chapel Hill.

9. *Louisiana Courier,* 17 November 1817. For another example of "liver ailment" as a cause of death, see *Morgan v. McGowan,* 4 Martin 209 (La., 1816).

10. *Louisiana Courier,* 26 November 1817; PCDV, 10: 85–86, 106; *House Journal* (1812), 6.

11. *Claiborne v. Police Jury of Orleans,* 7 Martin 4 (La., 1819).

12. PCDV, 9: 1–20.

13. Joan Cashin, *A Family Venture: Men and Women on the Southern Frontier* (Oxford: Oxford University Press, 1991); Walter Johnson, *Soul by Soul: Life inside the Antebellum Slave Market* (Cambridge: Harvard University Press, 1999).

14. Breckinridge to Jefferson, 10 September 1803, Carter, 9: 48.

15. Brown to Clay, 26 February 1809, *Clay Papers,* 1: 453.

16. Perry H. Howard, *Political Tendencies in Louisiana* (Baton Rouge: Louisiana State University Press, 1971); Joseph G. Tregle, *Louisiana in the Age of Jackson: A Clash of Cultures and Personalities* (Baton Rouge: Louisiana State University Press, 1999).

17. *Acts Passed* (1812), 44–47.

18. The government enacted piecemeal changes to the state's legal structure. See ibid., 24–45.

19. Warren M. Billings, ed., *The Historic Rules of the Supreme Court of Louisiana, 1813–1879* (Lafayette: Center for Louisiana Studies, 1985), xiii.

20. *Louisiana Courier,* 1 December 1820.

21. William B. Hatcher, *Edward Livingston: Jeffersonian Republican and Jacksonian Democrat* (Baton Rouge: Louisiana State University Press, 1940), 230–31, 320–30, 354–56, 417–22.

Bibliography

Unpublished Sources

ARCHIVAL SOURCES

HNO. Thomas Butler Broadside.
———. 1811 Orleans Territory Tax Record.
———. Edward Nicholls and William H. Percy Letters.
———. Thomas B. Robertson Broadside.
———. James Sterling Memorandum.
———. Jacques Philippe Villeré Papers.
LC. Albert Gallatin Papers.
———. Thomas Jefferson Papers. Microfilm Collection.
———. James Madison Papers. Microfilm Collection.
———. James Monroe Papers. Microfilm Collection.
———. David Dixon Porter Papers.
LSU. James Brown Papers.
———. Buhler Family Papers.
———. Thomas Butler and Family Papers.
———. William C. C. Claiborne Papers.
———. Nathaniel Evans Papers.
———. Charles E. A. Gayarré Collection.
———. J. Fair Hardin Collection.
———. Daniel P. Hickey Papers.

——. Philip Hickey Papers.

——. Frederick Kimball Papers.

——. Louisiana Congressional Election Papers.

——. John McDonogh Papers.

——. David Morgan Papers.

——. Fulwar Skipwith Papers.

——. Henry Wilson Papers.

NA. Dispatches from Consuls. Record Group 59.

——. Domestic Letters of the Department of State. Record Group 59. Microfilm Copy M-40.

——. Letters Received by the Secretary of the Navy from Captains. Record Group 45. Microfilm Copy M125.

——. Letters Received by the Secretary of the Navy from Commanders. Record Group 45. Microfilm Copy M147.

——. Letters Received by the Secretary of War: Registered Series. Record Group 107. Microfilm Copy M22.

——. Letters Sent by the Secretary of the Navy to Officers. Record Group 45. Microfilm Copy 149.

——. Miscellaneous Letters of the Department of States. Record Group 59. Microfilm Copy M179.

——. Territorial Papers of the United States. Record Group 59. Microfilm Copy M116 (Florida); T260 (Orleans).

NOPL. Letters, Petitions, and Reports Received by the Conseil de Ville.

——. Mayor's Minute Book.

——. Messages from the Mayor to the Conseil de Ville.

——. Proceedings of the Conseil de Ville.

TUL. De la Vergne Papers.

——. Antonio de Sedella Papers.

——. Louis Toussard Papers.

——. War of 1812 Series.

University of North Carolina–Chapel Hill. Magdalene Claiborne Papers. Southern Historical Collection.

DISSERTATIONS, THESES, AND PAPERS

Adams, Mary P. "Jefferson's Military Policy with Special Reference to the Frontier, 1805–1809." Ph.D. diss., University of Virginia, 1958.

Deen, Isabelle Claxton. "Public Response to the Louisiana Purchase: A Survey of American Press and Pamphlets, 1801–1804." Master's thesis, University of Virginia, 1972.

Fernandez, Mark F. "The Appellate Question: A Comparative Analysis of Supreme Courts of Appeal in Virginia and Louisiana, 1776–1840." Ph.D. diss., College of William and Mary, 1991.

McGrath, Rosemarie Catherine. "The Issue of the Foreign Slave Trade in the Louisiana Territory, 1803–1810." Master's thesis, University of Virginia, 1967.

McMichael, Andrew. "Reluctant Revolutionaries: The West Florida Borderlands, 1785–1810." Ph.D. diss., Vanderbilt University, 2000.

———. "Slavery on the Southwestern Borderlands: Anglos, Slaves, and Receding Spaniards." Paper presented at the 1999 meeting of the Society for Historians of the Early American Republic, Lexington, Ky.

Nguyen, Julia Huston. "Worldly Rites: The Social and Political Significance of Religious Services in Louisiana, 1803–1865." Ph.D. diss., Louisiana State University, 2001.

Saucier, Earl Noland. "Charles Gayarré, the Creole Historian." Ph.D. diss., George Peabody College for Teachers, 1935.

Socola, Edward M. "Charles Gayarré: A Biography." Ph.D. diss., University of Pennsylvania, 1954.

Spear, Jennifer M. "The Louisiana Purchase and the Gens de Couleur Libre in New Orleans." Paper presented at the 2002 meeting of the Society for Historians of the Early American Republic, Berkeley, Calif.

Tregle, Joseph G., Jr. "Louisiana in the Age of Jackson: A Study in Ego-Politics." Ph.D. diss., University of Pennsylvania, 1954.

Weiss, Adolfo Arriaga. "The Domestic Opposition to the Louisiana Purchase: Anti-Expansionism and Republican Thought." Ph.D. diss., University of Virginia, 1993.

Winship, Marion Nelson. "The Territorial Aspirations of William Charles Cole Claiborne: A Western Success Story from the Jeffersonian Empire." Paper presented at the 1998 meeting of the Society for Historians of the Early American Republic.

Published Sources

BOOKS, ARTICLES, AND COLLECTIONS

Aberbach, Alan David. *In Search of an American Identity: Samuel Latham Mitchill, Jeffersonian Nationalist.* New York: Peter Lang, 1988.

An Account of Louisiana, Being an Abstract of Documents, in the Offices of the Departments of State, and of the Treasury. Washington, D.C.: Duane, 1803.

Acts Passed at the General Assembly of the State of Louisiana. New Orleans: Thierry, Baird and Wagner; Peter K. Wagner; J. C. de St. Romes, 1812–20.

Acts Passed at the Legislature of the Territory of Orleans. 6 vols. New Orleans: Bradford and Anderson, 1806–12.

Adams, Charles Francis, ed. *Memoirs of John Quincy Adams, Comprising Portions of His Diary from 1795 to 1848.* 12 vols. Philadelphia: J. B. Lippincott, 1874.

Adelman, Jeremy, and Stephen Aron. "From Borderlands to Borders: Empires, Nation-States, and the Peoples in Between in North American History." *American Historical Review* 104 (1999): 814–41.

Alexander, Gregory S. *Commodity and Propriety: Competing Visions of Property in American Legal Thought, 1776–1970.* Chicago: University of Chicago Press, 1977.

Amar, Akhil Reed. "The Bill of Rights as a Constitution." *Yale Law Journal* 100 (1991): 1131–1210.

Ambrose, Stephen A. *Undaunted Courage: Meriwether Lewis, Thomas Jefferson, and the Opening of the American West.* New York: Simon and Schuster, 1996.

American State Papers: Documents, Legislative and Executive, of the Congress of the United States. 38 vols. Washington, D.C.: Gales and Seaton, 1832–61.

Ammon, Harry. *James Monroe: The Search for National Identity*. Charlottesville: University Press of Virginia, 1990.

Anderson, Benedict. *Imagined Communities: Reflections on the Origin and Spread of Nationalism*. London: Verso, 1991.

Appleby, Joyce O. *Capitalism and a New Social Order: The Republican Vision of the 1790s*. New York: New York University Press, 1984.

Arena, C. Richard. "Philadelphia–Spanish New Orleans Trade in the 1790s." *LAH* 2 (1961): 429–45.

Ariela, Yhoshua. *Individualism and Nationalism in American Ideology*. Cambridge: Harvard University Press, 1964.

Aron, Stephen. *How the West Was Lost: The Transformation of Kentucky from Daniel Boone to Henry Clay*. Baltimore: Johns Hopkins University Press, 1996.

Arthur, Stanley C. *The Story of the Kemper Brothers: Three Fighting Sons of a Baptist Preacher Who Fought for Freedom When Louisiana Was Young*. St. Francisville, La.: St. Francisville Democrat, 1933.

Baade, Hans W. "The Law of Slavery in Spanish Luisiana." In *Louisiana's Legal Heritage*, ed. Edward F. Haas Jr. Pensacola: Perdido Bay Press, 1983.

Bailyn, Bernard. *The Ideological Origins of the American Revolution*. Enl. ed. Cambridge: Belknap Press of Harvard University Press, 1992.

Ball, Terence, and J. G. A. Pocock, eds. *Conceptual Change and the Constitution*. Lawrence: University Press of Kansas, 1988.

Banner, James M., Jr. *To the Hartford Convention: The Federalists and the Origins of Party Politics in Massachusetts, 1789–1815*. New York: Knopf, 1970.

Banner, Stuart. "The Political Function of the Commons: Changing Conceptions of Property and Sovereignty in Missouri, 1750–1860." *American Journal of Legal History* 41 (1997): 61–93.

Banning, Lance. *The Jeffersonian Persuasion: Evolution of a Party Ideology*. Ithaca: Cornell University Press, 1978.

———. *The Sacred Fire of Liberty: James Madison and the Founding of the Federal Republic*. Cornell: Cornell University Press, 1995.

Baseler, Marylin C. *"Asylum for Mankind": America, 1607–1800*. Ithaca: Cornell University Press, 1998.

Beeman, Richard, Stephen Botein, and Edward C. Carter II, eds. *Beyond Confederation: Origins of the Constitution and American National Identity*. Chapel Hill: University of North Carolina Press, 1987.

Beiner, Ronald, ed. *Theorizing Citizenship*. New York: State University of New York Press, 1995.

Bell, Caryn Cossé. *Revolution, Romanticism, and the Afro-Creole Protest Tradition in Louisiana, 1718–1868*. Baton Rouge: Louisiana State University Press, 1997.

Bellesiles, Michael A. *Revolutionary Outlaws: Ethan Allen and the Struggle for Independence on the Early American Frontier*. Charlottesville: University Press of Virginia, 1993.

Beltman, Brian W. "Territorial Commands of the Army: The System Refined but Not Perfected." *JER* 11 (1991): 185–218.

Bemis, Samuel Flagg. *Jay's Treaty: A Study in Commerce and Diplomacy*. New Haven: Yale University Press, 1962.

———. *John Quincy Adams and the Union*. New York: Knopf, 1956.

Berkhofer, Robert F., Jr. "The Northwest Ordinance and the Principle of Territorial Evolution." In *The American Territorial System*, ed. John Porter Bloom. Athens: Ohio University Press, 1969.

Berlin, Ira. "From Creole to African: Atlantic Creoles and the Origins of African-American Society in Mainland North America." *WMQ*, 3d ser., 53 (1996): 251–88.

———. *Many Thousands Gone: The First Two Centuries of Slavery in North America*. Cambridge: Belknap Press of Harvard University Press, 1999.

———. *Slaves without Masters: The Free Negro in the Antebellum South*. New York: New Press, 1974.

Berquin-Duvallon. *Travels in Louisiana and the Floridas in the Year 1802*. New York: I. Riley, 1807.

Berthoff, Rowland. "Conventional Mentality: Free Blacks, Women, and Business Corporations as Unequal Persons, 1820–1870." *JAH* 76 (1989): 753–84.

Bevans, Charles E., ed. *Treaties and Other International Agreements of the United States of America, 1776–1949*. 13 vols. Washington, D.C.: Government Printing Office, 1968–76.

Billings, Warren M. "From This Seed: The State Constitution of 1812." In *In Search of Fundamental Law: Louisiana's Constitutions, 1812–1974*, ed. Warren M. Billings and Edward F. Haas. Lafayette: Center for Louisiana Studies, University of Southwestern Louisiana, 1993.

———. "A Neglected Treaty: Lewis Kerr's Exposition and the Making of Criminal Law in Louisiana." *LAH* 38 (1997): 261–86.

———. "Origins of Criminal Law in Louisiana." *LAH* 32 (1991): 63–76.

———, ed. *The Historic Rules of the Supreme Court of Louisiana, 1813–1879*. Lafayette: Center for Louisiana Studies, 1985.

Biographical Directory of the United States Congress, 1774–1989. Washington, D.C.: Government Printing Office, 1989.

Brasseaux, Carl A. *Acadian to Cajun: Transformation of a People, 1803–1877*. Jackson: University Press of Mississippi, 1992.

———. *Denis-Nicolas Foucault and the New Orleans Rebellion of 1768*. Ruston: Louisiana Tech University, 1987.

Brasseaux, Carl A., and Glenn L. Conrad, eds. *The Road to Louisiana: The Saint-Domingue Refugees, 1792–1809*. Lafayette: University of Southwestern Louisiana, 1992.

Brasseaux, Carl A., Keith P. Fontenot, and Claude F. Oubre. *Creoles of Color in the Bayou Country*. Jackson: University of Mississippi Press, 1994.

Brazer, Samuel. *Address, Pronounced at Worcester, on May 12th, 1804, in Commemoration of the Cession of Louisiana to the United States*. Worcester, Mass.: Sewall Goodridge, 1804.

Breen, T. H. "Ideology and Nationalism on the Eve of the American Revolution: Revisions *Once More* in Need of Revising." *JAH* 84 (1997): 13–39.

Brown, Charles Brockden. *An Address to the Government of the United States, on the Cession of Louisiana to the French and on the Late Breach of Treaty by the Spaniards*. Philadelphia: John Conrad, 1803.

Brown, Everett S. *The Constitutional History of the Louisiana Purchase.* Clifton, N.J.: Augustus M. Kelley, 1972.

Brown, James, and Louis Moreau-Lislet. *A Digest of the Civil Laws Now in Force in the Territory of Orleans . . . Adapted to Its Present System of Government.* New Orleans: Bradford and Anderson, 1808.

Brubaker, Rogers. *Citizenship and Nationhood in France and Germany.* Cambridge: Harvard University Press, 1992.

Bryan, Violet. *The Myth of New Orleans in Literature: Dialogues of Race and Gender.* Knoxville: University of Tennessee Press, 1993.

Burr, Aaron. *Political Correspondence and Public Papers of Aaron Burr,* ed. Mary-Jo Kline. 2 vols. Princeton: Princeton University Press, 1983.

Calhoun, Craig. *Critical Social Theory: Culture, History, and the Challenge of Difference.* Oxford: Oxford University Press, 1995.

Calhoun, John C. *The Papers of John C. Calhoun,* ed. Robert L. Meriwether et al. 28 vols. to date. Columbia: University of South Carolina Press, 1959–.

Campbell, Randolph. *An Empire for Slavery: The Peculiar Institution in Texas, 1821– 1865.* Baton Rouge: Louisiana State University Press, 1989.

Canny, Nicholas, and Anthony Pagden, eds. *Colonial Identity in the Atlantic World, 1500–1800.* Princeton: Princeton University Press, 1987.

Carp, E. Wayne. *To Starve the Army at Pleasure: Continental Army Administration and American Political Culture, 1775–1783.* Chapel Hill: University of North Carolina Press, 1984.

Carroll, John. *The John Carroll Papers,* ed. Thomas O'Brien Hanley. 3 vols. Notre Dame: University of Notre Dame Press, 1976.

Casey, Powell A. "Military Roads in the Florida Parishes of Louisiana." *LAH* 15 (1974): 229–42.

Cashin, Joan. *A Family Venture: Men and Women on the Southern Frontier.* Oxford: Oxford University Press, 1991.

Catterall, Helen Tunncliff, ed. *Judicial Cases Concerning American Slavery and the Negro.* 5 vols. Washington, D.C.: Carnegie Institution, 1932–37.

Cayton, Andrew R. L. *Frontier Indiana.* Bloomington: Indiana University Press, 1996.

———. *The Frontier Republic: Ideology and Politics in the Ohio Country.* Kent: Kent State University Press, 1986.

———. "Land, Power, and Reputation: The Cultural Dimension of Politics in the Ohio Country." *WMQ,* 3d ser., 47 (1990): 266–86.

———. " 'Separate Interests' and the Nation-State: The Washington Administration and the Origins of Regionalism in the Trans-Appalachian West." *JAH* 79 (1993): 39–67.

Chase, Philander. *Bishop Chase's Reminiscences.* Boston: J. B. Dow, 1848.

Claiborne, William C. C. *The Letter Books of William C. C. Claiborne, 1801–1816,* ed. Dunbar Rowland. 6 vols. Jackson: Mississippi State Library and Archive, 1917.

Clay, Henry. *The Papers of Henry Clay,* ed. James F. Hopkins et al. 10 vols. Lexington: University of Kentucky Press, 1959–91.

Coles, Harry Lewis. *History of the Administration of Federal Land Policies and Land Tenure in Louisiana, 1803–1860.* New York: Arno, 1979.

Connor, Walker. "The Politics of Ethnonationalism." *Journal of International Affairs* 27 (1973): 1–21.

Constitution or Form of Government of the State of Louisiana. New Orleans: Jo. Bar. Baird, 1812.

Cook, Brian J. *Bureaucracy and Self-Government: Reconsidering the Role of Public Administration in American Politics.* Baltimore: Johns Hopkins University Press, 1996.

Cox, Isaac J. "The Border Missions of General George Mathews." *Mississippi Valley Historical Review* 12 (1925): 309–333.

———. *The West Florida Controversy, 1798–1813: A Study in American Diplomacy.* Baltimore: Johns Hopkins Press, 1923.

Crackel, Theodore J. *Mr. Jefferson's Army: Political and Social Reform of the Military Establishment, 1801–1809.* New York: New York University Press, 1987.

Crenson, Matthew A. *The Federal Machine: Beginnings of Bureaucracy in Jacksonian America.* Baltimore: Johns Hopkins University Press, 1975.

Cress, Lawrence Delbart. *Citizens in Arms: The Army and the Militia in American Society to the War of 1812.* Chapel Hill: University of North Carolina Press, 1982.

Cunningham, Noble E. *The Jeffersonian Republicans in Power: Party Operations, 1801–1809.* Chapel Hill: University of North Carolina Press, 1963.

Curti, Merle E. *The Roots of American Loyalty.* New York: Columbia University Press, 1946.

Cutter, John R. "The Administration of Law in Colonial New Mexico." *JER* 18 (1998): 99–115.

Dargo, George. *Jefferson's Louisiana: Politics and the Clash of Legal Traditions.* Cambridge: Harvard University Press, 1975.

Davis, David Brion. *The Problem of Slavery in the Age of Revolution.* Ithaca: Cornell University Press, 1975.

Debates and Proceedings of the Congress of the United States. 42 vols. Washington, D.C.: Gales and Seaton, 1834–56.

DeConde, Alexander. *This Affair of Louisiana.* New York: Charles Scribner's Sons, 1976.

DeGrummond, Jane Lucas. *The Baratarians and the Battle of New Orleans.* Baton Rouge: Louisiana State University Press, 1961.

———. "Cayetana Susana Bosque y Fanqui: 'A Notable Woman.'" *LAH* 22 (1982): 277–94.

Detweiler, Philip F. "The Changing Reputation of the Declaration of Independence: The First Fifty Years." *WMQ*, 3d ser., 19 (1962): 557–74.

A Dictionary of Louisiana Biography, ed. Glenn R. Conrad. 2 vols. New Orleans: Louisiana Historical Association, 1988.

Din, Gilbert C. *Francisco Bouligny: A Bourbon Soldier in Spanish Louisiana.* Baton Rouge: Louisiana State University Press, 1993.

Din, Gilbert C., and John E. Harkins. *The New Orleans Cabildo: Colonial Louisiana's First City Government, 1769–1803.* Baton Rouge: Louisiana State University Press, 1996.

Domínguez, Virginia. *White by Definition: Social Classification in Creole Louisiana.* New Brunswick, N.J.: Rutgers University Press, 1986.

Dormon, James. "The Persistent Specter: Slave Rebellion in Territorial Louisiana." *LAH* 18 (1977): 389–404.

Dowd, Gregory. *A Spirited Resistance: The North American Indian Struggle for Unity.* Baltimore: Johns Hopkins University Press, 1992.

Drinnon, Richard. "The Metaphysics of Empire-Building: American Imperialism in the Age of Jefferson and Monroe." *Massachusetts Review* 16 (1975): 666–89.

Eblen, Jack Ericson. *The First and Second United States Empires: Governors and Territorial Government, 1784–1912.* Pittsburgh: University of Pittsburgh Press, 1968.

Egerton, Douglas R. *Gabriel's Rebellion: The Virginia Slave Conspiracies of 1800 and 1802.* Chapel Hill: University of North Carolina Press, 1993.

The Election of a President. Pittsburgh, 1812.

Ellis, Richard. *The Jeffersonian Crisis: Courts and Politics in the Young Republic.* New York: Norton, 1971.

Evans, Peter B., Dietrich Rueschemeyer, and Theda Skocpol, eds. *Bringing the State Back In.* Cambridge: Cambridge University Press, 1985.

Examination of the Rights of the United States and the Claims of Mr. Edward Livingston on the Batture in Front of the Faubourg Ste. Marie. New Orleans: Thierry, 1808.

Farnham, Wallace D. " 'The Weakened Spring of Government': A Study in Nineteenth-Century American History." *American Historical Review* 68 (1963): 662–80.

Fernandez, Mark F. "The Rules of the Courts of the Territory of Orleans." *LAH* 37 (1997): 63–86.

Finkleman, Paul. *An Imperfect Union: Slavery, Federalism, and Comity.* Chapel Hill: University of North Carolina Press, 1981.

The First Constitution of the State of Louisiana, ed. Cecil Morgan. Baton Rouge: Louisiana State University Press, 1975.

Fliegelman, Jay. *Declaring Independence: Jefferson, Natural Language, and the Culture of Performance.* Stanford: Stanford University Press, 1993.

Foley, William E. *The Genesis of Missouri: From Wilderness Outpost to Statehood.* Columbia: University of Missouri Press, 1989.

Foner, Laura. "The Free People of Color in Louisiana and St. Domingue: A Comparative Portrait of Two Three-Caste Slave Societies." *Journal of Social History* 3 (1970): 404–30.

Fortier, Alcée. *A History of Louisiana.* 4 vols. New York: Manzi, Joyan, 1904.

Freeman, Joanne B. "Slander, Poison, Whispers, and Fame: Jefferson's 'Anas' and Political Gossip in the Early Republic." *JER* 15 (1995): 25–58.

Gayarré, Charles E. A. *History of Louisiana.* 4 vols. New Orleans: F. F. Hansell and Bro., 1903.

Gitlin, Jay. "Children of Empire or Concitoyens? Louisiana's French Inhabitants." In *The Louisiana Purchase: Emergence of an American Nation,* ed. Peter J. Kastor. Washington, D.C.: CQ Press, 2002.

———. "On the Boundaries of Empire: Connecting the West to Its Imperial Past." In *Under an Open Sky: Rethinking America's Western Past,* ed. William Cronon, George Miles, and Jay Gitlin. New York: Norton, 1992.

———. "Private Diplomacy to Private Property: States, Tribes, and Nations in the Early National Period." *Diplomatic History* 22 (1998): 87–99.

Gleason, Philip D. "American Identity and Americanization." In *The Harvard Encyclopedia of American Ethnic Groups,* ed. Stephan Thernstrom. Cambridge: Belknap Press of Harvard University Press, 1980.

———. "Identifying Identity: A Semantic History." *JAH* 69 (1983): 910–31.

Glover, Richard. "The French Fleet, 1807–1814: Britain's Problem and Madison's Opportunity." *Journal of Modern History* 39 (1967): 233–52.

Gough, Robert. "Officering the American Army, 1798." *WMQ,* 3d ser., 43 (1986): 460–71.

Green, Fletcher M. "Listen to the Eagle Scream: One Hundred Years of the Fourth of July in North Carolina." In *Democracy in the Old South and Other Essays,* ed. J. Isaac Copeland. Nashville: Vanderbilt University Press, 1969.

Green, George D. *Finance and Economic Development in the Old South: Louisiana Banking, 1804–1861.* Stanford: Stanford University Press, 1972.

Greene, Jack P. *Peripheries and Center: Constitutional Development in the Extended Polities of the British Empire and the United States.* New York: Norton, 1986.

Greenfeld, Liah. *Nationalism: Five Roads to Modernity.* Cambridge: Harvard University Press, 1992.

Haas, Edward F. "Odyssey of a Manuscript Collection: Records of the Surveyor General of Antebellum Louisiana." *LAH* 27 (1986): 5–26.

Hackett, David G. "The Social Origins of Nationalism: Albany, New York, 1754–1835." *Journal of Social History* 21 (1987–88): 659–81.

Haggard, Villasana. "The Neutral Ground between Louisiana and Texas, 1806–1821." *LHQ* 28 (1945): 1001–1128.

Hall, Gwendolyn Midlo. *Africans in Colonial Louisiana: The Development of Afro-Creole Culture in the Eighteenth Century.* Baton Rouge: Louisiana State University Press, 1992.

Hall, Kermit I. "Hacks and Derelicts Revisited: American Territorial Judiciary, 1789–1959." *Western Historical Quarterly* 12 (1981): 273–89.

Hamilton, Peter Joseph. *Colonial Mobile. An Historical Study, Largely from Original Sources, of the Alabama-Tombigbee Basin from the Discovery of Mobile Bay in 1519 until the Demolition of Fort Charlotte in 1821.* Boston: Houghton Mifflin, 1897.

Handler, Richard. "Is 'Identity' a Useful Cross-Cultural Concept?" In *Commemorations: The Politics of National Identity,* ed. John R. Gillis. Princeton: Princeton University Press, 1996.

———. *Nationalism and the Politics of Culture in Quebec.* Madison: University of Wisconsin Press, 1988.

———. "On Sociocultural Discontinuity: Nationalism and Cultural Objectification in Quebec." *Current Anthropology* 25 (1984): 55–71.

Hanger, Kimberly S. *Bounded Lives, Bounded Places: Free Black Society in Colonial New Orleans, 1769–1803.* Durham, N.C.: Duke University Press, 1997.

———. "Conflicting Loyalties: The French Revolution and Free People of Color in Spanish Louisiana." *LAH* 34 (1993): 5–34.

Hatcher, William B. *Edward Livingston: Jeffersonian Republican and Jacksonian Democrat.* Baton Rouge: Louisiana State University Press, 1940.

Hatfield, Joseph T. *William Claiborne: Jeffersonian Centurion in the American Southwest.* Lafayette: University of Southwestern Louisiana, 1976.

Hatzenbuehler, Ronald L., and Robert L. Ivie. *Congress Declares War: Rhetoric, Leadership, and Partisanship in the Early Republic.* Kent: Kent State University Press, 1983.

Hawker, Henry A. *Trumpet of Glory: Fourth of July Orations, 1786–1861.* Granby, Conn.: Salmon Brook Historical Society, 1976.

Henderson, Harry McCorry. "The Magee-Gutierrez Expedition." *Southwestern Historical Quarterly* 55 (1951): 43–61.

Hietala, Thomas R. *Manifest Design: Anxious Aggrandizement in Late Jacksonian America.* Ithaca: Cornell University Press, 1985.

Hilb, Claudia. "Equality at the Limit of Liberty." In *The Making of Political Identities,* ed. Ernesto Laclau. New York: Verso, 1994.

Hill, Peter P. *French Perceptions of the Early American Republic, 1783–1793.* Philadelphia: American Philosophical Society, 1988.

Hoadley, John H. *Origins of American Political Parties, 1789–1803.* Lexington: University of Kentucky Press, 1986.

Hobsbawm, E. J. *Nations and Nationalism since 1780.* Cambridge: Cambridge University Press, 1990.

Hobsbawm, Eric, and Terence Ranger, eds. *The Invention of Tradition.* Cambridge: Cambridge University Press, 1993.

Holmes, Jack D. L. "The Abortive Slave Revolt at Pointe Coupée, Louisiana, 1795." *LAH* 11 (1970): 341–62.

———. "The Historiography of the American Revolution in Louisiana." *LAH* 19 (1978): 309–25.

———. "Showdown on the Sabine: General James Wilkinson vs. Lieutenant-Colonel Simón de Herrera." *Louisiana Studies* 3 (1964): 46–76.

Holton, Woody. "'Rebel against Rebel': Enslaved Virginians and the Coming of the American Revolution." *Virginia Magazine of History and Biography* 105 (1997): 157–92.

Horsman, Reginald. "The Dimensions of an 'Empire for Liberty': Expansion and Republicanism, 1775–1825." *JER* 9 (1989): 1–20.

———. *Expansion and American Foreign Policy.* East Lansing: Michigan State University Press, 1967.

———. *Race and Manifest Destiny: The Origins of American Racial Anglo-Saxonism.* Cambridge: Harvard University Press, 1981.

Howard, Perry H. *Political Tendencies in Louisiana.* Baton Rouge: Louisiana State University Press, 1971.

Huff, A. V., Jr. "The Eagle and the Vulture: Changing Attitudes toward Nationalism in Fourth of July Orations Delivered in Charleston, 1788–1860." *South Atlantic Quarterly* 73 (1974): 10–22.

Hutchinson, William T. "Unite to Divide; Divide to United: The Shaping of American Federalism." *Mississippi Valley Historical Review* 66 (1959): 3–18.

Hyde, Samuel C., Jr. *Pistols and Politics: The Dilemma of Democracy in Louisiana's Florida Parishes, 1810–1899.* Baton Rouge: Louisiana State University Press, 1996.

Ingersoll, Thomas N. "Free Blacks in a Slave Society: New Orleans, 1718–1812." *WMQ,* 3d ser., 48 (1991): 173–200.

Instructions from the Inhabitants of the Territory of Orleans. New Orleans, 1810.

The Invitation: A Poem Addressed to General Wilkinson, Commander in Chief of the United States Army. Natchez: Andrew Marschalk, 1807.

Ireland, Robert M. *The County Courts in Antebellum Kentucky.* Lexington: University of Kentucky Press, 1972.

Jackson, Andrew. *The Papers of Andrew Jackson,* ed. Sam B. Smith et al. 6 vols. to date. Knoxville: University of Tennessee Press, 1980–.

Jackson, Donald, ed. *Letters of the Lewis and Clark Expedition, with Related Documents, 1783–1854.* 2 vols. Urbana: University of Illinois Press, 1978.

Jacobs, James Ripley. *Tarnished Warrior: Major-General James Wilkinson.* New York: Macmillan, 1938.

Jacobson, Matthew Frye. *Whiteness of a Different Color: European Immigrants and the Alchemy of Race.* Cambridge: Harvard University Press, 1998.

Jefferson, Thomas. *Jefferson: Public and Private Papers,* ed. Merrill D. Peterson. New York: Library of America, 1990.

———. *Jefferson Writings,* ed. Merrill D. Peterson. New York: Library of America, 1984.

———. *The Papers of Thomas Jefferson,* ed. Julian Boyd et al. 29 vols. to date. Princeton: Princeton University Press, 1950–.

———. *The Works of Thomas Jefferson,* ed. Paul Leicester Ford. 10 vols. New York: G. P. Putnam's Sons, 1904–05.

John, Richard R. "Leonard D. White and the Invention of American Administrative History." *Reviews in American History* 24 (1996): 344–60.

———. *Spreading the News: The American Postal System from Franklin to Morse.* Cambridge: Harvard University Press, 1995.

Johnson, Jerah. "Colonial New Orleans: A Fragment of the Eighteenth-Century French Ethos." In *Creole New Orleans: Race and Americanization,* ed. Arnold R. Hirsch and Joseph Logsdon. Baton Rouge: Louisiana State University Press, 1992.

Johnson, Walter. *Soul by Soul: Life inside the Antebellum Slave Market.* Cambridge: Harvard University Press, 1999.

Journal of the Executive Proceedings of the Senate of the United States of America. 36 vols. New York: Johnson Reprint, 1969.

Journal of the House of Representatives of the State of Louisiana. New Orleans: Thierry; Baird and Wagner; Peter K. Wagner; J. C. de St. Romes, 1812–20.

Journal of the Senate of the State of Louisiana. New Orleans: Thierry; Baird and Wagner; Peter K. Wagner; J. C. de St. Romes, 1812–20.

Kaplan, Lawrence S. *Entangling Alliances with None: American Foreign Policy in the Age of Jefferson.* Kent: Kent State University Press, 1987.

———. *Thomas Jefferson: Westward the Course of Empire.* Wilmington: SR Books, 1999.

Kastor, Peter J. " 'Equitable Rights and Privileges': The Divided Loyalties of Washington County, Virginia, during the Franklin Separatist Crisis." *Virginia Magazine of History and Biography* 105 (1997): 193–226.

Kedourie, Elie. *Nationalism.* London: Hutchinson, 1960.

Kenneally, Finbar, ed. *United States Documents in the Propaganda Fide Archives.* 7 vols. Washington, D.C.: Academy of American Franciscan History, 1966–81.

Kerber, Linda K. *No Constitutional Right to Be Ladies: Women and the Obligations of Citizenship.* New York: Hill and Wang, 1998.

———. *Women of the Republic: Intellect and Ideology in Revolutionary America.* Chapel Hill: University of North Carolina Press, 1980.

Ketcham, Ralph. *James Madison: A Biography.* Charlottesville: University Press of Virginia, 1990.

Kettner, James H. *The Development of American Citizenship, 1608–1870.* Chapel Hill: University of North Carolina Press, 1978.

Kilbourne, Richard Holcombe, Jr. *Debt, Investment, Slaves: Credit Relations in East Feliciana Parish, Louisiana, 1825–1885.* Tuscaloosa: University of Alabama Press, 1995.

Klein, Rachel N. *Unification of a Slave State: The Rise of the Planter Class in the South Carolina Backcountry, 1760–1808.* Chapel Hill: University of North Carolina Press, 1990.

Knott, Stephen F. *Secret and Sanctioned: Covert Operations and the American Presidency.* New York: Oxford University Press, 1996.

Kohn, Hans. *American Nationalism: An Interpretive Essay.* New York: Macmillan, 1957.

——. *Nationalism: Its Meaning and History.* New York: D. Van Nostrand, 1965.

——. *Prelude to Nation-States: The French and German Experience, 1789–1815.* Princeton: D. Van Nostrand, 1967.

Kohn, Richard H. *Eagle and Sword: The Federalists and the Creation of the Military Establishment in America, 1783–1802.* New York: Free Press, 1975.

Kondert, Reinhart. "The German Involvement in the Rebellion of 1768." *LAH* 26 (1985): 385–98.

Konig, David Thomas. "Jurisprudence and Social Policy in the New Republic." In *Devising Liberty: Preserving and Creating Freedom in the New American Republic,* ed. Konig. Stanford: Stanford University Press, 1995.

Kruman, Mark. *Between Authority and Liberty: State Constitution Making in Revolutionary America.* Chapel Hill: University of North Carolina Press, 1997.

Kruse, Paul. "A Secret Agent in East Florida: George Mathews and the Patriot War." *Journal of Southern History* 18 (1952): 193–217.

Kukla, John, ed. *A Guide to the Papers of Pierre Clément Laussat: Napoleon's Prefect for the Colony of Louisiana and of General Claude Perrin Victor at the Historic New Orleans Collection.* New Orleans: Historic New Orleans Collection, 1993.

Kurtz, Donn M., II. *Kinship and Politics: The Justices of the United States and Louisiana Supreme Courts.* Baton Rouge: Louisiana State University Press, 1997.

Lachance, Paul F. "The 1809 Immigration of Saint-Domingue Refugees to New Orleans: Reception, Integration and Impact." *LAH* 29 (1988): 109–41.

——. "The Foreign French." In *Creole New Orleans: Race and Americanization,* ed. Arnold R. Hirsch and Joseph Logsdon. Baton Rouge: Louisiana State University Press, 1992.

——. "The Formation of a Three-Caste Society: Evidence from Wills in Antebellum New Orleans." *Social Science History* 18 (1994): 211–42.

——. "The Politics of Fear: French Louisianans and the Slave Trade, 1786–1809." *Plantation Society* 1 (1979): 162–97.

Ladd, Barbara. *Nationalism and the Color Line in George W. Cable, Mark Twain, and William Faulkner.* Baton Rouge: Louisiana State University Press, 1996.

Landers, Jane. *Black Society in Spanish Florida.* Urbana: University of Illinois Press, 1999.

——. "Gracia Real de Santa Teresa de Mose: A Free Black Town in Spanish Colonial Florida." *American Historical Review* 95 (1990): 9–30.

Langley, Lester. *The Americas in the Age of Revolution*. New Haven: Yale University Press, 1996.

Larson, John Lauritz. "Jefferson's Union and the Problem of Internal Improvements." In *Jeffersonian Legacies*, ed. Peter S. Onuf. Charlottesville: University Press of Virginia, 1993.

"Letters of James Brown to Henry Clay, 1804–1835." *LHQ* 24 (1941): 922–34.

Levasseur, Alain A. *Louis Casimir Elisabeth Moreau-Lislet, Foster Father of Louisiana Civil Law*. Baton Rouge: Louisiana State University, 1996.

Lewis, James E., Jr. *The American Union and the Problem of Neighborhood: The United States and the Collapse of the Spanish Empire, 1783–1829*. Chapel Hill: University of North Carolina Press, 1998.

Limerick, Patricia Nelson. *The Legacy of Conquest: The Unbroken Past of the American West*. New York: Norton, 1987.

Liss, Peggy K. *Atlantic Empires: The Network of Trade and Revolution, 1713–1826*. Baltimore: Johns Hopkins University Press, 1983.

———. "Creoles, the North American Example and the Spanish Imperial Economy." In *The North American Role in the Spanish Imperial Economy, 1760–1819*, ed. Jacques A. Barbier and Allen Kuethe. Manchester: Manchester University Press, 1984.

Long, David F. *Nothing too Daring: A Biography of Commodore David Porter, 1780–1843*. Annapolis: Naval Institute Press, 1970.

Louisianais [Pierre Derbigny]. *Esquisse de la situation politique et civile de la Louisiane* . . . New Orleans, 1804.

Lyon, E. Wilson. *Louisiana in French Diplomacy*. Norman: University of Oklahoma Press, 1934.

———. *The Man Who Sold Louisiana: The Career of François Barbe-Marbois*. Norman: University of Oklahoma Press, 1942.

Madison, James. *Letters and Other Writings of James Madison*. 4 vols. New York: R. Worthington, 1884.

———. *Notes of the Debates in the Federal Convention of 1787*, ed. Max Farrand. New York: Norton, 1987.

———. *The Papers of James Madison*, ed. William T. Hutchison et al. 17 vols. Charlottesville and Chicago: University Press of Virginia and University of Chicago Press, 1962–91.

———. *The Papers of James Madison: Presidential Series*, ed. Robert A. Rutland et al. 4 vols. to date. Charlottesville: University Press of Virginia, 1986–.

———. *The Papers of James Madison: Secretary of State Series*, ed. Robert J. Brugger et al. 6 vols. to date. Charlottesville: University Press of Virginia, 1986–.

———. *The Writings of James Madison: Comprising His Public Papers and His Private Correspondence, Including Numerous Letters and Documents Now for the First Time Printed*, ed. Gaillard Hunt. 9 vols. New York: G. P. Putnam's Sons, 1900–10.

Magruder, Allan Bowie. *Political, Commercial, and Moral Reflections on the Late Cession of Louisiana to the United States*. Lexington, Ky.: D. Bradford, 1803.

Maier, Pauline. *American Scripture: Making the Declaration of Independence*. New York: Knopf, 1997.

Malone, Dumas. *Jefferson and the Rights of Man*. Boston: Little, Brown, 1951.

——. *Jefferson the President: First Term, 1801–1805*. Boston: Little, Brown, 1970.

Martin, François-Xavier. *A General Digest of the Acts of the Legislatures of the Late Territory of Orleans, and the State of Louisiana* . . . New Orleans: Peter K. Wagner, 1816.

——. *The History of Louisiana*. New Orleans: J. A. Gresham, 1882.

——. *Reports of Cases Argued and Determined in the Supreme Court of Louisiana and in the Superior Court of the Territory of Orleans*. St. Paul: West Publishing, 1913.

——. *A Treatise on the Powers and Duties of Executors and Administrators* . . . New Bern, N.C.: Martin and Ogden, 1803.

——, ed. *The Office and Authority of a Justice of the Peace* . . . New Bern, N.C.: Martin and Ogden, 1804.

Matson, Cathy D., and Peter S. Onuf. *A Union of Interests: Political and Economic Thought in Revolutionary America*. Lawrence: University Press of Kansas, 1990.

Matthewson, Tim. "Thomas Jefferson and Haiti." *Journal of Southern History* 61 (1995): 209–49.

McConnell, Roland C. *Negro Troops of Antebellum Louisiana: A History of the Battalion of Free Men of Color*. Baton Rouge: Louisiana State University Press, 1968.

McCoy, Drew R. *The Elusive Republic: Political Economy in Jeffersonian America*. New York: Norton, 1980.

——. *The Last of the Fathers: James Madison and the Republican Legacy*. Cambridge: Cambridge University Press, 1988.

McKee, Christopher. *A Gentlemanly and Honorable Profession: The Creation of the U.S. Naval Officer Corps, 1794–1815*. Annapolis: Naval Institute Press, 1991.

Melville, Annabelle M. "John Carroll and Louisiana, 1803–1815." *Catholic Historical Review* 64 (1978): 398–440.

——. *Louis William DuBourg, Bishop of Louisiana and the Floridas, Bishop of Montauban, and Archbishop of Besançon, 1766–1833*. Chicago: Loyola University Press, 1986.

Merrill, Orasmus Cook. *The Happiness of America: An Oration Delivered at Shaftsbury, on the Fourth of July*. Bennington, Vt.: Anthony Haswell, 1804.

Miguel, Jesús Lorente. "Commercial Relations between New Orleans and the United States, 1783–1803." In *The North American Role in the Spanish Imperial Economy, 1760–1819*, ed. Jacques A. Barbier and Allan J. Kuethe. Manchester: Manchester University Press, 1984.

Mills, Gary. *The Forgotten People: Cane River's Creoles of Color*. Baton Rouge: Louisiana State University Press, 1977.

Monroe, James. *The Writings of James Monroe*, ed. Stanislaus Murray Hamilton. 7 vols. New York: G. P. Putnam's Sons, 1898–1903.

Moore, John Preston. *Revolt in Louisiana: The Spanish Occupation, 1766–1770*. Baton Rouge: Louisiana State University Press, 1976.

Moreau-Lislet, Louis. *Examination of the Judgment Rendered in the Case between Jean Gravier and the City of New Orleans*. Washington, D.C.: A. and G. Way, 1809.

Morgan, Edmund S. "Slavery and Freedom: The American Paradox." *JAH* 59 (1972): 5–29.

Morris, Christopher. *Becoming Southern: The Evolution of a Way of Life, Warren*

County and Vicksburg, Mississippi, 1770–1860. New York: Oxford University Press, 1995.

Murchland, Bernard. "The Rigors of Citizenship." *Review of Politics* 59 (1997): 127–34.

Murrin, John M. "A Roof without Walls: The Dilemma of American National Identity." In *Beyond Confederation: Origins of the Constitution and American National Identity,* ed. Richard Beeman, Stephen Botein, and Edward C. Carter II. Chapel Hill: University of North Carolina Press, 1987.

Nasatir, Abraham. *Borderland in Retreat: From Spanish Louisiana to the Far Southwest.* Albuquerque: University of New Mexico Press, 1976.

Nash, Gary B. *Forging Freedom: The Formation of Philadelphia's Black Community, 1720–1840.* Cambridge: Harvard University Press, 1988.

Nedelsky, Jennifer. *Private Property and the Limits of American Constitutionalism: The Madisonian Framework and Its Legacy.* Chicago: University of Chicago Press, 1990.

Nelson, John R., Jr. *Liberty and Property: Political Economy and Policymaking in the New Nation, 1789–1812.* Baltimore: Johns Hopkins University Press, 1987.

Newton, Lewis William. *The Americanization of French Louisiana: A Study of the Process of Adjustment between the French and Anglo-American Populations of Louisiana, 1803–1860.* New York: Arno, 1980.

———. "Creoles and Anglo-Americans in Old Louisiana: A Study in Cultural Conflicts." *Southwestern Social Science Quarterly* 14 (1933): 21–48.

Nobles, Gregory H. *American Frontiers: Cultural Encounters and Continental Conquest.* New York: Hill and Wang, 1997.

Oaks, Robert F. "Philadelphians in Exile: The Problem of Loyalty during the American Revolution." *Pennsylvania Magazine of History and Biography* 96 (1972): 298–325.

O'Neil, Charles Edward. "'A Quarter Marked by Sundry Peculiarities': New Orleans, Lay Trustees, and Père Antoine." *Catholic Historical Review* 76 (1990): 235–77.

Onuf, Peter S. "The Expanding Union." In *Devising Liberty: Preserving and Creating Freedom in the New American Republic,* ed. David T. Konig. Stanford: Stanford University Press, 1995.

———. "Federalism, Republicanism, and the Origins of American Sectionalism." In *All Over the Map: Rethinking American Regions,* ed. Edward L. Ayers, Patricia Nelson Limerick, Stephen Nissenbaum, and Peter S. Onuf. Baltimore: Johns Hopkins University Press, 1996.

———. *Jefferson's Empire: The Language of American Nationhood.* Charlottesville: University Press of Virginia, 2000.

———. *The Origins of the Federal Republic: Jurisdictional Controversies in the United States, 1775–1787.* Philadelphia: University of Pennsylvania Press, 1983.

———. *Statehood and Union: A History of the Northwest Ordinance.* Bloomington: Indiana University Press, 1987.

———. "'To Declare Them a Free and Independent People': Race, Slavery, and National Identity in Jefferson's Thought." *JER* 18 (1998): 1–46.

Onuf, Peter S., and Nicholas G. Onuf. *Federal Union, Modern World: The Law of Nations in an Age of Revolutions, 1776–1814.* Madison, Wis.: Madison House, 1993.

Owsley, Frank Lawrence, Jr., and Gene A. Smith. *Filibusters and Expansionists: Jeffersonian Manifest Destiny, 1800–1821.* Tuscaloosa: University of Alabama Press, 1997.

Paquette, Robert L. "Revolutionary Saint Domingue in the Making of Territorial Louisiana." In *A Turbulent Time: The French Revolution and the Greater Caribbean,* ed. David B. Gaspar and David Patrick Geggus. Bloomington: Indiana University Press, 1997.

Parsons, Lynn H. *John Quincy Adams.* Madison, Wis.: Madison House, 1998.

Patrick, Rembert. *Florida Fiasco: Rampant Rebels on the Georgia-Florida Border, 1810–1815.* Athens: University of Georgia Press, 1954.

Perkins, Bradford. *The First Rapprochement: England and the United States, 1795–1805.* Philadelphia: University of Pennsylvania Press, 1955.

———. *Prologue to War: England and the United States, 1805–1812.* Berkeley: University of California Press, 1968.

Peterson, Merrill D. *Thomas Jefferson and the New Nation: A Biography.* Oxford: Oxford University Press, 1970.

Pitot, James. *Observations on the Colony of Louisiana from 1796 to 1802.* Baton Rouge: Louisiana State University Press, 1979.

Plumer, William. *William Plumer's Memorandum of Proceedings in the United States Senate, 1803–1807,* ed. Everett Somerville Brown. New York: Macmillan, 1923.

Poydras, Julien. *A Defense of the Right of the Public to the Batture of New Orleans.* Washington, D.C.: Julien Poydras, 1809.

———. *A Speech by Mr. Poydras, President of the Legislative Council of Orleans.* New Orleans, 1804.

Price, Edward T. *Dividing the Land: Early American Beginnings of Our Private Property Mosaic.* Chicago: University of Chicago Press, 1995.

Prichard, Walter, ed. "Selecting a Governor for the Territory of Orleans." *LHQ* 31 (1948): 269–393.

Prucha, Francis Paul. *The Sword of the Republic: The United States Army on the Frontier, 1783–1846.* New York: Macmillan, 1969.

The Public Statutes at Large of the United States of America. 8 vols. Boston: Charles C. Little and James Brown, 1845.

Quincy, Josiah. *Speech of Mr. Quincy . . . on the Bill Admitting the Territory of Orleans in to the Union.* Baltimore: Benjamin Edes, 1811.

Rakove, Jack N. *The Beginnings of National Politics: An Interpretive History of the Continental Congress.* New York: Knopf, 1979.

———. *Original Meanings: Politics and Ideas in the Making of the Constitution.* New York: Vintage, 1997.

Ramsay, David. *An Oration on the Cession of Louisiana to the United States . . .* Charleston: W. P. Young, 1804.

Rankin, David C. "The Tannenbaum Thesis Reconsidered: Slavery and Race Relations in Antebellum Louisiana." *Southern Studies* 18 (1979): 5–31.

Reflections on the Cause of the Louisianians Respectfully Submitted by Their Agents. Washington, D.C., 1803.

Remini, Robert V. *Andrew Jackson and the Course of American Empire, 1767–1821.* New York: Harper and Row, 1977.

———. *Henry Clay: Statesman for the Union.* New York: Norton, 1991.

Richardson, James D., ed. *A Compilation of the Messages and Papers of the Presidents, 1789–1897.* 16 vols. Washington, D.C.: Government Printing Office, 1896–99.

Robertson, Andrew W. " 'Look on This Picture . . . and on This!': Nationalism, Localism, and Partisan Images of Otherness in the United States, 1787–1820." *American Historical Review* 106 (2001): 1263–80.

Robertson, James A., ed. *Louisiana under the Rule of Spain, France, and the United States, 1785–1807.* 3 vols. Cleveland: Arthur H. Clark, 1911.

Rodgers, Daniel T. "Republicanism: The Career of a Concept." *JAH* 79 (1992): 11–38.

Romero, Sidney J. *"My Fellow Citizens . . .": The Inaugural Addresses of Louisiana's Governors.* Lafayette: University of Southwestern Louisiana, 1980.

Rossiter, Clinton. *The American Quest, 1790–1860: An Emerging Nation in Search of Identity, Unity, and Modernity.* New York: Harcourt Brace Jovanovich, 1971.

Rousey, Dennis C. *Policing the Southern City: New Orleans, 1805–1889.* Baton Rouge: Louisiana State University Press, 1996.

Rowland, Eron, ed. *Life, Letters, and Papers of William Dunbar.* Jackson: Mississippi Historical Society, 1930.

Royster, Charles. *A Revolutionary People at War: The Continental Army and American Character, 1775–1783.* New York: Norton, 1979.

Russell, Sarah. "Ethnicity, Commerce, and Community on Lower Louisiana's Plantation Frontier, 1803–1828." *LAH* 40 (1999): 389–405.

Sahlins, Peter. *Boundaries: The Making of France and Spain in the Pyrenees.* Berkeley: University of California Press, 1989.

Salmond, John. "Citizenship and Allegiance." *Law Quarterly Review* 17 (1901): 270–391 and 18 (1902): 49–363.

Saunt, Claudio. *A New Order of Things: Property, Power, and the Transformation of the Creek Indians, 1733–1816.* Cambridge: Cambridge University Press, 1999.

Scanlon, James E. "A Sudden Conceit: Jefferson and the Louisiana Government Bill of 1804." *LAH* 9 (1968): 139–62.

Schafer, Judith Kelleher. *Slavery, the Civil Law, and the Supreme Court of Louisiana.* Baton Rouge: Louisiana State University Press, 1994.

Schwartz, Philip J. *Slave Laws in Virginia.* Athens: University of Georgia Press, 1996.

Segal, Daniel, and Richard Handler. "How European Is Nationalism?" *Social Analysis* 32 (1992): 1–15.

Sidbury, James. *Ploughshares into Swords: Race, Rebellion, and Identity in Gabriel's Virginia, 1730–1810.* Cambridge: Cambridge University Press, 1997.

Skocpol, Theda. *Protecting Soldiers and Mothers: The Political Origins of Social Policy in the United States.* Cambridge: Belknap Press of Harvard University Press, 1992.

Skowronek, Stephen. *Building a New American State: The Expansion of National Administrative Capacities, 1877–1920.* Cambridge: Cambridge University Press, 1982.

Sloan, Herbert E. *Principle and Interest: Thomas Jefferson and the Problem of Debt.* New York: Oxford University Press, 1995.

Smith, F. Todd. *The Caddo Indians: Tribes at the Convergence of Empires, 1542–1854.* College Station: Texas A&M Press, 1995.

———. "The Kadohadacho Indians and the Louisiana-Texas Frontier, 1686–1870." *Southwestern Historical Quarterly* 95 (1991): 177–204.

Smith, James Morton. *Freedom's Fetters: The Alien and Sedition Laws and American Civil Liberties.* Ithaca: Cornell University Press, 1956.

Smith, James Norton, ed. *The Republic of Letters: The Correspondence between Thomas Jefferson and James Madison.* 3 vols. New York: Norton, 1995.

Smith, Joseph Burkholder. *The Plot to Steal Florida: James Madison's Phony War.* New York: Arbor House, 1983.

Smith, Rogers M. *Civic Ideals: Conflicting Visions of Citizenship in U.S. History.* New Haven: Yale University Press, 1997.

"Some Letters of James Brown of Louisiana to Presidents of the United States." *LHQ* 20 (1937): 58–136.

Spinner, Jeff. *The Boundaries of Citizenship: Race, Ethnicity, and Nationality in the Liberal State.* Baltimore: Johns Hopkins University Press, 1994.

Spivak, Burton. *Jefferson's English Crisis: Commerce, Embargo, and the Republican Revolution.* Charlottesville: University Press of Virginia, 1979.

Stagg, J. C. A. "James Madison and the Coercion of Great Britain: Canada, the West Indies, and the War of 1812." *WMQ*, 3d ser., 38 (1981): 3–34.

———. "James Madison and the 'Malcontents': The Political Origins of the War of 1812." *WMQ*, 3d ser., 33 (1976): 557–85.

———. *Mr. Madison's War: Politics, Diplomacy, and Warfare in the Early American Republic, 1783–1830.* Princeton: Princeton University Press, 1983.

Stampp, Kenneth J., et al., eds. *Records of Ante-bellum Southern Plantations.* Bethesda: University Publications of America, 1985–.

Stuart, Reginald C. "Special Interests and National Authority in Foreign Policy: American-British Provincial Links during the Embargo and the War of 1812." *Diplomatic History* 8 (1984): 311–28.

———. *United States Expansionism and British North America, 1775–1871.* Chapel Hill: University of North Carolina Press, 1988.

Sugden, John. "Jean Lafitte and the British Offer of 1814." *LAH* 20 (1979): 159–67.

"Summary of Trial Proceedings of Those Accused of Participating in the Slave Uprising of January 9, 1811." *LAH* 18 (1977): 472–73.

Tannenbaum, Frank. *Slave and Citizen: The Negro in the Americas.* New York: Knopf, 1947.

Taylor, Alan. "Land and Liberty on the Post-Revolutionary Frontier." In *Devising Liberty: Preserving and Creating Freedom in the New American Republic,* ed. David T. Konig. Stanford: Stanford University Press, 1995.

———. *Liberty Men and Great Proprietors: The Revolutionary Settlement on the Maine Frontier, 1760–1820.* Chapel Hill: University of North Carolina Press, 1990.

———. *William Cooper's Town: Power and Persuasion on the Frontier of the Early American Republic.* New York: Norton, 1995.

Taylor, Georgia Fairbanks. "The Early History of the Episcopal Church in New Orleans, 1805–1840." *LHQ* 22 (1939): 428–78.

The Territorial Papers of the United States, ed. Clarence Edward Carter. 28 vols. Washington, D.C.: Government Printing Office, 1934–75.

Thorne, Tanis C. *The Many Hands of My Relations: French and Indians on the Lower Missouri.* Columbia: University of Missouri Press, 1996.

Thorpe, Francis Newton, ed. *The Federal and State Constitutions, Colonial Charters, and Other Organic Laws of the States, Territories, and Colonies Now or Heretofore*

Forming the United States of America. 7 vols. Washington, D.C.: Government Printing Office, 1909.

"Three Letters from Robert Miller to Richard Claiborne, 1813–1817." *LHQ* 24 (1941): 729–43.

Travers, Len. *Celebrating the Fourth: Independence Day and the Rites of Nationalism in the Early Republic.* Amherst: University of Massachusetts Press, 1997.

Tregle, Joseph G. "Andrew Jackson and the Continuing Battle of New Orleans." *JER* 1 (1981): 373–92.

———. "Creoles and Americans." In *Creole New Orleans: Race and Americanization,* ed. Arnold R. Hirsch and Joseph Logsdon. Baton Rouge: Louisiana State University Press, 1992.

———. *Louisiana in the Age of Jackson: A Clash of Cultures and Personalities.* Baton Rouge: Louisiana State University Press, 1999.

———. "Political Reinforcement of Ethnic Dominance in Louisiana, 1812–1845." In *The Americanization of the Gulf Coast, 1803–1850,* ed. Lucius F. Ellsworth. Pensacola: Historic Pensacola Preservation Board, 1972.

Tucker, Robert W., and David C. Hendrickson. *Empire of Liberty: The Statecraft of Thomas Jefferson.* New York: Oxford University Press, 1990.

Tucker, St. George. *Reflections on the Cession of Louisiana to the United States.* Washington, D.C.: Samuel Harrison Smith, 1803.

Usner, Daniel H., Jr. *Indians, Settlers, and Slaves in a Frontier Exchange Economy: The Lower Mississippi Valley before 1783.* Chapel Hill: University of North Carolina Press, 1992.

Villeré, Sidney Louis. *Jacques Philippe Villeré, First Native-Born Governor of Louisiana, 1816–1820.* New Orleans: Historic New Orleans Collection, 1981.

Viroli, Maurizio. *For Love of Country: An Essay on Patriotism and Nationalism.* New York: Oxford University Press, 1995.

Waldstreicher, David. *In the Midst of Perpetual Fetes: The Making of American Nationalism, 1776–1820.* Chapel Hill: University of North Carolina Press, 1997.

———. "Rites of Rebellion, Rites of Assent: Celebrations, Print Culture, and the Origins of American Nationalism." *JAH* 82 (1995): 37–61.

Weber, David J. *The Spanish Frontier in North America.* New Haven: Yale University Press, 1992.

Webre, Stephen. "The Problem of Indian Slavery in Spanish Louisiana, 1769–1803." *LAH* 25 (1984): 117–35.

"The West Florida Revolution of 1810, as Told in the Letters of John Rhea, Fulwar Skipwith, Reuben Kemper, and Others." *LHQ* 21 (1938): 76–202.

White, Leonard. *The Federalists: A Study in Administrative History.* New York: Macmillan, 1948.

———. *The Jeffersonians: A Study in Administrative History, 1801–1829.* New York: Macmillan, 1951.

White, Richard. *"It's Your Misfortune and None of My Own": A New History of the American West.* Norman: University of Oklahoma Press, 1991.

———. *The Middle Ground: Indians, Empires, and Republics in the Great Lakes Region, 1650–1815.* Cambridge: Cambridge University Press, 1991.

———. *The Roots of Dependency: Subsistence, Environment, and Social Change among the Choctaws, Pawnees, and Navajos.* Lincoln: University of Nebraska Press, 1983.

White, Shane. *Somewhat More Independent: The End of Slavery in New York City, 1770–1810.* Athens: University of Georgia Press, 1991.

Wilds, John, Charles L. Dufour, and Walter G. Cowan. *Louisiana, Yesterday and Today: A Historical Guide to the State.* Baton Rouge: Louisiana State University Press, 1996.

Winfield, Betty Houchin. "Public Perception and Public Events: The Louisiana Purchase and the American Partisan Press." In *The Louisiana Purchase: Emergence of an American Nation,* ed. Peter J. Kastor. Washington, D.C.: CQ Press, 2002.

Winship, Marion Nelson. "Enterprise in Motion in the Early American Republic: The Federal Government and the Making of Thomas Worthington." *Business and Economic History: The Journal of the Business History Conference* 23 (1994): 81–91.

Wood, Gordon S. *The Creation of the American Republic, 1776–1787.* New York: Norton, 1969.

———. *The Radicalism of the American Revolution.* New York: Knopf, 1992.

Wunder, John. "American Law and Order Comes to the Mississippi Territory: The Making of Sargent's Code, 1798–1800." *Journal of Mississippi History* 38 (1976): 131–55.

Wyllys, Rufus Kay. "The East Florida Revolution of 1812–1814." *Hispanic American Historical Review* 9 (1929): 415–45.

Young, Henry J. "Treason and Its Punishment in Revolutionary Pennsylvania." *Pennsylvania Magazine of History and Biography* 90 (1966): 287–313.

Zernatto, Guido. "Nation: The History of a Word." *Review of Politics* 6 (1944): 351–66.

Zink, Frances Pirotte. *Julien Poydras: Statesman, Philanthropist, Educator.* Lafayette: University of Southwestern Louisiana, 1968.

NEWSPAPERS

Aurora General Advertiser. Philadelphia.
Charleston Courier. Charleston, S.C.
Louisiana Courier. New Orleans.
Louisiana Gazette. New Orleans.
Moniteur de la Louisiane. New Orleans.
National Intelligencer. Washington, D.C.
Orleans Gazette. New Orleans.
Richmond Enquirer. Richmond, Va.
Union. New Orleans.
Weekly Chronicle. Natchez, Miss.
Alexandria Advertiser. Alexandria, Va.

Index